It's All One Case

THE ILLUSTRATED
ROSS MACDONALD
ARCHIVES

ALSO BY KEVIN AVERY

Everything Is an Afterthought:
The Life and Writings of Paul Nelson

Conversations with Clint:
Paul Nelson's Lost Interviews with Clint Eastwood,
1979–1983

It's All One Case

THE ILLUSTRATED ROSS MACDONALD ARCHIVES

BY

PAUL NELSON & KEVIN AVERY

WITH JEFF WONG

FANTAGRAPHICS BOOKS

Fantagraphics Books
7563 Lake City Way NE
Seattle, Washington 98115
Editor: Gary Groth
Designer: Jeff Wong
Associate Publisher: Eric Reynolds
Publisher: Gary Groth

IT'S ALL ONE CASE
The Illustrated Ross Macdonald Archives

Paul Nelson's interviews with Ross Macdonald used courtesy of Special Collections and Archives,
University of California, Irvine Libraries. Kenneth Millar Papers. MS-L001. Box 43.

Unless otherwise indicated, all quoted material by Paul Nelson courtesy of Mark C. Nelson.

Cover photo of Kenneth Millar/Ross Macdonald
by Jill Krementz.

Photos of Jeff Wong's Kenneth Millar/Ross Macdonald collection and associated captions
by Jeff Wong.

Visit www.fantagraphics.com.
You may order books at our web site or by phone.
Distributed in the U.S. by W.W. Norton and Company, Inc. (800-233-4830)
Distributed in Canada by Canadian Manda Group (fax 888-563-8327)
Distributed in the U.K. by Turnaround Distribution (44 (0)20 8829-3002)
Distributed to comic stores by Diamond Comics Distributors (800-452-6642 x215)

ISBN 13: 978-1-60699-888-5
ISBN 10: 1-60699-888-9

First Fantagraphics Books printing: September, 2016

For my father,
Donald R. Avery (1923–2013).
For all our fathers.

CONTENTS

FOREWORD

ROSS MACDONALD AND HIS SHADOW PORTRAIT
by Jerome Charyn

I couldn't have written crime novels without Ross Macdonald and *The Galton Case*—Macdonald's book was my maiden voyage into detective fiction. What enthralled me was the mysterious music of the language, a poetry of mosaics, of stone built upon tiny stone, or as Macdonald himself says in *It's All One Case*: "an aesthetic of rapid, uncluttered prose and vivid imagery," where the crime only deepens the further we delve into the book.

I'd never read anything quite like *The Galton Case*, a book haunted with ghosts from the past, and an unsolved crime that left its own cacophony of rattling bones. And yet I felt something extremely personal in the novel, as if these mosaics were a piecemeal portrait of Macdonald himself. Ross Macdonald was only a "stage name," another ghost. The crime novelist was born Kenneth Millar in 1915, and seemed to feel he was an orphan without a real sense of place. His mother was a registered nurse who had caught typhoid fever from one of her patients and remained an invalid for the rest of her life, while his father ran out on the family when Macdonald was three or four. The boy became a kind of Bedouin, who was shunted from relative to relative, and would live in fifty different houses before he was sixteen. "And that's the real background to my writing," he would tell rock critic Paul Nelson, who managed to seduce Macdonald into a series of interviews in 1976. These interviews were collected and archived by author-editor Kevin Avery in *It's All One Case*.

As Avery suggests, Nelson has "fallen from our collective memory." But Nelson was the most prominent rock critic of his era, and he hoped to sculpt these interviews into an article for *Rolling Stone* and a book on Macdonald. He was one of the first critics to glean the relationship between rock & roll and the new, emerging pop culture: "the Western, noir, screwball comedy, and, most especially, the detective novel," writer Kit Rachlis tells us.

The article was never written, and now these interviews suddenly resurface after a lapse of forty years. They contain a treasure of material about Ross Macdonald, crime fiction, modern literature, jazz, and Macdonald's iconic private detective, Lew Archer. Why was I startled to learn that Macdonald adored Vladimir Nabokov, and admired Thomas Pynchon and Flannery O'Connor? He himself was a modernist in his own way, who found his craft and his voice with the creation of Lew Archer, the most *reliable* unreliable narrator since Nick Carraway in *The Great Gatsby*, Macdonald's favorite novel. Archer, Macdonald insists, "is the man who *sees* but is not *seen*," a kind of "shadow portrait." Macdonald himself was a great puzzle, with "those chilly little blue eyes," according to book dealer Ralph Sipper.

"I'm the ruins of what could have been a man of action," Macdonald declared. But he was a man of action in the turbulent dreamscape of his own texts. Macdonald took the notion of genre out of crime fiction, turned it into an art form with its own borders, limits, and, in his words, "wild masonry." "Music," he told Nelson "strikes deeper … than the written word." And Macdonald sought his own enchanted syncopation in his writing. His novels are so disturbing, because they dredge up the narrow containers of Ken Millar's past—the "orphan" whose parents were still alive, the boy who can barely trace his own shadow, who can only survive as a wanderer in one place (Macdonald would live in Santa Barbara for over thirty years with his wife, Margaret Millar, who was also a crime novelist).

Perhaps he found solace in the false stability of Archer's own voice. *If* Archer represented the author, then "everybody else in the stories is just Archer's dream." This is why novels such as *The Galton Case* continue to haunt us. They provide no resolution, since a crime that burrows out of the past leaves a wound that can never heal. Macdonald reinvented the *polar*, as French critics dubbed those crime novels that dug into the underbelly of American culture with a nervous edge that couldn't be found in any other art form. Together with his celebrated forebear, Dashiell Hammett, Macdonald took the private detective and turned him into a deadly angel, who hovers above the crime and is almost a chastened mirror of the criminals themselves.

May 31, 1994   Jill K Robertz

Ken and his wife Margaret "Maggie" Millar outside their Hope Ranch home.

INTRODUCTION

This book is not about Paul Nelson, but it could not exist without him. For those of us who remember his writing and the way his words embraced what he was writing about, Paul Nelson is a key figure in rock & roll, someone who, because of his unique understanding of the music in its formative years and what it meant to popular culture, remains just as important as the artists he wrote about. One of the first writers on the scene in the mid-Sixties, he recognized that something was happening (unlike that other thin man, Dylan's Mr. Jones, Paul *did* know what it was) and as a result helped invent rock criticism. According to Kit Rachlis, Paul's friend and fellow *Rolling Stone* contributor, "He linked rock & roll to the great genres of American pop culture: the Western, noir, screwball comedy, and, most especially, the detective novel." The detective novel was important to Paul. More than anything else in the realm of writing, he, in his own words, "wanted to write a series of detective novels, be the next Ross Macdonald."

That never happened. Instead, Paul discovered that in this world there are many different ways for life to go wrong. By the early Eighties, he and his writing disappeared from public view altogether. Not unlike a character out of one of Macdonald's mysteries, the reasons why were tragic and close to the heart. More than once on his way down and out, Paul probably tried to find solace in one of his favorite quotes, from Jean Renoir's *The Rules of the Game*: "You see, in this world, there is one awful thing, and that is that everyone has his reasons."

Things were already going awry for Paul as far back as the winter of 1970. In New York City, he had finished the last Ross Macdonald book he could get his hands on, having collected all but a couple of early ones in hardcover first editions. But he was hungry for more. He was also, he would later write, "Close to explosion.… My own existence was certainly a mystery in which the psychic murders seemed to keep piling up …" In conversation with friends, however, he described his first encounter with Ross Macdonald—real name Kenneth Millar—this way: "I was a mystery fan and I was working on a mystery novel. I just got brave one night and said, *Well, I'll see if his phone number is in the Santa Barbara telephone book*, and called him up on the pretext of asking where I could get the two early books." In truth he was looking for what he had found between the covers of Macdonald's books, something he was desperately lacking in his own life. "He was very open and really interested, and I sort of gave him an excuse to get off, you know, saying, 'I don't want to take up a lot of your time.' And he said, 'No, no, let's keep talking.' We talked like for an hour and a half. Now that I've met him and realize that he is very quiet, I'm kind of amazed that I was that lucky. You know, it doesn't appear to me that he would talk an hour and a half to a lot of

people. I certainly wasn't that intelligent over the phone—it wasn't that—but he just seemed to sense that I was genuinely interested."

Five years later, Paul, then a freelance writer, convinced his editor at *Rolling Stone* that a feature article on Ross Macdonald would find favor with the magazine's youthful readership. The Summer of Love had long given way to the fall, and there were plenty of disillusioned ex-idealists out there in need of comfort and understanding of their own. As Paul would write in a book proposal: "Macdonald's books have a huge following among young people, who view his detective, Lew Archer, as an honest, compassionate, and understanding father figure." In his mind there couldn't be much of a difference between Macdonald and his fictional creation, but he was soon to discover that the on-page persona was much easier to deal with than his flesh-and-bones counterpart.

> My 1976 interviews with Ross Macdonald—I have approximately forty-seven hours of tape with him; another fifteen or so hours with the people who knew him best, including his wife—were all formal question-and-answer sessions, not just unstructured gab about whatever crossed our minds.[1] Macdonald did not make small talk easily (his past seemed to have cost him dearly in that respect: he was a very *serious* man) and preferred specific questions, so I had to spend five or six hours preparing carefully for each session. Whenever I tried to wing it, there would be silence—a kindly, comfortable silence for him; not so for me—and I knew I'd have to do more homework next time.

Though by the time he was finished interviewing Millar, Paul was less afraid of these "dead spaces" (as he came to call them), it was tough going from the start. "The first day was about four, four and a half hours in which I felt like I played five straight basketball games. I was just literally exhausted. For an hour I thought, *Gee, does he want to do this? Should I say something so somebody's saying something?* There just wouldn't be a response and it didn't seem to bother him, you know. A minute or two went by, and I just realized that's the way he is." Listening to the recordings today with their deep, almost painful pockets of

---

1 Whether this is an addition error on Paul's part or if some of the recordings got lost over the years, for the purposes of this book we had access to thirty-nine hours of interviews with Millar and thirteen hours with the other key players.

silence, it's not difficult to imagine what it felt like being on the receiving end of the cold stare that accompanied Millar's frequent bouts of taciturnity. What bookseller Ralph Sipper once described as "those chilly little blue eyes."

"Throughout these sessions," Paul wrote, "both of us were striving to cover almost every aspect of his life and work. His friends held the view that he was determined to get his life down on tape, to tell his story—or as much of it as he was willing to—to someone whom he felt had studied and understood his books." By the time he was finished, Paul amassed dozens of audio cassettes and sheaves of notes bearing his small scribble. "How the heck are you going to take all this material and organize it?" someone asked him. "Throw it up in the air," Kit Rachlis joked.

Certainly it was a question that Paul asked himself many times in the ensuing years. Finally, unable to produce either the magazine article or the book, in 1991 he sold the tapes for a reported $3,000 to the University of California, Irvine, for inclusion in their Kenneth and Margaret Millar Collection. He needed the cash. It wasn't the first time in his career that a significant project had fallen victim to his recurring writer's block. But those are other stories for other books.

"I think he gathered so much information that he didn't know where to jump into it," Rachlis says today. "You know, I think sometimes you get so close to something that finishing it might be a way of letting go of it, and you don't want to. Sometimes as much as you like a subject, sometimes it's just easier not to do something. You find the reasons not to do it."

That word again: *reasons.*

One major reason for Paul's not finishing at least the magazine article certainly had to do with Millar's daughter Linda Jane, who had, according to a source, died from a drug overdose in 1970 (the same year that Paul placed his first phone call to Millar) at the age of thirty-one. Kenneth, however, and his wife Margaret Millar, a successful mystery novelist in her own right, had told everyone that Linda's death had been due to a "cerebral incident," and he stipulated in writing at the outset that Paul couldn't include anything in the piece about Linda or the troubled life she'd led. At the age of sixteen while driving drunk, she'd struck three young boys, killing one of them. As a college student three years later, she became the target of a well-publicized search when she disappeared with two men.

Perhaps Paul couldn't figure out how to write honestly about Millar without mentioning such a tragic loss, one that he believed was central to understanding the author and so many of his books, what with their fractured families and wayward children. "I think there's a real truth to that," Rachlis says, "and a more hard-hearted writer might have independently verified the story around the daughter and written about it, and then honored that nothing Ken Millar said was going to be on the record and could have written about it. Paul, I think, would never betray a subject that way."

When Paul Nelson died thirty years later, in 2006—the medical examiner ruled the cause of death as heart disease, but the less clinical, sadder truth is that one day he just lay down and never again got up—Kenneth Millar was not far away. All the Macdonald first editions had long ago been traded in and replaced by a stack of inexpensive Lew Archer paperbacks, and open near his bedside was Tom Nolan's *Ross Macdonald: A Biography.*

In my previous writings about Paul Nelson, I used to wonder how a man whose brilliant and insightful writing, once so highly regarded and accessible, having contributed so much to our culture, could have fallen so quickly from our collective memory. But the same can now be said about Ross Macdonald. It doesn't seem all that long ago that his books were on the bestseller list and being made into movies starring that other Paul (Newman). Indeed, almost forty years have flown by and the books of Ross Macdonald are seldom any longer found on the

shelves of the local bookstore, be it indie or Barnes & Noble. But such wasn't always the case. As Paul wrote in his proposal:

In the field of detective fiction, only three names stand out as genre masters *and* important American novelists: Dashiell Hammett (who published his first novel, *Red Harvest*, in 1929), Raymond Chandler (who published his first novel, *The Big Sleep*, in 1939) and Ross Macdonald (who published his first detective novel, *The Moving Target*, in 1949 after writing four non-private-eye mysteries under his real name, Kenneth Millar). While it's somewhat surprising that within the relatively short time span of twenty years, all three major figures of the modern American detective novel—each very different—made their entrances, it's truly remarkable that, since 1949, there hasn't been a single writer of detective fiction who has successfully and consistently taken the genre into new territory. After Macdonald, who died of Alzheimer's disease on July 11th, 1983, no worthy successor exists.

(LA1) LOS ANGELES, June 10--SEEKS MISSING DAUGHTER--Mystery writer Kenneth Millar, left, confers with Sgt. Edward Berger of the Los Angeles police department yesterday in the search for Millar's missing 19-year-old daughter, Linda. A picture of the missing girl lies on the desk. The search for Linda, who has been missing since May 31, turned to Southern California when a Hollywood grocery store operator informed police the girl had cashed a $10 check last Friday night.
AP Wirephoto)(see story)(mw40730tms) 1959

AP wirephoto filed under "Missing Persons" from June 12, 1959.

ABOUT THE INTERVIEWS THAT MAKE UP THIS BOOK:

In April of 1976, Kenneth Millar was in New York City to attend a cocktail party thrown on his behalf by his publisher, Alfred A. Knopf, Inc. and to participate in a National Book Critics Circle symposium on criticism. He also spent several days being interviewed by Paul Nelson. On Sunday afternoon, April 26, he met for four and a half hours with Paul, Kit Rachlis, and Dave Marsh at Paul's apartment on East Fifty-Eighth Street. Marsh, then an associate editor at *Rolling Stone*, remembers: "The comfort level was very high in that room. It was like sitting around and talking with friends, you know?" Listening to the tape today, it sounds as if Rachlis and Marsh are sitting at the feet of their literary master. "In my mind, I'm sitting to Millar's right, Paul's right in front of him, Kit is sort of a little back of Paul, and it's dim. Whatever light there is is kind of being shared by Macdonald and Paul, and there's not a lot of natural light. But whether that's because it's cut off or because it was a gray day, I do not remember. It doesn't seem gray in my memory because of anything dismal that I associated with Millar, because he was *fantastic*, man." Rachlis recalls that Millar wore a trench coat to the get-together, "which just seemed so grown-up to me." Even so, he didn't think of the older man as being part of the previous generation—the generation of his father, who had introduced him to Ross Macdonald's books in the first place.

"That was one thing," Marsh agrees, "you did not feel a generation gap. And that was something that I had liked about him as a writer. If you know his book *The Instant Enemy*, to me that had an empathy with the dilemma of young people like very few other books people in his generation have written. Of contemporary young people. Of course, we now know the biographical reasons for that. I think that we had begun to know them already. I think that Paul had kind of scoped some of that out, about the daughter and all."

"What I mostly remember," Rachlis says, "was being in the presence of a writer I truly admired and who spoke with great precision and great care. Unlike most of us, he composed his sentences before he spoke, and so they came out near perfectly.

"Not to make too much and too little about how Paul was like Ken Millar and Ken Millar was like Paul, but what they shared—in addition to a kind of fundamental sense of privacy, which expressed itself I think as shyness—what drew each of them to each other were certainly two things I can think of and probably much more: One was that each truly had, and lived by and thought a great deal about, a moral code. The other was that they approached writing with a level of care and precision about voice that is truly striking. You can find voice as a writer in a lot of different ways—Lester Bangs, you know, has a voice, Edgar Allan Poe has another—but what Ken Millar and Paul shared when they approached writing was that every word was carefully thought out and placed one in front of the other with precision. Everything was measured and everything was precise. I think that they shared a literary sensibility and a moral vision that they had devoted their life to and given enormous thought to."

Three months later, with America's coast-to-coast bicentennial celebration already fading from memory, Paul flew to California to conduct the remaining interviews, which lasted from Sunday, July 25 to Monday, August 16. Twenty years separated the men: Paul was forty and Millar was sixty. The meeting locales were almost evenly divided between Millar's study at his and Margaret's Santa Barbara home in the exclusive Hope Ranch neighborhood, or the Millars' cabana at the Coral Casino Beach and Cabana Club, which was adjacent to the Biltmore. At home the tone was hushed, almost funereal, the only interruptions coming from the barks, growls, and whimpers of one of the household dogs, or from Margaret passing through the room and whispering in transit, "Hi, Paul." The Coral Casino interviews were something else altogether. Small planes constantly buzzed overhead, on their way to or from the Santa Barbara Municipal Airport ("the tiniest airport in the world," according to Rachlis, "like flying into the airport of *Casablanca*"). Club members chattered about, dined and drank, and wished Millar well as they passed by on their way to water and sun. Waves crashed on the beach in the near distance while children splashed in the swimming pool, calling out, "Marco! Polo!" Both men tolerated all these distractions remarkably well. Other than the occasions when his memory would fail him, Millar's focus never faltered, not even when Paul's chronic sinusitis flared up and his sniffling and sneezing would culminate in loud and strident nose-blowing. Still, there were those "dead spaces."

Rachlis remembers how, when he joined Paul in Santa Barbara for the last few interview sessions, Paul brought him up to speed. The comfort level he and Paul had enjoyed with Millar in New York had dissipated. "One, he wasn't allowed to smoke at the beach club, and how difficult he found that. At that point I smoked, too, so that was a warning. Two, is that there was unspoken, or not so unspoken, tension with Kenneth Millar's wife Margaret Millar that Paul interpreted as kind of jealousy that he was being the subject of this long, lengthy interview and profile.

"Paul had also warned me that he had already had the conversations with Ken about their daughter. I think that's certainly part of Margaret Millar's deep concern about the interviews. The stuff around the daughter had been a source of obviously great turmoil and emotional distress, but I think also a source of real tension, between Ken and his wife."

One night Rachlis and Paul ventured south to Los Angeles for dinner at Musso & Frank. Thirty years later, at Paul's memorial service, Rachlis recalled: "We then spent the rest of the night looking for where Lew Archer and Philip Marlowe's offices had to be. It turned out Lew Archer's place [at 8411½ Sunset Boulevard] was now a Denny's, which just crushed Paul."

The Santa Barbara sessions also included, for one afternoon, singer-songwriter Warren Zevon and his wife Crystal, ardent Ross Macdonald fans who, at Paul's invitation, had driven up from Los Angeles. Friendships were formed and, almost five years later, Millar played a heroic cameo in Paul's classic *Rolling Stone* cover story, "Warren Zevon: How He Saved Himself from a Coward's Death." At one of the lowest points in Zevon's alcoholic life, Millar showed up on his doorstep. Lew Archer-like, he had come to save Zevon's life. Zevon later told Paul: "I said to him, 'This is a real experience for me because to meet someone I'm so much in awe of *and* to be in such a vulnerable condition at the same time is really something.' And he just said, 'Don't be scared of ol' Ken.'"

On the last morning that he met with Paul and Rachlis, when asked what time it was, Millar looked at the hands on his wristwatch and said, "It's twenty to two, which means it's ten-thirty." Later he explained: "It runs on a battery and it needs a replacement. I just haven't had the time to get it done." He had just published his twenty-fourth and, though he didn't know it yet, last novel. In the seven years that followed these interviews, leading up to his death in 1983, the Alzheimer's disease that had afflicted him as early as 1971 continued to worsen.

ABOUT THIS BOOK:

Because the focus is on the interviewee, not the interviewers, the questions are not given attribution. Suffice it to say, the bulk of the questions came from Paul. Anyway, the answers are more important than the questions. More than just a collection of interviews with Kenneth Millar about himself and his impressive writing career, this book is intended to be compendium of his thoughts on, as evidenced by its table of contents, a wide variety of topics. Paul attempted to encapsulate the breadth of their conversations when he pitched his book proposal:

> We talked about everything imaginable: Hammett, Chandler, other writers; how Chandler, in his later years, had consciously tried to destroy the careers of up-and-coming mystery writers, particularly Macdonald's; "high" and "low" culture; Macdonald the teacher-scholar and Macdonald the popular novelist; the formation of and changes in his literary style; how and when to use slang; the influence of F. Scott Fitzgerald's *The Great Gatsby*, his favorite book, on his work (e.g., Macdonald consciously used Archer as the narrator but not the most important character in his novels just like Fitzgerald used Nick Carraway in *The Great Gatsby*); Canada; California; all of his novels and how they related to his life; his themes; his beliefs; his relationship to Archer; his thoughts on a final Archer novel—my God, everything.

Without sacrificing the truth of what was said—if anything, to preserve it—the interview material has sometimes been reorganized to make more chronological or thematic sense.

Regardless the setting and despite any distractions or "dead spots," what emerged for Paul then and now for us as readers was Millar's wisdom, his no-nonsense philosophies, a sharp eye (private and otherwise) and ear for criticism,

and a wealth of genuine knowledge about writing—and the life of a writer—that's indispensable (and sometimes self-contradictory).

"He's the only writer that I've ever approached," Paul told friends in 1976. "Why don't I go bug Norman Mailer or other writers who I like equally well? But I don't. He strikes this chord among a whole lot of people. I mean, it's something beyond his books that draws us to him personally. Whatever it is that we're drawn to comes from the books, but what we are drawn to isn't that he's the greatest writer in America—because he's not. It's something extra-literary in that sense. He does hit some primal thing that seems to set us all off and wondering, *What is he thinking of us now?* Better writers haven't done that for me."

Kevin Avery
Brooklyn, New York
March 7, 2015

ROSS MACDONALD BIBLIOGRAPHY

The following list constitutes all novels and short-story collections written by Kenneth Millar and published in his lifetime. Unless otherwise indicated, all were written under the Ross Macdonald pseudonym and were published by Alfred A. Knopf, Inc. Books reflecting an asterisk are non-Lew Archer novels or short-story collections.

1944   *The Dark Tunnel* (by Kenneth Millar, published by Dodd, Mead; a.k.a. *I Die Slowly*)°

1946   *Trouble Follows Me* (by Kenneth Millar, published by Dodd, Mead; a.k.a. *Night Train*)°

1947   *Blue City* (by Kenneth Millar)°

1948   *The Three Roads* (by Kenneth Millar)°

1949   *The Moving Target* (by John Macdonald)

1950   *The Drowning Pool* (by John Ross Macdonald)

1951   *The Way Some People Die* (by John Ross Macdonald)

1952   *The Ivory Grin* (a.k.a. *Marked for Murder*, by John Ross Macdonald)

1953   *Meet Me at the Morgue* (a.k.a. *Experience with Evil*, by John Ross Macdonald)°

1954   *Find a Victim* (by John Ross Macdonald)

1955   *The Name Is Archer* (by John Ross Macdonald, published by Bantam and collecting seven short stories: "Find the Woman," "Gone Girl," "The Bearded Lady," "The Suicide," "Guilt-Edged Blonde," "The Sinister Habit," and "Wild Goose Chase")

1956   *The Barbarous Coast*

1958   *The Doomsters*

1959   *The Galton Case*

1960   *The Ferguson Affair*°

1961   *The Wycherly Woman*

1962   *The Zebra-Striped Hearse*

1964   *The Chill*

1965   *The Far Side of the Dollar*

1966   *Black Money*

1967   *Archer in Hollywood* (omnibus collecting *The Moving Target*, *The Way Some People Die*, and *The Barbarous Coast*)

1968   *The Instant Enemy*

1969   *The Goodbye Look*

1970   *Archer at Large* (omnibus collecting *The Galton Case*, *The Chill*, and *Black Money*)

1971   *The Underground Man*

1973   *Sleeping Beauty*

1976   *The Blue Hammer*

1977   *Lew Archer: Private Investigator* (published by Mysterious Press and collecting the seven short stories from *The Name Is Archer* plus "Midnight Blue" and "Sleeping Dog")

1979   *Archer in Jeopardy* (omnibus collecting *The Doomsters*, *The Zebra-Striped Hearse*, and *The Instant Enemy*

May 31, 1974   Jill Krementz

Ken and Maggie share a laugh, though about what remains a mystery.

1. BEGINNINGS

KENNETH MILLAR: Some of my earliest memories go back to books. Picture books and things that were read to me before I could read. I'm talking about when I was three. I remember one, for example, about children having difficulty on stairs. One of the lines was: "Going down is difficult but going up is harder still." I know how old I was because I remember the place, and I left there when I was four. It was where we were living in Vancouver.

Who used to read the books to you?

My mother did. Books were very important to me. I started to draw at the same time, probably an imitation of the pictures in the books.

When you did start reading, what books made an impression on you?

Well, the first one I think of is *Heidi*. Offhand I can't think of anything else right away.

Did you write when you were a child? Or in high school were you taking journalism?

They didn't teach journalism in Canadian high school. Everything was just the classic disciplines. But, yeah, I started writing even before high school. I started writing when I was eleven or twelve.

You already had this feeling that's what you would want to do with your life then.

Yep. And I knew it for sure by the time I was fifteen. When I was in boarding school in Winnipeg—I went up there when I was eleven, I was there for a couple years—I started writing extensively on my own, both prose and verse. I wrote, for example, a long narrative poem about Bonnie Prince Charlie when I was about twelve. And a lot of other things.

It was mostly just plain fiction that I wrote. Then soon after that when I got into high school, by the time I was fourteen, I was writing serious verse—and a lot of it. I also wrote fiction, which I started trying on the magazines long before I was ready. I showed my verse to a cousin of mine who taught English and had studied English at the University of Toronto, and he encouraged me. He said

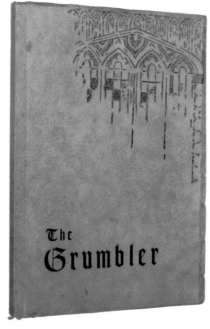

Later issue of The Grumbler *from 1932 featuring a Philo Vance parody by Ken Millar.*

what I was doing was worthwhile and I should stay with it. What he actually said, I remember, was that this early verse was similar to the verse that other people who later became writers had written.

I wrote all sorts of things. I wrote stuff that was supposed to be funny, too. My first published piece was a parody of Sherlock Holmes, which was I'm sure an imitation of Stephen Leacock. Stephen Leacock was the leading writer in Canada at that time and the father of *all* twentieth-century American humor. All the great American humorists, from Benchley and including Fitzgerald, acknowledged their debt to Leacock.

Where was the Sherlock Holmes parody published?

School magazine called *The Grumbler*. Age fourteen.[1] I went to high school in Kitchener, Ontario. It's Southern Ontario. It's about 200 miles from Detroit. It's quite close to Toronto.

You started reading poetry apparently.

It was traditional Romantic period poetry. I read on my own a great deal. I was what they call a bookworm in those days. Canada had quite a number of poets, too, you know, of its own. In fact, it's had a wonderful twentieth-century efflorescence of poetry. There are approximately a thousand active poets in twentieth-century Canadian literature. I've known some of the poets and one of my two or three

---

1 Published by what is now the Kitchener-Waterloo Collegiate and Vocational School.

ROBERT D. FORD
Honour English and History
LONDON, ONTARIO

ALBERT McWHA
Honour English and History
WINDSOR, ONTARIO

DONALD M. HERRON
Honour English and History
TILLSONBURG, ONTARIO

JOHN MIDDAUGH
Honour English and History
LONDON, ONTARIO

BETHEA McGILL
Honour English and History
ORILLIA, ONTARIO

KENNETH MILLAR
Honour English and History
LONDON, ONTARIO

WILMER McGUFFIN
Honour English and History
ETTRICK, ONTARIO

L. JEAN PHILLIPS
Honour English and History
LONDON, ONTARIO

Ford and Millar in the Waterloo College Yearbook, The Occidentalia 1938.

dearest friends is a Canadian poet. Robert Ford. He's the Canadian ambassador to Russia at the present time. We were very close in college. He won the Governor General's Medal for Poetry.[2]

Robert Burns was a particularly important writer to me because he was the Scottish laureate, so to speak. He was my father's main source of inspiration. My father was a poet in Scottish dialect.

A lot of the images in The Galton Case *are sailing images. Was your father a sailor?*

Yes, he was a captain. He had his captain's papers, and during the first World War he became a harbor pilot in Vancouver Harbor. Those are my first memories of him, in connection with the sea and going out on his tugboat and so on. That was something he just took up rather late in life. He was close to forty when he got his captain's papers. I think what he was doing was what amounted to his idea of war service. He had always been interested in the water. He was too old to be drafted.

Was he a good poet?

I don't know. He was a light poet, he wasn't trying to be particularly serious. He wrote a poem about my birth which I thought was pretty good, in Scottish dialect. It was probably recited to me back at the age of memory. I didn't actually see it written, of course, until I learned to read, but I don't remember when it was.

You must read a poem like that with a great deal of various emotions.

Well, it really does help someone to become a writer if the stars are right and there are other people who are writers in the family. Or painters or whatever. Any kind of creative work, I think, gets you used to the idea of artistic creation.

Did your father just write as a hobby?

Oh no, he was a professional writer. His main work was as a newspaper editor, like his father. His father came over from Scotland and founded a small Canadian newspaper called *The Walkerton Herald*, which is still in existence, by the way. My father, he taught school for a year or two and then started out on his own journalistic career, and he edited several different small papers in Canada. One of the most interesting ones was a paper which he established for the Canadian government at Athabasca Landing, which is on Great Slave Lake or Lake Athabasca in the Northwest Territories. The idea was to start some kind of cultural enterprise for the Northwest Territories. Of course, it was paid for by the Canadian government. There was a touch of the pioneer in that sort of thing. My father was profoundly interested in the Indians of the Northwest, and in fact at one period for several months he went and lived with an Indian tribe. He had an interesting life. But his active life was ended prematurely by a very severe illness. I guess he had his first stroke when he was only about forty or so, and he ended up flat on his back.

Your father left you and your mother when you were very young, is that right? And then he died when he was in his fifties.

Yeah, he was on his back for about ten years. The last few years he was in a hospital in Toronto, an Ontario government hospital. I lived seventy miles from Toronto. I rarely managed to get down there; I didn't have any transportation or any money at that time.

But no, most of my childhood I wasn't in contact with my father. He was out in the West and I was in the East. And then when I went to Winnipeg, he wasn't in Winnipeg; he merely turned up there for a week at one time. I would see him a week every two years. That sort of thing.

Was that very hard? Or was a week every two years better than not at all?

I'm sure it was. I certainly dwell on those meetings with interest and pleasure. He had never been, in my life, a man playing the full role of father. I was brought

<hr>

2 Millar credited Ford, to whom he dedicated *Blue City*, with getting the book published in a Russian literary journal. "He's very, very prominent in literary circles," he told Paul, "and I feel certain that he must've had some connection with drawing that book to the attention of whoever published it. Ford is not only a diplomat but he's also a very important poet. He translates from half a dozen languages in addition to his own poetry, including the Russian. So he has I think a unique position in Russia cultural life." Millar was concerned, however, about Paul referencing Ford in his article. "In connection with my diplomat friend in Moscow, it would be a good idea to conceal his identity, I think. I wouldn't want to have anything put in print that would interfere with his duties or his standing. You know what I mean. So just conceal his identity. He's not the Canadian ambassador and his name isn't Robert Ford. Just a 'Western diplomat.'" Ford passed away in 1998.

Drafts of letters to Bob Ford circa 1980.

up by my mother. See, they broke up when I was three or four, and I went with my mother. So I only saw my father incidentally after that, and I never lived in the same house with him.

Your books often deal with the sins of the father being passed down. In your life what sins of your father did you inherit?

Well, I've tried to not do some of the things that my father did. I've been luckier in my life, of course, and haven't been under the same compulsions as he.

Were these sins represented to you that it was your father who was to blame?

So it appeared to me. So it appeared to my mother, too. It always appears that way when couples separate; each one blames the other. I tried to avoid that. I

tried to avoid abandonment of my responsibilities, but of course none of us is totally successful in that respect. So I've probably inherited my father's fecklessness, too, to some extent. But when I look back over it now, I don't blame either of them.

I'm answering a different question than the one you asked, but it just happened to be the one that interested me. My father actually, apart from the simple fact that he didn't stay with me, didn't do anything wrong that I know of in his life. He was a good man and a highly respected man among the people who knew him. He had a tragic life, though, because things didn't go well with him after our family broke up. It was about that time that he had his first stroke, which ultimately completely paralyzed him. He had a very, very dreary and sad life in his later years. He came back, of course, a little bit later when he was very ill. My mother, who was a nurse, did her best to look after him.

Did your father have trouble speaking after the stroke?

Yes, his last few years, his brain centers wouldn't permit him to speak, but he was actually able to write poetry.

What was your father's full name?

John M. Millar.

What was your mother's full name?

Anne Moyer.

She died not too long after your father died, is that correct?

Within a few years. He was a little older than she was.

You didn't really grow up with your mother either in a sense, did you?

No, but I was much more in touch with her than I was with my father. I was raised by various relatives and I lived at times with my mother. Never or very seldom with her alone. It was generally in her mother's house. She lived with her mother after she left my father for the most part, and I lived in that house, too, for long periods of time.

Was that a happy time or an unhappy time, living with your mother?

It wasn't a happy time, no.

Undoubtedly there was a reason why she didn't bring you up.

Well, it's because she was physically incapable of looking after me really. My mother was a registered nurse in Winnipeg General Hospital at the time of a typhoid epidemic and she caught typhoid from her patients. It wrecked her physically. She was incapable after that of doing sustained work.

This was when she was a young woman in her thirties.

Yeah, it was before I was born.

Was the time with your mother unhappy strictly because of the illness or did you not get along in any way?

Well, I think we got along pretty well, but my mother wasn't capable of dealing with a child after her own illness. She just wasn't up to looking after somebody.

Could you understand that at the time or was that a later observation?

Oh, I think I understood it partly. I felt somewhat deprived in a family sense. I felt that I had been traded around quite a bit by the time I grew up. It wasn't anybody's fault. It just happened.

But that's not easy to realize at the time.

That's right. Children are very jealous of their rights, and if they're deprived of their rights they resent it. Family rights. I ran into bad luck, you know, with both my parents being disabled really. It was just bad luck.

One parent can satisfy a child. I think *any* human contact is desirable and especially a loving one, even if it's only once in a year. All these things are so significant to children. Any positive thing that you do for them is remembered. I must say that my whole adult development was *pieced* together from little things year by year, you know. Meetings with my father and father substitutes, memories, touches of kindness from men. Teachers, for example.

You mention somewhere—I think it's in one of the introductions—that your relatives would look at you and see that you were the son of a wandering man, and you refer to that as the paternal curse.

People don't attach the same importance to a fatherless boy that they do to one with a father who is there on the spot. People's judgments of children depend a great deal on the children's immediate background—I'm sure you know that—and this was particularly true in earlier generations. We're much more inclined now to take children on their own merits. That wasn't true in those days. In those days I was my father's son and if I were to turn out well that would be a miracle. You know what I mean.

In those days there were not that many broken marriages also.

But this applies to something more than just broken marriages, it applies to the whole spectrum of life. What was your question?

The paternal curse.

Oh. Well, you must understand that one dramatizes one's own life when one is young. You gradually *de*-dramatize it as you get older perhaps. Any writer will take his own life and make some kind of central, primal story out of it, and he will draw on that story time after time. This is true of all writers. It's particularly true of me because I've done it consciously and intentionally. I wasn't satisfied with the earlier versions, and I kept thinking that there was more to find out and more to say. And that's true. Even though what I say isn't necessarily an improvement in a literary way, it maybe hews closer to the truth. Or it may be that what a writer should do intentionally is what he does anyway: he writes on a curve so the reader can see the whole curve.

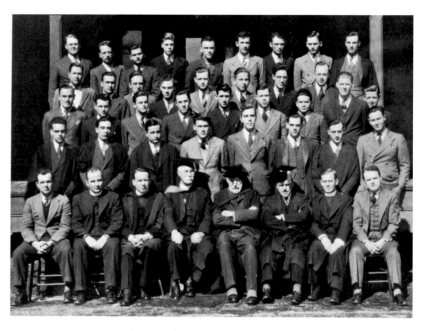

Back Row (left to right): D. Pitts, W. Smith, L. Hemsworth, H. Whicher, J. King, J. Henderson, L. Owen, F. Killer, L. Nelles.

Second Row: B. Ford, J. Rider, A. Jared, D. Pearce, B. Sanders, H. Hamilton, H. Johnston, R. Schippling.

Third Row: J. Lee, A. Sweeton, S. Horton, R. Kenney, W. Biehn, J. Douglas, B. Allen, K. Leckie, J. Watton.

Fourth Row: J. Doidge, L. Patterson, B. Martin, B. Rannie, W. Graham, D. Henry, B. Silcox, K. Millar.

Front Row: W. Cochrane, Rev. W. Brown, Rev. R. T. Appleyard, Dr. F. Anderson, Dr. C. C. Waller, Dr. J. D. Ralph, Rev. S. Rider, R. Crichton.

This page and next: Ford and Millar in the Waterloo College Yearbook,
The Occidentalia 1938.

Getting back to the sins of the father, it's natural for a child of a broken marriage to feel guilty. One of the sins in this case could mean that you felt guilty.

Well, it's a consequence. Whenever a child is separated from his father he blames himself. Always. My father's absenting himself from my mother wasn't necessarily a sin at all. It may have been a necessity—for both of them.

But it's difficult to reach that conclusion when one is four years old or five years old.

Well, you don't understand it. You have to think about it in mystical terms or whatever you want to call it because you don't know any other way to understand reality. Fairytale terms, that's what children understand, and there's a lot of truth in those fairytales when it's a beheaded father and son.[3] There's profound truth in them, in the images themselves. Children aren't always wrong. At the same time they don't understand reality. It takes a whole lifetime to understand your own life. And I suppose that's the basic reason why I recur to these themes. I have an idea that the truth is in the whole series of explanations on the curve. The truth is the curve. Because you've got an added truth in it—you've got the development of a mind, an imagination, from the beginning to the end—that reinforces the truth of your subject matter. I'm writing about that, too. You see, the whole purpose

3 In *The Instant Enemy*, three-year-old Davy Spanner's father is decapitated in a train accident, leaving the youth to spend the night alongside the headless body.

GAZETTE EDITORIAL STAFF

Back Row (left to right): George Weinstein, Hugh Knox, Bob Ford, Kenneth Millar, Ronald Ritchie, Donald Herron.
Front Row: Jean Ferguson, Ronald Bourne, Florence Elliott, Bob Syrett, Claude Turner, Mary Screaton.

of all these stratagems, all these problems and so on, is to make notations of the truth. The imaginative truth.

How old were your parents when you were born? Thirties?

No, they were both forty. My mother had previously lost three other children, and it was just lucky for me that I survived. And lucky for her, too. It was very important to her to have a child. She was very good to me.

You see, I lived for long periods in the same house with her. But then there were other periods, for example, when I was going to school in Winnipeg, I didn't see her at all except in the summers when I would go back to Ontario and spend the summer. And then the year after I left there, I lived with my mother's sister Laura in Alberta. And so on. About half the time I was with my mother and half the time I was just living with relatives. Or in boarding schools. I was in Winnipeg for two years.

And your mother wasn't in Winnipeg?

No. Then the following year I lived in Medicine Hat with my aunt. She wasn't there either; she was living with her own mother in Ontario for a time. But I'd say it was about half and half. Unless I were to lay it out year by year, I couldn't explain any better than that. I will lay it out by year if you want me to. I remember every place I've been since I was three.

Really?

Sure. Well, it helps, you know, if you live in a series of distinct places, because you can attach the time to them. Lots of memories of Vancouver. I remember the end of World War I, which occurred when I was three.

I was born in California.[4] I don't remember the occasion or the year or two after that, but I think that within the first year or so my parents moved back to Canada where I lived with them in Vancouver until I was four—no more than four. At that

time, my mother decided to move back East to her family, her mother, and she did and she took me with her. I lived with her and her mother and one of her sisters in my grandmother's house for several years, from the age of four to ten or eleven. Then my father's sister, Margaret, who lived in Winnipeg, took me for a couple of years and put me in this boarding school, St. Johns. That was terminated by not exactly the Crash but by economic events associated with the Crash at the end of the Twenties. And the next year I spent with another of my mother's sisters in Medicine Hat, Alberta. By this time I was in high school. The next couple of years I went back and lived with my mother and with her mother until I finished high school.

What I have left out, however, are long periods that I can't pin down so well: when I was with my mother, when I was a young child, over a period of several years and we lived in boarding houses and all that. Several of which I remember distinctly of course, but I can't pin them down in time. There was a period in British Columbia and then a period in Ontario later which I'm not too clear about.

Except when I was young, I was of course much, much clearer about these things, and I counted the number of places I had lived up through my teens, and it was fifty different buildings. I think I was sixteen when I made the count. I don't remember anymore nearly as distinctly now as I did then. I had just finished that period in my life.

That must've certainly left its mark.

Yes, it made for *varied* memories.

Was there a sense of resentfulness towards all that moving?

Well, not resentfulness so much as wondering why I should be unfortunate. I considered it a misfortune of course. You know, what's best for a kid is to live with his own family in one place and go to school there and have a chance to graduate and build a solid, single life. Now, of course, these are the subjects I write about in my books. I'm grateful *now* for having been exposed to so much experience when I was young because I think those things make a novelist.

Take a look into the early lives of other novelists, you very often find some of the same sorts of things. It wasn't pure coincidence that Dickens was the first great novelist that I really took to. I started reading him when I was eleven because he was writing out of a similar kind of experience and, of course, writing much better and more importantly than I ever have been able to—still. I felt a kinship there when I was a kid. You know, experiences like that, of finding a great artist who has made something of a life not wholly dissimilar from one's own, can help to convert a boy into a writer.

When did you become aware that Dickens had an effect like that on you?

It depends on what you mean by "aware." I wasn't aware of it at the time, but looking back I'm sure it's true. You can become aware of something by doing something about it. I became a writer. But as a critic and understanding the situation in, say, an autobiographical sense, I didn't realize it until I became a writer myself; you know, a published writer in my twenties.[5]

In one of your interviews you refer to Oliver Twist as the first important book you read.

4 Millar was born in Los Gatos on December 13, 1915.

5 Millar cut off Paul when he asked, "When you were writing in your teens, were you writing Dickensonian prose or—" "No," the older man, ever the teacher, corrected him. "The word would be *Dickensian*, Paul."

Yes. *Oliver Twist*, which I read when I was eleven, had a tremendous impact on me. I read it with such fascination that my mother could hardly stop me. I was able to identify with Oliver. While my situation was very much better than his, it was sort of parallel. There was a parallelism which I felt. But I think mainly I was carried away by reading, probably for the first time, a really great writer completely on my own. It was around about that period or soon afterwards that I started to think in terms of becoming a writer myself, and within the following year I was writing and I've been writing ever since.

Don't misunderstand me, I wasn't normally reading Dickens at the age of eleven. I can remember that at the same time I was reading *Tarzan of the Apes*. In fact, the whole Tarzan series. But it was Dickens that sort of lit whatever light it is that's been leading me ever since, rather than *Tarzan of the Apes*.

Do you reread Dickens frequently now?

Yes.

Do you reread Tarzan of the Apes at all?

I did the other month when a young friend of mine, a college student, was reading *Tarzan*. He was so fascinated by it that you could hardly get him to engage in conversation. So I took a look at it, and it didn't look that good to me. It no longer matched my fantasy, let's say.

You were saying that you lived in over fifty different places. Did your travels take you from one coast to the other?

No, I didn't live in fifty different municipalities, I lived in fifty different buildings by the time I was sixteen. And that's the real background of my writing, I think. Variegation. Social variegation. It's helpful to know how it feels on all the different levels, you know.

You must have gone to a lot of high schools, then, moving around as you did.

Just three. I went to the Kitchener, Ontario, high school [KCI: the Kitchener Collegiate Institute]; that's the one I've been talking about. That's where I went mostly. That's where I took my last two years of high school, and that's where I later taught. The same school. But I also went to a Medicine Hat high school in Alberta [Alexandra High School]. That wasn't quite as good, but it was good enough. And I spent two years at a boys boarding school in Winnipeg, St. John's, which I've mentioned to you. I think probably the standards there were not up to the public high schools, but they weren't markedly inferior either. And there were other advantages: contact with pretty good masters, mostly from England, and they had a darn good athletic program, which is important to teenagers. We had an excellent gymnastic coach … Sergeant Major Tompkins. He was in his sixties and he had been the British Empire gymnastic champ. He was a retired sergeant major from the British Army.

You grew up in rural or semirural areas in Canada.

Yes, a good part of my young life was spent in Kitchener, Ontario, which is the center of an excellent agricultural area planted by many of my own forbearers. My grandfather, my great grandfather had farms in that area. They were Pennsylvania Dutch people who came over to the United States in the middle of

GRUMBLER STAFF

Seated: Margaret Conrad: Wilda Graeber: Vi. Maxwell (*Business Mgr.*): Howard Schmidt (*Editor*): Susan Devitt: Marg. Sturm: Helen Kaufman: Eunice Kuntz
Standing: Eddie Knorr: Nelson Erb: Kenneth Millar: Clay Hall: William Wight: Henry Enns: Frank Brent: Garland Hallman: Graham Campbell: Clare Milhausen.

Margaret and Ken in The Grumbler *(1932).*

the nineteenth century for the most part. I had a chance to work summers and one whole year on a good general farm in the neighborhood of Kitchener.

How big a city was Kitchener?

It was about 25,000 in the days that we're talking about, and now it's 125,000. It has sought growth. In some respects it was fairly rugged. It wouldn't compare with the ruggedness of the big cities, though.

You said that you felt supported while you were in Canada by your American citizenship.

Yes. A lot of bad things happened to me in Canada, bad things in the sense of poverty and so on, being pushed around quite a bit, from one place to another. One family to another. One house to another. I was supported by the idea that, let's say, my life in Canada wasn't the only potential life I might have. Now, of course, it was more of a dream than a reality, but the dream actually did come true, so that lends it more validity than it would otherwise have. I did make my way back to the United States and became an American again, and in fact to California.[6] I came back to home base and sort of started over, and I did so not entirely by my own volition. San Diego is the first place I lived when I came to California because I was transferred to the naval base there from the East Coast. For example, the Navy sent me to California. I had no choice.

6 "His mother used to talk to him about California," Robert Easton told Paul. "He couldn't remember; he left when he was two, I think. His mother and father were happy here. The family was happy and united. So afterwards, when the mother and father separated, she would tell him, the little boy, about the happy time in California. California became a dream place to him. He's told me this. It became a place of happiness, where happiness might be found, and subconsciously this was working in his mind." Easton added, "He said that 'I was brought up to regard California as a kind of a promised land.'"

Do you think you would have come to California eventually on your own?

Yes. It probably would have been under less fortunate circumstances, maybe by way of Hollywood or something like that. This way it was I think really fortunate.

Do you ever think about returning to Canada?

I'd like to go back, but not for anything longer than a visit. I find as I get older I'm more interested in going back and sort of renewing acquaintances and completing a circle, so to speak.

Your wife was talking a little about how you'd met. The two of you went to tea once before you dropped out of the University of Western Ontario for a semester and went to Europe. You asked her to go to Ireland with you.

That's right. See, I had been in love with Margaret for years. She was, as you might gather, a really outstanding girl. She had and has a lot of life. She comes from a rather extraordinary family.

So you sort of admired Margaret from a distance?

Well, it wasn't exactly a distance. We knew each other but I never took her out.

Other than when you took her out to tea, until you came back from England.

Yeah, just one time before. I hadn't seen her, you see, for a couple of years before that. She went to a different university. She went to Toronto and I went to the University of Western Ontario in London.

There was some feeling between you, though, before you went, it sounds like.

There was on my part. We were, let's say, prepared to become close friends by our common background, and it's the sort of thing that happens immediately in some cases. We went to the same high school and had the same interests. Such as debating and reading.

When you ran into her after you came back, at the library, it was by accident?

That's right, it was accidental. But, you see, it was fated because we were both book people. The library is where we would naturally see each other.

And from that point then you saw her a lot?

Every day.

And how long was it from that time till you got married?

Well, it was a year and a half. That was the year and a half that it took me to finish college. We got married the day after I graduated. I got married when I was twenty-two.

Was your daughter Linda born when you were going to graduate school?

Actually she was born in the June before the September that I started teaching; but the preceding year I was studying to be a high school teacher at the University of Toronto. She was born really when I was a student teacher.

Your wife's background was quite similar to yours?

Well, in many ways they were very similar. We lived in the same city, Kitchener. Of course, she lived there right on through and I lived in many other places. We did go to high school together and we got essentially the same education, except

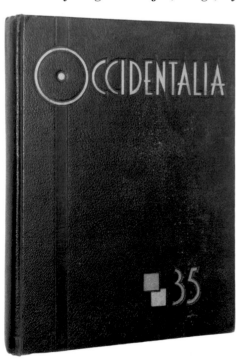
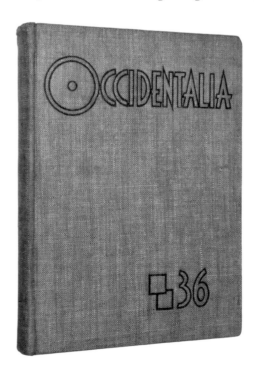
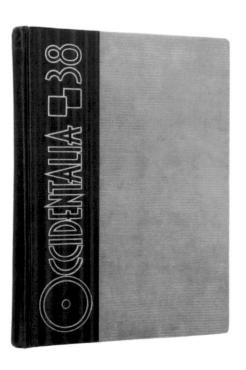

that she decided to take classics in her last year. So she took five years of Greek in one and got a classics scholarship at the University of Toronto. I went down to the University of Western Ontario and studied English and history. But while there are these minor differences in our backgrounds, the major cultural background is very similar indeed.

Just to go on for a minute, there were other important differences in our backgrounds. Her father was one of the leading men in the city of Kitchener. In fact, he was mayor and I think he sat on the city council for thirty-odd years and so on.

It was a wealthy family, is that right?

I wouldn't call it wealthy. It was important. I don't think he ever became wealthy. He was a successful businessman. He put a lot of his energies into other things than the business. He was a great sportsman.… [H]e was Canada's leading amateur hockey coach. Many of his players went right into the National Hockey League from the junior team that he coached. I have a lot of respect for him. He's a nice man, an extraordinary man.

I lived in comparative poverty. Not real poverty—there were always good middle-class relatives who were able to and willing to look after me.

The Summer Olympics are going on right now in Montreal. You were active in sports when you were in high school, weren't you?

I played baseball. I never played football except just in the scrub way, and I never boxed. Of course, I used to spend a lot of time with boxers because the wrestlers and the boxers used to travel together and be in the same meets. Swimming was really my best sport and it's the one that's persisted, and it's something that doesn't have any age limit. I swim half a mile a day. For one period in recent years, Margaret and I were bicycling over ten miles every day in hilly territory.

In connection with the Olympic games, I was struck by how many of the events I have actually participated in myself. I don't mean as an Olympic competitor. For

SWIMMING TEAM

Standing, left to right: Bob Smith, Kenneth Miller, Jack Levine, John Stevenson, Kenneth Symmington, John Forristal, Ward Smith, Em Orlick (Coach).
Seated: Carson Mark, Charles Froud, Tom Lawson, Dave Johnston, Scott Montgomery, Les Milton.

Ken Millar, swimming team photo, The Occidentalia 1935.

example, I was leader of the horse team at school, and I did a lot of work on the uneven bars and horizontal bar. I've won a lot of swimming and diving competitions. And running. I've been in skating. I was for a couple of years in intercollegiate competition in wrestling. While I never set the world on fire in any of these things, I was involved in them and enjoyed them. So you might say that I'm the ruins of what could have been a man of action. Of course, you have to make choices as to what you're going to be. When I went in seriously for scholarship, I pretty well gave up my physical pleasures—the ones we were talking about anyway.

Are you a religious man?

In a sense, but I don't know that I can define the sense.

Any particular denomination?

No, I'm not an anything. But I come from a somewhat religious background, and there's no way you can be brought up in a religious family with a Mennonite grandmother and that sort of thing without being touched by religion. I think religion is like a forest fire, which just simply has to be not put out but kept under control. I think that a great many errors have been committed in the name of religion—but only in its name, not in the truth of it. I think we have to constantly try to bear in mind and act in terms of a religion that doesn't exclude people or negate them but which also teaches them some of the limits and controls.

What are the evils of religion?

Well, the main evil of religion is a tendency to regard a nonbeliever as outside the pale, to be treated badly. That's the main thing. It's better to have no religion at all than an exclusive one, because religion turned upside down is just hell. T. E. Hulme described Romanticism as "spilt religion," but you can turn it around and describe certain kinds of religion as spilt Romanticism. Of course, this does not apply to the great historic religions. Far from it.

You're not an atheist, you're a believer in something? Or a hoper in something?

Oh, I believe in human values. I don't have any direct contact with the divine world. If I did have I'd be afraid of it. I don't know whether that makes me an atheist or not. I think I live in sufficient fear and trembling to qualify as a believer, but I don't want to know the source of my fear and trembling too intimately. Kierkegaard, whom I just referred to, is one of the major influences and has been at least in my life.

I've just been reading Greene quite a bit. Have you ever been interested in Catholicism from an intellectual standpoint, which he seems to be, rather than an emotional standpoint?

Graham Greene doesn't interest me intellectually. Please understand me, this is not in any way a rejection of Graham Greene, whom I admire greatly. He just doesn't seem to me to be an intellectual writer. His values don't seem to me to be particularly intellectual, they seem to me to be intuitive. Intuitive and religious. Now, of course, I may be making a mistake in drawing a distinction between the intuitive and the religious on one hand and the intellectual on the other, but that's the way I see it.

WRESTLING TEAM

Standing, left to right: Vic Lafontaine (Coach), Bruce Sloane, Stewart Patterson, Paul Elson, Kenneth Miller, Bill Bryden, Gordon Munn, Claude Turner.
Seated: Osler Lockhart, Lionel Munn, Pete Beach, Bill Duncan, Norman Anderson, Charlie Swartz.
Absent: Tom McGarry, Bill Ewener.

WRESTLING TEAM

Back row, left to right: Charlie Hayes, Ken Millar, Jack Lee, George Dodd, Ken Bodkin, Cecil Hiuser.
Centre row: Stu Carver (Manager), Lorne Spry, Lorne Brooks, Norm Anderson, Jim McGill, Stew Horton, Osler Loskhart, Claude Turner (Coach).
Front row: Jack Zomerplaag, Stu Patterson, Lionel Munn, Charlie Swartz, Bill Brydon, George Willis.   *Insets, left to right:* Bill Ewener (Captain), Bill Duncan.

Ken Millar, wrestling team photos in The Occidentalia 1935 *and* 1936.

I was just reading Journey without Maps and was struck by Greene's statement that he was interested in Catholicism not emotionally at all. So he became a Catholic strictly on an intellectual level, which is a sort of remarkable schizophrenia in a way to do that.

Well, I don't take Greene quite as seriously as you do. I think he's an awfully good writer, particularly a good fiction writer, but when he gets into theology I find him hard to follow. I don't find him particularly interesting in that field.

It seems like that's one way of dealing with the problem of faith or lack of faith: accepting the intellectual arguments for it and not worrying about the emotional arguments, if that is indeed possible.

Well, that's just a kind of standard Roman Catholic approach.

I know nothing much about Catholicism. Of all the professional religions that one appeals to me the most.

Well, it's got the highest intellectual content. Some Jesuits are among the great scholars of the world and have been traditionally. Much as I admire their scholarship, I don't go to them for religious instruction. [*laughs*] I don't trust professionals in the field, let's say.

I don't want to criticize Greene, but you asked me a direct question; I had to give you an honest answer. I find him a very interesting writer. I think one major source of his interest is the fact that he went through a psychoanalysis in his teens. A truly major event and at an early time in our modern history. That would be, well, almost sixty years ago. Fifty-five years ago anyway. My whole lifetime ago. I tend to regard that as one of the sources of his difference. I'm sure he does, too.

There are references in some of your books to Lew Archer in connection with priests. Is Archer Catholic?

Oh yes. He was brought up in the Catholic Church to the extent that he lived with his grandmother, who was a Roman Catholic and as you know wanted to make a priest out of him. This is a kind of transliteration of my grandmother's being an old-fashioned Mennonite, I think.

What do the Mennonites believe?

Well, the old Mennonites dress in black and don't use anything more mechanical than a buggy. They still drive a horse and buggy. They have their own community, their own traditions, their own morality, which is extremely strict, except perhaps as regards to sexuality. Their sexual life is fairly lusty.

As in Archer's background there was a split between my paternal grandmother and my paternal grandfather. He was a Methodist and a bit of an intellectual, you see, and she was considerably younger and in no way an intellectual—and a Mennonite who, however muted her religion, went to the Methodist Church all through her marriage, which lasted for about fifty years. She married him when she was sixteen, by the way, and had fourteen children. When he died, she immediately went back to the Mennonite Church. It was at that period that I entered her life when I was I guess four, and she sent me to the Mennonite Sunday school. So that was my first experience with church. My own father was an atheist; he never went to church at all.

How did you react to church?

I didn't have any particular reaction. It probably seemed a little strange to me. I kept on going to church as, you know, people do, especially when you're a small child. I kept on going to whatever church was favored by the people I was living with. That included the so-called United Church, which was primarily Methodist, which was what my grandfather was, and the Christian Science Church, which was what my mother belonged to. She sent me to Christian Science Church and

Sunday school for several years. I was a member of the choir in an Episcopalian boys school in Winnipeg for a couple of years. When I lived with my uncle in Medicine Hat, Alberta, who was a Presbyterian, I went to the Presbyterian Church, so I got a real good mix. Now I only go to church in order to attend the funerals of my friends.

I forget whether I told you what thing had happened at that Presbyterian Church in Medicine Hat which affected my feeling about the moral value of going to church. The regular minister was away on a vacation and a young minister took his place and preached a pretty good sermon, which was connected in some way with the season of the year. The following Sunday the regular minister came back and preached identically the same sermon, word for word. He just used the same book of sermons. I didn't think that was quite fair, to however accidentally make a church full of people sit through the same thing twice out of laziness. What was so funny was that the entire audience sat there and nobody moved, nobody left. Maybe they hadn't listened to it the first time around. Or maybe they were just transfixed by horror, as I was.

How old were you at the time?

Fourteen.

And that was the reason you stopped attending church?

No, I didn't stop going to church right after that. As I said, as young people have to do more or less, I followed the habits of whatever people I was living with. However, ultimately I did have to assert my dubieties about going to church. In the last year of her life, my mother and I lived together when I was in the university, shared an apartment, and she stopped insisting that I should go her way. We didn't quarrel about it anymore.

Here's a quote from The New Yorker: "I started drinking in Canada at twelve. I was a semi-juvenile delinquent, to say the least." Did the drinking at all persist past that or was it wild oats?

No, it was just something that occurred. And I think it's generally true of kids in my milieu at that time. I started drinking awfully young, though. I first got drunk when I was twelve, I think. I don't mean that I went right on drinking every day; I didn't have the opportunity. But alcohol was just as serious a problem socially and otherwise in the last generation as drugs are now. It's hard to believe, I know.

Isn't there a big difference, though, between minor hooliganism and shooting dope?

Drugs certainly do make the difference. Though there were drugs on the scene when I was young, too, I never used them.

You also had your pool hall days.

Yeah, I played a lot of pool. I don't know how I ever got through high school. Somehow I got through. I had a pool table for a while, but I don't have a room that I could put one in now.

My greatest feat—this is not for the record—was breaking into the public library in order to be able to read Hemingway, because they had him in a locked book room. Actually I didn't have to break anything; I climbed on a fire escape and went in an unlocked window. Nobody was allowed to read Hemingway or Flaubert, several other writers, they were just kept there for posterity. In a fairly puritan Canadian city they were regarded as unreadable. I must've been around fourteen. It gives you some idea, though, of how important writers were—not just to me but to that whole culture.[7]

When did you emerge from your semi-delinquent days to your not-so-delinquent days?

Well, when I was sixteen I graduated from high school. I went and worked on a farm for a year plus and I settled down pretty well. It was quite a satisfying life for a while. It was primarily a dairy farm, but they also raised other things.

So there wasn't anything like in The Doomsters, where a plainclothesman snatches a teenage Archer stealing a battery from a Sears Roebuck and lets him go—but not without first scaring him away from a life of crime?

Well, there was an incident in which I got let off, for which I was grateful.

Can I ask what you were let off for?

I don't think I'll answer.

People with any spirit eventually get into some kind of jam at least once.

Oh, everybody gets into some kind of a jam, sure. I had another experience that was probably formative for me in relation to this kind of writing. I had an uncle by marriage who I've since realized was a fairly big-time manager in the slot machine racket in Winnipeg. That explained the gun he carried in his Packard and stuff like that, you know.

You see, I was just a kid, and it wouldn't be talked about to me—it was undoubtedly known to everybody else—it's only in the last year or so that I put some of this together. I *think* that probably was very important in my life to be aware of this right in the immediate family. I really wasn't directly related to him; he married my father's sister. I still haven't got to the point of being able to write directly about that, but I'm planning to.

---

7 Tom Nolan, in *Ross Macdonald: A Biography*, reported that other forbidden writers' work that young Millar found behind the library's locked door included Hammett, François Rabelais, and Faulkner. On his way out of the library, Millar grabbed an armful of bestselling fiction, which he deposited down a manhole. This tale, that he had deemed "not for the record" to Paul, was related to Nolan by Millar's almost lifelong friend, Donald Pearce.

2. FIRST WORKS

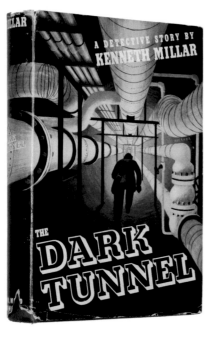

Your early books are a combination of the spy novel, the big-city novel, and the detective novel.

Well, the first two books were spy novels. One [*The Dark Tunnel*] was suggested by my visit to Nazi Germany in the Thirties, and the other [*Trouble Follows Me*] came out of my wartime experience. The book starts in Hawaii and moves from the West Coast to the East Coast. It's not a very well-constructed book but it gets some feeling of wartime in. One thing that is important in the book is the treatment of the black people in the United States, particularly in Detroit. I was very much struck by the Detroit riots, you know, though I lived in Ann Arbor at that time. I didn't see Detroit to any great extent when I was a kid. I paid a few visits to it but I didn't live there. I lived in Ann Arbor after I got in graduate school for the most part. If there's any validity in that book, it has to do with its treatment of the blacks at a time when they weren't generally given what might be called an evenhanded treatment. It was an unconscious withholding of human characteristics from blacks in American fiction. I got past that a little. It helps, you know, to have been raised in Canada.

I'm not sure I follow.

Well, there aren't a great many blacks in Canada and they are not treated as a separate segment of the population to the degree that they are in the United States. They're much more evenly matched, so to speak. But in Eastern Canada there is some black population dating from the days of the underground railroad, and I was brought up in that general area. They came over the border and settled. There's much less racial prejudice in Canada than there is in the United States; at least there was in the time when I was growing up.

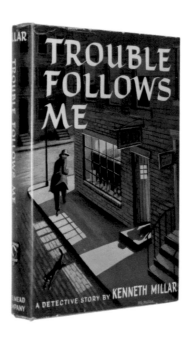

Did Trouble Follows Me *do slightly less well than* The Dark Tunnel?

Yes. I think it was not so good a book either. I wrote it under peculiar circumstances. I was in the Navy and I wrote sections of it in a room with two other guys.

On a ship?

Yeah, on a ship. That didn't help with the concentration. It's quite a wandering sort of plot.

How fast were those two books written?

I *think* no more than a month or two for *The Dark Tunnel*. A couple of months. I would go down to the Angell Hall at the University of Michigan at night and sit in my office and write eight or ten pages after the day was over. It's the kind of writing you do in between other jobs, as you know. The other one, I think it dragged on a bit because I had fairly demanding duties when I was in the Navy. I was in the communications department; I was responsible for all the coding business on the ship.

At this point you and Margaret had been married how many years?

I had been married for a number of years. We were married in 1938.

You joined the Navy in 1944 when you were twenty-nine and served as a communications officer. Did you see a lot of battle?

I was on an escort carrier for a year and we were only in one battle; it was Okinawa. But all the time we were out we were conscious of possible danger, you know. Most of my sea duty was after the war was over. The boat was transformed

 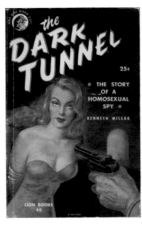  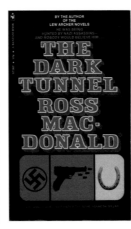 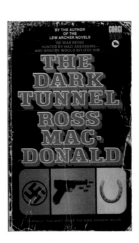 

into a troop carrier. We had the job of bringing troops back from the Philippines, for example. It was interesting.

How many planes are on an escort carrier?

Dozens. It's a big ship. It's not enormous, but it's big. It can go anywhere it wants to.

What was sea battle like?

Well, you don't see anything of it. The only thing you know about it directly is the planes taking off and coming back. There were Kamikazes in the air, but none ever got within sight of us. The main job in communications was the lines change every day, and then we'd get radio messages about the changes in the battle lines. We would have to communicate this information to our pilots, and they would go and take part in the actual battle. What I did, only for a few days, in that department was really more like being back at the desk than anything else.

How long were you in the Navy?

A little under two years.

And why did you join?

Well, I felt I wanted to get into the war, which was probably a stupid idea. [*laughs*] But that's what I thought.

Did your experiences in Germany add to that decision?

They probably had something to do with it.

Was being in the Navy a pleasant experience?

On the whole it wasn't too bad. I met some people that I liked and went some interesting places, did some work that was worth doing. Though it's just really a minor episode in my life, a long time ago.

You had already published The Dark Tunnel before you went in.

No. The novel was published while I was in Boston in the Navy.

And you managed to write Trouble Follows Me while you were in the Navy.

Such as it was.

And Blue City came out when?

After I got out.[1]

Did anybody else on the ship know that you were a writer?

Sure. The captain was a reader. He had access to more books than I had; he lent me books to read. As an officer in the communications department, I had direct contacts with the captain a good deal of the time. We got along fine.

I gather you weren't ultimately altogether happy with the spy novel form.

Well, my feeling now—and I think the reason I left it—was that the spy novel by definition is tied to current events, and I didn't particularly want to write political novels as such. At its best the spy novel becomes a kind of historical novel which represents a time. *The Confidential Agent* [by Graham Greene] is a perfect example of what I mean. It stands up as historical fiction long after it has lost its relevance as an immediate commentary on the world.

But I didn't feel drawn that way. I wanted to write something much more subjective and, let's say, person-centered rather than history-centered. The spy novel draws you toward history. I didn't particularly feel an urge to write history. I don't think I was particularly good at it either.

Why did you choose to write mysteries instead?

Well, I think it had to do with my wife's working in the field. I'm sure that she has a lot to do with my becoming a mystery writer at all. She sort of led the way. There has to be some strong urge or impelling reason that makes you embark on something like that, and I'm sure that my wife's doing it ahead of me had a lot to do with it. I used to read her manuscripts and work over them to some extent, so I learned in the process something about writing mystery fiction. But, of course, I'd been reading it for a long time. You don't really learn a thing, though, from a creative point of view until you start trying to write something. It just happened

1 *Blue City* was published in 1947, the year after Millar got out of the Navy.

À la déloyale!,
*the 1951 French edition
of* The Dark Tunnel
from Série Noire.

to suit both of us, obviously. It was the form that we were meant to work in.

And as is very obvious from what you know and what I've been saying, my initial efforts in those two spy novels came directly out of the contemporary world that I was living in: one, Nazi Germany; the other, the United States Navy with its race problems. I was deeply impressed by the race problems on American Navy ships and the existence of what amounted to a class of serfs in our society at that time.

I imagine that was particularly obvious in the Navy.

It was bloody obvious. And it was disgusting. So, you see, I was really writing about the same thing in both books: oppression. Other writers have done much better. But that was my beginning anyway.

Why had you gone to Germany and how old were you when you went there?

I was twenty. This was in the period of the Spanish Civil War and the period when Hitler was consolidating his power in Germany, and it just seemed to me a terribly interesting place. Of course, I'd already read Christopher Isherwood. I was in England before I went to Germany and in England I met several Germans, one of them a Jewish refugee from Germany, a young woman, whom I got to know very well in London. It was just a matter of interest. I found it intensely interesting. It was the shape of the problems of the world coming into focus, you know, and it still *is* to a great extent. I don't mean that Germany currently is a focus for the problems of the world, but the Nazi experience is an illustration of what we're teetering on the verge of all the time in one way or another: the potentiality of a criminal, antihuman government. It's what the main danger is in all countries, I think. It's not an immediate danger but it lurks there as a possibility, and there are elements in all of the Western countries that want that sort of country, that sort of government. A lot of people want it without knowing that they want it.

You mentioned Isherwood. Those books meant a great deal to you, I gather, at the time.

Yes, they still do. I think he's a very, very good writer. One of the most important writers in modern English.

Which books are we talking about?

Oh, I was talking about *The Berlin Stories,* which is probably his best book. *Down There on a Visit* isn't in the same class; it's much more in the realm of psychological fantasy. *The Berlin Stories* is very closely realistic. You might call it *fictional reporting* on a social situation. Nobody in English that I know of has described the immediate pre-Hitler period as well as Isherwood.

Have you used any of your experiences in Germany in any of your other books?

Yeah, I think really that the idea of that sort of government is a kind of shadow behind a lot of my books, though I don't write explicitly political novels. It seems to me we always seem to be teetering on the edge of some degree of fascism. That's the ultimate crime because it engulfs whole populations, it destroys their human futures.

Can you remember any specific things in Germany that triggered off a feeling?

You mean that illustrated what kind of a country it was and what was going to happen? Well, I got to know a lot of Germans, including some Jews, who were still in the country. Another friend of mine, who was somewhat anti-Hitler, a classicist, was the son of one of Hitler's generals. A woman I got to know well was the daughter of a member of Hitler's rump Reichstag. And so on. I got to know the situation in Germany quite intimately.

Was it a feeling of a bomb about to explode, or a threat that no one knew when it was going to happen?

Well, what had happened, or what was going to happen, had already happened, but not its consequences. Hitler *was* in power and the country *was* Nazified, and what came later of course, the attack on the rest of Europe, was inevitable. There wasn't any secret about it. Everybody in Germany knew that Hitler was preparing for war. It was obvious. When I so reported back in Canada, nobody took me seriously. They just couldn't believe it. Didn't want to.

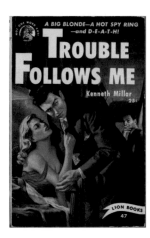

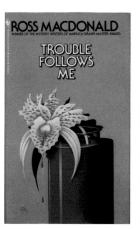

Above: Sempre nei Guai, *the 1953 Italian edition of* Trouble Follows Me *from Garzanti. Below: 2002 Russian edition.*

When everybody knew it in Germany, were most of them for it or against it?

They were for Hitler and he was for war. Don't forget that even at that time the German populace was denied facts. You know, there wasn't a free press, and they were more and more tending to believe what the government told them.

I'll give you an idea of how unreal the feeling was in Germany. You know, when King Edward retired from the throne—this was of course publicized on the German radio—I thought it was just Nazi propaganda when I first heard it. That's an illustration … that nobody believed anything—or else they believed everything perhaps. I guess a lot of the Germans believed everything.

Did you know people who were against Hitler?

The son of the general was and so was the daughter of the Reichstag deputy, but not actively. Passively. I imagine most of the active ones had already been picked up and put in camps, or else had left the country.

I don't imagine they knew anything about the camps.

I didn't know anything about them.

When you went to Germany at twenty, did you already think of yourself as a writer?

Oh, I was a natural writer. I was already writing. I hadn't published anything except in college papers and stuff like that, but I had done a lot of writing. I started writing when I was quite young, in my early teens. Actually, even before that. I never thought of any other possible career—except what most writers do: I taught for a while.

We talked earlier about Kitchener. Did it have any sense of being a company town? I mean, is there one major industry there?

Well, it wasn't a company town in a complete sense, but the rubber factories are kind of significant. It was a strange combination of an agricultural center and a factory town. It calls itself "the Industrial City." It's a big union town, too. Kitchener brings me to the third book that we were going to talk about, *Blue City,* because that's a kind of politicized version of Kitchener.

In one of the introductions you write that one of the reasons for writing Blue City ***was a reaction against academics.***

Well, not against academics but against the academic life. It's a valid way of life, but not if you have had a desire to be a novelist. I spent a number of years primarily studying other men's work and writing about it, which of course is good preparation for writing. But it shouldn't be the be all and the end all of your life if you feel that you're a writer. Critical writing is not nearly so satisfying in the emotional and imaginative sense. At least it wasn't for me at that stage in my life, and I wanted to do something different. Something of my own. Don't forget, I had already written a couple of novels before I went all out into the academic life. While they weren't much good, I wanted to try again. *Blue City* was my next try.

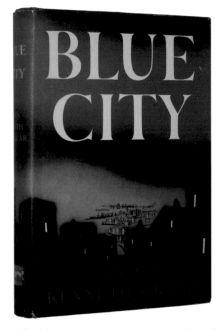

Did you think Blue City ***was a more personal try?***

Yes. It takes most writers—not all—quite a while to find out what their true subject is and so on. This was true even of Fitzgerald. His first novel [*This Side of Paradise*], successful as it was, was not real Fitzgerald by the standard that he later set.

Do you think there was any coincidence that Blue City ***is possibly the toughest book you wrote, in the hard-boiled sense? Is anything there a statement of reaction against academia? Is there a reason why that was the toughest book?***

Well, there's a reason. I'm not sure that that's the reason. I had a lot of anger in me and the book expresses that anger. The anger is directed against an imaginary city, which was based on cities I lived in when I was young. That was certainly an expression of anger, although there was more in it than anger. There were positive elements, too.

Was Dashiell Hammett a conscious influence on that book?

Yes, Hammett was a conscious influence on everything that I have done in the mystery field, and particularly those early books and particularly *Blue City*. That's definitely a Hammettesque, to put it mildly, book. Of course, I started reading Hammett when I was in high school, and he was really formative for me. I imagine I might never have written hard-boiled detective stories at all if it hadn't been for Hammett. He led the way for a lot of us, but particularly for me.

I had the idea in Blue City ***that you were writing about a much bigger city than Kitchener.***

I really was writing about a bigger city, but it was based on the basic mechanisms of Kitchener. I wasn't really writing about Kitchener. Kitchener's much more complex than Blue City, and Blue City is an American city with a black population and so on.

Blue City is the book where I first got the idea of tackling some of these things, to try to put the modern city into a version of popular art. It was all mixed up with my interest in jazz. The movement of the story and of the sentences is, I think, very much influenced by jazz. You can see the difference in the kind of movement between the two earlier books that we were talking about and *Blue City*, where I first got some kind of artistic control over what I was writing. With a lot of help of course from better writers than myself, notably Nelson Algren and Dashiell Hammett. They were the two main influences on me in that book.

Incidentally, Algren—a very nice coincidence for me—was sent it for review and he liked it.

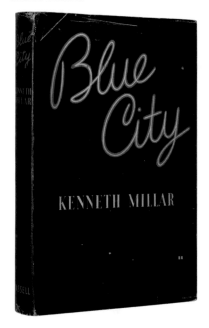

What publication?

One of the Philadelphia papers. Is there a *Philadelphia Inquirer*? I think that may have been it. And that meant very, very much to me that he should've liked it. He really gave me the first important review I ever got, on *Blue City*. I don't mean that he went overboard for it as a masterpiece or anything. He just plain liked it.

See, I was already a fan of his. To get a good review from somebody that you feel the way I felt about him is enormously uplifting. In fact, unless one or two things like that happen in the course of your life, you don't go on.

How is the police novel different from the detective novel?

I haven't thought too much about the police novel particularly nor have I ever really worked in it, at least not in twenty or thirty years, but the police novel implies a wholly different universe from the private detective. The difference is that the individual is the center of the private detective novel, the individual and the family group, whereas the *city* or the *state* in its various forms is the essential center of the police novel. There are many varying combinations of the two, but in their pure forms I think that's the difference, speaking off the cuff and not thinking about it much.

I think one could argue that the city is the subject, or one of the subjects, of your latest novel, The Blue Hammer, in particular, and The Moving Target, the first Lew Archer book. In both novels the city seems to be somewhat of a prevailing character that forces several of the new rich into doing things.

That's true. The city is *a* character, but it isn't the *center* of the novel where the author places his imaginative meaning. That belongs to the individual who is set up over against the city. Wouldn't you agree? The city is an enormously powerful force. In the police novel the hero is more or less in the service of the city, whereas in the private detective novel he is in one way or another fighting the city. Or at least trying to put it back in shape morally. You know, that's one of the two or three central themes of literature from Greek days down, from Sophocles and Aristophanes down to the present: the conflicting demands of the individual conscience and the state.

It's sort of inevitable that policemen should become servants of the city because that's literally what they are. When I set up this antithesis, I'm not really setting a rebellion antithesis, although my books always or nearly always take the side of the individual—but not the criminal individual, rather the somewhat free individual. The point is to keep alive all the various human elements that go to make up both a person and a city. A police state, where the police are in control and beyond criticism, degenerates rapidly into an inhuman place. Of course, I've seen examples of that in varying degrees. The most extreme example—it's an impure example but nevertheless I saw it—was Hitler's Germany.

You've never been tempted toward the police novel in your later years at all?

No, but I think perhaps my books have been influenced by the police novel to a certain extent.

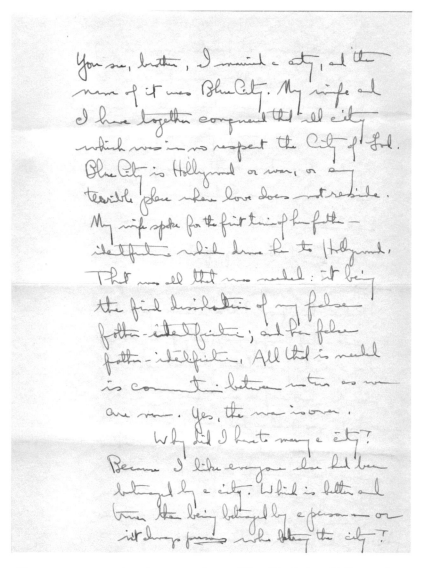

Three-page manuscript of an essay about a "Blue City," circa 1946 or earlier.

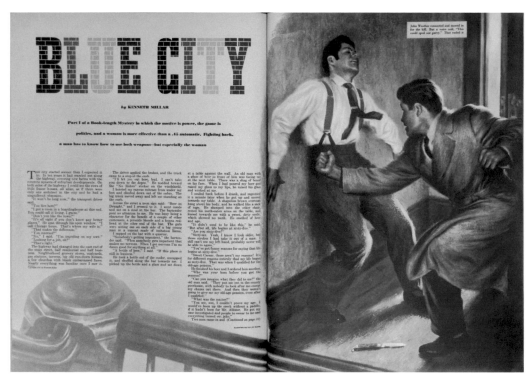

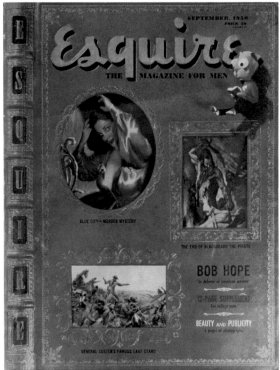

Blue City as serialized in the August and September 1950 issues of Esquire.

Kenneth Millar
2124 Bath St.
Santa Barbara, Calif.

Miss G. Pfleger
c/o Esquire, Inc.
Chicago 1, Illinois   February 20/48

Dear Miss Pfleger:

Mr. Wiswell asks me to send you some backstage autobiography in connection with your forthcoming one-shot of my mystery Blue City. Also a photo, which I'm sending under separate cover and hope you'll return if you can — because the photographer who took it has gone out of business and I can't get a copy and I don't look like that any more. I'm thinner.

I'm 32. Born in Los Gatos, California, but spent most of my early life in Canada because my parents were Canadian. My father was, among other things, an itinerant newspaperman, and I lived or went to school in Vancouver, Medicine Hat, Winnipeg, Toronto, London (Canada), and way stations. Attended the Universities of Western Ontario, Toronto, and Michigan. Also went to the University of Munich under Hitler for a couple of months, but that was for laughs. Few laughs, however. That was in the winter of 1936-7, which I spent in Europe, mostly in Germany, because

Nazism had interested me, in a painful way, for a long time. I wrote a novel about it in collaboration with James Meisel, a refugee German man of letters, but the novel has never been published. I spent a summer in Ireland, and have been talking about it so enthusiastically ever since that my wife still thinks of me as an Irishman, though I'm not.

My wife is Margaret Millar, the mystery writer and novelist. We were married in 1938, the day after I graduated from college, and have a eight-year-old daughter. I taught high school for a couple of years, and then was given a fellowship in English at the University of Michigan. I'd finished most of my work for the doctorate when the Navy took me and simultaneously Dodd Mead took my first book, The Dark Tunnel, a spy story about Nazis in Detroit. I was a Communications Officer on an escort carrier which operated off Okinawa in the closing weeks of the war. All I saw of Okinawa was a glow in the distance, but I'm not inclined to kick about that.

Since my release from the Navy in the spring of 1946 we've been living in Santa Barbara, partly because Santa Barbara is the place where we have a house to live in, partly because I like swimming. Before the war I did a good deal of writing for the Toronto Saturday Night: book-reviewing, political paragraphing, fiction, and even light verse; I've written stories for Ellery Queen's Magazine and American Mercury and for money. Blue City is my third book. While it speeds up reality, no doubt, it's much closer to life as some people live it in midwestern towns than other people might think. My fourth book, The Three Roads, will be published by Knopf in June. It's what publishers are calling now a "novel of suspense." I'm working on the second draft of a serious novel, tentatively

called Winter Solstice, about life in the lower and lower-middle depths of a blue midwestern city.

In the early summer of 1934, when I was a freshman in college, I wrote a letter to Esquire's "Sound and Fury" department which was just about my first appearance in print. I think I announced, among other things, that when I learned to write I was going to write you some fiction. See if you can find it in the files.

Yours sincerely,
Kenneth Millar

Two-and-a-half page draft of a letter by Ken Millar to Esquire *in 1948 providing biographical information for the upcoming serialization of* Blue City. *It mentions his travels through Germany and an unpublished novel about Nazism that he collaborated on with a German refugee, James Meisel. Especially interesting is it also mentions his abandoned autobiographical novel,* Winter Solstice. *In Millar's introduction to* Kenneth Millar/Ross Macdonald: A Checklist *from 1971 (see carbon typescript below), he wrote: "I left the manuscript, I think, in an abandoned blacking factory." But during his research, biographer Tom Nolan located different versions of the manuscript, either typed or handwritten, essentially complete. It remains unpublished.*

had less choice than the reader may suppose. My one attempt to write a regular autobiographical novel about my unhappy childhood turned out so badly that I never showed it to my publisher. I left the manuscript, I think, in an abandoned blacking factory. The deadly game of social Snakes and Ladders which occupied much of my youth had to be dealt with in another form, more impersonal and objective.

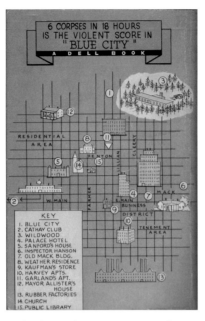
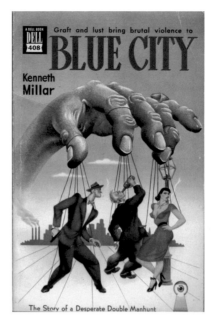

Dell mapback 363 from 1949, reissued as 408 with the same cover, and a signed copy of 363.

Do you think there's a metaphor there? The state being experience and the individual being innocence, which is certainly the great American theme? The private detective is, in a way, right in the middle.

Oh yes, very much in the middle. He serves almost as a messenger between what the state demands and what the individual wants.

Do you think that's why you were drawn to the private detective?

I have no doubt. There are a number of reasons why, and I'm sure that that basic interest in the state and the individual is the central reason why I write that kind of fiction.

On the other hand, one could almost see your books as political novels.

Yes, my books are political novels, but they're not about politics particularly except in the sense that the city as such represents the political. My books are partly political and partly, in a broad sense, anthropological, having to do with human behavior under various foundations.

You majored in English and history. Where do you think the interest in the state and the city, and the historical interest, date from?

Of course, a lot of it was unconscious or preconscious. I was interested in these sorts of themes before I was aware, in an intellectual sense, of any conflict between the state and the individual. I'm talking about when I was a kid. I was reading this kind of fiction from a very early age, including Hammett. Hammett is a good example of what I'm talking about. All his novels have to do with this conflict centrally.

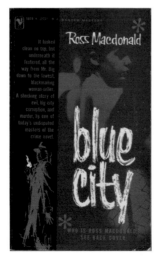

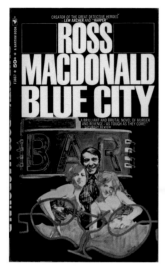 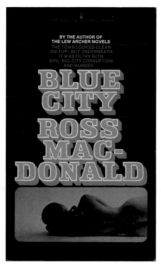   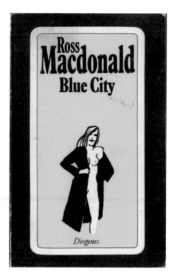

You came out here to California shortly after you came back from the Navy.

Margaret had already settled in Santa Barbara, bought a house. When I got out of the Navy in Boston, I just came here and settled right in.

How long had she been in Santa Barbara before you got here?

Pretty close to a year.

And at that point she had already published a number of books, I guess.

Three or four.

Then you both settled in to write full-time?

I was very fortunate that things worked out the way they did.

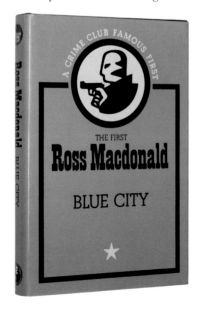

Has Margaret been a great help to you in your books?

Well, she got me started writing them. Not by saying, "Write them," but by example. And as far as being a help, no. She's not an editorial type. I've helped her on her books but she hasn't really helped me on mine. She *does* read them of course when I've finished them, express an opinion, but not a detailed, critical opinion.

She said that you were able to support each other's writing.

That's right. That means that neither one of us was ever forced to get a book out fast for money, the way most writers [have to]. You know, in order to pay the bills. It's never been quite that bad since we both became full-time writers.

You were never actually poor as writers, you and Margaret? I mean, in a desperate way, let's say.

We were in that situation before I started writing, mercifully, when I was in graduate school at the University of Michigan. We went through periods of extreme deprivation. I can remember an occasion when we didn't have any coal and the temperature was zero and we were burning old boxes in the furnace. *But* we did have a house with a furnace. We didn't own the house, we rented it. There was one Christmas when we had to borrow money to buy Christmas presents. That sort of thing. This was when I was in graduate school, and graduate students at that time were among the most impoverished species in the country, you know. Even a good fellowship wasn't really enough to live on. I may have held the best fellowship at the university; it was just a thousand dollars a year, and yet it required me to work full-time at my studies and dissertation.

 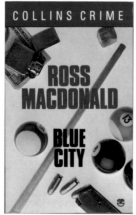 

So in those days the upper reaches of graduate school were generally pretty limited to people with money. It was a gentleman's preserve. Ordinary people couldn't afford to go all the way through it. So Margaret's contribution made

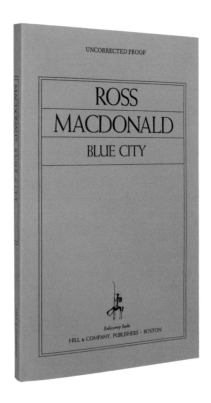

it possible for me to stay in graduate school. She wasn't the only working wife, of course. That was a common situation, for the wife to work and the husband to go through graduate school.

Well, certainly from The Galton Case on, the books were well received.

Yeah, but I had written a dozen books before *The Galton Case*. That's half my life. But I made a living. Of course, my wife was working very successfully. If she hadn't been a successful novelist, I wouldn't have been able to quit teaching and write full-time, obviously. It was her success that made it possible for me to become a full-time writer. Just as it was my teaching for a few years and supporting her that made it possible for her to become a full-time writer.

She wrote when you taught on your own.

Sure. She started writing when I was a high school teacher. I did, too, but I didn't have the time to write anything but very short things.

Is your story in Margaret's books?

You mean do Margaret's books refer to our marriage?

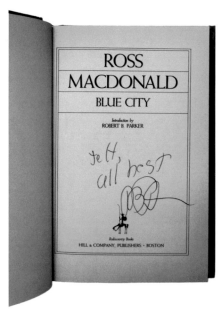

Yes, and do yours refer to the marriage also? Do you put secret messages in there to each other and other references?

No. I'm sure there are messages there, but I couldn't pick them out. It wouldn't be conscious. Unlike my books, which do have some autobiographical content as we've been talking about, Margaret's books don't seem to. They're pretty pure creations. Of course, major events in a writer's life are always reflected in his fiction, and that would be true of hers, too. But in general she just seems to make them up.

Was that a happy time for you when you were both starting out as writers?

Yes. We really had some nice years.

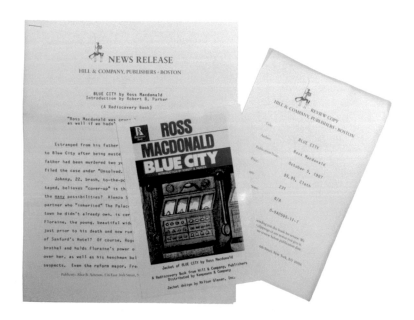

A feu et à sang, *the 1949 French edition of* Blue City *from Gallimard's Série Noire.*

3. JAZZ

Would it be correct to say that jazz is the music that is now the most important to you?

Yes, but that's primarily because I'm not really knowledgeable in music. Popular music is the only kind of music I know, and the popular music of my own youth primarily.

Had you come into contact with jazz earlier in your life?

Oh yes. I'd been familiar with all kinds of popular music from very early days, starting with my player piano days. You know, that was the source of music before we had record players. But I was fortunate in this respect, going back even further. My Uncle Rob Millar, who was the town electrician at Wiarton on Georgian Bay, was the first man in town to have a radio, because he built his own.[1] So from the age of seven I was listening to radio and hearing American popular songs. I'm sure it was absolutely formative in my life, *combined* with the fact that he also ran on Saturdays the local movie theater. Also he looked after me when nobody else was able to, for two years. So I was raised on popular radio music and Pearl White in *Plunder*. Perfect background for a writer in the popular field.

And you really liked it at the time?

I loved it. I still look back on it with pleasure. Not everybody, you know, is privileged to hear "Yes Sir, She's My Baby" on the radio at the time when it first came out.[2] So one lucky effect of a fairly scattered kind of young life was that I really did become immersed [in the popular arts].

And, you know, the kind of arts that we're talking about, these popular arts,

Left and above: 16mm print of Arthur M. Kaye's film Ross Macdonald: In the First Person *(1971). Below: Ken Millar's notes for the shooting script.*

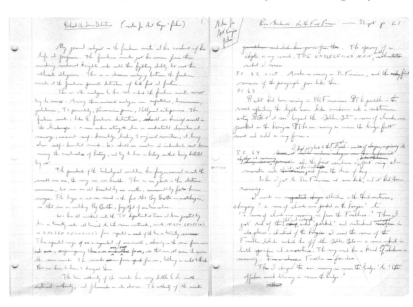

really exist in order to describe society as she changes and how people feel about things that happen to them, both individually and *en masse*. They provide means of coping with experience that otherwise couldn't be coped with and couldn't be brought under human control in the mind. It's all meaningful.

Isn't it interesting that there's this segregation of cultures? There's a serious culture and a popular culture, and the popular culture is more important to more people and maybe, ultimately, artistically more important.

1 "Uncle Rob" was a second cousin, not an uncle. In the 16mm film *Ross Macdonald: In the First Person*, Millar says: "When I was six, my mother, without resources, prepared to place me in an orphanage. But a cousin of my father, Rob Millar, took me into his home."
2 The song, whose correct title is "Yes Sir, That's My Baby," was written in 1925 (the same year that Millar's favorite book, *The Great Gatsby*, was published) by Walter Donaldson and Gus Kahn.

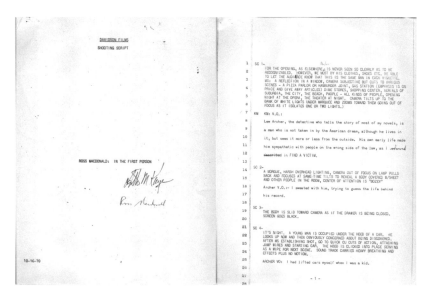

Cover of the shooting script signed by Arthur M. Kaye and Ken Millar (as Ross Macdonald), and opening scene with corrections by Millar.

Sure. And it's the succeeding waves of popular culture out of which the higher culture gets its vitality. Don't forget that within a very fast generation Elizabethan drama jumped from what could be called popular culture to the highest thing that ever came out of England. You know, the revenge tragedy really was a form of popular culture, just as much as it was a literary thing.

It may not be apparent in my writing but it was jazz rhythms that really struck me alive as a writer. I'm talking about books that go back a long way; I'm not talking necessarily about the end result, which has become, as indeed jazz has become, more and more involved. There was a powerful connection for me between listening to jazz and learning about jazz, and writing the kind of fiction that I write. You can see the connections in the rhythmic development. That's quite obvious, but there are deeper connections, too. They have to do with what the music means and what its sources are. For example, I don't doubt that modern jazz is the voice of the modern city in a sense and so is the hard-boiled detective story, that they really are connected with each other. They're not trying to do exactly the same thing, but their intentions are parallel. And if you understand one, it helps you to understand the other. But specifically, the imagery and rhythm and movements of jazz had a lot to do in forming my style in my early books. It's quite obvious in a book like *Blue City*. I think it becomes less obvious.

Actually, I think one of the sources of the modern detective story, as opposed to the traditional one, and one of the main differences, is the rise of jazz. I wouldn't go so far as to say that Hammett was directly influenced by jazz, but I bet he was, and he came up at the same time as modern jazz did. For me it was an enormously influential thing. It was probably the art that made the breakthrough for me into the possibility of popular writing: jazz. I was a jazz buff long before I was a writer.

Of course, I'm not talking about directly imitative parallels, I'm just saying that both the forms broke through into new country and that it was somewhat the same country for each. It had to do with life in American cities—actual life in American cities, not imagined life. Ellington is probably as much my master as any writer is.

And there's a direct connection, too, between what I ... said about the American Navy and the novel I wrote with some American blacks in it [*Trouble Follows Me*]

and my interest in jazz, which is the *par excellence*, the art, of American blacks and expression of a suppressed but un-suppressible group of people.

What kind of jazz were you listening to at the time you wrote the next book, Blue City?

Well, it was everybody on Fifty-Second Street at the time that I was there, and the time was 1943 or 1944.

Were you in New York City because of the service?

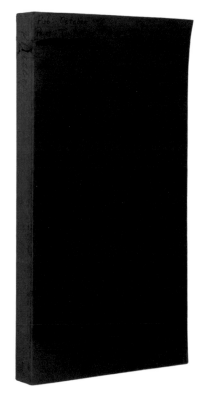

Yeah. I was very lucky, I got sent to Princeton for my basic training, and then Harvard. [*laughs*] That's the way I hit the Ivy League: two months in Princeton and three months in Harvard. I've often said that I got to those schools the same way that Gatsby got to Oxford. You only need a little bit of it.

My wife was a fairly prosperous writer by that time, and we rented a house on the main residential street in Princeton. It had five bathrooms, only one of which we used. I got some idea of how some people had lived in the East.

A friend of mine named Matt Bruccoli wrote a biography of O'Hara [*The O'Hara Concern: A Biography of John O'Hara*] in which he described a house in which O'Hara had gone to lunch, and it was the same house that we had rented five years before. That sort of tied it all up, you know. It was the Listerine Lambert house.[3]

In terms of jazz, I presume you're talking about the Duke Ellington time period.

Duke Ellington was the leading figure, but I'm really talking about *all* the good jazz players. Like J. C. Higginbotham, for example, who just played a very good trombone and wasn't an orchestra leader. People didn't last on the street unless they were good.

Did you see Billie Holiday?

No, I never saw her, but I learned about her quite early. I think I was telling you, Robert Hayden, the black poet, was one of my close friends and neighbors in Ann Arbor, and he put me on to Billie Holiday. Through records. That was long before I ever got to Fifty-Second Street.

---

3 Gerard B. Lambert invented and manufactured Listerine mouthwash.

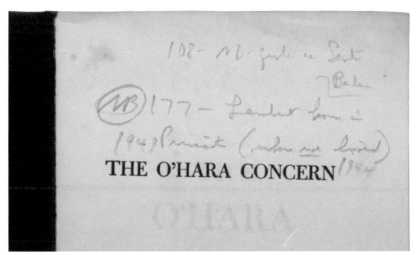

Ken Millar's penciled notation in his uncorrected proof of The O'Hara Concern: A Biography of John O'Hara: *"Lambert house in 1949 Princeton (where* we *lived) 1944."*

Had you ever been to New York before?

Yeah, I was in New York on my way back from Europe in 1937 for a few days. I went down to Harlem to the Cotton Club, and I saw *Pygmalion*, the play. Those were the two main events.

Who was playing in Pygmalion?

Somebody very, very good. I can't remember names.

There's a list of musicians and records mentioned in The Moving Target. Were they records that you had or that you liked, do you recall?

I don't remember the passage, but chances are that they were records that I liked. I was listening to a very great deal of jazz. I wore out my records; they wore out more easily in those days. For several years it was just about, apart from literature itself, the most important thing in my life.

You said that "modern jazz is the voice of the modern city … and so is the hard-boiled detective story."

You can certainly hear the city behind all of it. Oh, I think music has been really the prime interpreter of American cities, ahead of literature, year by year. Ever since Scott Joplin, I would guess. That's close to a hundred years. For every person that reads Dreiser, who was the first great literary interpreter of the contemporary city, there would be twenty that would listen to music on the same theme. Music strikes deeper, too, than the written word.

But for me, you see, although I'm not a musician—I'm not even particularly musical—it was the music that made the breakthrough. It saved me from a "literary" understanding of what goes on particularly in the cities. It was just more intimately tied up with my personal experience, from the age of seven when I started listening to the radio. As soon as you started hearing popular music. Maybe it isn't the same for everybody, but for me it was just absolutely central. We're talking about breakthrough into other experience than what we grew up with.

Did you know any jazz musicians?

I really haven't known any of them beyond just saying hello and telling them I like their work. When it was possible, when I was living in the East briefly in the Navy, I used to go down on the street and listen to all the good ones. I'd go from club to club.

Was the effect that jazz had on you principally in terms of composition?

No, I don't think so. I think it had to do with content also.

When you were visiting New York City in April, what did you think when I called you up late one night and invited you to go to David Forman's recording session?[4]

Well, I think my initial reaction was curiosity and the desire to satisfy my curiosity about how these things were done. I was also looking forward to meeting what would be called a different kind of artist.

You know, a friend of mine in the music business has said that the young people who are writing the new music and playing it are really assuming the position in our culture, to a great extent, of poets. Their essential message is similar to the kind of messages that the nineteenth-century poets provided us with. So I went in with the expectation of what might be called a poetic or an artistic experience, which would tell me more particularly about the younger part of our society. Because, while I've been following popular music ever since I was about seven and started listening to the radio, I really have had very little experience with the advanced contemporary kind of music that we're talking about. I was mainly curious—and also looking forward to the new experience.

Did you have any preconception going in of what to expect?

Well, I think listening to a lot of jazz, though it's a different kind of music, can prepare you for the experience of listening to different kinds of rock. One seems to me to lead into the other. There really isn't any sharp break either in the development of the music or my experience of it. I could go from a rock recording session to a jazz session without any sense of discontinuity at all. Of course, I don't have a terribly good musical ear. I don't think I live through music as musicians do or as music critics do. It's important to me but it's not absolutely essential to me.

I see stacks of records in your home, though, including the Beatles.

Sure. We like a lot of different kinds of music and the Beatles most particularly. Of course, they're the masters of the previous scene.

They're one of them.

As far as I know they are. I don't take a very critical attitude towards music. I listen to it. I seem to enjoy most kinds of music—and I always have, from the Anglican liturgy to rock.

---

4 Millar was staying at the Algonquin Hotel. Paul, who'd worked in A&R at Mercury Records from 1970 to 1975, had been unsuccessful in signing singer-songwriter David Forman to the label. The two men remained friends, however, and Forman had invited him to the studio where he was recording his eponymous debut album for Arista Records.

Was going back to the 21 Club to listen to jazz in New York in April a conscious revisitation of those days?

No, it was just a conscious enjoyment of what I was doing then and there. There wasn't anything nostalgic about it, it was just a continuation. I've never stopped listening to popular music.

I don't mean nostalgia. You just seemed like a man on a mission in many ways in New York, going to various places and seeing it all, hearing it all.

Well, you must remember that until that place opened, [jazz] wasn't terribly available. I did make a point of going there because I read about it in *The New Yorker* and knew about it. The last time I went, I went to hear Marian McPartland a couple of times. She was playing at one of the clubs in New York, Michael's Pub. She really sends me, I think she's just great. That's a continuation of what we've been talking about. There's a great deal of jazz, as well as the classical tradition, mixed into her creations. I never really got over that initial love of jazz.

Certainly one of the influences on Jack Kerouac's writing was also jazz, although it translated into his prose in a different way.

Yes. Well, it was a different jazz, too. It was later.

Although you listened to Charlie Parker, right?

Yes, but Parker, you see, was just at the *end* of the period for me; and it was the *beginning* of the period for Kerouac. There was no doubt Parker was the great watershed figure at that time. And it was about that time that I in effect turned my main attention to other things. But I don't see Kerouac as any kind of any influence on me, for good or ill.

No, but he was similarly influenced by jazz.

Yeah, but a quite different result.

I guess, though, that some of the people that influenced Kerouac also influenced you: Charlie Parker and Coleman Hawkins and Dizzy Gillespie.

No, I don't doubt that we were each in touch with the whole list, but I think he was much more deeply affected than I was. Well, he was philosophically affected. I have the impression that he was. I've never been terribly fond of Kerouac for some reason. He seems rather loose.

Are you talking about the short rhythms particularly? That's the way it comes out anyway. It comes out in the form of rhythms, but it probably has other things pressing it. I haven't thought critically very much about this, but of course it's basic to what we're talking about. What's the difference between popular art and the other kind? What are the various kinds of popular art, in prose and so on?

You know, if popular art wants to do some of the work of high art, it has to have the same artistic virtues, or at least comparable artistic virtues, otherwise it's not doing the job. And Kerouac really avoided the basic job, which has to do with, oh, creating fresh rhythms for thought to move in. That sort of thing. He just left things loose so you could play your own tune, so to speak. Well, he evidently had a meaning for a whole generation.

Of course, by the fact that I had an education as a graduate student—even at the University of Michigan, which wasn't old hat—it was still a pretty definite regime and an old-fashioned regime. It doesn't prepare you to learn much from somebody like Kerouac. You have an instant reaction against it when you start looking at it. And in fact that background that I had prevented me from appreciating the whole Beat movement until quite recently. I didn't really see it until I saw it in history.

That's strange to me.

It's strange to me, too, but it's true.

There's a cultist aspect of the Beat generation that drifted off into the Sixties generation and manifested itself in the hippies and Charlie Manson and est.

You mean the loss of sharply defined personality and that sort of thing? Yeah, well, Archer was written consciously in reaction against what we're talking about, and it has to do with what I was saying before about my inability to go along with Kerouac, for example, on account of what seemed to me a kind of vagueness as to what values were and even what a personality was. And that really worries me…. I see a lot of it. People are sort of vaguely wandering through life without expecting themselves to have definite reactions to anything.

To give an illustration, we have a kind of religious colony, called the Brotherhood of the Sun, in Santa Barbara. It's run by a guy who is a little nuts. He has been taking over a lot of young people who are in the last stages—or stages anyway—of drug addiction and straightening them out in that respect, and introduced them to religious experience and got them working for him on his ranches. It's become a very wealthy and successful agricultural operation, branching out into other fields.[5] But I'm concerned about it because I know one or two of the kids involved and they remind me a little bit of Jack Nicholson in the last scene of *Cuckoo's Nest*, after he had been lobotomized, you know. Just a little bit like that. And that's what we're talking about.

As time has gone along, have you felt more prepared to cope with that "vagueness" you described?

Well, it doesn't afflict me personally. My afflictions are in the other direction: you know, being too definite and too square and all that sort of thing. And too much a person of the past than rather of the present as she flows.

What do you mean by being "too square"?

Well, to put it very bluntly, I'm still dividing people into good people and bad people, although I recognize that there are in-betweeners.

Is that bad?

No, I don't think it is. It's just that there are larger ways of approaching the whole thing than my way.

5 The Brotherhood of the Sun was founded in 1969 by Norman Paulsen, based on the teachings of Paramahansa Yogananda. The organization, which became known as Sunburst, still exists today and, according to its website, "is dedicated to personal and planetary awakening and transformation through spiritual practice, conscious living and sustainable Earth stewardship."

Especially because in your books there is a recurrence of fascination with artists. Even in something like The Zebra-Striped Hearse, *where you moved very close to that haute bohemia that cropped up in the Sixties, even if you felt alienated in it, I always felt that you were interested in it.*

Oh, I was, I was. And my objection to the writers was stylistic, it didn't have to do with subject matter. I just was ill at ease with their style.

Because of that sort of perceived sense of sloppiness?

Well, that's what it seemed like to me, but it really isn't true. It's true of Kerouac, but it isn't true of Ginsberg. I've learned to really admire Ginsberg, for example. Especially the last time I saw him—the only time I saw him. It was during the bombing of Cambodia and he was at a public gathering playing on his little whatever and chanting: "They bombed Cambodia again." And so on. Yeah, he's a remarkable force.

Whether it's poetry or painting or writing detective fiction, there isn't just one way to do it, I don't think.

No. That's one thing you learn from these painters and musicianly poets: that there isn't just one way to do it. There are infinite possibilities, and they differ from each other sometimes in minor ways but very important ways. The way Parker and Lester [Young] differ from each other and yet are profoundly similar. I really think that popular music blazed the trail to a great extent for contemporary writing.

It comes out of the same consciousness, I think.

I mean, I think the musicians did it first and best and most completely. Maybe that's in the nature of music. There actually hasn't been any improvement on the great jazz musicians of the previous generation, wouldn't you agree? They just went to the complete limit, and that's where they live—at the livin' end.

Ken Millar, too, appeared on LP. Above: His personal transcription discs (two lacquer acetates with information cut on three sides, intended for radio broadcast) of a lecture he delivered at the University of Michigan in Ann Arbor, in July 1953, called "The Scene of the Crime: Social Meanings of the Detective Story." His friend Donald Pearce introduced him to the audience in Angell Hall. A printed transcription of the lecture was published in a slightly edited form in Ralph Sipper's 1984 Ross Macdonald tribute volume, Inward Journey. *Below: Assorted audio books on cassette and compact disc. Perhaps most notable is* Sleeping Beauty, *which is presented as a dramatic full-cast reading (thirty-five different voice actors) with Harris Yulin as Lew Archer.*

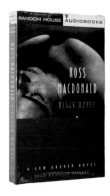 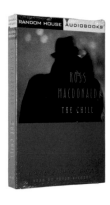  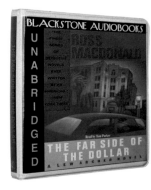  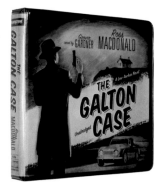

Photo of Ken Millar at home in 1961 by Ray Borges for Santa Barbara News-Press.

4. A BOOKSHELF FULL OF INFLUENCES

Do you think Dashiell Hammett is one of the influences on your style?

I expect so. Chandler was the immediate influence when I started writing the kind of books I write. He was a great liberating influence to me. The liberation was from the standards of the academy, which I was in at the time. Chandler wasn't in the academy in the sense that I was. I was in graduate school and his experience in the academy was in his teens. However, to say a general thing is true: he was brought up on the classics. Probably much more fundamentally than I was.

I never sensed in your books that sort of overripe Romanticism that Chandler had.

Well, I belong to a later generation. He really, you know, started writing shortly after 1900 in the late heyday of Romanticism, the lush heyday of Romanticism. That's one of the things he had to contend with in his style, one of the reasons why the colloquial American idiom was so useful to him: as a counter.

Do you think it's as much history as it is temperament?

I think both history and temperament. He really did start writing in the days of, well, Aubrey Beardsley, let's say.

I don't think of Chandler as being a very conscious craftsman in the overall sense that you are with your books. He doesn't tie his books together, I don't think, very much by symbolism, for example.

Well, these things came into American literature at a later stage really. It's only within the last couple of decades that American literature has been pervaded by these elements, such as symbolism.

They were certainly in **The Great Gatsby** *and they were certainly to a degree in Hammett's work.*

Of course they were in *Gatsby*, but that was the central novel of the century.

It's a novel certainly Chandler knew and one could argue was affected by in **The Long Goodbye.**

Well, he wouldn't get it just from reading Scott Fitzgerald; he would have to be subjected to the whole experience of the symbolist revolution, and I don't think he was. And the reason didn't have to do with him personally, it's just that, with the exception of a few people like Hemingway and Fitzgerald—in particular Fitzgerald—it didn't enter American literature until a later time. Now, of course, it's our standard manner of discourse, but it wasn't when Fitzgerald wrote *The Great Gatsby*. That was practically a breakthrough novel for American literature. What I mean is, something like that takes a generation really to pervade popular writing, and it happened too late to affect Chandler very much.

Other than Fitzgerald and Hemingway, what writers did the symbolist revolution impact?

Well, you really mentioned the two that are most obvious: Fitzgerald and Hemingway. Of course, there were many others. Katherine Anne Porter is an excellent example. She was a real pioneer, ahead of both those guys.

You would say that the impact, though, of their work didn't become fully apparent till, say, the Fifties?

Well, it didn't reach popular writing.

What about Albert Camus? Has he been an influence on you?

Yes. I became aware of him, I suppose, at the time when most people—most people interested in writing—became aware of him. I can't name the year but it was a long time ago. It goes back to my days in graduate school at least.[1]

I think Camus is a great moralist. It really is his central subject: What is good and what is proper in human life? He became no less so as he got older either. His later books are even more moralistic, I think. It doesn't necessarily make them better. I think *The Fall* is a profoundly moral book.

1 The first English translation of Camus's *The Stranger* was published in 1946. The original French publication date was 1942.

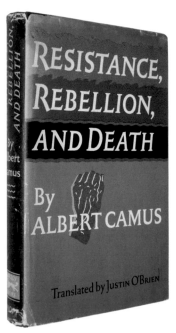

***Yeah, I like it. That and* The Stranger.**

I guess, according to my figuring, those are his best books.

The Plague *isn't one of them?*

No. It's a little too much of an explicit parable to work imaginatively for me. I know that a great many people hold it in very high esteem, but I don't.

It was taught a lot.

It's a very teachable book. You have the overt story and then you have the hidden story, the hidden meaning. But it isn't hidden enough in my estimation. [*laughs*] I hate to have anything critical to say about Camus. He's one of the great masters—one of my masters.

He's been an influence practically from the beginning, then. I wouldn't have guessed that. Maybe you better tell me some more of your influences, because I'm not very good at guessing them.

Well, I think a lot of these things have been coming out, Paul, in the course of our conversation. It's better, I think, for them to come out sort of under pressure, and with trailing clouds of meaning, than just a list. Because, hell, I could walk over blindfolded to that bookshelf and put my finger on any book on the shelf and open my eyes and look at the book and say, "Ah yeah, here's another influence." [*laughs*] I'm really not kidding.

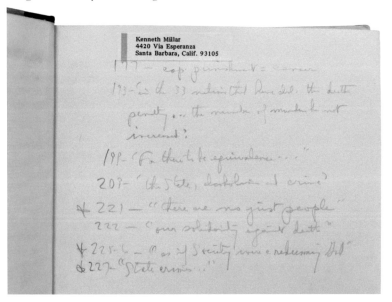

Ken Millar's copy of Camus's Resistance, Rebellion, and Death
from 1960 with his address label and penciled notes on the endpaper.

You know, for example, from where I sit, oh, the first name I see is Shaw. An enormous influence on me. I spent years very much under his influence—joyfully. And the next thing I see is *The Modern Tradition*, which is a collection of essays on aesthetic written, nearly all of them, by writers who influenced me. I took my doctorate in criticism, and that's a collection of modern criticism. And then next is *A Treasury of the Theatre*. Same thing goes: I was terribly in love with drama for years and wanted to be a playwright, and I read right through the modern theater.

Next is *Mrs. Bridge* by Evan Connell; that's one of my favorite novels. Next is *The Stories of F. Scott Fitzgerald*, a writer that has been profoundly influential on me and everybody else. Next is *The Nazi Primer*. It's a book about what was taught in the Nazi primary schools. As you know, I went to Nazi Germany and wrote a book about it. Next is Nabokov, a writer who has been extremely useful and influential to me.

And I skip over a little. *Ancilla to the Pre-Socratic Philosophers*. Well, I practically brought myself up on the pre-Socratic philosophers. I'm not kidding! And next is *The Collected Stories of Peter Taylor*. He's a writer that I've been following for, oh, twenty-five years. A good short-story writer. And next is Donald Davie, *Essex Poems*. Well, Davie is one of my closest friends in writing.

You see, those books are not picked at random of course because they're my books, but every damn one of them is significant in my life. I could start on the next shelf: *Major Poets of the Earlier Seventeenth Century*—mother's milk. Or I start at the other end and I have *The Twenties* by Edmund Wilson. He was practically my teacher for about ten years, you know. He was a teacher of all of us in his great period. And so on, all the way down the line. John Dewey. Carl Jung. Aubrey Beardsley.

How about* The Hard-Boiled Omnibus *by Joseph Shaw? Is that up there?

It sure is somewhere there, I don't know exactly where.

Any other French authors who influenced you?

Well, I'd been interested in the modern phenomenon of the *poète maudit*, particularly as exemplified by some of the great French poets like Rimbaud. Flaubert, too, for that matter. There's a strong element of what you could figuratively call *diabolism* in Flaubert and, in fact, in the whole modern French literary movement. Of course, my earliest and most powerful literary influence of all was Edgar Allan Poe. He's the American master of that sort of thing. I started reading him when I was a child and I've been reading him ever since. The size of his talent and his importance is gradually dawning on the whole civilization. He really is a central figure and he has been all through my life. When you think of the writers that he fathered or influenced, starting with Baudelaire and Dostoyevsky and so on, and a whole line of other writers in English. D. H. Lawrence was very much attracted to and influenced by Poe. I think that Lawrence's essay on Poe in *Studies in Classic American Literature* is the best thing that's ever been done on him. It says some of these things.

But you would cite Poe as an absolutely major influence.

Oh yes. In some respects an unconscious influence. You know, if you drank your mother's milk when you're young, you take it for granted, but it's an important part of your intellectual inheritance really.

Was Poe preceded by anyone, or was he startlingly original in some ways?

Oh, he was startlingly original. I don't know his sources; if they've been studied in depth, I haven't seen the studies. I don't think there's much doubt that he had European sources, though, in the early gothic and pre-gothic European development, particularly in Germany. But I don't know about them. I only know that there must have been something, that he couldn't have invented that whole world all by himself.

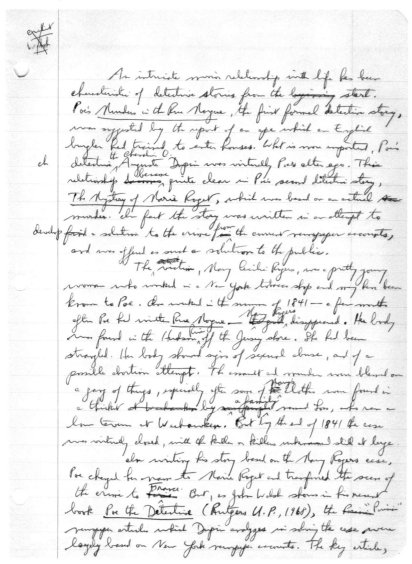

A page from one of the drafts of Ken Millar's 1973 essay "A Very Private Eye," which focuses on Poe.

But he was the first one in America pretty much?

Yes, and *I* think the leader in world literature in that field. Of course, there was a whole gothic tradition out of which he grew. Coleridge was one of the

spokesmen for it and one of the representatives, and Poe regarded himself as a disciple of Coleridge. Coleridge's great poems have a strong gothic element. In fact, Coleridge was in touch with the European gothic tradition right from the beginning. He reviewed Mrs. Radcliffe and "Monk" Lewis when their novels were coming out in the 1790s.

Then Frankenstein *must have preceded Poe, right?*

Yes. *Frankenstein*, too, came out of the same general literary movement that Coleridge was the critical spokesman for. So as far as England is concerned, you can identify many of the sources—in fact, I just have—but I don't know about the continental sources; I'm just ignorant of them. There would be intermediary steps and literature, too, that I just don't know about. I'm sure other people do.

I know that Poe is being studied now. For a long time he wasn't taken seriously because he was regarded as a mere popular artist and a writer about forbidden subjects. It's pretty absurd. But his content is extremely important to us. It's the whole dark side of our hemisphere that he's writing about. Incidentally, Mark Twain carried on from Poe in that field. Although I wouldn't call him a Poesque writer, there's a strong element of it in Twain and it's very important, too. You can trace it through generation by generation, jumping from Poe to Twain to Faulkner and so on. To Flannery O'Connor.

Was Twain less so an influence on you?

Poe and Twain are the two native American influences that are most important to me. I would say that the influence of Poe has survived and come through stronger in my later life.

Will you explain that?

Well, Poe wrote the kind of thing that I am interested in writing. After all, he did invent the detective story, and that's the obvious thing. Twain is a greater writer perhaps, I don't know. I don't know what constitutes a great writer. But Poe perceived the psychological essence of the American experience in ways that nobody else has, and Twain was a follower in that respect. He was behind Poe and he didn't trust his own explorations of his own psychology, so to speak, to the extent that Poe did. He wrote a lot of things of terribly secondary value. Well, I suppose Poe did, too. It's unfair to compare them because one's a novelist and the other is not. A novelist and a short-story writer and poet do rather different things and have different opportunities. But you can see the element of the gothic throughout Twain, throughout his work, including *Tom Sawyer* and *Huckleberry Finn*.

Bierce was a great original, too. He is certainly a Poesque writer and he influenced me, too.

None of these writers influenced me to *do* the thing that they do exactly but to do other things parallel. They opened up the possibilities. I'm just taking it for granted that there's a strong traditional gothic element in my work. It comes out in some of the books very strong and in others not so. My books are often gothic in more than one sense, in the sense of subject matter. Obviously murder stories are broadly in the gothic tradition. The whole detective tradition descends partly from the gothic.

What is a workable definition of the gothic tradition?

Well, it's a recognition of the psychological importance, and the philosophic value and the ethical relevance, of the dark side of human life and human experience.

It's a form, generally speaking, which emphasizes the strange, mysterious, and the unexpected. It ranges all the way from rather broad and coarse emphasis on the horrible, as in one or two of the books of two of the writers that I've mentioned, to an intense and illuminating psychological interest. You get that very strongly in Poe at his best and in Poe's best disciples. Dostoyevsky of course and Baudelaire, the two that I mentioned, are among his great European disciples. He opened up for Dostoyevsky—not that Dostoyevsky needed Poe to become what he became— the world that Dostoyevsky explored.

You know, [Dostoyevsky] lived in a period in Russian history when things were rather dismal and dark, particularly for him. His own experiences were pretty black until he had his fortunate late marriage. But at the same time there's an enormous strength and invigorating quality in the ability of somebody like Dostoyevsky and the other Poesque writers to face the darkness and explore it, and discover that it, too, is part of the human heritage and that we *can* live in it. To turn your back on it, you know, you lose *half* of yourself. You're like a man standing in sunlight without a shadow, which is a strange thing to be. And that's the way we have tried to live. So much of our life is lived in that shadow—and that's fortunate because we also rest and reinvigorate ourselves in the shade.

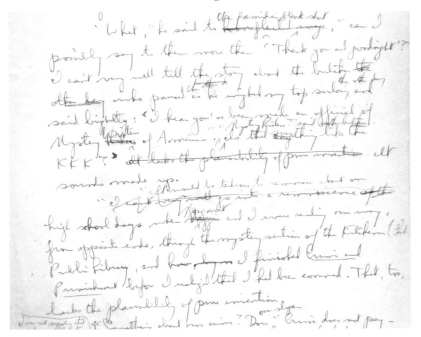

Draft of a speech or essay on being elected president of the Mystery Writers of America in 1965. The beginning of the speech (not shown) borrowed elements from Millar's piece "The Macdonald Case" (circa 1959). This excerpt (with quotation marks as written) reads as follows:
"What," he said to the familiar blank sheet, "can I possibly say to them more than 'Thank you and good night'? I can't very well tell the story about the butcher who paused as he weighed my top sirloin the other day and said brightly: "I hear you've been made an official of Mystery Writers of America." "Mystery Riders?" said another butcher. "Is that something like the KKK?" It sounds made up. "It would be tedious to reminisce about our high school days when Margaret and I were reading our way, from opposite ends, through the mystery section of the Kitchener (Ontario) Public Library, and how I finished Crime and Punishment before I realized that I had been conned. That, too, lacks plausibility of pure invention...."

Has French poetry been an enormous influence on you?

Well, I don't know how much of an influence it's been. French poetry and French fiction together have been naturally secondary to literature in English, but second to no other literature in importance to me. One reason for that is that I was lucky enough to take some courses in college that led me into French literature. I was forced—fortunately forced—to read most of Racine in French, most of Corneille, and most of Molière. That's an awfully good preparation for any writer, to acquaint himself with another literature and such wonderful poets as those were.

I went on by myself into modern French literature.... Arthur Rimbaud and Verlaine, both were very important to me imaginatively. I guess Rimbaud is the poet who really broke through the ancient poetic tradition into a new world and in a sense imaginatively created the modern world in which not only poets but all of us live now.

Would you connect them to Poe at all in America?

Well, certainly Poe had a great influence on French poetry of the nineteenth century, particularly on Baudelaire, who translated Poe. I don't know what the connection would have been between Poe and Rimbaud, although they were somewhat similar in certain respects. They were visionary poets who wrote out of what might be called psychological breakthroughs into a previously undiscovered or unexplored world: the world of the psyche and of the unconscious mind. Really Rimbaud was not in any sense that I know of a direct disciple of Poe, but they had the same antecedents. Coleridge, for example, was the master of both of them in a sense. He was, as far as English poetry is concerned, the founder of modern symbolism, and Poe was his direct and conscious disciple of course. I think Rimbaud must have been, too, but I don't know how pervasive the influence was. I'm sure that of course Rimbaud's "[The] Drunken Boat" was influenced by "The [Rime of the] Ancient Mariner." It's an attempt to do the same thing: to write a psychological epic.

When you say Rimbaud "imaginatively created the modern world," what aspects of the modern world?

The world of the perceptions that we now live in, particularly the connections between conscious and unconscious life. Poets have been doing it almost forever, but I think his breakthrough was the most striking *single* breakthrough of the nineteenth century.

He had a remarkable career in literature.

It was remarkable in the sense that he had a complete and *large* and important poetic career before the age of twenty and, so far as we know, never wrote anything after that. And it started, if my memory serves me, at the age of seven. He was some kind of a seer.

His poetry doesn't resemble Ginsberg's or some of the Beat poets'.

It's not classical poetry but it's classically *formed*, and the vocabulary and so on are classical. It's not a colloquial poetry, let's say. Ginsberg is primarily a colloquial voice and that's his great strength. I'm not saying that Rimbaud's poetry is remote from life, but *all* of the great French poets are classical in the basic sense. In their use of language and in their immense depth of consciousness of the past, they all go back to Racine and beyond.

Rimbaud, for all his breakthrough and all the pyrotechnics of it, is essentially in vocabulary and discipline what I would consider a classical poet, as opposed to the contemporary colloquial poets that you referred to. Ginsberg is the leader of them. *But* there's a tremendous connection and similarity between what Rimbaud did and what Ginsberg does. They both are poets that write out of a breakthrough knowledge of their own unconscious minds and they see *deep* into that life, far beyond the realistic classicists. It's almost as if their unconscious mind spews up a volcano of meaningful images. They have that in common. They have more in common actually than they have in difference. Rimbaud of course is the more important figure probably than Ginsberg, but not necessarily to us. I think there's another similarity: they both *lived* their poetry out. They're not closet poets. They live it.

Do you think this is a good quality? Rimbaud, for example, devoting his life to debauchery in the name of art?

Well, let's say it's a terribly significant event…. The actions that a poet goes through in life in order to become what he is are really beyond moral judgment. In other words, you can't use his life to criticize his poetry necessarily. I think it's a great boon to the world that that breakthrough was made—and it destroyed Rimbaud, let's say. At an early age he was done.

Because of the lifestyle?

No, I don't think because of the lifestyle. Volcanoes don't go on erupting forever. I think that the lifestyle is sort of incidental [to the work].

How so?

Well, it's incidental in the sense that it's not really important. It doesn't matter how the work got written. Naturally, it was important to him, and it was tragic, too. He was destroyed by the work, by the effort, I suppose. It takes more than a wild lifestyle to destroy a man. It takes more than that to destroy a man of twenty.

You know, a lot of the nineteenth-century poets, including Poe, did have this in common: that they wrote wonderful poems early on and petered out. Now, this has not been true so much of the English poets, who are generally a more controlled group than, say, Poe or Rimbaud. But Coleridge ran out rather young. When Keats died he was almost as young as Rimbaud was when he died poetically. Byron ran out in a hurry. Shelley didn't live long, he was only thirty when he went. So Rimbaud is a kind of concentrated summation of the Romantic experience, but he carries it further, he carries it into the world of the modern consciousness.

Were these people international figures at that point?

Oh yes. Byron was probably the best known writer in Europe at his peak. I mean, he was enormously well known. Shelley of course was not, but he became known. While he was not widely known in the sense that Byron was in his own lifetime, Coleridge was an enormous influence as a poet and a critic. And the team of Coleridge and Wordsworth, if I may use the expression, was as important in its way as the team of Rimbaud and Verlaine—and produced a lot more work in the long run. Wordsworth was enormously productive, and so much of it is wonderfully good. Wordsworth went on for about fifty years, and so did Tennyson.

When Rimbaud stopped writing by the age of twenty, had he simply written all that he had to write?

No. A great many people write poetry when they're young and stop. I could invent theories as to why he stopped, but I don't really know why. He had had his say and perhaps he then wanted to live a life of action.

Do you have any favorites among the current so-called serious novelists? Pynchon and Updike and people like that?

I've read both Pynchon and Updike with pleasure. I guess I read Updike first. I've read four or five of his books. He's a very good writer. Pynchon I like very much in parts. I find it difficult to get through a whole book by him, but I'm ready to believe that that's entirely my problem, not his. I certainly don't go back on a man because of one book that I didn't like. *Liking* doesn't have too much to do with what I'm talking about. Sheer literary promise is over and above whether you like something or not. I don't like half of Wyndham Lewis, but I regard him as a great genius, to give you an example of what I mean. There are writers I don't like at all that are extremely important.

I think Updike's an excessive who overwrites.

Yes, I believe he does overwrite. But, you know, you can be a good writer and overwrite. It's an excess or a virtue. Neither one of them, though, are my favorite writers.

Who are? Pulling names out of the air.

This is just off the top. I don't pretend to be a critic or a student of literature in the field that we're talking about now, and that's the immediate contemporary. I don't read enough of it to be anything but just another reader. It's hard for me to answer that. The first name I thought of was Nabokov, but I haven't read anything by him for a couple of years. I just happen to like everything he does. With the exception of Nabokov, who doesn't really make mistakes—I think *Pale Fire* is a masterpiece—so many of these guys changed their mode in midstream and lost me, and I think lost themselves. Pynchon, too, used to be what I considered a highly readable and brilliant wit. I suppose he still is, but there were so many words it's difficult to appreciate it. But I think some of his stuff is marvelously funny.

Have you read his new book, Gravity's Rainbow?

When books are enormously thick, you say, "Well, do I have a month of my spare time to give to this?" So I haven't read *Gravity* yet. I may, though. I haven't read *J R* either.[2] They sit inside my shelves, threatening me with their sheer size.

Let's talk about our visit to the bookstore yesterday.[3] When you picked up the Yeats book, you had quite a reaction to that. It seemed to thrill you.

Oh well, it came unexpectedly. I mean, there I was holding a book—I didn't know that Yeats's signature was on the front page. [*laughs*] It was a little bit like

2 The first editions of *J R: A Novel* by William Gaddis and Pynchon's *Gravity's Rainbow* were both over 700 pages long.
3 Joseph the Provider Books, in Santa Barbara. Its proprietor at the time, Ralph Sipper, was one of the first book dealers to trade in Ross Macdonald collectables.

picking up a live wire. Since I'm not a book man in the sense of buying and looking after books, I wouldn't be a particularly good owner for a valuable book with a great name in it. See, for me books are just something that I use. I don't look after them particularly. It just seems to me that a variorum Yeats with Yeats's signature in it shouldn't be wasted on somebody like me. I guess I just don't believe, oh, in converting that kind of a thing into a personal possession. In any case, I just turned away from my opportunity to buy it. I might go back and do it yet, though. [laughs]

Ralph said that there was another book that he thought that you really considered seriously for a moment, and that was a first edition of Joyce's Ulysses.

Oh yes. I don't see the point of a writer acquiring an extremely valuable rare book. I don't have the proper storage facilities—and if I *did* and put it away, what's the point? I love the idea of having a first edition James Joyce, but at the same time it doesn't fit in with my lifestyle. I've got a *Ulysses*. I had one when I was twenty and I read it then.

The basic reason why I didn't buy it, though, was that I really didn't consider myself an appropriate custodian. I'm not fooling. All I could have done with it would be to put it in a safety deposit box, and that's not an appropriate use for a book like that. It was nearly five thousand then and now it's close to ten thousand. That's another thing: I don't want to start dealing in books, you know, and being concerned about their money value. Perhaps that's the basic reason why I shy away from the acquisition of valuable books: I don't want that kind of value to get mixed up with other values. You know, I buy a bond and put it in a safety deposit box and that's okay. That's not going to louse up my feeling about my work. Let's say that there is a sense in which writers, no matter how well they do or how much money they make, they should *act* in some ways according to a vow of poverty. In some ways, depending on the personality and the needs and the lack of needs. Even if he becomes rich, which I haven't quite, it isn't good for a writer to start acting and living exactly like a rich man, even if he is rich. And most writers have recognized that, you know. They have their bare rooms and so on in which they work. You can't have everything.[4]

4 About Millar, Ralph Sipper told Paul this: "He buys first editions from me, but that's only because I'm a first-edition book dealer. If I were just an out-of-print dealer, he'd buy the out-of-print copies. In fact … there have been times when we've had two copies of a book in my catalogue. He's always selected the inferior copy, which is cheaper." About *Ulysses*, one of a signed edition of 100 with a hand-tooled leather binding: "I showed it to him, and he picked it up and he said to me, 'Do you know, this is the first time I've ever coveted something material.'"

Letter from Ken Millar to Mary Louise Aswell from August 12, 1973. Aswell was the fiction editor of Harper's Bazaar *and a lifelong friend of Southern writer Eudora Welty (dedicatee of Millar's* Sleeping Beauty). *"Immediately after writing a note to Eudora, ten minutes ago, I got up and went to a bookshelf I don't use much and got out a grey volume and saw that you had edited it—* The World Within, *of course, a book that has given me pleasure and instruction for many years, a really marvellous and original anthology, but I didn't connect it with you until now. Oddly enough, I've just been asked to try my hand at a suspense anthology which I wish I could start out with 'The Black Monk' but realize I can't. If you or Agi [Agnes C. Sims, Santa Fe, New Mexico artist and Aswell's long-time partner who purchased the Canyon Road house the couple lived in died from Alzheimer's in 1990] have any suggestions long or short I'd be glad to have them.* Beast in View *is at the head of my list, by the way…. Meanwhile it was great to hear from you—now and in 1947."* The World Within *was published in 1947 and can be seen on the shelf behind Ken Millar's ear in the detail from the Ray Borges photo (the book shown to the middle right is not Millar's copy).*

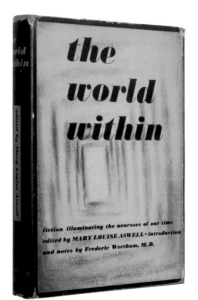

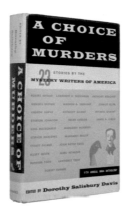

AUTHOR'S POSTSCRIPT: Most of my Archer stories come out of some emotional sense of conflict which is even vaguer than a plot idea. I try to find a situation for it. The characters tend to invent themselves; I disclaim responsibility for them; the working-out of the plot is my conscious problem. I suppose that this one got its start in a story told me about a gangster who checked into a hospital in fear of his life, and kept a gun with him in bed.

A Choice of Murders (1958) contains the Lew Archer story "Guilt-Edged Blonde" and Maggie's "The Couple Next Door"—each with a postscript by Ken, unique to this volume (shown above and below). Wicked Women (1960) contains the Joe Rogers version of "Find the Woman." Rogers was Millar's private eye predecessor to Lew Archer. In the Borges photo, A Choice of Murders can be seen to the right of Millar's head and Wicked Women third in the stack of books to the right of Millar's arm. Bottom: Detail from a list of possible stories for Great Stories of Suspense showing "The Couple Next Door" and "Guilt-Edged Blonde" with a note "(DO NOT LIKE)" next to the Macdonald story. It's interesting that Millar considered using both of these stories in his 1974 suspense anthology and that he didn't care for his own.

AUTHOR'S POSTSCRIPT, OR STRICTLY SPEAKING, AUTHOR'S HUSBAND'S POSTSCRIPT—ROSS MACDONALD, SPEAKING OF HIS WORK, AND OF MARGARET MILLAR'S: "Most fiction, especially our sort of fiction, seems to be based on unconscious fantasies which the conscious plotting mind tries to rationalize and generalize, both for itself and the reader. We all have the same unconscious, as a friend of mine once said, but writers are more aware of it." Inspector Sands, after appearing in several of Margaret Millar's Canadian novels, was transplanted to California with this story. He seems to have rooted well there.

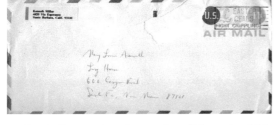

Letter from Ken Millar to Mary Louise Aswell from April 15, 1974: "It's wonderfully kind of you to invite me to Santa Fe and I feel badly that I can't do it. I won't bore you with my reasons, but they have to do with both health and family. After New York I have to go to Canada, primarily to visit my ancient father-in-law, and I'm hoping Margaret may meet me there. I know what a good time we'd have with you, if it were possible, because I remember how I enjoyed our time in Jackson. And I'm terribly sorry to miss Eudora, the more so on the occasion of her inaugural flight (is it not?). I hope she descends to you safely, and that you will remember me in your conversations with kindness and affection, as I remember you and A." In his postscript: "What Mystery Writers plan to give me is in Edgar [sic], not for any one book, but for the work in general. As I plan to tell them, in the eighteen years since M. was so honored her Edgar [for Beast in View in 1955] has been getting terribly lonely."

May 3, 1974

Ken Millar accepting his Grand Master Edgar® Award at the Mystery Writers of America award dinner on May 3, 1974.

5. DETECTIVE FICTION

Tell me about the day that you discovered **The Maltese Falcon.**

Well, I was in a tobacco shop in Kitchener, Ontario, and this store had a lending library which included some hard-boiled mystery which included Hammett's *The Maltese Falcon*. I picked it up and started reading it and, as far as I know, that was my introduction to Hammett. Well, I may have read stuff in the magazines that I didn't connect with his name, but that was my first consciousness of him. I stood there and read well into the book.

Did you take the book home?

I don't think I took the book home then. I just read part of it. I don't remember. But the interesting thing about this tobacco shop is that it had been managed by the man who became my father-in-law. This as far as I know had nothing to do with my picking up that particular book there, but my father-in-law was the manager of the place. Or had been.

When was this?

Well, it would've been 1929, I think. I would be fourteen. Thirteen or fourteen.[1] As for detective stories, well, when I was in my early teens and was admitted to the adult section of the Kitchener Library, I just set myself the project of reading my way down the shelves of mystery fiction. And not just Hammett; I read dozens and hundreds of mystery novels when I was in high school and before I got into high school. Hammett was certainly the one that stands out most and had the most influence on me, not just then but right on through. I had a very strong feeling that for the first time I had found something about the world as I knew it. He's the one I respect most now in the whole field.

Do you remember the first mysteries you read?

The earliest that I can remember offhand by name is Falcon Swift. You've never heard of him. He ran in serials in an English magazine called *Boys' Magazine*,

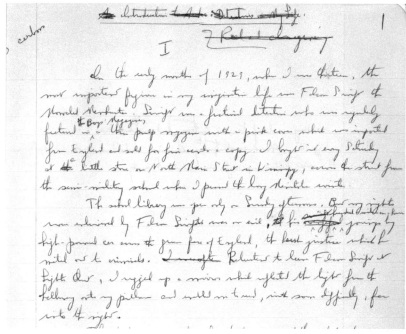

A *draft of the introduction to* Lew Archer: Private Investigator *(1977) mentioning Falcon Swift the Monocled Manhunter.*

which was available nearby in Winnipeg. That would be starting when I was eleven. Falcon Swift the Monocled Manhunter. I forget who wrote it. It was a serial that went on forever. Falcon Swift was not a private eye in the sense that we're talking about. He was more representative of the state in the English sense, you know.... He was a sort of semiofficial enforcer, as I remember, very much like Ian Fleming's character. In fact, they're very similar now that I think about it. He was a forerunner of the Ian Fleming character.

The majority of Canadian reading matter, in the time I'm talking about, which was in the Twenties, came from England.

Also from America?

1 *The Maltese Falcon* was published in 1930, which would have made Millar fourteen or fifteen at the time. However, the book had been serialized in *Black Mask* in five installments from September 1929 to January 1930, making it possible that he read one of those incarnations of the work.

Sure. It's half and half. And the local libraries handled a great deal of both English and American material. My upbringing, in the sense of what I read and in other ways, too, was Anglo-American.

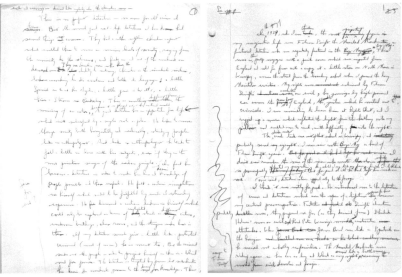

Other drafts of the introduction to Lew Archer: Private Investigator, *with the unlined page on the upper left being a new insertion (see the arrow on the right side of that page and the squiggly line on the page to its right).*

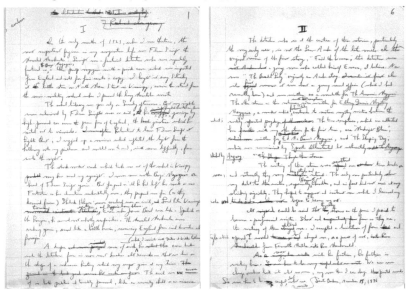

When you continued to read the pulps, say, even when you were in your mid-twenties, was Chandler being published at that point, and Paul Cain and these people?

Yes, but at this stage in time I can't really remember the names of the people I read. I'm sure I read both Paul Cain and Chandler, but I don't remember. I would pick up a magazine and just read the whole damn thing, you know. I read a lot of the pulps. And not just the mystery fiction in *Black Mask*, etc., and *Detective Story Weekly*, but also *Amazing Stories* and *Wonder Stories* and so on. I was a real fan of that in my early teens, too—science fiction.

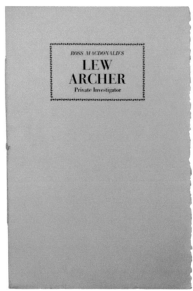

Introduction to Lew Archer: Private Investigator *published as a separate promotional pamphlet.*

Did you ever try to write any science fiction?

Not really, no.

When did you come back, then, to rereading, say, Hammett and Cain and Chandler and these people?

I never really left. You see, Margaret and I were reading mysteries right on through. We both learned the craft from reading detective magazines and detective novels. Of course, when I was teaching high school and preparing lessons for seven different classes and that sort of stuff, I didn't have much time for fun reading. I was reviewing books at the same time, but with one or two exceptions they were not detective stories, they were general novels. Later on, Margaret was ill for a winter after we were married. I used to bring home twenty or thirty books at a time from the library, and she'd go right through them in a few days; then I'd go back and bring back another pile. Most of these would be detective fiction. We're talking now about 1940. Well, the following year she wrote her first detective story.

Do you read it any less today?

Neither one of us follows detective fiction very much anymore. Naturally there are a lot of books I read, but I don't follow it in the sense that I'm talking about where you just eat it up. Writing it seems to use up the same energies that reading it does, and you have to sort of make a choice: you have to be either a consumer or a producer. So the real detective fans are detective fans, period, and the writers, well, of course we try to keep up with the best that are in our field. We don't read right across the board the way we did when we were primarily readers. Most of my reading in the genre is not recent, although I do read a detective story maybe every two or three weeks. I try to read the good ones. Let's say not a detective story but I read a crime story every two or three weeks. And there are many good ones that I miss, but sometimes you have to choose between writing and reading.

I'm fortunate, I get sent a lot of the good coming detective writers as they come out. I get sent them with the expectation, or the hope is, that if I like the

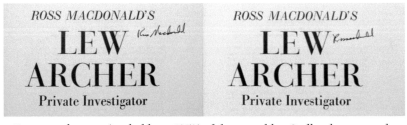

Two signed copies (probably in 1979) of the pamphlet. Sadly, the one on the right as "Rossacdonald," showing evidence of the onset of Alzheimer's.

book I'll say something. Very often I don't have time to read them all, though. I have my "serious" reading to keep on, too, you know.

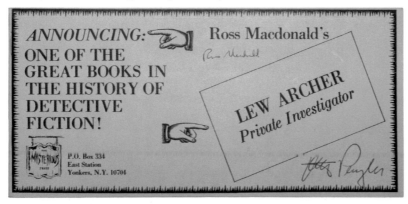

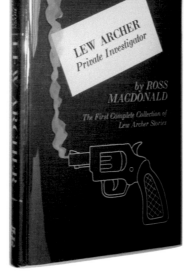

Clockwise from top: Pale blue Mysterious Press booklet catalogue signed by Ken Millar (as Ross Macdonald) and publisher Otto Penzler; trade edition of the story collection; slipcased signed limited edition; aqua blue version of the Mysterious Press booklet.

Certainly you could put your books under serious reading.

Of course I take the form seriously. I meant that as a joke. If I don't take it seriously, who will? I spent my life at it—the second half of my life anyway.

I guess I still read a fair amount, but I'm no longer omnivorous. A couple of books a week. Of course, sometimes I get into a book that takes me a long time to read. I like biography, for example.

When you write are you able to read, or will that disturb your concentration?

Oh no, I read all the time. I read something every evening. I'm reading more factual material and less fiction than I used to.

Any particular reason, do you think?

Well, I think the reason is that the world is changing rapidly and you sort of have to keep up with it. It didn't used to have so many interesting things going on in it as it does now. Things are changing very rapidly. You know, we live through a generation now in a few years. The whole atmosphere and feeling of the country has changed enormously in the last ten years. Our economy and technology have changed enormously just in the last decade. I think fact writing in general is certainly the form from now on.

Are you happy about that?

Well, it's not going to last. But for a period of time. Because we've finally discovered that you *can* look at yourself in the mirror—and how to do it.

I'm just afraid that people are going to stop reading novels then.

They already have stopped reading novels. I think fact has become terribly fascinating right at the present time because I guess we know we're living through some kind of cultural crisis and this is the record of it. Fiction comes a little

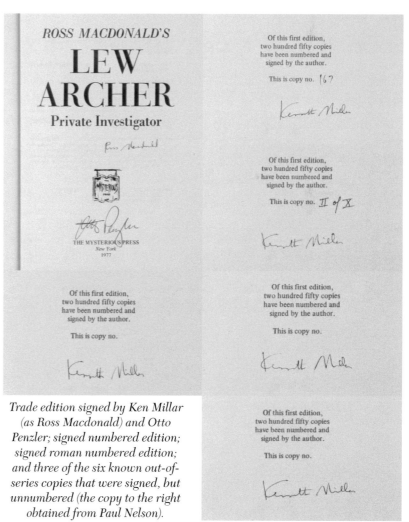

Trade edition signed by Ken Millar (as Ross Macdonald) and Otto Penzler; signed numbered edition; signed roman numbered edition; and three of the six known out-of-series copies that were signed, but unnumbered (the copy to the right obtained from Paul Nelson).

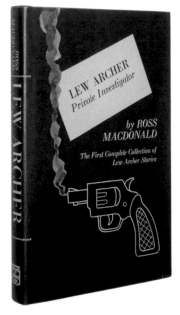

Left: Later printing of Lew Archer: Private Investigator *with a paper dust jacket instead of clear plastic jacket and business card mounted to front board. Above: Folded and gathered signatures of the second printing used as an advance reading copy for promotional purposes.*

too late, you know. It's always a time lag. It's not the latest news. One thing that happened was that we used to have generations and now we have weeks.

That great Andy Warhol quote, that "In the future, everyone will be world-famous for fifteen minutes."

That's exactly it. Except that we're not talking about celebrities, we're talking about reality changing rapidly. People really have to read the latest book in order to know what the reality is.

Getting back to detective fiction, did Margaret also have an interest in Hammett and some of the writers you liked?

She was just as interested in Chandler when he started coming out in the novels as I was, but that was later, when we even became aware of Chandler when we were in Ann Arbor. I can remember hastening down to the rental library when a new Chandler was going to come out. It was enormously important to me at that stage.

Was Hammett's name as well known then as, say, yours is now?

Not at the beginning, no. Leave me out of this for the moment. You made a comparison, but I'm dropping the comparison. I would say it's in the last ten years that Hammett and Chandler have become very significant national literary figures, wouldn't you?

I would. I was just wondering if at the time it was a significant event for an enormous amount of people.

Just for me. It wasn't for an enormous number of people. Chandler didn't sell that well, his early books didn't sell that well. They sold well but they were not bestsellers. And Hammett of course wasn't writing at all at that period.

I think, though, to answer your initial question, the whole school, headed by Hammett and Chandler and with me coming in late, and others of course that

we can both name, is riding as high now as it ever has, in popular estimation, in critical interest.

When you started writing, was that a terribly competitive time in that group of people who were doing similar kinds of books?

No, no more so than now or any other time. Mystery writers have generally flocked together fairly well. We compete with each other, but it doesn't generally make for bad friends. We flocked together and sought protection.

You said in New York something about mystery writers being an independent lot that demand to make their own mistakes.

It's true. You know, one of the main reasons why somebody goes in for writing a series of detective stories is because nobody's watching. You can actually go ahead and do what you damn please, provided that you meet certain requirements of the form and be a published novelist without anybody saying boo to you. You can develop for ten or twenty years without anybody noticing. It's a great advantage.

The same advantage, I guess, that the B movie directors had in Hollywood: they could make those really incredibly personal movies within the forms of Westerns and detective films.

Well, that's one of the advantages. But you can experiment without destroying yourself, without destroying your reputation, because you don't have any reputation to destroy. You're just there. It's much better just to be there than to be a reputation on the world scene, you know. But, of course, this ties in with my whole feeling about popular art and the joys and pleasures of it, both for the creator and the person who consumes it.

Starting out, you wrote some of your books at your sister-in-law's on Sola Street.

Yeah. That was the first five years in Santa Barbara. See, we had rather a small house, a four-room house, and a child, and Margaret was writing, too. It just seemed like a good idea for me to shift my operations to another place and, since my sister-in-law was working, as she still is, at the Sansum Clinic and her apartment was vacant all day, I moved over. I wrote *The Moving Target* in her apartment. Complete isolation was really helpful to me at that point. I was trying to develop a style and point of view and so on. I think that's the last book I ever sat down and wrote right through twice. It took me one solid year.

A first and a second draft, you mean, or with much greater differences than that?

No, the main differences were just stylistic. I rewrote it for style. That was where I formed my style. That was the first Archer book.

When I speak of serious writing, I don't exclude an earlier book like that. It took me many years to learn to write mature fiction. And while that's a good book in my opinion according to its lights, its lights are not my mature lights. In other words, I'm not disowning any of these books. I think the whole curve of them is more interesting than just a segment of the good ones, if you know what I mean.

THE MOVING TARGET

The Sampson family made their money in the Texas oil fields and spent it on the California coast. There was still plenty of it left when Ralph Sampson disappeared. Sampson was a slow man with a dollar when he was sober, but an easy touch when he was off on a spree. Which is why Mrs. Sampson, a paralytic blonde who had bad dreams, called Archer in to find him and his checkbook.

The trail that Archer followed took him down through the seven circles of California society. Sampson had mixed with thieves and murderers, a cult of phony sun-worshippers, a silent-movie star in the last stages of degradation, a boogie pianist who had served her time. In company like that you look for trouble, and Archer found plenty of trouble. He also found Sampson. But not before he had seen some plain and fancy evil, solved a series of violent crimes, and handed out some rough poetic justice.

Lew Archer is a new private eye, one that sees deeper than most. He travels faster than most, and with stranger people. His story is told in prose as fast and colorful as the events of his first case.

JACKET DESIGN BY BILL ENGLISH

Stored flat (for over fifty years) in the drawer of a lending library in Oklahoma, this is likely one of the finest examples of this rare and fragile dust jack extant.

The Moving Target *was your fifth book. Why do you suppose you didn't develop your style and the Archer character before that? Why did it take you that many books to decide that the private detective form was the form that you could do best, that interested you most?*

Well, everybody as he starts out finds out what he can do by trying it. Also, it was a very promising form. I felt that the American private detective story hadn't been fully developed at all when I started in on it, in spite of Hammett and Chandler. It seemed to me that, well, what it failed to do was to do all the things that other kinds of novels were doing. Or many of them. I mean, it failed to do *all* the things that other kinds of novels were doing, and yet it's a form that lends itself to any use that you want to put it to—as I've tried to do.

You felt that it had restricted itself meaninglessly.

Well, no, it hadn't restricted itself meaninglessly, it just hadn't gotten that far down the road. And Chandler, as we know from his letters, never really took the form very seriously. He always regarded himself with a certain self-contempt for being a mere

Left: The US Knopf edition of The Moving Target *(1949) signed as "John Macdonald." Above: The 1951 UK Cassell edition in which Lew Archer's name was inexplicably changed to Lew Arless.*

detective story writer. I don't feel that at all. I feel it's just as valid a form of the dramatic novel as there is in terms of what you can get into it. I'm not saying that my books are as good as some novels, I'm just saying that they're valid stratagems for doing what other novelists are doing in other ways.

And, of course, we keep talking about *Gatsby*. *Gatsby* is an example of what the crime novel can be developed into. It's much more than a crime novel, but its basic structure is close enough to the crime novel to make the comparison valid, I think. I don't think *Gatsby* could or would have been written if there hadn't been crime novels before it, providing Fitzgerald with rough blueprints of structure that he could use in *Gatsby*.

Do you feel any connection yet at all with the hard-boiled school or the Black Mask school?

Yes, I do, the same way I feel a connection with my grandfather—but in this case I am my own grandfather. Writers tend to be. I started out writing in the hard-boiled school—I mean that my first several books were very much in the hard-boiled school—and I haven't abandoned it entirely even now. You know, there's more to the hard-boiled school than just being hard-boiled. It also involves an aesthetic of rapid, uncluttered prose and vivid imagery, and interest in what in general can be

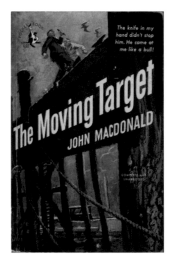

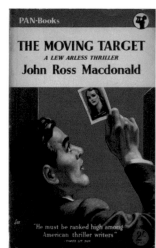

called civic problems. The whole thing of course is telegraphed and laid down for all time by Hammett's early work. That's what the hard-boiled school is. All of the writers for *Black Mask* and the allied magazines wrote with varying elements of that same mix in their work. They were *all*, in one way or another, socially or morally concerned; and however remote that may seem, I think it's true. You know, concerned about what was happening to American society, let's put it just in the broadest sense. Or in other ways: James M. Cain, who is one of the greatest and most extreme of all the hard-boiled writers—and of course he goes beyond being a hard-boiled writer, but that's what he primarily is—is a very subtle psychologist and I think a really leading dramatic artist, and extremely original.

You know, so often the established canons for readers—oh, like *The New York Times* the way it used to be—have gotten the hard-boiled school and the writers in it, many of whom are good writers and important writers like Cain, mixed up with their material, as if Cain were somehow fronting for the kind of people he writes about. Whereas the exact opposite is the case. He's writing socially conscious and tragic psychological material, which I know is important. Several of his books are extremely good, extremely important.

Which ones do you like?

I think [*The*] *Postman* [*Always Rings Twice*] and *Double Indemnity* and *Mildred Pierce* are all of first-rate importance. Nothing has ever been done in its field better than *Double Indemnity* in my opinion. I think it's a masterpiece. Beautifully done. He was a disciple and protégé of H. L. Mencken. One of the things that these writers have in common, and for the reason that Mencken was kind of their master in a sense, is the concern with the American vernacular language and the use of it.

I read Cain's latest book, Rainbow's End, which just came out a year ago. It's quite sad, quite disappointing. His grasp seems to be really evading him.

Well, Cain is now at an advanced age, close to eighty I would think, and very few writers are able to go on writing at that age successfully. Still, he wrote the book and he sold it. I think he got a $15,000 advance, and he can use the money. He has a right to go on supporting himself. He's a real pro in addition to being a real artist. I've had a letter from him.

In what connection?

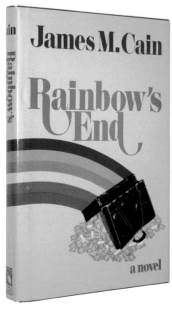
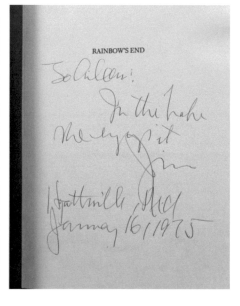

"A poet of the tabloid murder...Cain is particularly ingenious at tracing the tangles that gradually tighten around the necks of people involved in bizarre and brutal crimes...and the larger tangles of social interest from which these deadly little knots derive."   —Edmund Wilson

"One of the great inventors, a conscious and deliberate artist with a wonderful eye for everyday detail."   —Ross MacDonald

"More than any other contemporary writer, Cain has become the novelist laureate of the crime of passion in America."   —Max Lerner

"Mr. Cain is a real writer who can construct and tell an exciting story with dazzling swiftness—one of our hard-boiled novelists whose work has a fast rhythm that is rare."   —William Rose Benét

First edition of James M. Cain's Rainbow's End *with rear panel dust jacket blurb by Millar. This copy was inscribed by Cain to his ex-wife Aileen Pringle in 1975—the couple went through an acrimonious divorce in 1946.*

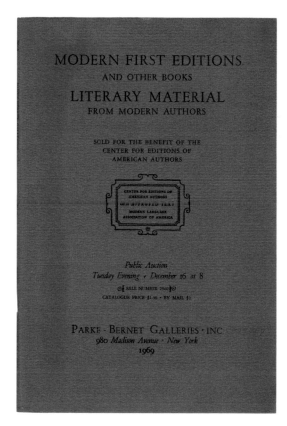

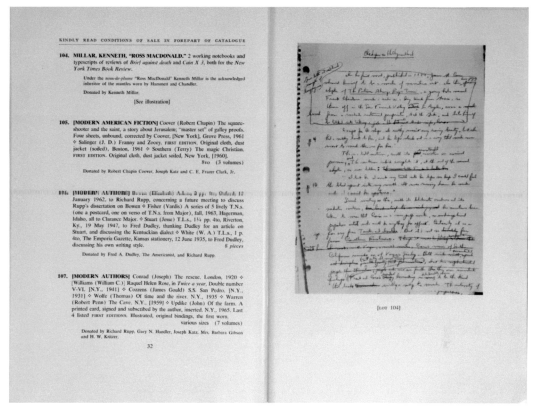

Ken Millar's own copy of the Parke-Bernet Galleries, Inc. auction catalogue (Sale Number 2960) from December 1969 with his penciled "(SOTHEBY)" notation on the cover. His notebooks and typescripts for his reviews of Edgar Smith's Brief Against Death *and James M. Cain's* Cain X 3 *(both written for* The New York Times Book Review*) were donated to the auction for the benefit of the Center for Editions of American Authors. Matthew J. Bruccoli was one of the organizers of the auction.*

I got a thank-you letter from him for a review I did of one of his collections. It was a front-page *New York Times* [*Book*] review, and he was pleased with it and wrote me.[2] I've written him once or twice.

A very favorable review?

Yes, and I think a true review. I think I gave him only his due.

Do you think Joyce Carol Oates has ever read detective fiction and been influenced in any way by it?

I imagine she has. She certainly belongs not in the detective genre but in the overall gothic genre. The gothic concession, you know, is a very handy way to refer to these writers because it includes both the highbrow and the lowbrow and a wide range of material, but it all hangs together by virtue of its combined interest in psychology and morality. The study of evil, you might call it.

I think she's potentially and perhaps actually a great novelist. It's difficult to assess somebody who is in mid-career. I don't doubt that her career is very important and very interesting. She's not unique but close to it. I'm glad you mentioned her. She's an example of somebody that I mightn't have thought of in this connection, you know, right in the middle of a conversation. She's a writer I've been interested

in for years. But I don't know her. She lives just across the border in Canada. She teaches at a branch of the same university that I went to, the University of Western Ontario, or what was once a branch of that university. All I know is what I've read about her or been told. I've known somebody who *has* been close to her and have gotten the report that she's a gentle, nice person. It was my friend Peter Wolfe who got to know her. He taught one summer at that same university and got to know her, and was very well treated by her and her husband.

She looks very small and fragile.

But what a mind.

I think you said once that you make it as difficult as possible for yourself when you write. You don't take the easy ways.

Well, I don't really set out to make things difficult for myself, but I'm interested in problems. We all, all of us serious mystery writers, really try to work in the most difficult problems that occur to [us], that are presented by life. In other words, it is a real grappling with life problems. Or at least that's what it comes out of. You have to distinguish between the wrestling and the fiction that comes out of it. They are two different things and you can't equate them, although one merges into the other.

2 "Cain X 3," March 2, 1969.

Do you think that's true for figures like Agatha Christie? Is there something serious, the wrestling of good and evil, in her books?

I think probably so, yeah. I wouldn't take Agatha Christie as the best example of serious structure, though. While she *has* written some things with tragic content, her general approach is fairly light and dry I think, what would be called in general *comic*, which is an art all in itself, but it isn't exactly what we're talking about.

Is it possible to write a really comic crime novel?

There have been a few that worked out fairly well, but only in a light sense. On the other hand, I love true comedy. Evelyn Waugh, for example. Margaret was just reading aloud to me from *Scoop* this morning. He was a wonderful comic artist, so wonderful I'm sorry he got serious in his late years.

You included one of Christie's books in your anthology Great Stories of Suspense. ***Is that the one you consider her best, or the one that best fit the theme of the book you edited?***

Well, it's one of her best books and it's one of the Miss Marple books, *What Mrs. McGillicuddy Saw!* I didn't want to just reprint one of the books that was, you know, very common, like *And Then There Were None*, which is probably her masterpiece. It seemed to me the one I chose has more human quality and more emotional interest, and also it's not exactly a detective story—it is more of a suspense novel. She hasn't written too many novels that can be called suspense novels, and this is one of them. See, I wasn't doing an anthology of detective stories, I was doing a suspense anthology. This was the one, among those of hers that I was familiar with, that seemed to me to be best. I prefer Miss Marple to

Poirot anyway. I think she's a much realer figure. You can't do an anthology of that sort anyway without including Agatha Christie.

Do people call you Ross Macdonald? Do you recognize that as yourself when somebody calls that name?

I answer to it, but I'm aware of the fact that my name is Ken Millar. Ross Macdonald is just a stage name, so to speak, and I feel it to be. I don't have a subjective response to it with any particular tone I can identify. I often get called Ross Macdonald. I suppose it serves a purpose in widening the distance between the living self and the writing self, and that is certainly in all mystery right now. It's one of the things that the mystery I'm sure is all about. It provides you with a form in which you *can* examine some of the consequences of your own actions or thoughts without identifying so closely that the results are bent. In other words, if you're writing about yourself at a sufficient remove of pseudonymity, you don't make allowances for yourself so much as if you were writing directly about yourself.

Macdonald was picked because it was a family name?

I have a cousin named Gordon MacDonald whose family lives in California. He's an ophthalmologist in Riverside, not too far from here.

I don't know another form that has that many pseudonyms.

Well, being an actor does, and maybe there's a parallel there. I'm sure there's a parallel. Because the mystery writer in his fiction acts out fantasies or possibilities. It's what an actor does. He starts with the self and works with the self, but becomes other than the self.

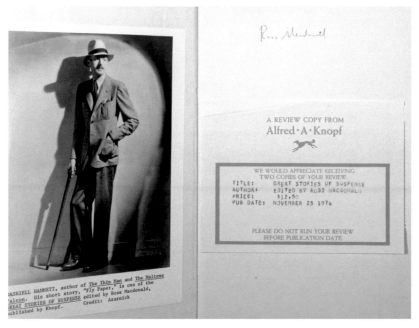

Lists of stories and novels for possible inclusion in Great Stories of Suspense.

Paul Nelson's signed review copy of Great Stories of Suspense.

Acting would've never occurred to me at all. Another reason an actor would change his name would be a more saleable or a more marketable name on the marquee, or a more heroic name than Schwartzburg or something like that, I guess. I don't know whether this would hold true in mystery writing or not.

Oh, I think it does. Ellery Queen is kind of a good example of a made-up name.

Of course, in that case it was necessary because there were two of them.[3]

It wasn't necessary but it was convenient.

It's also interesting that they made the character and the pseudonym the same.

Yes, I'd forgotten about that. That just reinforces what I've been saying.

Why do you think there is such a preponderance of pen names in the mystery field?

Well, in my own case the reason is obvious; it's because my wife was writing under my name, M-I double-L A-R, and we just hadn't foreseen the possibility that we'd both be writing the same kind of fiction, you know. And I changed my name.

There may be an element of conscious doubleness in the kind of people who write mystery novels. For example, so many of them, the new ones, are men who are prosecutors or working one way or another with the police and with the law, who write under pseudonyms. It also may have its social aspects, too. It seems to me that there must be some sort of psychological doubleness in anybody who chooses to write mystery novels in preference to straight novels.

Maybe it helps you to get out there or something, to have a pseudonym. To me it's really just a nuisance, at least so far as I consciously know. But not much of a one. I ran into a lot of trouble with names. But in the long run it didn't make much difference.[4]

Do you think John D. MacDonald is a figure of importance?

---

3 Behind the typewriter keys, Ellery Queen was actually a pair of Brooklyn cousins, Frederic Dannay and Manfred Bennington Lee—whose real names were, respectively, Daniel Nathan and Emanuel Benjamin Lepofsky.

4 Millar's first four non-Archer novels had been written under his own name, but for Lew Archer's debut novel, 1949's *The Moving Target*, he adopted the pseudonym John Macdonald. After John D. MacDonald made his displeasure known, Millar agreed to insert the initial *R* between the John and Macdonald. In 1950, with the publication of *The Drowning Pool*, he made the name difference even more pronounced, using the name John Ross Macdonald. Finally, with the publication of *The Barbarous Coast* in 1956, he dropped the John altogether and was forever more—yet apparently never to the satisfaction of John D. MacDonald—known as Ross Macdonald.

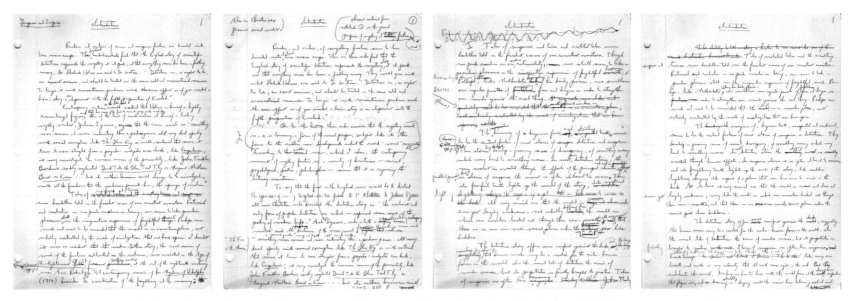

Various drafts to the introduction of Great Stories of Suspense. *The working title of the draft on the left was* Suspense and Surprise.

Obviously. He's an extraordinarily prolific and various writer. He's got great imaginative energy. But I don't particularly like his work, and he doesn't particularly like mine neither. You see, because of this unfortunate similarity of names there has been some amount of friction between us, and it continues.

He was angry because he thought you were capitalizing on his name, is that correct?

Well, he's a somewhat angry man anyway I think, by what I hear. Of course, I guess perhaps I am, too. There's a certain element of unfriendliness between us, I'm sorry to say.

Did you know who he was when you chose the name?

Well, he hadn't published anything. No doubt he had written some stories, but he hadn't published any books that I knew of. Or did know of. Obviously, I wasn't trying to steal his thunder.

   This is not for quotation, but he just recently wrote a letter to me to the effect that I and my publishers were trying to use a similarity in title in my last book to his titles in order to steal some of his readers. He wrote a letter to me to that effect. And this has been going on for years. So how can I give you a cool and pleasant answer about John D.? Just between us, without this thing listening in, I consider him a rather unpleasant man. I don't deny that he's got a grievance but, God knows, I didn't use the title *Blue Hammer* because he had used *blue* in a previous [book title].[5] But he wrote a letter to me to that effect, demanding that something be done.

It never really dawned on me at all that there could be any confusion at all between the two of you.

5 The book was the first in the Travis McGee series, 1964's *The Deep Blue Good-by.* As Tom Nolan noted in *Ross Macdonald: A Biography*, it wasn't specifically Millar's use of the word *blue* that MacDonald objected to but rather the common knowledge that all of the McGee books had utilized color-coded titles: *A Purple Place for Dying, A Deadly Shade of Gold, One Fearful Yellow Eye*, etc.

There isn't any confusion. I've never even had a letter addressed to him.

It's hard to believe anybody would think The Blue Hammer *was an attempt by you to lure his readers.*

You say nobody would, but *he* does, you see. This has been going on ever since he started publishing books. That's when the unfortunate accident occurred. I started out, you know, with the name John Macdonald. I changed it to Ross Macdonald, and I really feel he should be content with that.

   I don't want a perpetuation of a minor quarrel about nothing to go into print. I'm just explaining it to you. Obviously, he's one of the leading writers in the whole world in his field and an extremely effective writer. I'm not concerned about people using similar titles and that sort of thing, I'm concerned with anger and ill will. I don't blame somebody for getting angry, but when it goes on for so long and is renewed by silly little things like my use of the word *blue* in a title, well, it seems unnecessary.

   John D. MacDonald and I don't share political views or social views or any other kind of views. Or literary views either. But that's all right. I say thank God that there is diversity in the world.

Speaking of John D., what's your opinion of the Travis McGee series?

Zero.

Why?

Well, it just is not to my taste. It's just not my idea of how to do it. I don't object to its existence. They're not ambitious books. God knows, I've only read one or two of them. But I *have* read MacDonald. When I was putting together the anthology, I read quite a lot of his work. He's done a lot of good short fiction, and I know something about his writing.

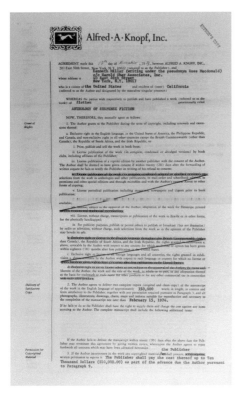

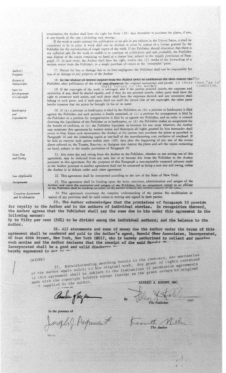

Ken Millar's copy of the contract for the anthology (then referred to as Anthology of Suspense Fiction).

Do you think the other books are better than the McGee series?

I don't know. I like them better. There's just something I don't like about the Travis McGee series. Obviously, it's because I have my own idea of what a fictional detective should be. It's just not along my line. He includes material that I don't. That's all, there's just a difference. I'm not talking in terms of quality, just in terms of kinds of material.

You described reading both Dickens and Tarzan when you were eleven. I'm wondering if at twenty-one, and again at thirty-one, that that same duality existed and you could be reading Dostoyevsky on one hand and Cleve Adams or some other private eye author on the other, and have fantasies in those worlds.

Yes. As a writer now more than I am a reader, I don't read detective stories with the fantasy accompaniment that I used to. I'm too busy seeing how they're being done. It's not a purely imaginative enjoyment, it's also a critical job. I don't get lost in them the way I used to. But you know, a critical enjoyment can be very keen. You know, keener, because you identify what you're enjoying as you enjoy it. I still love a first-class mystery—and even a second-class mystery.

The thing that you do in writing a good detective story is to simultaneously write a novel about, hopefully, new people in new situations, and yet you do it in sentences, not one of which violates the overall idea of a detective story. In other words, you don't put in anything merely because it will look good on the page or sound good to the ear. It all subserves the overall purpose of the

book. And what I've done, what I have accomplished in that line, is to extend and broaden, I think, the things that a detective story *can* do and is *supposed* to do.

Which are?

Well, I've sharpened the definition in the sentence, so to speak, and I've greatly increased the element of imagery. I use imagery, the simile and the metaphor, so extensively that they've become a structural element; they're actually part of the structure of the book. And so on.

You mean bringing in a lot more symbolism?

Yes. And a symbolism which isn't just there on the one page but which extends through the book and joins up with other symbolisms. That's what I mean: imagery as a structural element. Of course, that's the basic structural element of modern poetry and modern fiction generally. God knows, it should be. What we call imagery is simply the traces of our inner life. That's what it comes from, that's what it expresses. You use it to relate the overt action to the inner lives of the characters, and the inner life of the author, too. Because, don't forget, the author is always writing about his own inner life, too.

It seems your later books are much more consciously symbolic than the early ones.

Well, of course. I think the gradual development of symbolism in a lot of fiction is absolutely central. It takes a long time, you know, before you can convert your own personal material and your own observations into symbols. At least it took me a long time.

I think you've brought the detective story much closer to* The Great Gatsby *than to Hammett or Chandler.

Well, *Gatsby* of course is beyond my reach and also it's quite different from what we've been talking about. It's structurally really remarkable. Profoundly original. *Gatsby* is certainly the most important book in my life. I think this is true for all of Americans. It seems to be our central book. It opens doors in all directions, into the past and the future. And they're still open; it hasn't been closed off at all. It's still relevant. And it operates like poetry.

Do you write poetry?

Not very much. I'm not really particularly talented in that direction.

I think there are several lines in every book that contradict that.

Yeah, there are certainly poetic elements. But this was in the context of Auden, who is a really good poet. In that context I don't exist at all. He's not only a very good poet but he was enormously productive.

What strengths does symbolism bring to your books? And what weaknesses does it bring? Do you pay the price in another area?

Yes, I think you do. You sacrifice immediate impact for echoes. But also … the tendency of symbolism is to make imagery into a proviso structural factor. While

To Shepard Rifkin, from his symbol-minded friend, with warm regards, Ken Miller

YES! CAPRA CHAPBOOK SERIES (Ross Macdonald)

1. Henry Miller. ON TURNING EIGHTY.

2. James D. Houston. AN OCCURRENCE AT NORMAN'S BURGER CASTLE.

3. Anais Nin. PARIS REVISITED.

4. Faye Kicknosway. O. YOU CAN WALK ON THE SKY? GOOD.

Ken's chapbook On Crime Writing *as inscribed to Shepard Rifkin, author of* The Murderer Vine, *along with an explanation of how the "symbol-minded friend" inscription came to be.*

31 Jan '95

When On Crime Writing first came out I wrote to Miller.

I told him that I write detective fiction, and that I do not search for characters in order to find a symbol in their personalities and then work out the story.

I said that I find my character and let him or speak in their natural voices, without forcing them into what I said then were symbolic acts.

I added that I had read and enjoyed all his books.

I sent him a copy of On Crime Writing and asked him to inscribe it for me. This is the result of my letter to him.

Shepard Rifkin

Shepard Rifkin

that in a way greatly improves the *weave* of narrative, it also makes it somewhat more cumbersome. Or can. Now, in a thing like *Gatsby* it doesn't. That moves as rapidly as a lyric poem. At the same time, *Gatsby* is a comparatively simple structure, it needs that interweaving of symbol to give it depth and weight. But where you're dealing with a larger structure, being aware of all the symbolic overtones and undertones can strain you to your limits.

I would imagine it's particularly difficult in a suspense book.

Yes, where you have other laws to obey. You have, for example, a sign that says: DRIVERS WHO GO UNDER FORTY MILES AN HOUR IN THIS AREA WILL BE ARRESTED. However, I think it's inescapable. You have to write in the idiom that your time presents to you, obviously, and that other writers have prepared for you and done a better job than you can in. It certainly is worth doing. Besides, a writer owes it to himself to occupy his mind as completely and intelligently as possible, and symbolism does make it possible to pursue meanings into areas that they've never been found in before. You set up a reverberating symbolist structure—and I don't claim I have ever succeeded in doing this, because there are other things that I have to be doing, too—that's one reason. It means that a very slight hint or whisper or move can have rather profound reverberations in the meaning structure of your fiction.

When we talked in New York, I got the feeling that you felt this was possibly your major contribution to detective fiction: the incorporation of this kind of echo in detective fiction through symbols.

From the purely literary standpoint, it's probably true. I don't know. Well, I was brought up on symbolism. That's the whole point of what we were saying about Verlaine and Rimbaud and so on. I should mention Proust, too. He's almost the final example of that kind of writing in fiction. Wonderful writer. Well, he's the writer who does the things that are hard to do best perhaps and with the greatest skill.

What are the things that are hardest to do best? Giving this echo?

Oh no, that's just one of the things. I don't even want to imply that the chief merit of symbolist writing is the existence of echoes. What symbolist writing does is to find significant imagery and use it to the hilt. That's more than an echo, that's masonry. The symbols are real, you see, they're not just echoes of each other. They are actually part of a structure which is just as valid as a building—in which you also find repetitions. For example, one side of a building is always exactly like the other side, so to speak. There's that symmetry.

Is Proust a symbolist?

Yes, he's a symbolist. That doesn't comprehend him, but certainly his use of imagery and recurrences and so is very much at one with the symbolist poets that he learned from.

He's also obsessively concerned with the past, is that correct?

Not really. It's in the nature of his book [*In Search of Lost Time*] that it should be about the past because he was writing about his whole life, beginning with child-hood. *But* towards the end he was writing about the immediate present, almost as he lived it. I don't deny really that he *was* obsessed with the past, I just mean to say it wasn't his only subject. He was writing about the civilization of Paris and how people lived in it. And that's not really past. What he wrote is still valid.

He was an autobiographical writer, wasn't he? Was it an open way or an indirect way?

Both. There was indirection. He avoided identifying himself directly with the sins of his characters, an avoidance which later writers haven't felt it necessary to make. But that's incidental. You know, the personal relationship to one's fiction is really an incidental matter. It's what enables the fiction to get written, but the exact nature of the relationship is not important. It's interesting but it's not really significant. It's different for each writer.

But would there be a fiction if there were not a personal reason?

Yeah, but it doesn't matter what the personal reason is. I mean, we don't have to know the personal reason in order to enjoy the fiction.

I suppose you're right except I guess my approach is always somewhat more person-drawn than that. The man who writes the poem is as important to me as the poem.

But you're a critic and a writer.

I may be like an Archer figure in that I'm somewhere between the city and the state, or in this case the poet and the poem or something. I want to know about them both, I guess.

I do, too. It's the interaction very often that I find so interesting in reading fiction by writers about whose lives I know something. *But* the fiction does stand by itself and you don't have to know anything about the writer in order to understand the fiction. That's all I meant to say. Naturally, almost the greatest pleasure I have in life is drawing the relationship between fiction and reality. In the life of a man like Fitzgerald, for example.

In New York you also said you felt the need to do a bigger book, a longer book, where you could experiment with slower rhythms.

Yes. I'm not taking any of that back. Remember, we were talking in terms of, well, the history of the form and influence on me, and my reaction to the influence. I was really talking about what I've done in relation to these other writers.

You talked a lot about what you've learned from Hammett and Chandler, but it seems to me that a novelist would also react against his masters.

Yes, I certainly have. You know, one of the most important and difficult things that a writer has to do is clear a space for himself which hasn't been preempted by other writers. You have to find it, or invent it and develop it, and make it your own. When you've done that, you hate like hell to abandon it. And it could be a mistake, you know, to make any large gesture or step away from what you've been doing. I don't know.

You see, the only thing a writer can do when he's been profoundly influenced by another writer, as I have been by, well, let's say starting with Poe and coming

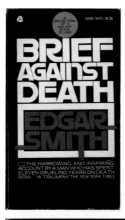
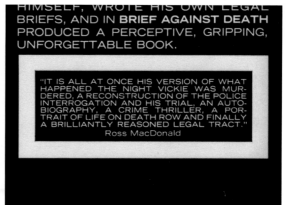

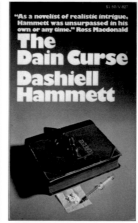

Paperback blurbs for Edgar Smith and Dashiell Hammett.

on down—and obviously Chandler and Hammett are the two main influences on me in the American detective story—my relationship to them is not simply that of a critic, it's somebody trying to assimilate and use and *become* an influence. I don't pretend to talk about Chandler particularly from a cool, critical standpoint. I'm struggling with forces—and other forces—that they represent in the form, and trying to do something with my own, which compels me of course to take a dim view of what they've done, even though I draw my strength from them. It's somewhat like a younger swimmer or wrestler—those were my two main sports—competing with another swimmer or wrestler and *depending* on the other guy for having taught him what he knows, and at the same time wanting to pin him as a wrestler or beat him in a swimming race. One thing that you don't want to do is what the other guy has done. You have to find your own thing based on your own life, your own experience, and your own peculiar vision. Your own limitations even. All these things become positive forces in one way or another in a book. Books are made out of limitations as well as possibilities, you know. You have to depend heavily on your limitations. Learn what they are and work like hell inside of them.

Everything turns out to be a strength for a writer if he follows his own light all the way.

You *are the space now of the private detective novel, I guess. Today's writers have to figure out a way to occupy a different area than Lew Archer somehow and yet incorporate Lew Archer as well as Hammett and Chandler. They have to assimilate that history.*

Yes, and some of them are doing it, too. [Michael Z.] Lewin, for example. He has taken it somewhere else. I'm not predicting anything, I'm just pointing out what I read. I mean, I can't predict what his development will be.

I don't want to be forced into the position of criticizing my own work in favor of his work, but it seems to me that there's a nice, natural liveliness and a humorous acceptance of self and other people, which is certainly lacking in my works to the extent that he has these things. Also—and this is very important—he has had the courage and the ability to take over a new and wholly different cityscape. He's the first major detective writer in that area and he's done it well. He's not at all backward or diffident about it—he goes right ahead and makes it his own. Right from the start. Those are some of the things that I value in him. He's got a very nice, humorous touch, too.

What of Hammett and Chandler have you reacted against in your work?

Well, over-simplicity essentially. Stylistic simplicity, thematic simplicity, and simplicity of plot, too. I've tried in all three fields to write more as if I were writing serious fiction in a popular form than just writing popular fiction. Of course, a whole generation elapsed between Hammett's best work and Chandler's best work on the one hand and my best work, which came pretty late.[6] It took me at least a dozen years to hit my stride, I would say. Something like that anyway. Meanwhile, the European developments that we associate with symbolism and so on had become available to American writers. That's the main difference. I'm a generation later, culturally speaking, and great changes occurred during that generation, and I benefited from them I think. Or at least I learned from them—enough to be different from Hammett and Chandler. You know, when you're following and learning from and imitating at the beginning such extremely powerful writers as they are, it's extremely difficult to be different, to find *ways* to be different, and still be valid and yourself, you know. So I would say that I've introduced some of the modern literary complexities into the form. Found a use for them. Psychological complexities, too. That may be the basic one. I think the psychology that I write out of is a deeper psychology than either Chandler or Hammett. I don't mean to downgrade them, but you asked me for the differences. Obviously, they're my two masters.

My own literary education was long and drawn out. I spent too much time being educated and not enough time putting the education to use. But in the end I think I found some uses for it in revising the hard-boiled American style to some extent. But now it's medium-boiled.

Do you think that after Chandler there were some other hard-boiled writers who were very important? Did Mickey Spillane make any contributions to the form?

Well, he didn't make any contributions to me, but he certainly did to the form.

What contributions did he make?

Oh, strength. In subject matter I think he went further in self-exploration than any of us did in a way. But I don't take his novels quite seriously as fiction. They're more, oh, almost compulsive writing in a sense. That's not an objection to them, it's just a kind of description of them.

Would you rank him a major figure?

Well, he's a strong writer and he's an original. Very much of an original. He's not imitating anybody. I think he has to be counted as a major figure. He's not a major literary figure, but he's a major cultural figure.

That reminds me of the question somebody asked a Frenchman—this was some time ago: "Who was your greatest poet?" And the answer was "*Hélas, c'est Victor Hugo.*"[7] I say, "Alas, it's Mickey Spillane." I don't mean to compare him with Victor Hugo.

A lot of Spillane's books are very dumb and very right-wing, but they do have some merits.

Journey to the End of the Night [by Louis-Ferdinand Céline] is right-wing, too, and it's one of the greatest novels of this century.

It seemed like the hard-boiled style went into excess very fast.

Well, it's very hard to keep it clean, to keep it morally clean, because simplicity is the most difficult of all tools to use. When you're writing what purports to be the spoken word, you're constantly having to differentiate between what's valid and

---

6 Dashiell Hammett wrote from 1922 to 1934, followed by Raymond Chandler, who wrote from 1933 to 1958. Millar wrote from 1944 to 1979.

7 André Gide first answered the question in *L'Ermitage* magazine in February 1902.

what's ephemeral in the spoken word. Most slang dies, for example, so you have to be very careful. You really have to write a purer style in a sense than the literary writers write; and I think Hammett does write a purer style than most of his literary contemporaries. His style in his best work is amazingly pure and accurate and simple. Well, that's not what I aim at of course. I don't aim at simplicity.

Do you think you're a prisoner of complexity in a way?

Yes, but a willing prisoner. It's sort of a happy imprisonment, though, to be imprisoned in something that you've made yourself.

It does seem to me almost inevitable. I mean, you spend your life working to hone this vision and this style to as fine a point as possible. It's not easy to walk away from that.

It's not desirable to walk away from it either as long as it's valid for your own imagination, as long as it's what grips you, you know. It would be an artificial thing to turn your back on it and deliberately start over. You can't start over anyway, you can't forget what you know.

Actually, my books are not getting any more complex. A book that I wrote fifteen or sixteen years ago, like *The Zebra-Striped Hearse*, as far as plot is concerned and perhaps style, too, it's just about as complex as the books I'm writing now. In fact my recent book, while the plot is as complex as any, I would say that the style is not. I think the style is somewhat simpler.

I think The Blue Hammer is an easier book to follow than The Instant Enemy.

I think the writing is simpler. It may be that there's more there line by line and page by page, but that's not what we're talking about. It may be *denser*, but it's simpler. And I think the plot is simpler, too. I tried to write it so that the readers would be able to follow it. I was more interested in making it clear what had happened, and in setting up the dramatic relationships among the characters, than in preserving the mystery right to the end in this book.

You've talked about moving your books closer to dramatic novels. I already regard them as novels.

I don't. I regard them as a restricted form.[8] It doesn't mean that you can't break *some* of the rules, but if you break all the rules, you're writing something different from a detective story.

I obviously by experience know that I need a form, a skeleton at least to a form, to give me my basic structure. Otherwise I get lost in the wilderness of material that's available. Of course, I'm not saying that that's the best way to do it; it's just the way that works for me. It's not the best way to do it. The best way to do it is to invent your form out of the material that you want to write about, and very few writers are able to do that—successfully.

A lot of the really good writing, though, has come out of genre writing. It's not inaccurate to say that Elizabethan and Jacobean drama came out of genre writing. They came a long way, but that's where they originated. I don't think the detective story is that hopeful, I don't really think it's going to lead to anything

very much larger than it already has, though I hope it does. It just seems to me there's an inherent moral limitation in writing about a crime and a solution to a crime. It doesn't offer the possibility of taking in enough life experience, when you consider the variety that you get in English drama and so on.

It seems to me that allegorically anyway it covers a pretty vast range of experience that one could write about.

Well, allegorically you're still restricted to the contest between good and evil. When you think of the complexities that you find in Elizabethan and Jacobean drama, which includes a lot of comedy, I don't see how the form can really compete historically. But it may be the form that is kind of central for this present society.

Evil wins in life, but it shouldn't win in the ultimate sense in books. It should be contained by books rather than expressed by them. That's my feeling. You see, that's the opinion of a moralist and a detective story writer. It could be that the exploration of evil *without* those moral controls is more important and more necessary. I'm suggesting that Céline, for example, may be one of the really great writers of our time because he does that. The mystery and the detective story, almost by definition, can't perform that function of exploring evil on the side of evil, so to speak. We're really just talking about categories anyway. Anything that's true and involves the human can't be completely evil. The act of writing it down is not an evil act, you know. It's very significant and desirable. I'm just using Céline as an example to break down the idea that the contest between good and evil is necessarily an ultimate one for literature. It is for me apparently and for other detective story writers, but I don't know whether that's desirable.

Is that viewpoint also in your life as well as your books, do you think? That of the moralist?

What I was saying was a literary argument and it wasn't about life. I really was suggesting that life steps outside of those boundaries and that it should. I'm not saying that that's necessarily a way to have a *happy* life or a good life, but it's obvious in this century that we're in a period of testing, testing limitations and limits, and in the long run what we'll do is set up new limits, new standards. That can't be done simply by reapplying old standards to contemporary situations, which is to some extent what the detective story does, almost by its nature.

Perhaps the central idea that I came up with … was the idea of the exploratory nature, which *can't be met* by a form like the detective story, which tends to begin with definite standards of good and evil rather than *seek* what its standards will be as an end rather than a beginning. I think that's one reason why so much

---

8 Warren Zevon told Millar: "Maybe there's a parallel in songwriting; that's a very restricted form. I tend to overwrite if I step out of the boundaries of that form." Millar replied, "What you just said about yourself is true about me, too."

detective fiction is psychologically unsatisfying: because it doesn't really explore the various possibilities of moral attitude. It just assumes certain moral attitudes. One reason a writer like Camus is so refreshing is that, while he writes out of a moral background certainly, he doesn't impose it on the events of his fiction. At least he doesn't in *The Stranger*; he does in some of his other work.

It's present, though, isn't it?

Yes, of course. But it's not rigid, it's not a rigid framework that affects the action itself. There's nothing moralistic in the action. Of course, he has a moral attitude, but he is not condemning his murderer, for example, as a detective story almost automatically does. I'm making very broad statements which don't fit a subtle work like that, but I'm talking about how in the detective story moral prejudgments do tend to predetermine the action.

Do you think there's been a movement, though, away from black-and-white towards very heavy areas of gray in the detective fiction?

Sure. Of course there are gray areas, and some of the most interesting people and people that we feel for most *can* be the people who are most guilty—which I think is desirable. But this is true of any kind of writing that is good enough to be called tragic writing.

Do you think the detective story can achieve that level?

Probably the form can, but it has to be changed and developed in that direction. I don't really think it has been. I consider *The Maltese Falcon* a tragic novel, I think it has the true tragic attitude.

It seems to me that a great deal of your work has the quality you were talking about: being morally exploratory.

To the extent that that's true of some of my books, particularly some of the later ones, it's a secondary characteristic. The books are still based primarily on the traditional detective story skeleton, and this is a variation and an amelioration of that, but it isn't a complete change.

If there is a limitation to the detective story, can't that be transferred into a strength almost through the use of inevitability to some extent? You know what's going to happen, but you can underline it and make it really work for you?

I suppose there are certain advantages in that, but you pay very heavily for them. I much prefer the idea of a story that "makes itself up" as it goes along and then doesn't lean at all heavily on a basic structure that's laid down by the convention. That's what I'm objecting to, and what I would like to break free from.

 A perfect example of what I'm talking about, a book that really has broken free, is *The Great Gatsby*. We've discussed it before. That's obviously influenced by the genre that I've been criticizing, but at the same time it's not contained by it. It steps outside. It takes the same materials and does more with them—in the direction of tragedy, tragedy written in a contemporary form with contemporary materials, including the detective story. It could never had been written quite as it was without a background in detective fiction.

You were talking earlier about the detective novel having "definite standards of good and evil." Whereas oftentimes life doesn't.

That's true. The detective form is an invitation to sacrifice subtlety. You have to try to reintroduce it into the form perhaps and recognize that the rough, obvious conflicts that you get in detective fiction don't really offer, well, subtle, not complex enough solutions.

Did you have a problem fitting your own life into a black-and-white genre, so to speak?

That question isn't specific enough to have an answer.

Did you have difficulty fitting the material of your own life into a form that has its limitations of good and evil? Say, in The Galton Case.

What *The Galton Case* forced me to do, for the first time quite successfully although I made earlier attempts at it, was to change the black-and-white form into a white-gray-and-black form which would correspond a little more closely to our emotional experience. I think the step that that particular book, *The Galton Case*, exemplifies is a step into the gray area where we all live, out of the black-and-white area in which the traditional detective story has been imagined. I regard the central character in that novel as definitely gray and subjectively so.

Wouldn't it have been in a sense easier, at least on this one level that we're talking about, not picking a genre that was so morally defined?

Well, it was already my genre, and I went into it right from the beginning because it appealed very strongly to me. It, so to speak, fitted the autobiographical elements that I wanted to write about. Though of course I didn't know consciously quite what they were when I chose the form, I knew that I was powerfully drawn to it and I knew that it contained the sort of materials that I wanted to write about. No other form does or will probably. Everything I write is in that form and everything of book-length that I've ever written that I've published has been in that form. Conflict between good and evil, or whatever you want to call it, seems to be my subject. At the point that we're talking about, in *The Galton Case*, I first succeeded in making it subjective as well as objective.

Do you think it was an advantage almost? Because you had to more or less fit personal experiences into a tight pattern, it made it somewhat easier to define them?

That's true, that's true.

Is perhaps another reason why you picked the form because one of the advantages of popular art would seem to be that it has a visceral impact and a speed and a faster definition?

Yes, and it simply gives you a definite form to work in. It gives you, so to speak—we've been watching the Olympics and the gymnasts—apparatus to work out on. You're not just all by yourself standing in the room.

On the other hand, sometimes high art can give you an opportunity to work if you perhaps don't have the ability to make visceral impact—visceral impact that's essential to the detective story.

By all means. Or to put it another way, if the kind of conflict that you get in the detective story simply doesn't appeal to your mind, you know, you may be seeking something much more complex and much subtler. It can be done in any kind of popular art. I'm speaking now about the person who doesn't choose the popular art. My attempts to write outside of genre haven't worked well.

I think there are probably instances where, just as there are superior talents working in popular art, there are people working in high art who wouldn't be able to make the impact necessary to make a piece of popular art work.

Or who are not interested in making that kind of impact. Most of us end up doing what we can and, if we're lucky, it's what we're best at. Although the two don't necessarily always go together.

One of the difficulties of talking about this kind of fiction, detective fiction, is until recently it didn't attract any serious critical attention, so there is not really a vocabulary to talk about the kind of the problems and solutions that really go to create a good mystery novel. I don't know of anybody that has really gone into it in the way that the more traditional forms have been studied. But this is no doubt happening right now. I know that this form is very popular in the universities now, and that means that there will be works of scholarship and criticism on it and that some of them will probably be enlightening. But in talking about it to you, I sort of have to make it up as I go along, the kind of vocabulary and also the kind of things we talk about that to me, personally, seem to go into detective fiction. Many of them are highly subjective really, more subjective than autobiographical, if I may make a distinction. They have to do with theory of psychology and everything else. Why does the mystery satisfy? You can't even begin to discuss that without some psychological ideas. And historical ideas, too, history of culture, it comes in immediately. Why in the past century has the detective and mystery novel become almost our central form of printed communication in fiction? You really have to have a theory of history, a theory of psychology, a theory of aesthetic and so on. And not just an old one, because the old ones don't comprehend the new occurrences.

How do you feel about the increasing academic recognition of the hard-boiled detective? It seems to me it's really hitting a peak these days.

Yeah. I like to see the books in the schools. You know, I started out as a teacher, in high school and then in college. It just comes natural to me that the books should get into the schools. My own and others. I've been told, by people who know, that I'm being taught at Harvard and Yale and a number of other schools. And the University of California. I have heard from both students and professors all over the country. My books are being taught in high schools, too, on quite a large scale, and I hear from high school students. I like hearing from students.

The detective novel has re-risen to its greatest popularity in the last ten or fifteen years, say. So has popular music in a way. No one really took anyone in popular music probably quite as seriously as they took Bob Dylan, say, and the Beatles. In the same time span almost, the popular musician has risen to great heights as has the detective writer. I suspect there's a correlation there somewhere; I don't know what it is.

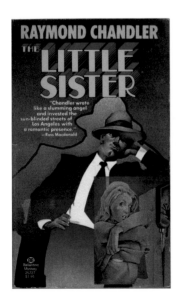  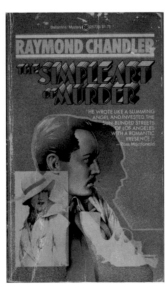 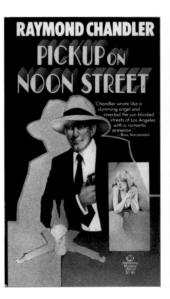 

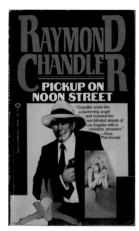 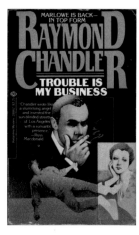 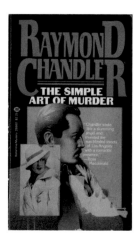

Well, we've discovered that the culture the popular culture is concerned with is our own, and it intimately molds us. There's been almost a reversal in the amount of serious interest.

It seems to me the highest form of the detective novels now, which I would say is your books, and the highest form of rock & roll, which I would say is Dylan and Jackson Browne and Warren Zevon and some other people, are equal to at least the lowest of the high art, if not the highest of the high art. I really don't see that aesthetically there's a whole lot of difference in them.

Well, I'm not ready to make that claim for my own work, but naturally my intentions are serious. I think we've just suddenly discovered—it's part of the democratization of the world—that we *are* the people. We ourselves are the people, we are the populous in word *popular*, and we're beginning to take our own lives more seriously. We're beginning to take what we used to consider a light amusement more seriously, as a way into ourselves and our lives. This is true about the popular music that you mentioned, and I meant the same thing when we were talking about jazz. I brought jazz in because that's the popular music that I grew up with.

Would you rank Ellington lower than some middle-of-the-road classical composer because he was in jazz? I would guess no.

No, I wouldn't.

At one time classical music was a popular art. The Beethoven symphony was an event in popular music as much as in the court. And I don't think that's true of the classical writers today or composers today. I can't think of a serious composer writing symphonic music today that's really writing for a mass audience. That's why the form is becoming more and more anachronistic.

It's true of serious music nowadays. What little I know of it smells of the graduate school, doesn't it, to a great extent? And this of course is true of the kind of fiction that popular fiction is an alternative to. I'm just struck by the fact that what you say about music is also true of the sort of thing that we've been talking about in fiction. I just wanted to mention that probably the *basic* impulse behind my writing, so far as it can be interpreted historically, is as a reaction against the academic in literature on the part of somebody who has been there. And in fact my whole writing life is a kind of alternative life to the life of scholarship, which is what I started out in.

One reason why Auden was so important to me was that he legitimized the kind of writing that I wanted to do. He was the first important critic to take detective fiction seriously, so far as I know. He said the things that sort of liberated me. I had him as a teacher for a semester at University of Michigan. He did a lot of lecturing across the whole range of modern literature. He read it all. As a matter of fact, his first critical writing was as a critic of detective fiction for the London newspapers when he was in his early twenties. He was a fan.

You've probably written more private detective novels, and certainly more good private detective novels, than anyone who has ever lived actually.

No comment.

I didn't think I'd get much of a response out of that question.

Well, what every writer hopes for of course is to do good work and do a lot of it. Just to have written one good book like *The Zebra-Striped Hearse* is a lucky event, you know. I really feel lucky. I was lucky in my background; you know, a good education and a highly-charged literary background, and artists there. It's much easier to become an artist if you know some.

It must be more than background. Chandler and Hammett did not die young and they only wrote five and seven books, respectively.

They had to invent the tradition, in a sense, that I didn't, and they passed it on.

Chandler didn't invent the tradition.

Well, he did, though. He did invent the contemporary literary hard-boiled detective story.

More than Hammett?

Oh no, I'm just making a distinction between the particular thing that Chandler invented and the particular thing that Hammett invented. There's a difference of a generation between them, that's all I mean. He was the next generation. He invented the appropriate vehicle. There are a lot of things in Chandler that there aren't in Hammett. You know, much more detailed characterization and sociology and so on. I'm not comparing their respective values, I'm just talking about what's there.

I was wondering what you felt your prevalent flaw, as a young writer entering the form, was at the beginning.

Oh, I underestimated my medium, even though there were Hammett and Chandler there to show me the difference and the potential. It took me years of working in it to realize the potential of the detective story and to learn how to turn it in what I will call *literary directions*. Whether that's the right word or not, I don't know, but you know what I mean.

You were always drawn to it, though, in a personal way.

Sure, sure. But I had to learn it. I had to learn how to do it. I'm not claiming that I have learned all about how to do it, because that's the work of not just one lifetime.

6. A SHADOW PORTRAIT

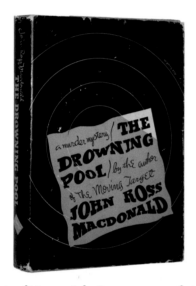

Did you know after you wrote The Moving Target there would be a second Lew Archer novel?

Yes. I wrote *The Moving Target* with the idea of training myself in the form. At that point I was committing myself to the form and trying to learn it, and trying to master the style at that point.

When you began writing Archer, then, you did so with the intention that he'd be a series character?

Yes, but I didn't have the conception that I have of him now, developed over the years *pari passu* with my own development. He reflects my own maturation at a distance. I don't mean to say that we're twins by any means—far from it. Because he has to meet certain narrative needs and so on, he doesn't develop as fully as a one-book character can; there always has to be more of him later on. And that's fine. This is true of everybody as he goes through life: he doesn't use himself up in one single action—unless his name is Harry Crosby or all the people who are like that.

I think that's one of the elements of reassurance in these books: that a man *can* survive a lot of troubles and even learn from them. You know, it's customary for tragic novels to use up the characters, *bang*, like that, and to many readers it must seem that that's the way life is or should be. But it really isn't. Life goes on for a long time.

I intended Archer to be a series character, but of course I didn't know it was going to be such a long series. All these things depend on how things turn out. Of course, the form and the character of Archer have both changed and developed a very great deal since I wrote *The Moving Target*. I've been doing my best to change the form in the direction of my own lights, you know, and that takes time. It's a very persistent and strong form. Just to master it is an effort, and then to *change* it is a further effort. Of course, I've been changing it as I go along and as *I* change. I've learned how to use the form in various directions and so

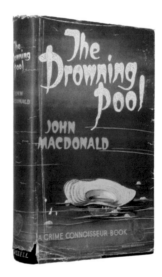

have the other serious writers in the field. I'm interested to know what the next move will be in this field. I'd like to make the next move, but it's very tough to know what to do.

Would you say you're still interested in the mythology of the form?

That must be the case. It's the mythology I'm working in terms of, still. I've changed it in some ways. One way I've changed it is to reduce the story significance of the detective in his relation to the other characters. My detective is not actually the hero in the classic sense. He does act, but more to *promote* the story than to be the centerpiece of it. As I've said before, it's the stories of the other people that really interest me more. Archer is just a means of getting to them and showing them as they are.

What do you think of Archer?

Archer of course has his Romantic elements. He survives better than people usually do in real life, although not always. I regard Archer as a fairly realistic representation of a detective. I base the judgment, not him, on detectives that I've actually known; and detectives relate to him as a representative of themselves.

One difference is that Archer is certainly not as much an idealized mythic figure as Chandler's Philip Marlowe was. He's more realistic than Marlowe.

No, he's somewhat idealized. He's better probably than the average detective. That's an idealization. As I said, detectives themselves relate to him. I had one successful, youngish detective, who had operated in Santa Barbara and the Bay Area, who came to me one night out to my house and wanted to collaborate on a statement of ethics for private detectives, based on the Archer series. He wasn't kidding. He was a guy who had broken about fifty burglaries, most of them connected with dope. He wanted to do this. A local organization existed which he thought he could interest in promulgating a code of ethics. Well, that was his opinion of Archer. Obviously he took it as a valid presentation.

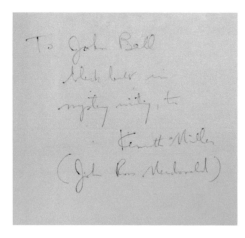

John Ball's copy of The Drowning Pool, *inscribed to him by Millar as John Ross Macdonald. Ball (author of* In the Heat of the Night) *was trained in the martial arts, hence the "black belt" inscription. The rear panel of the dust jacket features a shadow portrait of Millar by Dey Studio.*

What did you say to him?

I said I would be interested in working on it with him. But a case came up which required him to go underground, and that was the end of it. What happened immediately after that was the trial of the students that were arrested in Isla Vista and he became their detective. After that he left town.

I know very little about the trial.

Well, after the so-called riots at the university here, a number of students were put on trial.[1] Most of them got off. One or two, I guess three, were convicted. Two of them ran away and one stayed and spent a year in jail. A brave man, he's now holding public office in this area, showing the quality of man that he is. In any case, the detective that I'm talking about was employed by those students to get evidence that would help them. That's what he went underground for.

What did you think when he came to you with the idea to base a code of ethics on your Archer series? Did you take that as a compliment?

I took it as a compliment, yeah. I was rather surprised. Because, while I try to make Archer real, I've never been much concerned to try and make him an exact replica of a real-life detective. In fact, a writer, when he uses a first-person narrator as I do, doesn't really try to conceal the fact that he's speaking somewhat in his own voice through the detective. The combination of the two, the detective and the auctorial voice, is known to the reader and it's one of the sources of his pleasure. The combination of the two things: the real and the unreal, so to speak. But which is the real and which is the unreal?

1 More than 1,000 protestors participated in the student unrest. In the early morning hours of February 26, 1970, some of them burned a local Bank of America to the ground.

Do you think there's any validity to the statement that in effect Archer is a father figure, created so that in your writing you can relive your story in a somewhat more orderly fashion? I'm thinking about The Doomsters in particular.

It sounds as if it might be correct. That specific aspect of my fiction is something that I haven't thought about very much. I've done an awful lot of thinking about fathers and sons, though, and a lot of feeling, too. But I haven't tried to tie it up with that specific book.

Oh no, I don't mean necessarily that specific one. It's quite conceivably in all of your books, for thousands and thousands of readers, that Archer is in many ways a father figure.

Well, he certainly serves some of the functions of a father in the fiction. Maybe he's the kind of figure that you invent in the absence of an actual father. This is something that I really haven't thought about very much. The idea of the father figure is important to me, but I haven't worked out its relationship to the actual.

To me, it would be impossible to think of Sam Spade or Philip Marlowe as a father figure.

You think of the father figure as someone who not only represents the *active* and *forceful* elements in the male but the nurturing elements. God knows that's what I believe in. I think that a man should be a nurturer as well as an actor on the world stage.

The figure of Archer is almost continually a figure of mercy.

Well, by comparison with other hard-boiled private eyes perhaps.

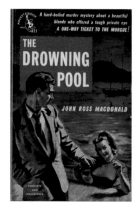

By comparison with the other characters in the books also.

That's true, that's true. He's a man who tries to *save* situations.

And also he tends to become aware of all of the characters, and quite a few in depth, so that he pretty much can dole out mercy and understanding to them.

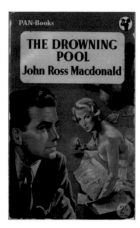
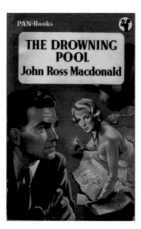

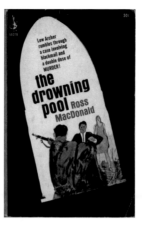
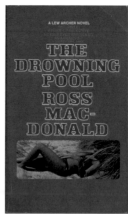
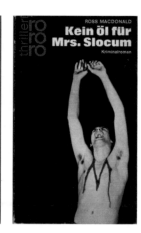

Of course, he's naturally limited by his profession and the kind of stories that he's projected into, but he represents in general my idea of how a man should act. Naturally, he makes mistakes. There are certain things built into the form that prevent him from being a full-fledged tragic figure. The basic thing is that he's both the narrator and the man who makes things right at the end. Those two aspects of a first-person narrator figure get in the way of a full-scale tragic treatment of a character.

Get in the way technically?

Well, not just technically. It's a matter of, you know, what a man does expresses what he is, and the form to a great extent determines what Archer does—that is, the sort of thing he does. There's a limitation there of which I'm very conscious.

One of them being that he has to wrap it all up in the end?

Oh no, that's not so bad. It's just that he is consistently on the side of the light. The more significant figures in crime fiction—or in psychological fiction, whatever you want to call it—are *not* on the side of the light; they partake of both darkness and light. In fact, they live in tragic struggle, an internal struggle. So there's a sense in which Archer is doomed to be a comic figure. I'm just thinking about the stresses that are built into the form and the things that are denied it, too. It's a terrible limitation on the detective story. The central figure always has to be a good guy, so to speak, and does solve things. At the same time, it enables you to write about subjects in great detail and great depth which otherwise you wouldn't be able to handle, I think.

How so? Why in great depth in a crime book and not in a novel?

Well, it just seems that the gothic pattern enables you to work deeper into the thing than the novel has ordinarily been able to do. It just lends itself to the purpose because it's been used for that purpose for 200 years. You know, it's a highly developed form. And we do properly include Dostoyevsky in it because he really did learn from Poe how to handle some of this material. *The Brothers Karamazov is* a detective story. I don't mean to say that it's that in a limited way; it's the prime example of detective fiction—what it *can* become in the hands of a world genius. I regard Dostoyevsky as probably the greatest of all fiction writers.

Can we talk about some of the other limitations? Of why Archer can't develop more than he has, and the fact that he's sort of forced to be a good guy?

Well, you can put it that way, that he's forced to be a good guy, or you can say that the initial conception of him that can't be changed completely is that of a problem-solver, a man who is on the side of virtue, in a broad sense. I'd go further and say that Archer—this is not necessarily inherent in the form, but it does have to do with my use of it—can never risk himself ultimately either. In other words, unlike truly tragic figures, his soul is not at stake. He's in that sense a secondary figure, and it's the other people in the fictions who are tragically involved and threatened.

Why can't he risk himself? Who draws that limit?

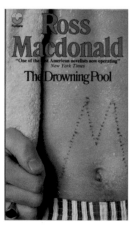

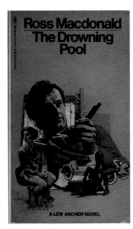

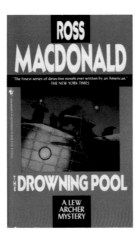

Well, the form as I use it draws that limit. The essential reason is that he's a continuing character and only a little bit of him really comes out in any one book. He is not revealed actually in any depth, the way the other characters are. He's the man who *sees* but is not *seen*.

Do you think it would explode the form if he did take great risks? He takes some risks in The Blue Hammer when he gets romantically involved with Betty Jo.

Yes, but of a very minor nature. That's a good example of what I'm talking about. The nature of the form precludes his taking over the book. I'm sure you'll agree, Archer's a central figure and, in the technical sense, *the* central figure. The books are always about the other people, and Archer's involvement in their tragic lives is always *incidental*

Condensed version of The Zebra-Striped Hearse, *September 1962, published as* A Zebra-Striped Hearse.

to his life. Even in the last book where he falls in love with a young woman, the affair is peripheral to the main action really. The girl is threatened and so on, but compared with the complexity and the depth of the main action and the difficulty of it, this other stuff is probably unimportant. I'm just thinking in emotional and structural terms.

I'm not so sure that I agree with that.

Well, let's put it another way: Archer's problems are not the central problems that the book is dealing with. If they were, it would be a different kind of book, he'd be a different kind of character, and he would be used up by that book.

You made the point that the romance with Betty Jo had to be minor and that otherwise it may destroy the book-by-book containment. That she was an unimportant segment of the book.

Yeah, and there's a sense in which Archer is less important than some of the other characters.

But Archer will be in the next book—Betty Jo may or may not.

I know that.

Another way that Archer is unlike Spade and Marlowe is that Hammett's and Chandler's books are about Spade and Marlowe, not the other characters. They are the central characters. Would you agree with that?

Oh sure. I always regard Archer's private life as being essentially secondary to the lives of the people in whatever the book is. That's one reason why I can go on writing him. I don't, so to speak, use up either him or my interest in him. Because there's a lot more at any time if I wanted to use it.

Leaving aside Marlowe, who's a special case and a very complex case which I'm not even prepared to understand fully—I think I understand Spade. Notice that he was used up by that one book [*The Maltese Falcon*]. That's very often the mark of a great book: that it consumes its materials completely.

In addition to The Maltese Falcon, there were three Sam Spade short stories.[2]

2 "A Man Called Spade," "Too Many Have Lived," and "They Can Only Hang You Once."

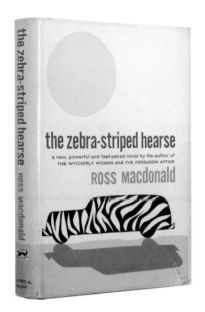

That doesn't count in the sense that we're talking about. He was used up. It was a tragic book and he was the tragic actor in the middle. Don't forget, he really did fall in love with a really bad woman, and he laid it on the line for her and ended up having to turn her over to the cops. And that's it. It's a tragic novel in which he is the central tragic figure. He's morally torn in two. Nothing like this ever happens to Archer.

Are there a lot more details about Archer's life that you could use?

It would be easy for me to write it, let's put it that way. I know essentially what his life is and has been, but I don't write it. I merely try to imply it in the course of the books. You know, it's the strangest thing, but by saying a bit less about a character you can actually tell more. If I went into some detail about his daily life—where he lives, who his friends are, and so on—his essential nature would be somewhat obscured, I believe. See, what he is now is essentially a style, and that style is reticent. You can get fairly strong effects in a reticent style with very small input. That's the real reason why I don't say more about Archer.

To go off to a different medium briefly, I think that's the basic strength of American acting. People like Jimmy Stewart and Gary Cooper and Clint Eastwood—that reticence, that less is more quality, is very powerful.

Yes. I'll give you one of my favorite literary examples. In *The Saga of Grettir the Strong*—which is an Icelandic saga, one of my favorites, and I'm sure had something to do with the development of Archer—Grettir is trapped in a small building, it's just really a hut, by his enemies. They take a tree trunk and start to batter down the door, and Grettir says, "You're knocking rather loud." It's a fairly short saga and one of the most interesting literarily. A lot of them are just, oh, lists of exploits, so to speak, but this one has form.

Do you think it's possible that you underrate Archer's influence?

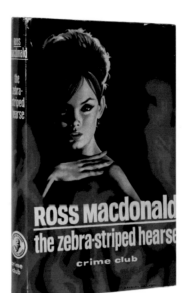

Oh, it could well be. I don't mean particularly to underrate him but to draw a distinction between what he represents and what he doesn't. He doesn't really represent me; it's the book that represents me.

I'm not so sure they're separable.

They're not, they're not. Since he's a major part of every book.

What first really involved me with the books, and one of their major strengths, is the wonderful sensitivity of Archer and, again, his role as father figure. Also, his moral certainty and moral strength, which I find Hammett-like. There's something extraordinarily solid and sensitive and dependable and, as you said, "how a man should act" in the viewpoint of those books. It permeates those books. It may be invisible, but it's just like the air: it's all out there, and I don't think those books could live without that air. I think a great many people respond to that air rather than this tree and that bush and things like that.

Could be. I've merely spent my life working on it. I really don't think I underrate it. No, I'm really just putting on the record some corrective aspects. I don't mean to deny my profound connection with Archer. I mean, if you want to define him, he's the sensibility of the books and, to a degree, that's my sensibility, too. But only to a degree. It's the difference between the poem and the poet. I'm just the poet, and the poem is much better than the poet. Always. It has to be. In any case, the poem is what we're talking about.

Not necessarily.

Sure. You're talking about Archer, and he's the poem.

But overall I would just as soon talk about the poet.

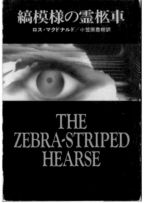

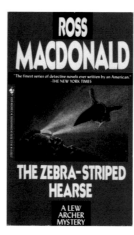
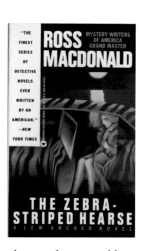

Well, maybe you would just as soon talk about the poet, but I'd rather talk about the poem. Because I'm too personally involved with the poet. I don't mean to say that I'm unwilling to talk about anything, I'm just continuing what we were saying. I think it's useful to a writer not to be too totally aware of his very close personal involvement with everything that he writes. In other words, it's good for him to think that he's writing something out there about something even further out there and it's just not all in his head.

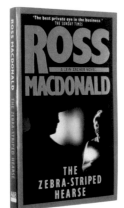

I'm sure you understand your books better than I do.

Oh, on the contrary. I probably haven't even read them as recently as you have.

But you wrote them.

That doesn't necessarily constitute you an expert.

Do you feel sometimes in rereading some of your early books that they were almost written by someone else? That they were written by a stranger who once was you?

Yeah, but I also read them as being by the writer that I used to be. And I read them, say, as early traces of the writer that I hoped to become.

I read an interview where you said that Archer's "primary interest is understanding other people's lives."[3] Isn't that an unusual position for a fiction character to take? I mean, why not his own life?

Well, I don't know. You'd have to ask him.

[laughs] ***That's hard to do. Is that a statement that at all holds true with you? That your primary interest is understanding other people's lives?***

No. But it's generally more true of detectives than it is of writers. I mean, there has to be a reason why detectives are detectives, and it has to do partly, in the cases

I've known, with simply, well, there are men who like to live in what seems like a family group. Wherever they are, whatever they do, they like to relate intimately to the people around them.

Are you talking about the kind of male camaraderie that appears in Howard Hawks's films?

No, I'm talking about how a good detective operates with other people. He really does *feel* a closeness and an interest—up to a limit. I'm not talking about criminals necessarily, I'm talking about the clouds of witness that every detective has to deal with all the time. He has to deal with innumerable people. Obviously, he wouldn't go into the work if he didn't among other things *like* dealing with people.

That also suggests, since his primary interest is in other people's lives, that there is something in his own he's unsatisfied with.

Yes, and I think that may be true of a good many detectives. But as regards the question of whether Archer is a valid presentation of a detective, I've known some detectives and some have read me, and I haven't had any complaints.

Had you met detectives before you started The Moving Target ***and the short stories?***

Sure. I've actually known detectives since I was a small boy.

3 "Ross Macdonald: at the Edge" by Sam Grogg Jr., *Journal of Popular Culture*, Summer 1973.

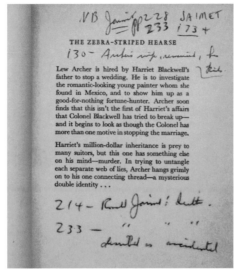

THE ZEBRA-STRIPED HEARSE

Lew Archer is hired by Harriet Blackwell's father to stop a wedding. He is to investigate the romantic-looking young painter whom she found in Mexico, and to show him up as a good-for-nothing fortune-hunter. Archer soon finds that this isn't the first of Harriet's affairs that Colonel Blackwell has tried to break up—and it begins to look as though the Colonel has more than one motive in stopping the marriage.

Harriet's million-dollar inheritance is prey to many suitors, but this one has something else on his mind—murder. In trying to untangle each separate web of lies, Archer hangs grimly on to his one connecting thread—a mysterious double identity . . .

Ken Millar's 1971 UK paperback of The Zebra-Striped Hearse *with his penned notation that Archer's ex-wife has remarried and has kids.*

Because you were in trouble? Or just acquaintances?

I haven't been in trouble. I was thinking about people that I just knew in a town where you knew a lot of people.

Were you interested in the detective as an occupation at that point because of a fascination in them?

Well, I started reading detective stories when I was in my early teens. I was reading Hammett by the time I was fourteen. I would say that while there is certainly a strong element of realism in my interest in detectives—that is, it's not a dream particularly—that it's also been strongly influenced by my literary interests. Detective stories are interesting to me not only because they've got detectives in them but because they're written in a certain way and they imply certain attitudes towards the world. In fact, they depict a world that was not available in any other form, but a world that corresponded to a world that I recognized.

Do you think you made those differentiations at fourteen?

You bet.

In looking back over Archer's life, if I can put it that way, how does it connect with your own?

Well, I think, while he is not a self-portrait, he's what might be called a possible imaginary self-portrait. My own personality and life are much more complex and explicit of course than Archer's have been. You might call him not a self-portrait but—I can't think of a good word—a *shadow* really. A shadow portrait, where you don't really get to know the person—that is, the live person: myself—in any great detail, but you have a good strong sense of the general outlines of the personality and what that person cares about. Of course, the basic difference between me and Archer is that I sit in a chair and write, and he gets out and acts.

Are you envious of that part of it?

Not particularly. I've moved around a good deal in my life.

Generally speaking, Archer reflects your viewpoint?

Yes, but his mind is much more limited, considerably more limited, than mine.

You're not at odds with him?

No. Let's say that I'm smarter and he's better.

Better at what?

[*chuckles*] Just better. He goes out and does good things, so far as he's able to.

Well, I think you probably do, too.

No. That's because I'm smarter.

More modest I would say.

Oh, he's a man of action. It's his job and his duty to do good things. And in spite of all the sadistic detective stories that have been written, most of the detectives that I've known have been angels of mercy in general. Their purpose is to improve the situation in the human world. That's the way they talk and that's the way they act, and that's the way their results turn out, too.

Would these be detectives that you would know had not you written these books about

Condensed version of The Chill, *August 1963.*

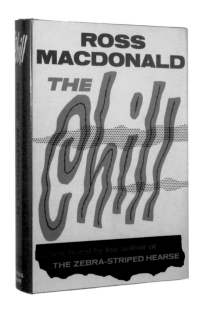

detectives? I mean, would you have met, say, the average run-of-the-mill detective who didn't know who you were and what Archer represented? Or are you liable to meet only the best of detectives?

No, I think I've just met a good sampling. It's true that one of them is one who came to me through the books, but the others I met just in the course of life. I was really talking about private detectives, but this is true of police detectives, too. I was on very close terms for several years with a local policeman who rose through the ranks and became an official in the detective department and later became head of the probation department. There was absolutely nothing in that man but a desire to do the right thing. He wasn't the smartest man that I ever knew, but he was a good one. Still is. Now retired.

As I said, I've gotten to know half a dozen private detectives, and they were all men who were trying to improve things and treated malefactors with forbearance. I don't mean that they let them go; they treated them okay. They had a feeling of mercy toward them.

Now, I do know that there are a lot of bum detectives in the world. There have to be. I mean, it's just that's the way things are. There are a lot of bum cops. But that isn't exactly what we were talking about.

You said Archer is "somewhat idealized."

I suppose he is, but I wouldn't present him as a better man than detectives I have known. He certainly isn't as good to other people as one pair of detectives, a man and wife, whom I came to know. They were people just burning up with desire to do things for other people. They would detect in the days of the week and on Sundays they actually held a kind of neighborhood seminar for the problems of their neighbors in a fairly poor district in Reno. I was using the word *seminar* poetically. What he actually did was to set up a family court, not with any punishments but just problem-solving for problems.

Did you continue to know them after you concluded your business with them as well?

No. But you get to know people awfully fast and awfully well under stress.

Have they appeared in your books?

Just in passing, just as friends of Archer.[4] But the main point of what I said is that private detectives really are often good guys, and the guys who write

4 In three books, *The Zebra-Striped Hearse, The Chill,* and *The Far Side of the Dollar,* Lew Archer sought the help of husband and wife Arnie and Phyllis Walters, who ran a detective agency in Reno. Their real-life inspirations, Reno detectives Armand and Thelma Girola, located Linda Millar when she disappeared with two men in 1959.

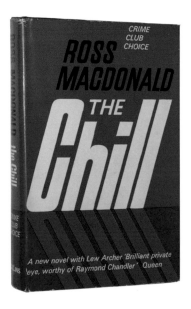

about them as just being crooks who are getting away with something don't really know the field. They're just writing fantasy, in my opinion. And this includes Chandler.

How did you come to know them?

Through my life.

Do you want to talk about that or would you prefer not to?

Well, the less I talk about my daughter the better.

Oh, I see. I wasn't aware your involvement with the detectives concerned her.

A great deal of my life has been. The reason why I don't want to talk about it is that I don't want anything in our interview to *depend* on that, if you know what I mean.

If your daughter is in your books, as I believe that she probably is, I would like to find some way to talk about that without mentioning or alluding to her. Primarily in this case I'm just interested in the two detectives. It doesn't matter the connection.

That's right.

I sort of blundered onto the connection.

Oh sure. I know that.

Among the different roles that Archer fulfills, including historian and observer, is it possible to see him also as psychologist?

Oh yes. You can see him as a representative of *all* the roles that a novelist has to assume in order to write a book.

Can you explain that?

Well, I was just responding in spades to what you said. He's a psychologist. That is to say, he reflects whatever psychological knowledge or understanding goes into the books. They go, to some extent at least, by way of him. He's the conduit for these things. Of course, a lot of these ideas are developed dramatically. Archer merely records them. He's the psychologist as commentator instead of the psychologist as recorder. He also is a powerful motive force in the books. He causes things to happen and in fact he enacts a good deal of them himself. In a muted way he also plays the role of psychiatrist, you know. Understanding people and bringing them to a point of self-understanding and changing lives.

Why do people want to tell Archer things?

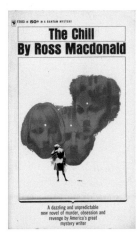

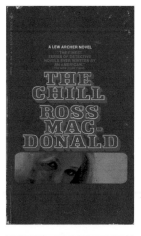

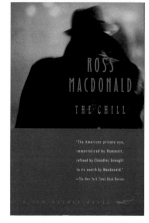

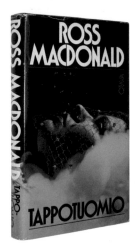

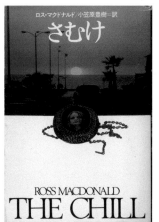

Well, people always want to tell other people things. All they need is a listener and they'll tell strangers more than they'll tell their brother-in-law.

What are the philosophical/psychological/ personal implications of Archer's statement in The Zebra-Striped Hearse, "It's all one case"?

Well, he would only be saying it about the case in that particular book, in any particular book. He wouldn't be saying that his whole series of cases are all one case. But in general, although there are major plots and subplots in the books, they're all related to each other, and you can't solve the main case without also—*solve* is the wrong word; let's say *understanding*—the others. And this reflects my feeling that we're all members of a single body, to degrees that we have no idea except in moments of what might be called revelation.

It seems to me almost like a very good philosophical statement, that they are all literally one case.

Oh, I believe it. It also has a religious echo in it. You know, the idea of all of us being members of a single body, so to speak, has a religious connection. But I think

it's literally true: we live or die together. The influences just of one person on another, any two people who know each other, are absolutely staggering if you trace them. It's the essence of our lives, that interrelationship. We don't really live full or even adequate lives without interrelationship. Everything that happens happens between two people. Or more.

In The Instant Enemy, Archer says the following, and I'm wondering if this is a rather personal statement about writing as well: "I had to admit to myself that I lived for nights like these, moving across the city's great broken body, making connections among its millions of cells. I had a crazy wish or fantasy that some day before I died, if I made all the right neural connections, the city would come all the way alive—"

[*in unison with Paul*] "—like the Bride of Frankenstein." Well, that's Archer as novelist talking.

Is that you as novelist talking as well?

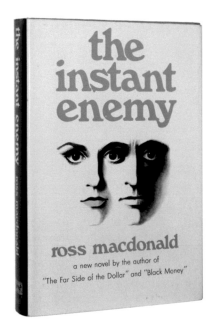

Well, that's a little more Romantic than I would express it. I don't attach any terrible importance to that paragraph. It's just one way of summing up what Archer is aiming to do. But it's an expression of a feeling rather than an intention. He knows he's not going to be able to put it all together.

Isn't that also your intention?

Sure. I was just going to say: But the artist *can't* put it all together. He doesn't have to work among the difficulties of the actual [world], although he has to take them into account because those are the difficulties he's trying to surmount imaginatively.

Why the Bride of Frankenstein? It's very startling to read that.

It's a semi-satiric comment on the civilization that he's trying to put or hold together. It has other meanings, too, of course. The Bride of Frankenstein is a woman, and you can imagine Archer as trying to construct Los Angeles, in an imaginative sense, as a bride. Don't forget he doesn't have a woman. At least he doesn't have a permanent woman—or he didn't until recently. Is that sufficient?

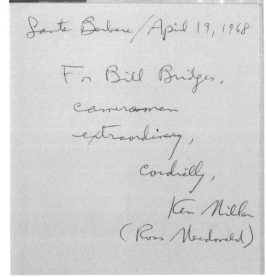

Above: Knopf review slip. Right: US 1st inscribed to Bill Bridges, who took the photos for the endpapers of Kenneth Millar/Ross Macdonald: A Checklist *by Matthew J. Bruccoli.*

I'd like to talk about it just a little bit more. What you said about the woman is interesting because the words body and cells almost seemed to refer to a person. It also seems like the Bride of Frankenstein is sort of a humorous way to defuse the obvious poetry of the previous sentences.

Yes. It takes the ambition out of it and just lets it sort of merge with what's around it.

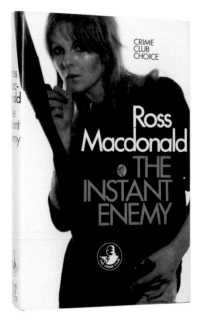

It's pretty much the same thing as saying, "It's all one case."

Yeah, I would say so. It's also a crack at Los Angeles. But it's not a denial of Los Angeles; it expresses essentially caring for Los Angeles *and* the potentiality of its coming alive even, as a whole, as a community.

It seems to me it's also an excellent credo for a novelist.

It was intended that way. Many of the things that Archer says may be a little out of character for a detective but are quite in character for a novelist.

It also seems to me a rejection of cynicism.

Yes, but, you see, the image of the Bride of Frankenstein *retains* an element of cynicism. I wouldn't say *cynicism* exactly. I'd say *skepticism* or *satiric feeling*.

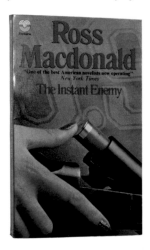
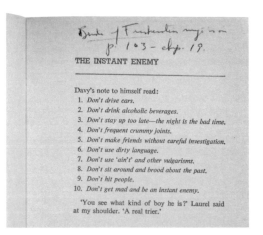

Ken Millar's 1972 UK paperback of The Instant Enemy *with his penned notation of where the Bride of Frankenstein image appears.*

It seems to me that one of the characteristics of the detectives that Hammett and Chandler created was their cynicism. Yet with Archer there's a skepticism but not a cynicism, and that seems to me a crucial difference.

I think it's a crucial difference, too, and it implies a degree of complexity that Hammett wasn't interested in and that Chandler was incapable of.

Is that also a reflection of your own attitudes and feelings, that you prefer skepticism to cynicism?

Yeah, I'm not a cynic at all in any way, I don't think.

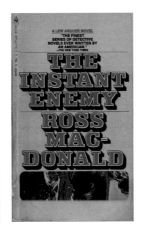

Still, I'd hardly call Archer an optimist.

Of course, Archer is the narrator but he's not the voice of the books. Do you accept the definition?

Yeah, I accept that. Again, in no way am I trying to make you synonymous with Archer.

No, I know that. I feel the books say a lot of things that Archer doesn't even know or is not recognizing himself as knowing. But you know, the symbolic action in the books often says a lot more than Archer ever does. So I just wanted to get that in. Archer is *a* voice that I would accept as my own, but only one of the voices in the narrative; and the whole narrative in its complexity, if I'm lucky, says what I want to say.

If the books cannot be described as optimistic and not pessimistic, how can they be described?

Well, they're not exactly realistic either. I think they have to be taken as members of a genre which is both popular and serious. Now, what I mean by the popular in this context is that the books are written in forms that are sort of handed down from other writers. In other words, you don't create your own form. You take a popular form and speak through it.

Yet you said that you prefer realism.

Realism in life. That means understanding the meaning of what you say and what you do, and what other people say and do, too. Very often the implications are hidden from the people who are doing the acting and the speaking. The realist should be able to understand what's happening around him.

In The Moving Target someone asks Archer if he judges people, and he says, "Everybody I meet." In that way, I was wondering if you consider him a moral center in the book because he indeed judges everyone he meets?

Yeah. That doesn't necessarily make him a moral center, though, because that's true of everybody. He is in a rather crude sense the moral center of some of the books. He's the moral center in the sense that he's the one who experiences all of these things, either on his own or through other people. The function that a man assumes as a character in a book has to be a little separated from the function that he has as teller of the story. They are two different functions, and he might make judgments in one side of that and not on the other.

Yes, he judges. Almost sentence by sentence he judges. The way the sentences are weighted, their tonal qualities and so on, have to do with his making judgments—which are really just stand-ins for my judgments. *Except* that I make broader judgments than he does. See, my judgment includes making judgments about his judgments. That's literally true, you know. He might have an idea, and I could indicate that he's too limited or even wrong.

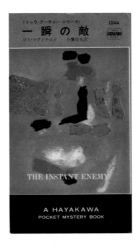
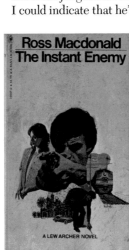

What I *have* done is to enlarge on his judgments. I do that on every page. You know, there are various ways to do it. You can do it by imagery and tone, what the characters do, what they say to each other, or even just by rhythm.

I'm not saying that you created him this way at all, but do you think Archer would be a good moral model for someone?

No, he's too much interested in other people's lives and not nearly enough in his own—as we know him in the books. Of course, this is the fault of novelists, too. All their best energy goes into describing the lives of other, imaginary people.

In The Blue Hammer, somebody says, "I guess you can't go home again," and Archer wonders who would want to. Isn't that what a lot of the runaways and troubled people are trying to do in a lot of your books? To go home or to at least understand home?

I'm not responsible for what Archer says. I really am not.

What do you mean by that?

I don't consider him my spokesman. Is that clear? Why should I? He's just a character in the books. I don't pretend that he's expressing my views—although he is to a considerable extent. But he and I have totally different backgrounds. I'm not kidding. Archer is certainly not my representative.

He's a man you like, though.

Not particularly.

Why did you write eighteen books about him, then?

I didn't. The books are about the other people. Archer is just the means—

Let me rephrase it: Why did you put him in a dozen and a half books if you didn't like him?

There are better reasons than liking somebody for putting them in a book.

You don't think he's a heroic figure, an honorable figure, in any way?

If he's a hero, he's certainly a modest kind of one. Modestly conceived.

Isn't that in some way a reflection on what happens to heroes, or what kind of heroes you admire?

No, I don't think so because the heroes that I admire are artists and intellectuals, and Archer isn't either of them.

In The Blue Hammer Archer says that "nearly everything [makes sense] when you understand it." Is that a personal philosophy of yours, as well?

Well, within the terms that Archer is talking in, yeah. Of course, there's always the edge and beyond the edge, where we don't understand but we know it exists.

In the article that you gave me yesterday you talk about making Archer a divorced man and how, as a result, loneliness now seems to be the central part of his life, even though it was unplanned and grew organically out of the story.

Loneliness itself in real life is unplanned, too. It's not unwilled, but it's unplanned. You don't consciously plan to be lonely.

It seemed that you were surprised by the importance that that theme took on in the books.

Well, this is true of all of the characteristics of Archer that he started out with. You see, he wasn't conceived as a figure who would be taken as seriously as he is being taken—by me as well as by some readers. I tried to make him true to life and interesting and decent and so on—and different from Marlowe—but he was essentially a figure who came out of the tradition. But I gradually filled him with more definite human characteristics which arise from my own observation and my personal experience. And my own feelings. He has become more my character as the books have progressed. Of course, one reason I made him divorced was the obvious thing of making him more mobile. I didn't want to write another one in the series of husband-and-wife detectives, which were going pretty strong at the time that I started. His being divorced, as you point out, has become a more significant factor in his life than it was at the beginning. Obviously I was doing something that had been done several times before, but I wasn't consciously doing that. It's quite true, even Spade, while he wasn't divorced, was awful close to being a divorced man.

Do you think Archer has mythic proportions?

I don't know, I never really gave it much thought. I suppose I tried to deprive him of things that would prevent him from having general relevance. That is, he can stand as a figure that represents a number of different constituencies. Let's put it that way. I tried to keep him out of being too especially himself.… One reason

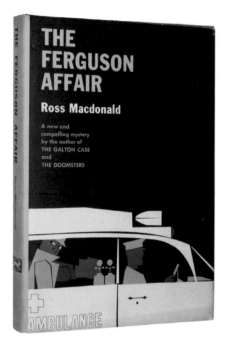

for that is that I wanted him to be more or less transparent so that you can look right through him into the action.

Do you mean that you are making reference to mythology with him when you do that or de-mythifying him?

Well, I'm not trying to de-mythify him but just rob him of too many specific qualities which would get in the way of his purpose, which is to be a witness and a narrator primarily. It's true he does a lot of things, but he doesn't do the essential things in the novels. Those things are done by the people who live and die in the novels.

When Archer acts as historian, isn't that an essential thing? That's a mythic role it seems to me.

Yes, that's his mythic role and of course it does relate to the action in a sense. But what he does is always the same thing: he observes, records, and comments. And he discovers, too. To me the essential things in the books are what he discovers, not what he is.

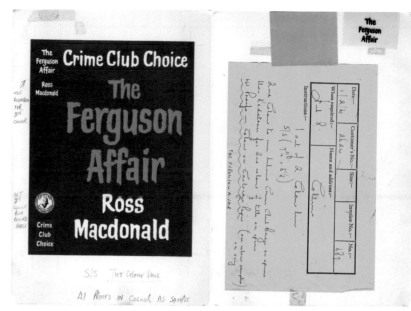

Unused original art for the UK edition of The Ferguson Affair *from January 1961. There were a number of Collins Crime Club Choice books in the late Fifties and early Sixties that did use a similar typographic design for the jackets.*

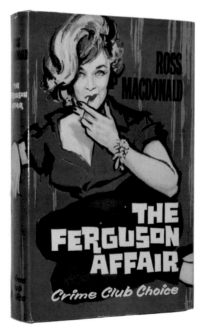

It seems to me that one of the paradoxes that you've created is that it's Archer who is the most difficult character. It's the symbol of the stories.

Yes. And to the extent that Archer represents me as author, there is a sense in which everybody else in the stories is just Archer's dream.

Can you explain that?

I just mean something rather literal, although I expressed it in a slightly poetic way. All I mean to say is the story goes on entirely in the mind of Archer. We know *nothing* except through him, and what he knows is of course limited. The story is constantly insisting on the limits of his knowledge as well as its specificity.

That Jean-Luc Godard quote that "cinema is truth twenty-four frames per second" suggests that film, too, in a sense plays the role of historian.[5] But it's also clear that the camera has an effect on the action. If you carry the analogy further, Archer, too, has an effect on the action.

Oh yes. In fact, his mind is the theater of the action. But I was just giving, let's say, a preliminary and temporary response in order to differentiate between him and the other characters. Of course, his mind is the theater and also his sensibility is the style—or rather the style is his sensibility.

I think it's better in dealing with a problem like this to take out small bites and chew them a bit rather than make some general statement to the effect that it's symbolic. The truth is, I regard the whole story and all the people in it as in one way or another symbolic. Within the intricacies of the story, what they symbolize is gradually and closely defined. Archer is the one who is not closely defined because his story has no beginning and no end really. Although there is a bit of a biography running through it, that's not what I'm concerned about. There's just enough there to give him human interest and human proportions.

Would Lew Archer have turned his girlfriend in to the police the way that Sam Spade did at the end of The Maltese Falcon?

He might or he might not have depending on the situation. I don't know. It would depend upon the whole book. But that wouldn't be so important because, I repeat, Archer really isn't the dramatic center. He may be the center of the books in some ways, but he's not the dramatic center. In other words, the books come to

5 From Godard's 1960 film (which wasn't released until 1963), *Le Petit Soldat.*

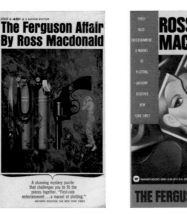

a head in a way that somewhat excludes him. He's not the main character in any of the stories except in senses that you mentioned. He's not the dramatic lead in the way that Spade is, or the way that Marlowe is either.

What about in a similar book?

It would be a similar book, but it would still embody different values from the ones that Hammett's book does. I don't really think it's the kind of choice that I would call on Archer to make. It would make him too important in the book.

Why are you reluctant to make Archer important?

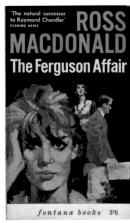
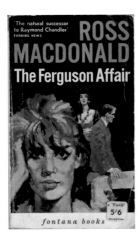
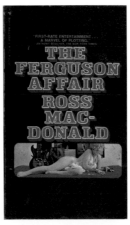

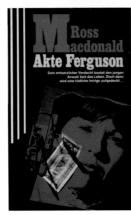

Well, it's just that I'm not writing a book, I'm writing a series of books, is my basic reason. Until I finish the series—if I ever do—I don't want to either destroy or inflate Archer to the extent that the series is no longer functional.

After what happened to Spade, you really can't write about him again. That's it. But Archer, you see, is not so totally committed *by me* in the novel, and that means committed as a person in the books. But as a function in the novel he's not so central and not so totally significant as Spade is. I could conceive any of these stories as being told without Archer, couldn't you? But you can't conceive of *The Maltese Falcon* being told without Spade. I could change Archer into a Chinaman and it wouldn't make a hell of a lot of difference to the actual structure of the books. It would make a great difference to the tone and style and so on.

He would have to have the same sensibility as Archer, no matter what you called him.

If he were going to be taken as the narrator, but it would be quite simple *not* to. Naturally I have to lend Archer the qualities that make him a suitable narrator.

You also have to supply him with the tone that sort of permeates the books.

Sure, but that's not really Archer; the tone would be there without him. I mean, certain parts of it would of course.

You're suggesting that taking Archer out of the books would not be as sweeping a change as it sounds like. The substitution, though, would have to be almost a repeat of Archer under a different name.

Condensed version of Meet Me at the Morgue
published as Experience with Evil, *March 1953.*

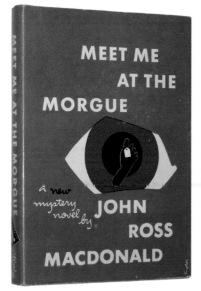
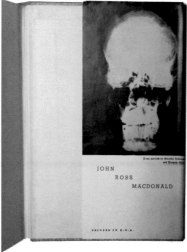

First edition of Meet Me at the Morgue. *Back flap author x-ray portrait done by Ken Millar's sister-in-law, Dorothy Schlagel, and Herman Mills.*

He's sort of an omniscient eye. No pun intended.

Yeah. Also, the presence of Archer enables me to write in a combination of the literary and the subliterary style. So it's kind of a speaking voice rather than an auctorial voice. That's very important to me, to have the right kind of language. Well, it's midway between high literary and the actual spoken language. It pretends to be the actual spoken language while trying to contrive to be literary, too. That is, more purity than the spoken language. Not so much purity of diction as purity of structure, sentence structure and so on.

Most of the UK Pan Macdonald titles can be found with three cover variants: one with a domestic UK price printed on the cover, one with no price made for export, and an export version with a price sticker affixed (often for English-speaking countries like Australia or South Africa, which sourced their books from the UK).

Yes, if I wanted the books to have exactly the same qualities that they have now, they would have to be written very much as they are now. Sure. But we're talking about something a little different. We were talking about the central figure *not* as somebody who tells a story but as somebody who enacts it, and I can see these stories being enacted completely without Archer. I'm not saying the story could be told the way I want it to be told without a narrator like Archer, but that's a different question. It's true that the narration and the narrator do become part of the story in inextricable ways.

But Archer could be taken out of the books and it wouldn't actually change them terribly in their structure or their meaning. In other words, the same story could be told without Archer. Isn't that a remarkable fact? In spite of his apparent all-importance in the books, I could sit down and take him right out of all of those books. I don't mean that it would be technically easy, but it could be done. *Why don't I?* That's the question!

Why don't you?

Well, it's probably because it seems to me the right way to tell the stories. Perhaps the imaginative validity of the stories *depends* on that kind of narration. Anyway, that's the way it might feel; it may not necessarily be true.[6]

You do it remarkably well. Archer uses a lot of metaphors and similes.

He sure does. Well, I keep straining of course in the direction of trying to say more. But I think the essential contribution that Archer makes, as far as I'm concerned, is the combination of the two styles. That's why he's there really.

6 It wasn't just Paul who struggled with the idea that it was not Lew Archer's heart that beat at the center of those books in which he was the private detective of record. Kit Rachlis, who sat in on some of those discussions, reflected shortly thereafter about Millar's stand on the subject: "His de-emphasis of Archer I found startling. So startling that it's caused me to reread some books in a new way. And they do come off differently. But I think that my initial reading of his books as Archer as the hero, and in fact Archer as the focus of the books, is not entirely my fault nor the readers' fault."

  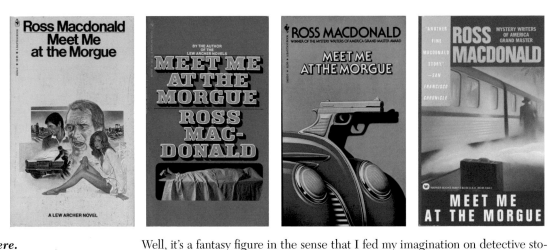 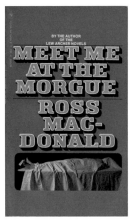 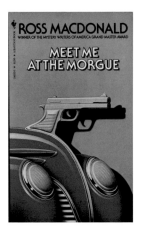 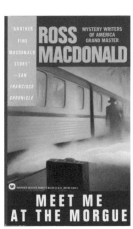

You'd have to find a whole new tone if he wasn't there.

I'd have to find a new way to tell the story and it would mean a new style, too. And in fact the couple of times that I've done that, the style *has* changed.

You're talking about The Ferguson Affair.

Yeah, and also the pre-Archer books.

When you were growing up, was the private detective a fantasy figure to you?

Well, it's a fantasy figure in the sense that I fed my imagination on detective stories starting at age eleven. I was simultaneously reading Poe and fiction that was written for boys about detectives. And also, I've always been concerned about good and evil in relation to the law. I was, to put it mildly, a semi-delinquent from an early age. You might say that Archer represents a choice for the better but in the same milieu, so to speak.

So did you ever want to be a detective?

No. I just wanted to be a writer.

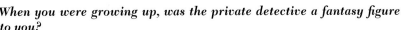

    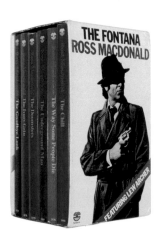 

Above: Two views of the 1971 US Bantam box set 5 Great Lew Archer Novels, *containing* The Goodbye Look, The Instant Enemy, The Galton Case, The Zebra-Striped Hearse, *and* The Chill. *Another 1971 US Bantam box set,* Six Great Ross Macdonald Novels, *contained* The Moving Target, The Way Some People Die, The Zebra-Striped Hearse, The Chill, The Goodbye Look, *and* The Ivory Grin. *Two views of the 1974 UK Fontana box set,* The Fontana Ross Macdonald, *which collected* The Underground Man, The Chill, The Goodbye Look, The Doomsters, The Way Some People Die, *and* The Ivory Grin. *Right: From the UK, Allison & Busby's* The Lew Archer Omnibuses: *Volume 1 (1993) featured* The Drowning Pool, The Chill, *and* The Goodbye Look; *Volume 2 (1994) contained* The Moving Target, The Barbarous Coast, *and* The Far Side of the Dollar; *and* Volume 3 (1997) *collected* The Ivory Grin, The Galton Case, *and* The Blue Hammer.

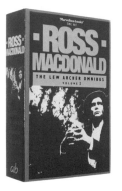 

7. HAMMETT

You seem to respond to Hammett almost as much as the kind of person he was as to the kind of writer he was.

Of course, when I first read Hammett I didn't know what kind of a person he was, but his books do reflect the kind of person that he was. I'm sure both the Sam Spade novel and stories and *The Glass Key* are somewhat autobiographical. I say, "I'm sure"—well, I *feel* that they are. I think the self comes through very strong in the books and in the short stories. I think he really is writing about himself.

Is that inevitable when you're as good a writer as he was?

No, I think it's peculiar to only a few American writers. Hammett writes fiction *as* action in the same sense certain French writers do. Like Camus, for example.

It's no coincidence that Camus liked Hammett a lot.

Yeah, that's true. He learned a lot from Hammett. It's in the French tradition to use fiction as a direct personal language and statement, and also to dramatize yourself.

I think I know what you mean by "fiction as action," but I'm not sure.

Well, the writing itself becomes a form of action at its best. It's so rapid and strong. It's a mental action of course, but it goes along *pari passu* with the physical action of the story. I haven't really tried to work out the definitions that would fit Hammett's style, and that's just really an imagistic way of putting it. But he really was one of the good stylists of his time, hard-boiled or not. The style is clean, direct, penetrating, strong. Its strength is not just a muscular strength but an imaginative strength. By the correct choice of language, he manages to put a great deal into simple language. The dialogue has overtones for that reason. I don't want to overuse the word but it does have *symbolic* overtones, and he's obviously aware of it line by line. It's written as if it were poetry, although it doesn't follow the formal rules of poetry. Of course, very often it falls down. Hammett's short stories particularly are very uneven in style. Very often, I suppose, he was writing something to get it out and support himself. But at his best I consider him a marvelous stylist, and at his worst he's not bad. An error that he made frequently was to become too colloquial. When he's bad it's just in the direction of too much colloquialism and a failure to listen through his *other* ear, listening to tradition.

I don't have the critical language to explain myself well, I just have a feeling when I read a Hammett book that I'm in *direct* contact with a particular man, or a particular mind, and that that mind is stating itself in the work. There's no attempt to put another character in between the writer and the reader, the writer himself is right there in the writing. That's fairly rare in American fiction. It isn't what Fitzgerald does at all. Fitzgerald is always the artist standing to one side and letting his characters speak for him in parables. But there's no sense of parable or secondary meaning or echo or anything in Hammett. It's just right there. It's both the dream and the reality, and the two things are fused in the consciousness of the writer as a person. This is sort of unique, fairly, in American writing. Stephen Crane did it, too.

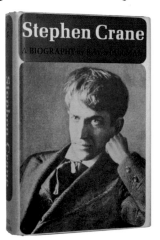
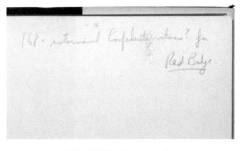

Ken Millar's copy of
Stephen Crane: A Biography *from 1968*
with a notation on the endpaper possibly for
a book review or research for a section of
The Goodbye Look.

What aspect of Hammett's work do you feel is autobiographical?

I think he was depicting the kind of man that he himself was or tried to be. Naturally, a very limited version of the self. The detective hero is always a limited version of the self, I think. That's one of the definitions as compared with the hero of a novel in the broader sense, not a genre novel. The limitation is actually sought by the writer because he wants to work within that limitation. Of course, Hammett also chose that kind of limitation in life—he actually chose to *be* a detective, too.[1] It's a limitation in the sense that the hero/the protagonist/the detective uses himself as an agent for some specific purpose rather than lives freely through life.

So you think Hammett had that quality in his actual life?

Not so much in his actual life as in his fiction. Don't forget, he lived out a long and full life before he died, and there's a lot in the life that never got into his fiction because he lost his writing strength through illness and so on. He would've had a lot more to write, I feel sure of, if it hadn't been for illness and other difficulties. I really regard him as a rather heroic figure, a man who didn't get all of himself onto the paper. His actual writing career was rather short. Too short.

About ten years or so.

Yeah. But his life went on and remained significant. His whole life was significant. He followed his own lights and they were pretty good lights. Now, I don't agree with him about everything, particularly in politics. What he did was manly.

  I think he was a consciously mythic self-creation. But not mythic in any imaginative sense—it was the real thing. He really lived it out according to his lights, and it wasn't playacting and he wasn't imitating his books. His books are an imitation of his life, rather. I wrote somewhere that Sam Spade represents the frontier male as thrown for his sins into the modern urban inferno. Or something like that.[2] I think that would describe the situation. There's a historical connection, too, between the frontier and Hammett. The firm of detectives that he worked for really did originate as a kind of rough and ready, frontier law-and-order business, you know. It really does go back into, well, the middle of the last century or thereabouts.[3] It has direct connections with these historical developments.

I guess what you said, about his life not following his fiction but his fiction following his life, was all true.

I think it's true in a broad sense anyway. I don't know what he wrote when he was young. Probably Romantic poetry like all of us. Maybe not. He was an extraordinary original, and he's just as important as a man as he is as a writer, historically, I think. Just as part of our national history. Really a beautiful figure. What I would consider a moral man and a brave man. When I say he was my favorite writer, I was including the whole image of the man, too. Actually Fitzgerald is my favorite writer, as he's every writer's favorite writer—but he wasn't always. *But* I read Hammett before I read Fitzgerald. I started reading Hammett when I was in my early teens, and I never got over it.

Important to you also as a man? Was he in any way a model, let's say?

No, my admiration for him is aesthetic and detached; I don't regard him as a model at all. He's entirely different from me. His life was entirely different. He

was primarily a man of action—who wrote about the action. I'm not a man of action at all in the same sense.

DASHIELL HAMMETT, author of <u>The Thin Man</u> and <u>The Maltese Falcon</u>. His short story, "Fly Paper," is one of the <u>GREAT STORIES OF SUSPENSE</u> edited by Ross Macdonald, published by Knopf.   Credit: Azarnick

Publicity still from Paul Nelson's signed review copy of Great Stories of Suspense *from 1974, featuring Dashiell Hammett.*

Writing twenty-four books is action.

It's the opposite of action. You know what I mean by "a man of action." Obviously Hammett took extreme pleasure in getting out into the physical world and fighting for what he believed in or for what his client needed and that sort of thing. Quite antithetical to the kind of life that I value for myself, which is a bookish and fairly sedentary and thoughtful life. Not a life of action. Except very sporadically.

---

1 Hammett worked for the Pinkerton National Detective Agency from 1915 to 1922, taking time off to join the US Army in 1918 and serve in World War I. It was there, as a sergeant in the Motor Ambulance Corps, that he contracted tuberculosis.

2 What he wrote about Spade, in "The Writer as Detective Hero," was: "He possesses the virtues and follows the code of a frontier male. Thrust for his sins into the urban inferno, he pits his courage and cunning against its denizens, plays for the highest stakes available, love and money, and loses nearly everything in the end."

3 Allan Pinkerton founded the agency in 1850. Pinkerton's trademark logo, a single unblinking eye accompanied by the slogan "WE NEVER SLEEP," became the origin of the term *private eye*.

It's sort of an irony, I guess, that leading that kind of life you should write detective novels.

I think most writers live in general the kind of life I do when they reach the point where they can make a choice. Of course, a great majority of younger writers have to do what I did: make a living with one hand, then write with the other. It goes on like that for many years. And that's good, too. It keeps you in contact with your sources and life itself.

The first appearance in print of "The Writer as Detective Hero," in the January 1965 issue of Show.

I've always had the impression that Ned Beaumont, the character in **The Glass Key,** *is probably the closest to a mirror of him in the finality of it.*

That's what I feel, too. It's the only profoundly sexual book that he wrote. The other stuff just has, well, you know—the girls are in there as girls. But *The Glass Key* is a very serious book about American life. At the same time it's autobiographical, I'm sure.

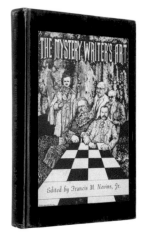

The first book appearance of "The Writer as Detective Hero," in The Mystery Writer's Art *edited by Francis M. Nevins Jr. in 1970.*

More so than **The Thin Man?**

Oh yeah.

Do you still find that feeling of an enigma about him? Because I agree with everything you say, that he presents himself very clearly, yet that clear portrait is almost totally enigmatic in many ways. In a way he doesn't tell you why anything.

No, he just presents himself.

My impression from what Lillian Hellman has written is that's pretty much the way he was, too.

So I gather. A lot of this recent understanding of Hammett comes from Hellman. She not only loved him and knew him very well, but she understood him. She understood what he was getting at and in fact she learned from it. She learned style from it, as she repeatedly says. I think her introduction to

the short stories is by far the best thing that's ever been written about Hammett.[4] That's really lovely. That's very fine writing, and I think it's true, too. What'd she call him? A "… Dostoyevsky sinner-saint"? Something like that.

It certainly helps to have known a man like him—directly—because so much of his work is personal. It's like a lyric poet: you can't really write about him without knowing him—accurately, that is. Most of the critical and scholarly work on him hasn't recognized his true value, in my opinion. Some of the great contemporary French writers I think have recognized Hammett for what he is. Now, I don't think in general that scholarly critics are equipped to judge something like Hammett. He's outside their range in a way. I've never seen an adequate critical review of Hammett's work.

The only one that comes to my mind is yours.[5]

Well, I'm glad you think so, but I would really like to see him done much fuller justice than I did in a really short piece. I just feel that there's a great figure there who hasn't been adequately defined. But he will be. Sometimes it takes a hundred years for a really good and new kind of writer to get his meaning across. I think Hammett is a tragic writer. Anyway, he certainly hit me right between the eyes when I first came to him, and he still does. There's an incandescence about his best work that is really quite unusual.

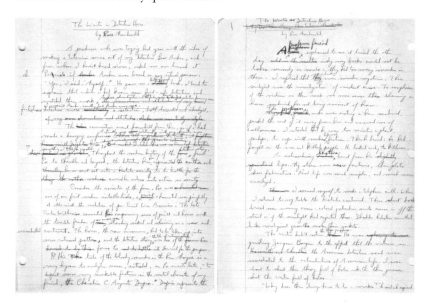

Two different manuscript drafts of "The Writer as Detective Hero."

What do you think the best work is?

Well, I think the best work are the two novels that we've discussed, *The Glass Key* and *The Maltese Falcon*. There are a great many stories that are good work, but I wouldn't include them among the best work. I don't really feel that any of his stories compares in importance with the kind of writing that he did in those novels.

Why did you pick Hammett's short story "Fly Paper" for the suspense anthology you edited?

4 Hellman edited *The Big Knockover: Selected Stories and Short Novels by Dashiell Hammett* in 1966.
5 "Homage to Dashiell Hammett" was published in *Mystery Writers Annual* in April 1964.

Oh, it's just bursting with life, and I think the style is good. Strong. Clean. It's one of my favorites. There isn't any of the stories that completely satisfies me in the sense that the novels do, but I like a lot of them. I've really read several dozen of them that I like and will probably reread.

Original manuscript for "Homage to Dashiell Hammett" from 1964 with a note to Millar's typist Alice Kladnik in the upper left corner requesting three carbon copies instead of two.

He wrote sixty or so stories, and I think only twenty are possibly available.

Is that right? It's time for a complete edition. Well, it's up to his publisher to do something about that, I would think. They've been garnering thousands and thousands of dollars in royalties from Hammett; they should take some of that money and put out a complete Hammett.[6]

6 To date this has not yet come to pass.

Well, I think Lillian Hellman may be the problem there to some extent also.

Could be since she owns them. She bought them.

I think that she doesn't necessarily want to see many of them reprinted, that her opinion is that the short stories are vastly inferior and shouldn't come out.

It's true, too. Very few of the short stories have any real claim on perfection. Over the years I've read a good many of them. I still think he's the best. Oh, he's important enough to merit a complete edition, and he will have, there's no doubt about it.

Do you like the three Sam Spade stories?

Well, they certainly vary in value. They're extremely well written, but Sam Spade just belongs in that novel really. He's a tragic figure in the novel and in the short stories he isn't, he's just a detective.

But those three stories stylistically seem to be among the tightest of all of Hammett's stories.

Oh, he's a great stylist. I don't agree with the commonly brooded idea that Hammett was just a comparatively crude operator and that Chandler put the final gloss on the form. I regard Hammett as the leading stylist in the school, and I don't really feel he's ever been improved on. That's just my own feeling.

Do you think Chandler's short stories are better than Hammett's short stories?

I don't. I wouldn't try to defend that because I haven't read them recently.

I like Chandler's Romantic qualities. They're I think both his strength and his weakness.

Well, I'm just talking about style, which of course is rather central. There's something very clean and very sparse and strong about Hammett's style. It's a classical style.

Do you like The Thin Man?

No. I think it's almost totally a loss. I didn't used to think so, but I do now. Of course, it was written under quite bad circumstances. It was sort of forced out. He had to produce a book, and I don't think he was too well at the time. The story is that Mrs. Knopf used to go around to his place and collect a manuscript from him every day.[7] I don't know whether that's true or not.

I think the basic plot idea is very good. It's probably one of the origins of the basic plot idea of *The Underground Man*.

The Thin Man was a sad book, I thought. The constant drinking all the way through seems not necessarily a comic note to me.

Yeah, he was drinking heavily at the time that he was writing the book.

7 Blanche Knopf cofounded the famed publishing house in 1915 with Alfred A. Knopf Sr., the man who became her husband the following year.

I always felt that Hammett was just almost verging on caricature or absurdity sometimes with his characters. Maybe it's particularly the stories from **The Continental Op,** *where they're almost pushed over the line into ridiculousness sometimes. In* **The Dain Curse** *they are pushed way over into ridiculousness.*

A later page from the "Homage to Dashiell Hammett" manuscript that quotes the story of Flitcraft from The Maltese Falcon.

I think really that he was trying to write, or capable of writing, a new kind of fiction, but he wasn't capable of inventing it all by himself. I just feel very strongly about many of those stories, that they are attempts to do the tragicomic. As I said, it isn't his stylistic resources that were lacking so much as the resources of the genre itself. You would have had to remake the genre; that's really what he was trying to do. He succeeded, but he didn't succeed in all directions, and that's a direction in which he didn't succeed. In doing tragicomedy, that is to say. In general, you need what might be called an educated style to do tragicomedy.

And while he was an educated man with a style, he wasn't trying to write what is supposed to be an educated style, he was writing something somewhat more colloquial. And the colloquial only has one note, so to speak, there's only one way you can hit it. I'm exaggerating, but—

I guess that's certainly one of the limitations of the hard-boiled school. It's difficult to set up that many resonances.

Yes, you can't introduce too many elements into it, or the whole thing comes apart. This has happened to a lot of American writers.

He has these scenes that ring really strangely because of that. I'm not sure how much of it was intended or what

I think a lot of it is experimental. He was using the stories to try to hit new notes. God knows, he hit a wonderful new note and he hit it very hard in *The Glass Key*. That's stylistically a marvelous book. The control of tone is just remarkable. It justifies those experiments.

It is all on those pages, but it's not quite all there. You don't know why whatshisname is getting beat to a pulp and what drives him to do what he's doing. In effect, a lot of the essentials are left out.

And they turn out not to be essentials. A lot of the art is leaving out. Well, he wasn't writing a novel of explanation. It's really rather surreal in some respects. I don't know how much Hammett knew about the history of writing in his own time. He certainly picked up a lot of the, oh, advance warning signals from the future. That's why he's made such a strong comeback now. Hell, he turns out to be a master, a master of American style. He's not on quite the same level as Fitzgerald … but he belongs in the same block. He was self-educated—and apparently very well educated by himself.

Did you think Joe Gores's project was well-taken or ill-taken? The fictionalized novel **Hammett** *that he did?*

It didn't add up to a likeness, a true likeness, of the Hammett whom I value, but he wasn't writing about the imaginative, creative Hammett. Although there are a few passages where he brings that in, in a sort of a perfunctory way, he was writing about Hammett as a man of action. It's written from the outside, it's an external book. In that respect it succeeds. Well, you know how difficult [it is], when you're reading about your favorite writer, to be satisfied by what somebody else has written about him.

Do you think that may be the Hammett image we're going to be saddled with?

I don't think so. I think Hammett left that image for himself. It just seems to me his fiction books represent him so well. I guess Miss Hellman's essay about Hammett has been quite widely read, and her autobiographical books have been bestsellers and they certainly give a speaking likeness of Hammett.[8] I think her likeness of Hammett is much preferable to any of the others that I know of.

8 Millar is referring to *An Unfinished Woman: A Memoir, Pentimento: A Book of Portraits*, and *Scoundrel Time.*

Homage to Dashiell Hammett

by Ross Macdonald

I have been given some space to speak for the hardboiled school of mystery writing. Let me use it to dwell for a bit on the work of Dashiell Hammett. He was the great innovator who invented the hardboiled detective novel and used it to express and master the undercurrent of inchoate violence that runs through so much of American life.

In certain ways, it must be admitted, Hammett's heroes are reminiscent of unreconstructed Darwinian man; McTeague and The Sea Wolf stand directly behind them. But no matter how rough and appetent they may be, true representatives of a rough and appetent society, they are never allowed to run unbridled. Hammett's irony controls them. In fact he criticized them far more astringently and basically than similar men were criticized

A detail from one of the three requested carbon typescripts of "Homage to Dashiell Hammett."

No one used to pay a whole lot of serious attention to directors like Howard Hawks and John Ford until the last fifteen years or so. Liking their films along with Ingmar Bergman's used to be not unlike liking Fitzgerald's books and Hammett's now, I think. You discover that there isn't that distinction that used to put one of them way out in left field and the other one way out in right field. There isn't that much difference between them.

Or between high and low art. If you compare the writing line by line you find they're quite similar. We're still talking about Hammett and Fitzgerald. Fitzgerald had the advantage of a fuller experience in a sense, a fuller imaginative and intellectual experience. It took in what you can learn in Europe, for example. But Hammett was very much in the native grain, writing completely out of American materials. In fact, the influence regarding Europe has gone the other way. It's Hammett who has influenced people like Camus and Gide, not the other way around. Gradually—the respect that we have for a man like Hammett, a growing respect—this country is going to value its native culture in ways that it hasn't. It's going to stop regarding itself as a kind of international cultural stepson and realize that it's a great originator. In every way. As we realize that, our culture will become mature. As we come to value what we have and learn how to add onto it in its own voice.

It's only in the last decade or so that those two great originators, Fitzgerald and Hammett, have been recognized as such. Naturally, Fitzgerald was recognized by his fellow writers, but now he's a national influence and a moralist. And Hammett, while I don't suppose his total work adds up to quite what Fitzgerald accomplished, he didn't have the experience or the background or the *need* to write something like *The Great Gatsby*, which is unique. But he's a very important figure in the same movement towards an American culture.

Do you think Hammett romanticized Sam Spade?

I don't think he idealized Spade at all except as a very powerful force. I think he was deliberate in trying to present Spade as a somewhat amoral man, and that's Spade's tragedy.

That he's an amoral man?

Amoral in the broadest sense. He has a code, but that's no substitute really for a morality. I'm not talking specifically about his final act, I'm talking about his whole approach to life. It isn't moral in the accepted sense.

I'd sort of like to go back and start over on the subject, though. You know, what we do is we plunge immediately into very deep subjects and we really get beyond our depth.

Can we start with what you said about his code being no substitute for morality?

That's what I meant and I'll stand by that. He was willing to do things that were illegal and also ruptures of friendship. There are two codes that he broke that you can think of immediately. If he's to be described as a moral man, what morality does he represent, or what morality does he bow down to? I would say that he is a man who is, to a considerable extent, outside the law.

Don't you think that he was also a self-projection of Hammett? That his code was Hammett's code?

Yes. He was a self-projection of Hammett, but not by any means a projection of *all* of Hammett. It's a narrow version, and that's true to a lesser extent of Archer, too. That's what I was trying to say before.

Do you think Hammett's code was no substitute for morality?

I don't know. We haven't even decided what Hammett's code was. You know, when you talk about Hammett's code you might mean something a little different from what I mean. We were talking first about Sam Spade and then about Hammett. It's terribly necessary to distinguish between the two. You can't discuss them at all as if they are the same thing. They are somewhat related, but Hammett wasn't writing about himself as Sam Spade. Hammett was an extremely sensitive late Romantic poet-novelist, and Sam Spade was just what I consider a rather tragic creation of a man who saw through the sort of men that Sam Spade was. What we mean by the hard-boiled detective. Although he had experience as a detective, and apparently was pretty good at it and wrote about it, Hammett himself was not that man. At least by the time he was writing the Sam Spade stories, he was an urban poet. A tragic poet. So then the question is, well, What's the tragedy? I would say Sam Spade's tragedy is precisely the loss of civilized urban qualities that a man should have.

Can you explain that?

Well, Sam Spade is a tragic figure precisely because he fell short of a complete humanity. I just don't identify Hammett with his creation at all. Why should he be identified any more with Sam Spade than he is with the hero of *The Glass Key*? No, I'm trying to find a way of saying what we're both trying to say. If you do it in pure abstraction you don't get anywhere because it really has to be tied down to examples, and that's what we're doing: trying to tie it down to examples.

Let me make a broad statement: Now, to me in the contemporary world, particularly in an urban setting among intelligent people, morality *cannot* be expressed in broad simple statements—it has to be known and expressed in rather delicate aperçus, the whole web of which constitute the moral framework of our civilization.

Even a fairly simplistic story like *The Maltese Falcon* is so complex that you can go on reading it and rereading it and finding things in it for the rest of your life. So it can't really be summed up in a narrow moral statement.

How do you think Hammett viewed Spade?

I think he regarded Spade as a man who fell short of full moral standing and that that was his tragedy. I could be quite mistaken, but I don't think I am. I think that's one of the main things that the book is about.

It seems to me that he's also a heroic figure.

Sure, but there are heroic figures of all differing moral statures.

Part of his heroism to me is precisely his ability to take a full accounting of himself.

But we differ. Because I don't feel that Sam Spade did come up with a full accounting of himself.

Dashiell Hammett: A Casebook *from 1969 by William F. Nolan was anonymously edited by Ken Millar.*

What do you think he held back?

Caring—the ultimate thing. Caring and all the things that go with it. All the expressions of feeling that are civilized. It seems to me necessary to recognize that he's a projection of a rough and narrow and rather shallow civilization. And Hammett knew it. A *dangerously* shallow civilization. I'm talking about the actual civilization that Hammett was writing about.

You know, this doesn't reduce the importance or the moral interest of Spade, to recognize that he himself was a creature of that civilization. But if we miss the point that this is the tragedy of the society and not just of Spade, I think we miss one of the writer's main points. In other words, Spade is exemplary. He's an exemplary character, but he exemplifies what was wrong as well as what was right with San Francisco in the Twenties. I don't think that Hammett romanticizes him at all. Except that giving a central character that much force is a form of romanticizing him.

How can Spade exemplify San Francisco in the Twenties when he is very specifically someone who lives outside of society and does not conform to its moral code? How does that fit into your strategy?

You mean how does he represent a society while living outside of it? Well, let's say it was a somewhat fragmented society which was in conflict with itself. He represents some central aspects of the society. He doesn't represent the whole society.

Archer represents the whole society to a greater extent—through his use of language, though his relationships with people, and so on. Spade represents the individual, *but* we get to know society through the individuals that he chooses. There is validity for me in this version of Spade.

There's something that should be mentioned also: I don't know at what point Hammett became a radical philosopher, but there is a great deal of the radical even in an early book like *The Maltese Falcon*. He's really denying the values of the society that he's operating in. Even by what he makes Spade do himself, he's satirizing and rejecting the values of San Francisco society as he knew it.

Don't forget that San Francisco had a long history of radicalism. Henry George, for example, lived and wrote there. A book like *McTeague* [subtitled *A Story of San Francisco*, by Frank Norris] is really quite a radical book. *The Octopus* [*A Story of California*, also by Norris] is definitely a radical book. These are all books a generation or more earlier. I'm sure it was the radicalism there that took my father there and caused me to be born in the San Francisco area.

Was your father a radical?

Yes. He was a great admirer of Henry George.

Hammett wrote somewhere that Spade was a kind of dream figure and the kind of detective that every detective wishes he were.

I seriously doubt, though, that it's true that that's the kind of person a private detective would want to be. There's a deliberate numbness of feeling about Spade that contemporary detectives would *hate* to have to admit to. This is a tragic numbness. Hammett was writing about himself to a certain extent. One of the aspects of the hard-boiled is that tragic numbness. It's the hurt that goes beyond words and that sort of thing. Hemingway, for example, has it, too, in his stories of that period. They're writing about a pretty sick society and a society that not only didn't know itself but *refused* to know itself. The literary heroes of that time, with the exception of Gatsby, were largely devoted to concealing from themselves what they were, or just to sort of brazening it out.

Isn't the code sort of an attempt to live with some kind of honor or with that numbness? In most cases maybe it's self-deluded, but it seems like an honorable attempt.

Yes, but I don't know whether any of the heroes of that numbness were actually, in ordinary terms and ordinary standards, particularly honorable men. They operated according to codes of their own rather than some generally accepted morality. Now, this of course doesn't reduce their stature at all; it's more important to be truly representative of the problems of your society than it is to be a good guy. Very much more so. And none of the tragic heroes are good guys, they all do terrible things. Spade did a terrible thing when he turned his girlfriend in, for example. Not by the standards he was operating under or the constraints perhaps that he was operating under, but by any other standards. The standards based on human feelings. He loved her.

But what would happen if he didn't turn her over? Which is the more terrible thing?

Well, it just depends on how the dice are loaded in the particular book. In other words, moral values are lent to certain actions by the way the book is put together and imagined, and moral weight given to certain actions and so on. There's no easy way to answer that question. The tragic situation *always* involves making choices, neither of which are any damn good. That's what modern tragedy is anyway.

I think it was more tragic for Spade to have to turn the girl in than simply to violate the police code. The whole point is that he was caught in a bind where nothing he did was right—or could be right. That's the beauty of it.

He's very eloquent about his whole code at the end when he spells it out. He's violating more than a police code, though, if he doesn't.

Yes. We were talking about the love code on the one hand; I just said the police code on the other. By that I meant simply the code that would be implied by his turning her over to the police, and is. I didn't say that he wasn't violating other things. He would have been violating his professional code, too, as well as all the standard moral codes. All the obvious ones.

Do you think her feeling for him was at all genuine in the book?

Sure. I think people often tend to have the feelings they have to have in circumstance, and that's how many feelings are born, particularly in the crime novel. And that's where that woman lived.

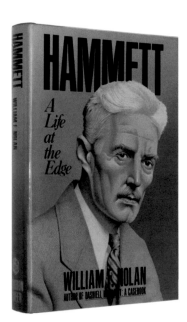

I'm just wondering if you think that they did have some chance to make it. Or if indeed she wouldn't have stabbed him in the back as she had everyone else.

No doubt she would have. No question he was caught in a bind. There was no reasonable out. But he also loved her, you see, and that's a very powerful value in the book as well as in life.

Let's face the fact: I regard this novel as a Romantic novel. It attaches much greater importance to the relationship between Spade and the woman than a contemporary realistic novel would. She's a Romantic figure and Spade's relationship with her is romantic in a rather old-fashioned sense.

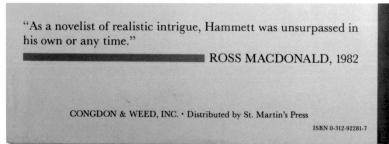

"As a novelist of realistic intrigue, Hammett was unsurpassed in his own or any time."

ROSS MACDONALD, 1982

CONGDON & WEED, INC. · Distributed by St. Martin's Press

ISBN 0-312-92281-7

Dashiell Hammett: A Life at the Edge *by William F. Nolan from 1983 with a 1982 blurb by Ken Millar.*

We've been talking about Spade a lot. How would you characterize the Continental Op?[9]

He's much closer to real-life detectives I have known. He's essentially a man of action who understands his actions and other people's actions. I don't think he's a significant tragic figure the way Spade is.

Do you think his moral code is any different than Spade's?

Yes, it seems to be. He's a company man. He does more or less what he has to do as the employee of a detective agency, and his code is essentially just a working code. You know, what the good detective will do.

Does that justify his actions?

Well, I don't know whether his actions need justification. They're not being judged on a stringent moral basis, by the author or by the reader, but we accept him as a well-intentioned man.

But doesn't Red Harvest call into question his actions?

I wasn't really thinking about *Red Harvest*. I even had forgotten that he was in *Red Harvest*. What I was saying had to do with the short stories, and I'm not prepared to debate with you on the subject of *Red Harvest*. I haven't read it for a long time, but I know it represents a quantum jump in the Continental Op series. You would admit that, too, wouldn't you?

Oh yes.

What happens in it cannot be used to explain *backwards* what he wrote before that. So you're going to have to let me off that one because I really haven't read it for years. I know generally what happens in it, though. It's a real bloodbath and a complete denial of human relationship among all the people involved.

And which he manipulates.

Right. But this isn't true of the Continental Op that I've read in recent years in the short stories; he's hard but not malign. He isn't centrally a moral figure. How can he be when he reports in to a boss? Even in *Red Harvest*, though correct me if I'm wrong, he's doing what the boss would tell him to do, or he's doing the things that will accomplish what the boss wants done. He's not an independent moral agent the way Spade is.

Are you saying we can't judge him morally because of that?

No, I'm saying that the book doesn't judge him morally in the same sense.

But I think we can.

Sure. I just did.

Can you do it again? [laughs] I missed the part where you judged him.

9 Hammett's character, a PI employed by the Continental Detective Agency in San Francisco, is never referred to by name in any of the books or stories.

I said he was a malign figure. He becomes, given the circumstances and who he's working for and so on, a malign figure.[10]

It seems to me that you can judge him as harsh or more harshly than Spade, that you can use the same argument used for the Nazis or with the Vietnam War: that he was just following orders. The Continental Op does indeed set up a bloodbath.

I wasn't denying that you can judge him morally. I just described him as an evil figure. But I'm really at a little bit of a disadvantage, talking with people who know this literature thoroughly—and I *don't*. I should be asking you … questions.

One of the interesting things that comes out of Lillian Hellman's discussions about Hammett is that he had a very upsetting experience union-busting in Butte, Montana. Apparently, he was offered $5,000 to kill Frank Little, a labor union organizer. According to Hellman, he never talked about it very much, but she was aware of the guilt that he had about the experience. She intimates that Red Harvest *in many ways is what came out of that.*

You don't really become a Communist for no reason at all. Well, you know, we weren't talking about *Red Harvest*. Everything that I said about the Continental Op, until you reminded me that he was also in *Red Harvest*, was about the stories. I wasn't talking about *Red Harvest* consciously. Criticism of the detective medium is not really my field. I don't consider myself an expert at all in the detective field. You must understand, in order to follow somebody like Hammett it's necessary to turn away from him, too. You learn everything that he can teach you, and then you have to turn away and find your own way to tell the same kind of stories differently.… And this is not a rejection or a criticism of the other guy, it's just a fact of life.

10 Millar did not say outright that the Continental Op in *Red Harvest* is "malign"; just that in the short stories he is not.

You see, I *have* written about Hammett, I've written about the Continental Op and particularly about Sam Spade. Some of it has been published and some hasn't been published, and I prefer to stand on what I've written rather than an attempt to resurrect in my memory a book that I haven't read for many years. I've read a lot of other books since, many of them detective stories—and my memory is not outstandingly good anyway.

Now, I don't want to leave Hammett with the idea that I'm a critic of Hammett. I admire him more than any other detective writer, and I think what he did was tragic writing. I have a feeling that our interchange, at least my part of it, didn't do him justice at all because I was being asked questions that I wasn't prepared for and really didn't answer adequately.[11]

Even in one of his very early stories, first published by Mencken in Smart Set, Hammett presents a character who might have been a parody of the Hemingway hero, except that he was pre-Hemingway. This huge brute is much attached to his beard. To make a short story shorter, the loss of his beard reveals that he used it to hide a receding chin and makes him a public laughingstock. This isn't much more than an anecdote, but it suggests Hammett's attitude towards the half-evolved frontier male of our not too distant past. Shorn and urbanized, he became in Hammett's best novels a near-tragic figure, a lonely and suspicious alien who pits a hopeless but

Another detail from one of the carbon typescripts of "Homage to Dashiell Hammett."

11 Shortly after this discussion, Kit Rachlis reflected on Millar's reaction to the line of questioning: "It was like somebody cutting back and forth across a football field but not going anywhere. He got very defensive and I just had no idea what was going on. Real tension on his face. Paul went to the bathroom or something, the tape was turned off, and [Millar] looked at me and said, 'You caught me really off-guard on *Red Harvest*. I'd totally forgotten that the Continental Op was in it,' and, 'Nobody likes to look bad in an argument.'"

May 4, 1974   Jill Krementz

8. CHANDLER

In an interview you made a point about Raymond Chandler that really puzzled me: "Raymond Chandler has shown how a private detective could be used to block off over-personal excitements while getting on with the story." I never felt that way with Chandler, and that seems to be somewhat of what you're saying now in connection with your work.

Well, I ask you simply to compare the Chandler of the stories as represented by Marlowe with the Chandler who wrote his letters. You see the difference? There's a much wider range of feeling in the letters than there is in the man in the story. A really remarkable range of feeling. By "over-personal excitements" I mean *over-personal* in terms of fiction. When he tried to get too much of his self-feelings into his fiction, it didn't work. You have to dole it out very carefully if you're the kind of writer that Chandler is—a writer of sensibility, almost of sentiment really. What I've just been saying about Chandler is true of myself in some degree, although we don't share the same psychic structures or anything like that. Far from it.

There's one sense in which the hard-boiled style, so-called, *is* a device which saves the writer from getting too deeply, too personally, involved with the characters. It stands between him and the characters and what happens to them, and it gives you a certain objectivity because the subjective element is sort of filtered off into the detective figure. But in the long run all these books, Chandler's and mine, are *totally* subjective really. I'm talking about strategies of getting them written and getting the stories told. I'm not talking about the ultimate fact that the stories are lyrical and subjective from beginning to end. But if you went at it directly, saying to yourself and the reader, "This is a lyrical and subjective account of life in Southern California," it wouldn't come off. You can't write fiction that way. Fiction is composed of endless stratagems, avoiding the over-personal. Most failed writers in fiction are people who never found out how to avoid the over-personal. Then of course there are others who never found out how to get the personal in at all, and that's worse.

Philip Marlowe wasn't ever used up the way Sam Spade was.

Marlowe, as I say, is another story, which I'm not prepared to tell. I haven't reread Chandler for a long time, and I don't take Chandler's overall intentions as seriously as I take his line by line style, which I think is really admirable. I've never found his books as morally interesting as I do *The Maltese Falcon*.

One could argue that Marlowe doesn't really probably take a risk in any of the books until **The Long Goodbye.**

I was just going to say that. *The Long Goodbye* is the only one where the risk is real. He really does lay himself on the line in love and friendship for a bad man. It's a somewhat similar situation to *The Maltese Falcon*. On the other hand, I don't consider *The Long Goodbye* to be a wholly successful work.

What don't you consider successful about it?

Well, it just doesn't have the strength and the movement and the style and the flair that his earlier books do. *For me.* I recognize its riches, but they are not quite primarily the virtues of a really good detective story. It's a book which is almost a new kind of creation.

If you can classify Dostoyevsky as a detective writer, I don't see why you exclude **The Long Goodbye** *from being—*

No, I'm not excluding it, I'm comparing it with his earlier books. Naturally, it's a detective story, but it doesn't obey the same rules as his earlier books. Wouldn't you say that he was deliberately trying to change the form in that book? Incorporate into it material that he had never touched before and so on?

Yes, I would.

Well, you have to remember that I'm talking about Chandler as a combination disciple and competitor. He's pretty close to me, and I'm really talking about what I would choose to do. I don't particularly mean to criticize him.

Do you feel that the idea of "fiction as action" works less well with Chandler?

Oh yeah, I think Chandler's writing in a much older form. To put it very obviously, his detective is a *conscious* self-image, but not intended to represent the complexities or the realities of the author's own nature or even his perceptions, is the way I feel about it. I feel that the whole thing is at least one remove from Chandler. It's natural that he should write that way because his subject really is the loss of the unitary central personality. It's what he's writing against, so to speak, in Marlowe. He's not intended to be a self-image—he's quite remote from the reality of Chandler—and Chandler wasn't really putting himself on record or on the line in the person of Marlowe. And Marlowe *is* a Romantic figure, quite intentionally so. The other characters are even more remote from Chandler. It's what I would call truly Romantic fiction, in the sense that he's not really aiming at a personal reality. In fact, he's writing something that could be described almost as a pastiche—a brilliant and witty pastiche. I really don't regard him as a realistic writer. I don't think he was planning to be.

Have you read the new biography, The Life of Raymond Chandler, by Frank MacShane?

I think MacShane's book, while it's not a book of criticism, really is a wonderful contribution. MacShane just tells you the facts and somehow they cohere into a very three-dimensional picture of Chandler. It's remarkably good, I think. Lots of good information. In fact, all you'll ever need to know, I think. Not that it's overfull. I think it really tells the whole story. He doesn't pull any punches.

The Italian edition of The Goodbye Look *was published in* Il Giallo Mondadori #1114 (1970) *and featured an exclusive interview with Millar. The answer to question eleven from the interview manuscript explores the contributions of Dashiell Hammett and Raymond Chandler to detective fiction.*

How does he handle Chandler's unusually close relationship to his mother and his relationship with his wife who was eighteen years older than him?

Well, he simply presents it in a factual way so that anyone can see the whole picture. Its form is narrative, but its effect is analytical. I don't think I'm reading too much into it. Of course, I did bring my own interest in Chandler to it. I've been a student of him. I think MacShane just managed to do both at once: tell a good narrative and also convey its meanings. He locked into very good material.

Does he deal with Chandler's remarks about you in the book?[1]

I don't think he mentioned it. [I'm discussing] that Chandler material in order to explain something to you. I don't want that to become such an important feature because, you see, for twenty years reviewers would pick up my books, take a quick look, and say, "Oh, it's just a Chandleresque writer," period. Because I'm aware of the differences. There's a whole element in my work which, so far as I can tell, doesn't appear at least consciously in Chandler, and that's the whole psychological/symbolic aspect of the action and the imagery.

I think Chandler's a much more sentimental, Romantic writer and a much less analytical one or structural one.

Yes, well, he represents an earlier period, of course. Now, what's your question?

There isn't any question. I don't want to make it a major point at all. No, the point I did want to make in the story wasn't so much that there had been a rift but rather how you reacted to it and how he reacted to it with other writers. You tend to help other writers.

Well, my training of course was different. I was trained as a teacher—and specifically a teacher of English and a teacher of writing. It comes both naturally and professionally to me that I should try to help other writers. Although certainly there are lots of writers who have done more for other writers than I have. On the other hand, I don't turn them away when they come along with a manuscript.

Yeah. You don't try to kill them.

I really can't read everything that's offered to me now, but for a long time I was able to. Once you've been trained as a teacher, you know, you don't lose the attitudes that go with teaching. I wouldn't want to either.

But I don't think it's just as a teacher. I mean, you like people, you like the young writers, I take it also.

Sure. Also, I think that one of the services we can do a craft is to pass it on. Any craft.

Where would you place yourself, with Chandler or Hammett? Of the two?

Well, a person can't place himself. Other people have to place him for him.

1 In 1949, after the publication of *The Moving Target*, Chandler wrote a letter to author and critic James Sandoe that was highly critical of Millar and his work. He cited Macdonald's "pretentiousness" and called him a "literary eunuch." Millar, undoubtedly hurt by the discovery, learned about the letter when it was published in 1962 as part of *Raymond Chandler Speaking*, edited by Dorothy Gardiner and Kathrine Sorley Walker.

  Paul Nelson, quoted in Tom Nolan's *Ross Macdonald: A Biography*, described what happened when he and Millar debated the merits of *The Long Goodbye*: "And I kept trying to explain what I thought was so good about *Goodbye*, and finally he just exploded. He said, 'To hell with Chandler! Chandler tried to kill me!' He had me stop the tape and insisted I erase that part, and he explained to me all about what Chandler had done: writing negative letters to people about Macdonald's first book and so on."

  Paul's friend Jeff Wong remembers that Paul recounted the story a little differently to him: "Paul told me that they got to talking about Chandler. After some time, Ken exploded and blurted out: 'Chandler tried to murder me!' which shocked Paul. Then he had Paul shut off the recorder and erase it, and they continued. But Paul specifically said *murder* as opposed to *kill* as in Tom's book. Paul and I talked about it numerous times and *murder* sticks in my mind as being the word used in the exclamation."

9. FITZGERALD

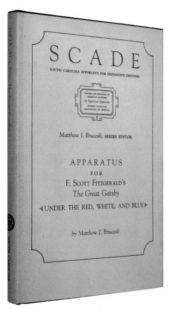

Limited and trade editions of Apparatus for F. Scott Fitzgerald's The Great Gatsby [Under the Red, White, and Blue] *(1974) by Matthew J. Bruccoli. The book was dedicated to Kenneth Millar.*

F. Scott Fitzgerald fell out of grace with the reading public in his own lifetime, then was rediscovered in the Fifties.

Well, he was recognized as a great writer by other good writers in his own time, but he didn't become a really significant literary influence. God knows, he wasn't taught in the schools, for example. Nobody ever heard of him in the schools when I was going to school. I found him for myself when I was an undergraduate.

Chandler did of course read *The Great Gatsby* and refer to it with approbation, but he did speak of it as a "little lost book" or something like that, which it was at the time. It isn't anymore. It's the most assured American classic of this century—and far more assured than Hemingway.

Yes. Although I persist in being a little pro-Hemingway. Right now he seems to be out of vogue.

At the moment. I'm pro-Hemingway, too. I'm just noticing the reversal.

And Steinbeck seems to have dropped entirely out of sight.

That's a little unfair. But his later fiction was not good. It would've been better if he hadn't polished it. But he has a valid reputation as a good writer. He's an original. That's terribly important. He wrote some very good short stories, too. However, he's not in the same class as either Fitzgerald or Hemingway. He just isn't a classical writer.

Speaking of Hemingway, did you like A Farewell to Arms?

No. I didn't even like it the first time around. I'm afraid not.

Did you like some of his short stories?

Oh sure. I like the whole bunch of the short stories without exception. And I like the first novel [*The Sun Also Rises*]. But *A Farewell to Arms* I don't go for at all. I think it's sentimental. It doesn't hold up stylistically even. Let's just forget about it, I fear. He did lots better work than that. *For Whom the Bell Tolls* is good second-rate Hemingway. I never finished it.

Now, you understand I'm talking as a reader, not as a writer. Anybody can criticize somebody like Hemingway as a reader, but as a writer it's a different story. He's one of the great, preeminent writers. As between Fitzgerald and Hemingway, though, I go for Fitzgerald. I think Fitzgerald has more lasting power. More depth and more lasting power.

Some of Hemingway's short stories, though, are awfully good. The Nick Adams ones.

Oh sure. I know that. I think Hemingway is at his best in his short stories. They're his greatest work. Hemingway's a good writer, but he failed to write a completely satisfactory novel. He best work was in his short stories. This isn't true of Fitzgerald.

Though he has written some really great short stories.

Yes, and he wrote great quantities of them, too. Many more than Hemingway. One thing about short stories like Hemingway's short stories or Fitzgerald's short stories: you can go back and reread them as many times as you want to because it doesn't take forever. I generally just read something once because there isn't time to read anything twice—except *Gatsby*. [*laughs*] God knows how many times I've read that.

Six or seven for me, probably more for you.

No. Perhaps six or seven would be about right.

Gatsby's very short, too.

I know. I don't suppose it's more than about 45,000 words. Something like that.[1] But you can't read it fast, or at least you can't *reread* it fast, because it's constantly stopping you to think.

Even the Robert Redford movie made me realize how great the book was—and the movie certainly wasn't altogether successful.

No, it had some mistakes in it. It was like an artist making colored illustrations to illustrate the book, so to speak. There's no harm in that. Lots worse movies have gotten rave reviews. It was over-promoted, too, of course.

The history of the book itself is instructive. It was certainly not over-promoted and it was just gradually discovered. Nevertheless, it was not generally recognized as a masterpiece until quite recently, except by the writers who learned from it. Innumerable writers have learned from it.

Do you think Gatsby and Daisy were representations of Scott and Zelda?

I don't know whether Daisy was a representation of Zelda in any portrait sense, but certainly the entire structure of the novel arose out of Fitzgerald's quasi-hopeless love for Zelda, I'm sure.

He wasn't sure whether he was going to be able to win her or not in the early courting days.

Yes, and probably he wasn't sure whether he wanted her or not, too. There's that element of the relationship. He was a very, very bright man, he must've recognized the signs of trouble. They're probably what drew him to her. You know, I'm just speculating, but if a man is troubled himself it can be useful to him personally to associate himself with a troubled woman who can, so to speak, be farmed

out as his trouble zone. You make a choice of the kind of trouble that you want, you know. Perhaps he wanted less a personal trouble than the trouble that you could be married to. I'm suggesting that they initially really shared the trouble and that she became the main custodian of it, in a sense, as long as she lived, but that the trouble was in both of them and developed probably as a result partly of their coming together.

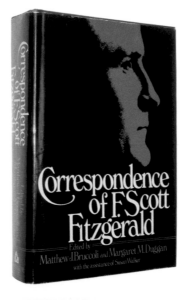

Blurb for Scott and Ernest *by Matthew J. Bruccoli on the back panel of* Correspondence of F. Scott Fitzgerald.

She was probably also part of the good as well as the trouble, don't you think?

Oh, by all means. She was his muse, of course. Also, potentially a very good writer and the source of a lot of Fitzgerald's understanding of life.

There's almost an Archer quality to Nick Carraway, who narrates The Great Gatsby.

It's the other way around: there's almost a *Gatsby* quality to Archer because I was so much influenced by it.

---

1 The book contains approximately 49,000 words.

Manuscript for an essay, "The Freelance Writer in Today's World," circa 1973, with a section on Fitzgerald and the Platonic dream.

Carraway never really describes himself in very much detail, but he's always present and always has a clear point of view of what's going on for the most part.

Oh, I think Fitzgerald taught us all how to do that sort of thing. There's a whole long string of novels that depend on *Gatsby*. Many of them are detective novels and quite a few aren't.

What did you think of Tender Is the Night? It's actually very much like Chinatown, the incestuous thing that's finally revealed at the end. Did you see Chinatown?

I saw it three times and I loved it.

Polanski changed the ending. In the original script, Nicholson helps the daughter get down to Mexico, away from John Huston.[2]

That was a dumb ending. Otherwise I liked the movie very much.

Polanski's pessimism seems to be in contrast to your books. You don't seem to share Polanski's pessimism.

No, and I felt that was somewhat superimposed even on the movie that we're talking about. The almost sadistic violence at one or two points seemed to me to be more an expression of Polanski than of the subject as a whole. I'm not objecting to it as such; I just feel that it was probably more Polanski's contribution than something that arose naturally out of the material. Particularly the shooting of the woman at the end.

Just speaking structurally, not as regards the execution, *Chinatown* is better than *Tender Is the Night*. Because Fitzgerald wasn't quite able to find out how to handle the material and that structure. He was writing very subjectively about conflicts that he was subject to himself, and he didn't manage to distance the narrative quite far enough from himself so that he could handle those dangerous subjects, those personal subjects, such as incest. He would've done well, I think, to put a narrator in between him and this novel. Because the narrator in *Gatsby* so obviously makes the whole thing possible. The writer can identify consciously with the narrator while semiconsciously writing about the other people who really *are* more closely related to himself. Fitzgerald was not a Nick Carraway at all in personality and imaginative quality and so on, but they did have one thing in common: they came from out West.[3] That in a way validated Nick Carraway as another persona of Fitzgerald. Actually, if you write a lot of books like this and become rather sophisticated, you begin to realize that all the characters are personae of yourself, and more so as you get older. Earlier on they're the personae of other writers who have created them and from whom you've borrowed them. Gradually you begin to learn to evolve the characters entirely out of self-knowledge, which is the only valid knowledge really in writing fiction.

That's one advantage of having an essentially uninvolved figure like a detective between the author and his life in fiction. That's the great advantage really of the detective story. I've been talking about some of the disadvantages of it, but the great advantage is that you can use it as tongs to pick up dangerously hot material—your own material—and deal with it as it should be and tell the truth about it. You can escape the knowledge that you're writing about your own life.

2 In the filmed version, Evelyn Cross Mulwray (Faye Dunaway) is shot and killed by the police during an attempted getaway on the streets of Chinatown, and Katherine (Belinda Palmer), her daughter/sister, is left in the clutches of Noah Cross (John Huston), Evelyn and Katherine's father.
3 More precisely, they both came from the Midwest. Carraway, like Fitzgerald, hailed from Minnesota—as did Paul Nelson.

May 31, 1974   Jill Krementz

10. FIRST PERSON

We've talked about how you see your books moving the detective novel closer to the dramatic novel.

Yeah, but only in their own terms. They're moving closer to the novel not by trying to become like so-called serious novels but by intensifying their own virtues, such as they are. There's no attempt in my writing to imitate the serious novel.

You're on record saying that you're impatient with stories that feature the detective's private life too much. Yet wouldn't that might be a way to move the two forms closer together? Showing the detective when he's not working on his caseload.

Well, it's not really what one reads detective fiction for. I'm not impatient with it, it's just something that I don't feel any particular desire to do. I don't object to other people doing it.

I'm asking ridiculously speculative questions about books that perhaps don't exist even. It's a tough question, but it does seem to me an intriguing possibility.

It's not a tough question, it's just that I don't have any particular response because it doesn't have to do with what I do. You know, I can answer why I do certain things that I do, but I can't answer questions about what other people do and why I don't do what the other people do. The reason is that I think this is the way to write detective stories, you see.

Which you think is the only way.

No, it's just the way for me to write detective stories. Even where it's extremely well done, as in the case of Rex Stout, I find the surrounding of the detective with a family entourage and so on *anti*-interesting. Instead of having half the space of the book go to essentially comic description and interplay and so on, I'd like to see [more about the case].

It seems to me that no one has ever shown what a detective does in the off hours of the case: if the person has an unhappy romance going, or if the person plays poker, or if the person likes films, or whatever—and it

wouldn't be wrong to present a complete picture of a man working for half the book on the case and how that interrelates to the other half of his life. It seems to me that's valid.

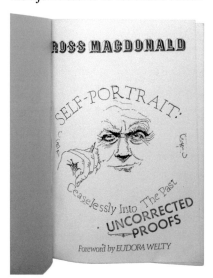

Uncorrected proof of Self-Portrait: Ceaselessly into the Past *(1981) and signed, lettered edition in slipcase that included a photo of Ken Millar and Eudora Welty by Virginia Kidd enclosed in a special pocket.*

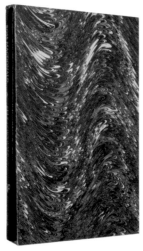

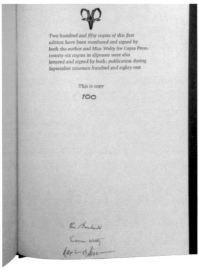

Signed, lettered edition and signed, numbered edition.
Although not called for, each copy is additionally signed by Ralph B. Sipper,
the editor of the collection.

Oh, it's valid. I'm not impatient with the idea, I just wouldn't want to do it myself. Because, you see, I have a different conception of the detective story from just another novel. For me, forgive my saying so, but on whatever level you want to take this, I consider it a poetic form. See, I'm not trying to write realistic novels; I'm trying to write drama.

I think you could write this kind of book on exactly the same—

Yeah, but nevertheless accept the fact that for me to write a novel in which the detective was, so to speak, the central figure in a different sense from what he is in the Archer books would mean a complete change in my understanding of what my novels do. At the risk of giving myself away, I have to confess that Archer is for me mainly an aspect of style and a narrative device which enables a great deal of ground to be covered rapidly and which can't be covered in any other way that I know of. It can't be done in the "realistic novel."

What does Archer enable you to do faster?

Get really into the heart of the material and also maintain a surface on which he can skate very rapidly across the face of the material. See, if I set up a realistic structure, in the first place I'd lose my rhythm, which is absolutely basic—the rhythm of movement in the books. It's not only fast in terms of external speed but it's psychologically fast. See, Archer becomes a mind in which a movement can be made from any one point to any other point, provided I set it up properly. He becomes a mind in which these events occur. He either sees and experiences them directly or he elicits them or remembers them.

Is Archer a buffer between you and the event?

He's not intended to be a buffer between me and the event because I'm on the other side of him, too. I suffer the event. Archer is essentially a means of writing what, if I were a better writer, would be poetic drama. Of a new kind. I don't think there's anything quite like the narrative moment that Archer enables me to set up. You see, it's all connected, and not only by his mind. In other words, this is not a personal matter, it's a matter of basic technique.

Limitation page that couldn't be used due to Ken Millar's advancing
Alzheimer's—he signed it perpendicular to and across the colophon text.
Compassionately, Eudora Welty followed suit.

I didn't mean that you should consider writing the kind of book I'm suggesting.

Yeah, it wouldn't be natural for me. If I have developed anything at all in the last twenty-five years, it's that technique.

So do you think that the kind of different approach I'm suggesting is nowhere for the detective story to go?

The trade edition reproduces a photo of Ken Millar on the rear panel of the dust jacket that is inscribed to Ralph and Carol Sipper and Larry Moskowitz (then proprietors of Joseph the Provider Books). The jacket is often mistaken for actually being signed by Millar.

I think it's a perfectly fine place for the detective story to go and I could even conceive of myself trying to take it there, but not very successfully. I think it's a natural development and it should occur. You must understand that I was speaking in defense of my own practice; I wasn't speaking as a critic at all.

There's also of course the factor of less is more. Archer seems to have become a more significant figure to readers by virtue of the fact that they *don't* know all that [much] about him. If I put more in, he'd be just more like the other guys. But he is a style of course. Not just a writing style but also a personal style. He has his personal style of action.

The kind of book that I was talking about, if indeed it did work, may well use up the whole subject. There may be nowhere for it to go after that.

Yes. I'm saying yes to the idea that it might use up the whole subject. Of course, the books do use up subjects, but I don't want them to use up Archer. Not completely. Even in making him as human as I have in the last book, with his girlfriend and so on, has represented a loss, too.

How is what you do different from the normal first-person book?

The normal first-person book is about the normal first person, and these books are not about Archer.

Well, is Gatsby about Nick Carraway?

That's a good question.

Somewhat?

Sure, but that illustrates my point. Of course, it was from Fitzgerald that I learned some of the basics of this technique. There wasn't any place else to learn this technique. You know what it is, it's the technique of psychological drama masquerading as a realistic novel. You begin to see why doing more with Archer would destroy the whole thing. And if Nick Carraway were more important in [*The Great Gatsby*], if he were the central figure in the book, it would be an entirely different book. The people who think he is the central figure don't understand how the book is done.

You don't think there's anything limiting at all about the first person?

Sure, it's limiting. It prevents you from getting literally inside of another character, but, you see, my approach is dramatic rather than subjectively lyrical. The dramatic sees *all* characters from the outside essentially. I mean, the stratagem is to see them from the outside and record what they say, and that's my stratagem. These stories are really substitutes for plays.

Or movies.

Or movies. On the level of technique you don't get inside the characters, but, if you'll think about the history of drama as compared with the history of other fictional forms, you couldn't say that drama fails to get inside of the characters. By comparison even with Proust, who's the ultimate in fiction. Your stratagem doesn't really determine your end, it's just a way of attaining it.

I consider myself essentially a dramatic writer. My books could be played as written. They would last endlessly long, but they could be played.

Do you ever wish you could write a detective book in the third person about Archer?

No. You see, the reason I write detective stories is that first-person device, and I think the primary reason is technical. It serves my purpose. It's really just a pretense because, once I'm into a story, I'm writing as subjectively as I care to. Very subjectively. In fact, the presence of another figure between me and the story enables me to be more subjective in the story than I otherwise could be. So these books are in a quite literal sense terribly autobiographical in terms of my sensibility and so on and even certain subjective events. They're as subjective as lyric poetry, which isn't so terribly subjective either, really. They're both stratagems getting at the expression of feeling.

Do you ever plan to write an autobiography?

I think I have been.

I think you have been, too.

I might write an autobiography. It will be an intensely painful thing to do for me. Not just because it will force me to recall in detail my own life but also the lives of other people who lived not too happily. If I live past the term of novel-writing and have nothing to do *but* write a biography, I may be forced into it. Naturally, it's one of the things that every writer has in his mind as a possibility.

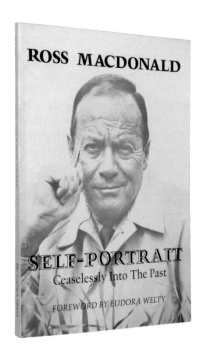

Do you think there's a certain point—beyond "the term of novel-writing"—where you won't have the energy to write the novel?

I think it's possible to write factually beyond the point of imaginative writing. Because when you're writing fact, you have that to lean on, you don't have to create it.

It's harder to write fiction.

It takes more energy. Anybody can write an autobiography anymore and do it passably well.

You seem to do very well using Archer as a sort of surrogate in your books, an indirect method of approaching your own life.

Yes, indirect. A true autobiography is direct.

Is the pain the only reason for the indirect approach?

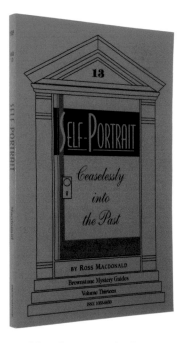

No, I don't think it's the only reason. I think that it's in the nature of fiction to require an indirect approach, if you think about how *any* novelist writes about reality. Take Greene as an example: he's using his own experience constantly. At the same time, it's imaginatively modified as he works it.

Modified for what reasons?

Well, perhaps in the direction of more general meaning; that would be one central reason. For other reasons, too. Life doesn't contain within it the forms of art; you have to modify the raw material, make it more assimilable.

You think it would be an area of a lot of painfulness, though, to write an autobiography?

To write one that would be honest would require writing about things that were painful at the time and reliving them to some extent. Of course, there again, I've been doing that. I'm not afraid of pain, I'm just pointing out that it would occur. I really think we're in this world to try to make sense out of the pains of it. It's one of the things we're here for.

11. MYTHOLOGIZING

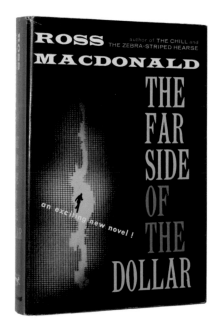

What is The Far Side of the Dollar? What is its theme?

Well, the trouble between the generations is the obvious thing. I suppose its central image or its most deeply reaching image is right at the beginning: the school for troubled children. I suppose its subject is why children get troubled. It goes back into the—oh, I wouldn't say immorality exactly—but the uncertain morality of the parents. While they have strong elements of realism, this book and others like it are not really intended to be literal social documents about American society. They're rather highly colored and dramatic, and there's an intended element of tragedy in them. I don't conceive of them as straight realistic novels at all. I tried to put into them, both into the structure and the writing, a minim of tragic poetry. Of course, a great deal of the time it doesn't come through or come off. My point is that the intention is not simply to depict society as I see it around me but to heighten the realism in a somewhat poetic direction.

I think that's what, when we were talking in the car yesterday, I was referring to as the mythic.

Yeah. I aim not at traditional tragedy but at something that could be called tragic or somewhat tragic, and that always includes the mythic. I think the mythic is a necessary element of the tragic. The characters stand for a little more than themselves; they are representative.

They sort of rest on realism basically. I don't think there's anything in the books that couldn't have happened. The realizations are not realistic, let's put it that way. They're not intended to be either. And while they have some kind of a poetic undercurrent, the method is generally realistic. They're

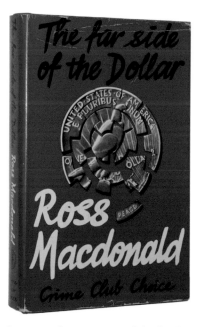

not grandly ambitious. I'm not writing about ordinary people, but on the other hand I'm not writing about the heroes of a civilization either. I'm not by any long shot.

Is that the difference between a social and psychological tragedy and Greek tragedy, do you think?

It certainly is a salient difference between the two. Greek tragedies are about culture heroes.

You said yesterday that Archer was a modest hero.

Yes. While he's got some courage, he doesn't have self-destructive courage, which is practically characteristic of Greek tragic figures. Anyway, he's not the tragic figure in any of the books. He's a much more muted kind of hero, if he's a hero at all. I think one of the things that runs through these books is that what you should basically emit is survival, which is a modest goal. In this civilization it's not so terribly modest. It's quite an achievement to survive, and to do it happily and constructively is even more of an achievement. I don't mean that many people aren't accomplishing it. Of course they are. The majority of us one way or another are.

You know, one of the things that sort of mixes up the record and makes it difficult to follow is that all of our main literature is tragic. It's about lives that end, if not in total destruction, then something pretty close to it. That's not really a reflection of life as we know it. All our very best writers are writing at the extreme edge, so to speak. I'm speaking of our modern writers, let's say from Hawthorne and Melville down. It seems to be *the* prime characteristic of modern writing, and I suppose that means that the people who do that writing regard it as essential. Speaking for myself, I've always written on what for me was the extreme edge. I don't mean as a person writing but as regard to my subject matter. Sometimes, of course, what I said about being on the extreme edge applies to me personally as I was writing, too.

There's one thing that should be mentioned about taking the detective out of mythology and using him in a novel which is essentially realistic in intent: it enables a writer to write without the embarrassment of regarding the central figure as a self-image. You can evade the problems of self-writing—and they are many. At the same time you can put as much of yourself into the detective character as you want to, as seems appropriate. So it gives you a kind of objective framework for subjective experience. And that's for me the real purpose of the detective story. That's why *I* write them.

Have you ever thought of carrying characters other than Archer through into later novels to a larger extent than you have?

Well, I have carried a few characters from one book to another, but I don't really want to form a family group and then perpetuate it as Rex Stout did, for example. It seems to me that that freezes you into one kind of story and one kind of atmo-

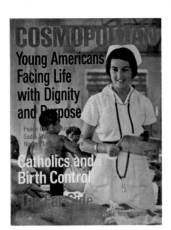

sphere in a way that I want to avoid. The essential thing about Archer is his freedom permits him to move in and out of situations and in and out of places. As you say, by virtue of repetition and constant reoccurrence, he's the most important figure in the books. I don't want him to take over the books. I'm not interested in building him up really into a superhuman figure or anything of that sort, which I think was the mistake of an earlier generation of detective writers. They really deliberately and rather grossly mythologized their central characters. This is true of Sherlock Holmes, too.

Shall I read Chandler into that, too?

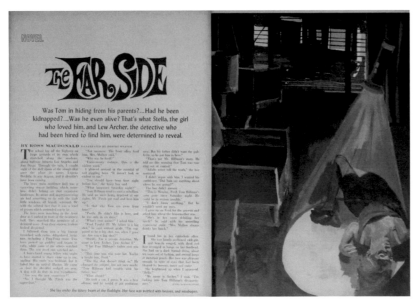

Condensed version of The Far Side of the Dollar, *September 1964, published as* The Far Side.

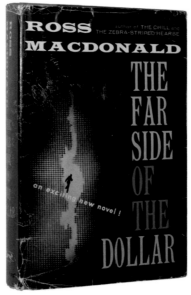
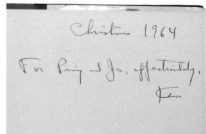

Above: W. H. "Ping" Ferry's copy of The Far Side of the Dollar *(1965) inscribed Christmas of 1964. Ferry was the dedicatee of* The Instant Enemy. *Below: Tom and Mary Hyland's copy. The Hylands were fellow bird watchers and appear in the book* The Birds and the Beasts Were There *(1967) by Margaret Millar.*

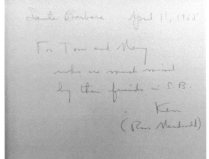

I wasn't thinking about Chandler and I don't know whether what I said is true of Chandler, certainly not to the extent that I would apply it to the earlier ones.

No, I was thinking of the references to Marlowe as a modern-day knight, and the kind of flowery language that Chandler used in that essay of his.[1]

That's true. I think his books are truer than his essay. He's a good critic but not a good critic of himself. And he was, it seems to me, romanticizing his books in a way that they don't romanticize themselves when he said that about the knight. Of course, if you took a close look at an actual knight, a wandering knight of the Middle Ages, then he'd come much closer to what we're talking about. But that isn't what he was talking about.

I think a lot of that is just literary trappings in Chandler and that the truth of Marlowe is not expressed in those trappings. Those are the things that he compares himself with and finds himself wanting perhaps, but the real description of the guy is in the conflict between the Romanticism and his sense of what's real. Now, it's not handled with complete aplomb all the time by Chandler because he himself is writing about his own mood swings to a great extent, I would think. It's a terribly personal kind of writing that he's doing, and that's not true of my writing; it's not personal in that same sense. Although all writing is personal.

1 In his essay "The Simple Art of Murder," Chandler wrote: "But down these mean streets a man must go who is not himself mean, who is neither tarnished nor afraid. The detective in this kind of story must be such a man. He is the hero, he is everything."

Can we go back to what we were talking about in the car? What your definition is of mythology?

I was trying to work out a definition as a result of what you said. You mentioned that a movie had a mythic quality, and I asked you whether that meant that it was something you felt related to you. What's the requirement of something that makes it mythic? You said something to the effect that it was larger than life. Is it something that embodies a kind of generalization? Not a verbal generalization but a philosophical generalization? Perhaps something that's valid for more than one person, more than one city, or even maybe more than one culture? And it may be that it's something that is continually significant for various people and times because it relates to human nature, a permanent aspect of human nature or human experience. *Relevance* is really what I would say is the essential, and the wider the relevance the more important it is.

Front and back of a wirephoto for The Far Side of the Dollar, *January 1965.*

Of course, there are other ways of establishing relevance than through the mythical. A philosophic statement is not mythical. It seems to me that myth also requires the presence of a symbol, it has to be embodied in a symbol, rather than simply an abstract statement. Then the question arises, What is a symbol? Well, we're going around in circles. It's something that is valid for more than one situation in a sense. You can take it out of its context or at least put it in a varying context, and it still has meaning or some trace of its original meaning. Symbols, like words, are to a great extent defined by their context, though. You put something in a different context and it will have a totally different meaning. You can even turn its meaning right upside down.

Do you think it has to be embodied in a symbol?

It has to be embodied in something. An action.

According to Tolkien's definition, you are writing mythology. His definition is, "To tell the past is history; but to explain the past, and make it meaningful to the present, is mythology."

He's talking of a historic past, and I'm merely writing about a past which is psychological and personal, more than historic. It depends on the emphasis of the writer of course. I *do* refer to the historic past, and my characters are affected by the past and by the general past, which is historic, but it isn't what I'm writing about. You know, I might refer to somebody being a child of the Depression or something like that, but I'm not writing about what the Depression did to people.

Right. You are writing about in some way what the present is doing to them.

Yes, but it's more about the very recent past. There is a sense, though, in which the past enters in. Psychology replaces history as my discipline. I'm writing a history of psychology, in a sense, not of overt behavior. I'm speaking now about the past that enters into the books. Events are important because of their psychological impact. The continuity is essentially, in the lives of the characters, a psychological one—or moral, if you want to put it that way. A moral/psychological one. But my concern is not to depict an external known past, like the history of the United States from 1920 to 1940 or something like that.

Are cowboys and detectives sort of the American equivalent of gods and legends?

If this is a mythology that we're talking about, it's a greatly reduced mythology. Greatly reduced in scale. The ancient mythology, Greek mythology, that we're talking about I suppose is related to a whole pantheon and a whole philosophic structure which persisted for centuries. We just don't have that sort of thing. What I'm writing about and what we have would be more comparable to the half-known mythology of a savage tribe with shamans rather than priests. What I'm trying to do is change the scale of what we're talking about. But, you see, what I just said applies better to my books than the idea of comparing it with classical mythology, which was, well, part of a religious establishment as well as a governmental, a political, establishment.

Do you think it's possible that psychology is the modern form of mythology?

I think the modern form of mythology is psychology, yeah. It's psychological. Of course, it has many other aspects.

The reason I said modern, *I guess I was thinking that the reason that cowboys and detectives may be gods now is that we're in sort of an existential society. Gods do not fit into a modern society, so we have to have heroes. Legends would be another way to put it, or mythic alter egos.*

That's true. And these people are people precisely, they're not gods and they're not even demigods. They fill the gap, let's say, to some extent.

And the American hero seems to me to be derived from the cowboys and the detective. Therefore, I think Archer is a mythological figure in that sense and also in the sense that Tolkien says.

It's just that in comparing what we're talking about with a mythology you have to make certain conscious adaptations. You can't set up large equivalences. Of course they perform some of the same functions in some way, but it's much more complex and malleable, the mythology of the civilization that we live in. You know, it's constantly being changed as we go, to fit new problems.

  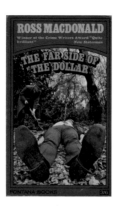 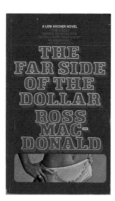   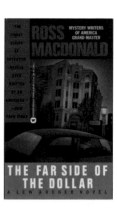

I think the detective is a symbol of that change. The cowboy wouldn't work anymore, so now we have a detective. I don't know what we'll have after that.

The cowboy turned out to be too dangerous. He always ends up shooting or getting shot. Actually, the detective figure did historically grow out of the cowboy. What was the name of the detective firm that Hammett worked for?

The Pinkertons.

Since Pinkerton was an outgrowth of California society and that one of the things they did was to take part in any range warfare and that sort of thing, Hammett wasn't making that up.

Is this the obvious connection between the Western novel and the detective novel? Has that novel moved from the frontier to the city?

Yes. I mean, the Wild West is still very much alive in certain parts of the West, including California. There really isn't anything wilder than any American city. Cities have lost their claim to be centers of civilization—or if they are that they're also centers of violence. So the difference is a little old-fashioned, between the wild open country and the sedate city. It's also the wild city.

The development is not just literary, it's historical. Every now and then in the books I've had Archer refer to himself as a modern Deerslayer.[2] The detective firm that Hammett worked for actually developed in the middle of the nineteenth century, in reaction to frontier conditions, as a kind of private police in places where there wasn't an adequate policing and so on. It represents a movement that was necessary to get our human and physical wilderness under control and gradually urbanize it. The detective became an urban man simply as part of that historical development.

On the frontier there were really very few choices as to, well, the way you made a living and what your lifestyle was, how you felt about yourself, and so on. What characterizes the city is the almost infinite multifariousness of possible life. So what you get is an *extreme* complexity gradually infiltrating a basic country simplicity. That country simplicity involved a hell of a lot of violence and so on, but it was really pretty simpleminded violence. You know, good guys and bad guys and rich guys and poor guys, and the poor guys taking it away from the rich guys and the rich guys oppressing the poor guys. That sort of thing. Whereas in the orchestration of life that a growing city like San Francisco

provides, you start getting an extremely interesting, highly civilized variety of possible experience. Of course, fiction follows that. I think the man who made the transition most consciously was Frank Norris. Around about 1900 was when the transition occurred. A thing doesn't really occur in a civilization until it's written by a good writer—before that it's just sort of vague—but Norris marks the event.

Are you thinking of any particular book? His naturalist writing?

The Responsibilities of the Novelist. Naturalism is a name for the writer's response to the city. He saw the thing as a struggle between economic interests on the one hand and human needs on the other. That's what *The Octopus* is about. I'm using *city* in the broadest sense to mean any developed environment, such as is represented by California with its railroad. It's the railroad that makes the difference and the concentration of wealth that it represents. He used it symbolically, too, of course, in the bad sense. I mean, he used it as a representation of the oppressive power of wealth. He was, most obviously in his feelings, on the side of the rural kind of life that was being destroyed or damaged.

Norris is one of my favorite writers, incidentally. Of course, Dreiser is a lot better writer than Norris. But I object to putting Norris and Dreiser in the same category. I regard Dreiser as a somewhat greater writer. Greater intention and greater fulfillment, too. I mean, he did what Norris would have liked to be able to do and what Norris talked about in his criticism. But Dreiser actually did it, he *did* write working-class novels.

Do you think there wasn't much choice for Western fiction? It had to almost in effect follow life.

Fiction always does. Very occasionally it creates life. A writer like Camus can actually influence a whole society and change it—or at least *help* to change it—as much as anybody I can think of offhand, you know. I think he presented a vision. The vision of course is never really ahead of life—it has to be taken from life—but it promotes what you depict. The vision promotes what it sees and also how it should understand. That's the important thing: I think Camus was a source of deep understanding. At the same time he tied up his perceptions with classical myth and so on. He's a central figure in our time, and in quite simple ways. He's quite a simple writer, he has a classical simplicity.

Would it be right to say that Archer is opposed to the values that Camus discovered?

2 Deerslayer is one of the nicknames of Natty Bumppo, the protagonist of James Fenimore Cooper's "Leatherstocking Tales." The five books—*The Deerslayer, The Last of the Mohicans, The Pathfinder, The Pioneers,* and *The Prairie*—follow Bumppo from 1740 to 1804.

The discovery itself is what constitutes the value. Archer wouldn't be opposed at all to what Camus did, which was discover and explain, or at least widen our understanding of—

No, not what he did, but the existential behavior.

Well, I don't know what existential behavior is. Of course, a writer is not necessarily favoring what he represents.

Yesterday in the car we got onto another subject, sort of a spinoff of the Western-detective subject, and that was our national preoccupation with lone wolves. America's heroes, they're always lone men pretty much. It would have to have some kind of psychological meaning, don't you think?

I can't answer that question. It's a very difficult question, why men and women have turned their backs on each other in this country to the extent that they have.

It's also in Gatsby, the great book, which is pretty much about the un-attainability of—

The un-attainability of sexual love.

You take the cowboy and the detective, it's just absolutely essential that they are womanless and they are alone in those genres. I don't think it's a rule that can be broken.

Well, I broke it deliberately.

Only in a simplified way, I think.

Oh, of course. I'm not offering myself as counter to what say you're saying, but I did break it deliberately in *The Ferguson Affair*. I presented as my hero a young lawyer with a wife and a child on the way, and I did that knowing that I was writing something counter to the genre. It worked out all right, but it didn't work out so well that I wanted to go on doing it. Now, *why*? I don't know. I don't know why, in many departments of our fiction, we're writing monosexual material.

I think it goes all the way back to Natty Bumppo. He's womanless and committed to a doomed way of life.

Sure. But don't forget that from Natty Bumppo on down the detective story is not the only story. There are other stories being told. It's true the central figure is male. He's a man of action. The point I've made is that very often, while the eye of the reader is focused on what this central man of action is doing, more important events are occurring among the other characters. Including women. I've tried to get away from the idea of the terribly central figure of the male and give a more complete and variegated version of the society.

Somewhere in that conversation in the car, about why these heroes are womanless, you said that part of that may be that it's a defense of the man-woman relationship. I'm not quite sure what you meant.

A defense of the man-woman relationship by not subjecting it   I'm just making this up now, but it may be what I had in mind—to the stresses and the searching. You know, not to go into a subject can be a means of protecting it and protecting the mind against it. I mean, actually not dwelling on a subject or not doing something about a subject *overt* can be a means of preserving it the way it is. The man alone is just a refusal to look *into* the other subject, and this is true in real life, too. The loner is a man who doesn't want to—or for other reasons, doesn't—go into the full life of sexuality. The man who abjures marriage and refrains from sexual activity is in a sense a preserver of marriage now. That's what a priest could truthfully say about himself. But that's not what I was saying yesterday.

No, it's not.

I just can't remember what was said yesterday.

Do you consider yourself a loner?

I really never have lived as a loner, no. But I probably think like one.

Does that fact please you or displease you?

Well, I would hate to be an actual loner in my life, but Archer, the loner in my books, does represent values as well as deprivations. He makes his own decisions, and I think that's the most important thing that a man can do. I think it's important in the moral world, which is where private detectives operate if they are worth anything. It's important to be able to make a moral decision involving other people without referring to some higher authority. I really feel that we have to learn to be able to do that. Now, I'm not talking about decisions that are destructive of authority or destructive of the community. I'm just talking about decisions that

 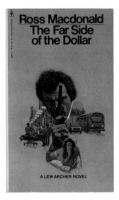   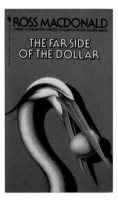  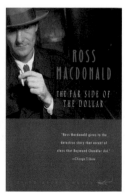

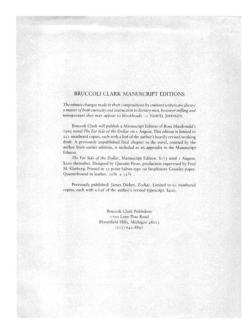

men and women have to make day by day in their lives about what to do next. I think we do have to assume a fairly high degree of moral responsibility for our own lives, for good and ill. God knows, we're not going to make the right decision all the time—or even the majority of times. I believe in the individual conscience.

Of course, we go on learning. I'm not suggesting that we stop listening to other people or learning what our own lives are. I'm really talking about circumstances that arise frequently in the kind of life that I write about, the life of crime and detection and punishment and that sort of thing, where decisions have to be made and they have to be made rapidly. And we shouldn't be afraid to make them. We should always try to make them in the direction of more and better life rather than less and worse life. Sometimes we have to make a choice between one evil and another. Not doing anything, of course, is a choice, too.

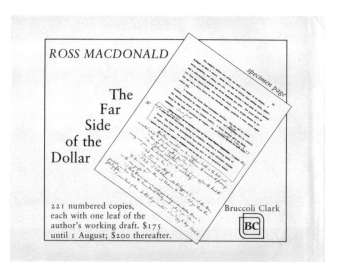

The Far Side of the Dollar: Manuscript Edition *(1982) was intended to consist of 221 copies, each with a revised typescript leaf attached. The edition included a previously unpublished chapter and was withdrawn from sale after review copies (without the inserted typescript leaf) were distributed. According to publisher Matthew J. Bruccoli: "The printer spoiled the copies, and I destroyed them. I decided not to start over because by that time Ken was unable to sign copies." The previously unpublished twenty-ninth chapter was issued as a separate pamphlet with the limited hardcover edition of the complete Lew Archer short stories,* The Archer Files, *in 2007.*

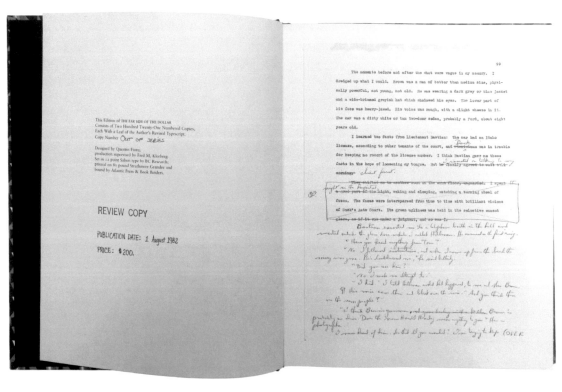

12. ROMANTICISM

Lew Archer seems a less Romantic detective figure than Sam Spade or Philip Marlowe, I would say.

Romanticism has been described as "spilt religion." There are other ways to think of Romanticism, though. The Romanticism I started talking about was the whole compendium of literary attitudes that have determined literary development for the last two centuries. The gothic movement in which the detective story belongs is a very powerful and important element in the whole Romantic development.

We're all Romantics in the broadly historical sense. We're living on towards the end of the Romantic period, and let's say that Archer is consciously the end—but not yet a figure of the end. Archer stands with his back to a cliff and every now and then he turns around and peeks over, but he doesn't jump.

You compared mystery writers to actors because they both start with the self but become other than the self.

I think it's true that imaginative people in general have to work out their own identities. That's part of the work that's given to them by their natures. They're generally not content to just accept the kind of identity that's given to them by their immediate family or their society. It's particularly true of the writers of the last two centuries—let's call it the Romantic period. The breakdown of traditional identities occurred partly as a result and partly as a cause of this Romantic development. It had to do with the complete disruption of traditional religion and society by things like the French Revolution and so on, and the tremendous philosophical revolution of the late eighteenth century. The forms—the selves, the egos, or whatever you want to call them—with which people had lived and done business, or within which people had lived their lives, gradually disappeared and people had to invent themselves again. Of course, that was the job primarily of writers and philosophers. I suppose Jean-Jacques Rousseau had as much to do as anybody with the creation of the modern self by writing his autobiography. It was the first—maybe not the first, but the first that occurs to me—statement of a modern man who was willing to describe himself. He stepped outside of all the rubrics and all the ancient forms of the self and just said what he did and what he felt. Well, that's the beginning. The answer might seem to be to just do again what Rousseau did or what Byron did.

I suppose Byron is the supreme example in English literature of the new creation of the self that I'm talking about in the breakdown of all previous selves.

That's what he wrote about: the breakdown and creation of a modern self. He did it as well as anywhere in his letters, which I've been reading, incidentally, and which show us simultaneously the creation of a modern self and a modern style. Just with his left hand in the course of his career he created the modern English style, which is why he's such an enormously important figure. I mean the English style of writing. But, you see, it also represents a style of living. The two go together. There's an outspokenness in his style and a willingness to pursue subtleties of feeling and thought and wit to the end, which becomes also a style of living. It's not just a literary style, it's the way he *was*, the way he became and taught some of his friends to become.

Now, obviously when a writer creates himself in the sense that we're talking about, he has tremendous dubieties and weaknesses and fallings away, too. It's almost like flying, literally flying, which is not a natural thing for men to do. And yet that's what the great Romantics did with the support of course of a lot of convention and literary and culture background. They weren't just flying naked, they had their spacesuits. But from Byron to Hemingway and Fitzgerald is a short jump.

Is it such a long jump to Norman Mailer, say? To the modern equivalent?

No, but Hemingway was an obvious example of a Byronic figure, not necessarily imitating Byron but doing some of the same things with some of the tools that Byron provided him with, or some of the insights. Maybe he wasn't a great reader of Byron, but these things feed into the culture, you know, they become part of the culture. What I just said about Hemingway is I think equally true of Fitzgerald, but I think Fitzgerald took it a step further, in the direction of originality. He isn't as close to Byron, he's closer to the writers who are writing now and of whom he was the master.

I think that sort of did Hemingway in. It seems to me that he couldn't keep up that ambivalence between the image and who he really was.

I'm not going to try to explain Hemingway in conversation. He's an enormously complex figure. I don't really feel that he had the sufficient interest in culture to become our prime explorer of contemporary culture. But Fitzgerald did. Fitzgerald was frankly more profoundly educated than Hemingway was, and he was more fortunate in the people he spent his time with, too, in spite of the sadness of his life. He had Edmund Wilson as his mentor, for example. Best critic of his time.

Now, Hemingway went it alone. I think he *overdid* the Romantic prescription in a sense. He overlooked the importance of the social support—I'm talking about the social support of his own country or his own readership—and I think that's why he got tired. He was going it alone too much. Byron didn't go it alone. He was surrounded by a coterie of other writers and he was in constant communication with them and they supported each other.

Hemingway seemed to be quite vicious to other writers in many cases.

He was jealous without reason. He had no reason to be jealous of any other writer, not when you write as well as he.

I do think he sort of got tagged harder than he should have with that unfeeling tough-guy image, which I don't think is true at all.

No, of course not. No, he had a very tender sense about him. People, you know, are so influenced by language, and because he used the spoken rather than the written language, so to speak, it made people think he was, well, a tough guy. Of course, he also dealt with violent subjects. So many of his short stories are centered in violence.

He promoted that image also.

Yeah. And he did celebrate the manly arts, you know, like shooting and boxing and so on. According to mutual friends, he was not really a good boxer at all.

Condensed version of Black Money, *December 1965, published as* The Demon Lover.

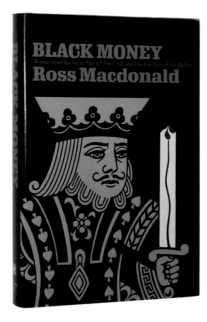

Towards the end he was misunderstanding his subject matter and his own talent. Well, you know, he wasn't an intellectual in the sense that Fitzgerald was. He wasn't really a particularly profound student or philosopher of fiction, and it's not surprising that he should have misunderstood. So many people were saying false things about him, it's not strange that he should have believed them. He didn't have an intellectual armature to protect him. He went directly out of high school into the war and from there pretty directly into writing. He didn't have much non-imaginative intellectual experience, which a writer really can use to protect him from false ideas. And to protect him from too much awareness and emphasis on the self. I think that was Hemingway's real misfortune: he didn't know how to escape from the subject of himself. And, of course, it takes philosophical work to do it.

The Romanticism got completely out of hand. Though I like the book very much, and although it's pretty flawed, Across the River and into the Trees, **is almost a childish fantasy.**

Yeah. It's suffused with self-pity. Of all the emotions, that's one of the emotions that hasn't served many writers very well. I suppose there were some pretty good poets that have been able to write out of self-pity and do it well, but I can't think offhand of any prose writers. When you compare Hemingway's attitude to himself and his self-heroes with Fitzgerald's *extremely* hard—I speak now of intellectually hard— and sophisticated treatment of Gatsby, who is a self-image, there's all the difference in the world. Which makes Gatsby a much more interesting figure—an endlessly interesting figure. Fitzgerald saw all through him and around him and right into the society. I think, when I mentioned society, that Hemingway's great loss was that loss of society. He never really wrote in the society in the sense that Fitzgerald did.

You brought in somebody else's name there that I passed over. Who was it?

Norman Mailer. I was just thinking that the description of Byron sounded very much like it could almost describe Mailer in a certain sense.

Yes. Except that Byron frankly wrote better, that's the main difference. But the men are equally serious in intention and they're dealing with the same themes: the growth of a new self in a world that's changing. If you don't grow a new self, you lose what self you have in a truly changing world. I think Mailer is just doing his damnedest to be our intellectual leader. We badly need somebody like him, trying out attitudes and finding new perceptions.

He's certainly not afraid to look like a total fool. Not very many people would be willing to go out on the limbs that he's gone out on.

That's right, he takes all the chances there are. No, I think he regards all that as an important part of the record. And it is. You know, the total fool of one generation can be the saint of the next.

I started out being a great Mailer fan, but I've gradually slowed down, I'm sorry to say. I'm really very limited in my tastes. I don't pretend to be a broad-gauge critic.

Do you find him to lack a little discipline as a writer?

I don't really think he lacks discipline, he just can't be bothered with it. He's aiming at something different. What he's after is full expression. I haven't really studied Mailer enough to talk about him critically. I've read a good deal of him. You know, the generation problem does come in here. I started reading Mailer when he was a young American novelist and now he's an old American fact writer. The change has gradually tended to leave me behind. I've lived through two generations of Mailer and I haven't gotten over my disappointment about his turning from a novelist into a journalist. Now, he may have gone on to better things than I know about even or better things than the early fiction.

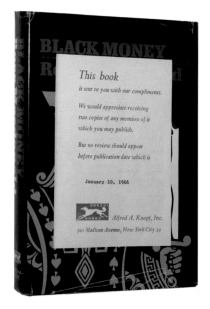

Review copy of Black Money.
Ken Millar considered this book his version of The Great Gatsby.

Going back to the original premise of the identity problem of writers, has this applied to you at all? Have you reinvented yourself in your books?

Not as much as I would have liked to.

I don't know what it means, but in the books Archer is often tracking down an artist. It must mean something.

Of course, the detective is often tracking down a lot of other people, too, but certainly the artist is represented. Because you've been reading my books, you're more familiar with what I'm talking about than I am because I haven't been rereading them. With the exception of *The Zebra-Striped Hearse*; I did reread that as part of the work connected with this interview because I regard it as sort of central. You obviously do, too—we're talking about it.

But I regard the artist, at least imaginatively in my books, as a profoundly ambivalent figure, which I suppose places me where I belong: in the Romantic strain. That's the Romantic view of the artist and it's the view that the artists in the Romantic tradition took of themselves, starting with Rousseau. Rousseau, who sort of invented the modern Romantic, portrayed himself as a man both good and evil.

The Romantic artist, from Byron down to the present, is a profoundly ambivalent figure to himself and to other people. He's like a witch doctor who deals in black arts, he's like a shaman who can both heal and destroy, and who doesn't have total control of the human and superhuman forces that he's dealing in. Of course, this is true of artists. To put it in a less melodramatic way, it's true of anybody

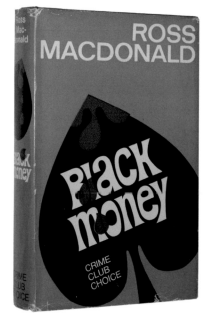

who writes music or paints or writes books. He can't do his work without to some extent being taken over by the daemon, or himself becoming a daemon in all kinds of senses. At least in the Romantic world, which we still live in to a great extent—and that is to say our minds are formed by Romantic doctrine and image—the artist is a daemon.

Why demon?

Well, it's D-A-E-M-O-N. By *daemon* I don't mean an inhabitant of hell. *Daemon* has several connotations. That's why I used the word. Do you want me to look up a few of them? [*pulls out a dictionary*] *Daemon*: it means "spirit." It also means "evil spirit." It means "divinity." It means "genius." It means "tutelary deity." Need I go on? Now do you understand why I used the word *daemon*? It's an extremely large and explosive word. But anyway it reflects, among other things, all the attitudes that the human beings have had towards the creative spirit.

You picked a good word. It represents the highest and the lowest.

Yes. And that's *precisely* what I'm trying to write about when I write about somebody like the painter. I don't hit the extreme heights or the extreme depths, but I do indicate the potential of them when I write about the painter in a book like *The Zebra-Striped Hearse*.

Archer isn't just tracking down the artist; he's trying to understand the artist.

Yes, well, Archer represents the more dry, intellectual side of man—he's not a creator himself—and he's doing in the fiction what I did as a scholar. I spent years tracking down Coleridge and the whole idea and the psychology of the Romantic artist. I'd been fascinated by it ever since I was in my teens. I started with Poe, who is the prime example of what I'm talking about in American literature and the prime example of the traditional Romantic artist. He exemplifies it. Poe was, you might say, my first master. Profoundly psychological, too. He wasn't just expressing feelings, he was understanding a very great deal about himself and other people. He was a great psychologist. Isn't it interesting that he also invented the detective story? He literally did, you know. And the detective story hasn't changed much. The detective is still the intellectual man trying to track down the sources of violence. And get it under control, as Poe did through ritual poetry, for example.

It's one-half of an artist tracking down his other half.

Of course. The intellect and the imagination. If my books were to be taken as allegories that would be the substance of the allegory.

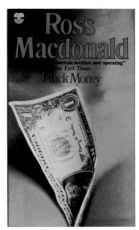
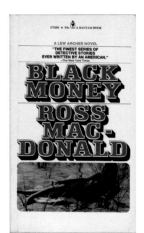

So you regard yourself as a Romantic novelist?

I think I fall within that general description, yeah. I think the whole gothic tradition, to which I belong, is a Romantic tradition. It's practically coterminous with Romanticism. It may even be one of the central definitions of Romanticism, when you consider that the major Romantic writers were very often touched by precisely this, the gothic. I think of Byron, Shelley, Coleridge, Poe, just in the Anglo-American tradition. You find a lot more both in the French and German. I think while gothicism and Romanticism are not the same thing, the gothic, well, it partly encloses Romanticism and is partly enclosed by it. The gothic really was invented before there was any Romanticism, at least in England. It was invented in the middle of the eighteenth century. And you have to consider somebody like Swift, a definite precursor of the gothic, I believe, if you look at it in broad terms. This whole emphasis on the darker side of life, this fascinated emphasis on darkness and strangeness and the unexpected and so on, is what lies behind the gothic tradition. Of course, I try to do more than just continue a gothic tradition. I've tried to marry it up with contemporary social realism and that sort of thing, and with modern psychology, which includes the gothic in its interest but goes far beyond it. Still, my central tradition is the detective story, and that's historically the gothic tradition. And Poe is the master.

I see Romanticism in a less classical sense but more in a psychological sense.

Yes. Of course, I gave you a scholar's answer.

Would you consider Hammett a Romanticist?

I was just going to say there's much less difference between Poe's detective stories and Hammett's detective stories than you think when you first read them. Just take a really close look at Poe's two or three short detective stories and take a close look at two or three of Hammett's short detective stories; more similarities than differences really in almost every respect. I'm talking about style, content, and the shape. I'm not talking, you see, about anything but Poe's detective stories right now, and they're written in what could be called the American voice.

Hammett's really do connect up with S. S. Van Dine and back to Poe.

Sure they do. His detective is a typical Romantic hero pitted against an alien or a world from which he is alienated. But his execution is not Romantic in the bad sense. He's got everything under such strict stylistic control. And that's what we really value, it's the meeting of these opposites and the fine balance that he maintains at his best. *The Glass Key* is a Romantic novel, too. Very much so. But really it's hard to mention anything of the period in fiction that isn't Romantic. The only major difference between Poe and Hammett is that Hammett writes about men of action and Poe writes about intellectuals. But Hammett's man of action is a concealed intellectual, as he himself was. Actually an important intellectual. He proved it in his art.

Signed French edition of Black Money *from 1972.*

You said at one point that Hammett's prose is an action prose. That he's almost inherently in the prose somewhat. Would that make it different from Poe's to some extent?

Yes. What we were just saying about Hammett and Poe could be said about Romanticism in general. The writer becomes ego-involved with the material that he's writing, and that's one of the defining characteristics of Romanticism. He's not writing about other people entirely, he's writing about himself *qua* other people.

Would it be too strong a statement to say that Chandler's Romanticism ultimately destroyed him?

It didn't destroy him, it simply set limits to his vision. You know, he started out as a late nineteenth-century Romantic poet, so to speak, and in the end his values didn't go beyond the values of the late nineteenth century. *Realism* was to him a bad word—or let's say that *the real* was to him a dangerous quantity and a frightening thing, the real itself—and Romanticism was an escape from it. There was a sort of pendulum swing in his style and also throughout his work between those two rather limited choices.

Is that so different from saying that his Romanticism destroyed him?

No, it merely limited him. He wasn't destroyed.

You don't think so?

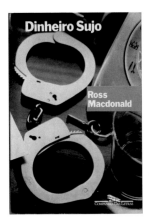

You mean as a person? Well, I certainly think it's dangerous to depend on the Romantic hype, if that's what you're talking about. Let's say that Chandler's work, which was profoundly influenced by Fitzgerald's, which Chandler referred to in a peculiar way as "that little lost novel," words to that effect—

You mean Gatsby?

Yeah. Chandler's work was a step backward from what Fitzgerald accomplished. He learned from Fitzgerald, but he didn't learn the ultimate thing, and that is how to handle tragedy. I mean the kind of contemporary tragedy that Fitzgerald did so well in *Gatsby*. In order to handle tragedy you have to have a standpoint which is beyond the personal and beyond the pendulum swings between realism and Romanticism, neither one of which will provide you with either a terminal or a safe place to stand on to look around from. There's a tragic irony beyond those things in Fitzgerald, from which he surveys the whole battlefield. Tragic irony is the answer for him.

I think there's a tragic irony in The Long Goodbye, and the irony is probably that Chandler didn't have that distance that you describe, and it was tragic to him personally.

Well, the tragic irony exists in *The Long Goodbye*, but it wasn't created by Chandler. He merely fell into it.

I'm speaking less on a literary level than, I guess, as to what their personal lives were like. You have, it seems to me, wonderfully managed not to have that problem.

Not to have a personal life.

No, not at all!

I meant that as a joke.

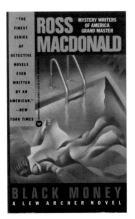

No, not to be consumed by "spilt religion." On the one hand I really admire people who are wallowing in Romanticism, and on the other hand I realize it usually winds up doing them in or narrowing their vision down to an often useless point. You're one writer and man who seems to have balanced that out rather nicely it seems.

Well, knowledge of history is a great corrective. Fitzgerald had an intuitive knowledge of history. I don't mean that he was by any means illiterate. I really think he was a genius—obviously he was—and any knowledge of history tends to protect you against the swings.

Were you ever at a point where you felt this lunge toward Romanticism in the sense that I'm talking about?

Oh sure. When I was in my teens I went through the whole bit. I regarded, well—who would be a typical Romantic figure? Not Byron. I like Byron now better than I did when I was younger, I understand him better. Oh, Shelley and Keats and that sort of thing. D. H. Lawrence is the greatest twentieth-century Romantic figure, at least in England and perhaps in the English language. I was enormously taken by Lawrence because he opened so many gates, you know. As you get older you tend to realize that some of those gates should not have been so carelessly flung open without seeing what was on the other side. I still admire Lawrence as an artist, but not so much as a philosopher.

I don't mean excesses in terms of alcohol or drugs or any of that.

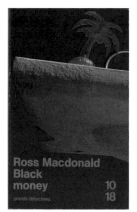

Lawrence didn't go in for alcohol or drugs, but he did have a Romantic view which, carried to excess, tends to identify the ego with God. That's the danger, paranoia of one kind or another.

Yet that's a danger with writing to some extent: you have to have the ego to do it.

Yes, it is. That's one reason why some of us use a middling kind of character like Archer: it keeps reminding us of our limitations and our human connections, our direct class situation, and so on. Things that tend to hold you *firm* in the body of the republic, both the republic of letters and the republic of the United States.

I haven't mentioned it until now, but the essential thing about Archer as compared with Spade on the one hand and Marlowe on the other is that Archer really *is* a democrat with a small *d*. Spade, in spite of his self-irony, did have delusions of grandeur, and Marlowe is very much a Romantic creation intended to satisfy the longings of the author in one direction or another.

"Spilt religion" is the key phrase here. If you spill it on yourself you're sunk. At least that's my opinion. I believe in a kind of prosaic sanity, but not a world devoid of sunsets. One of the things I try to do is to handle hard subjects in a way that they *can* be handled by the human mind without damage—or let's say without mistake.

I know he didn't have a detective, but how would you place Fitzgerald within this discussion?

Yeah, well, he did have a narrator who served as a kind of, oh, commentator and moderator. I regard Fitzgerald as the technical source of the contemporary detective story. That's clear I think in the case of Chandler who's the next great figure after Hammett. I don't know about a relationship between Hammett and Fitzgerald, but it doesn't matter.

Hemingway may have been a father figure, or at least a brother figure, to Hammett in some sense, I suspect.

Could be. They certainly started with somewhat the same aims and somewhat the same subject matter, too, and they both came out of the First World War. So did Chandler. He also fought in the First World War, in the Canadian Army.

Thinking of Gatsby in terms of emotional autobiography, a symbolic autobiography, how do you think Fitzgerald handled this problem of Romanticism?

He handled it by expressing it rather completely and then looking beyond. The story of *Gatsby* is a Romantic story but with a hard core of realism which emerges at the end. Then the next great novel, *Tender Is the Night*, is the aftermath of

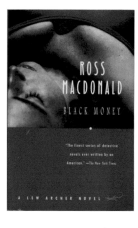

the Romantic dream. But of course an aftermath like that *to* a Romanticism is itself a further form of Romanticism. *Tender Is the Night* is also a Romantic novel. It's a Romantic tragedy, not quite a full tragedy.

Why?

Because it's too subjective and because the materials that he deals with are too limited.

You wouldn't classify Gatsby as "spilt religion" in any sense, would you?

It's not really spilt, it's *held*. It's held, but it's there.

Before I turned the tape recorder on we were talking about the mad painters and cursed artists in your books, and that in some cases those characters represented yourself as well.

Oh sure. Well, it's a shape into which a modern self has to learn to fit because so much of our experience—I don't mean just our external experience, I mean our inner experience—can best be expressed in those terms.

I have trouble seeing you as a mad painter somehow.

Well, I don't see myself as a mad painter. That's just a version. It occurs to me the curse and the art go together, and almost at the same time. It's what crime writers write about to a great extent, you know: the sources of evil in the self and in society and so on. But particularly in the self. The self is almost by obvious definition the source of our knowledge of evil.

But there's no such thing as an impersonal sense of evil. It's something that you feel—you put your finger in the electric socket and you get a shock. That's the way we recognize some of these valuable dangers. I wouldn't say the dangers are valuable—the recognitions are valuable because they keep you from destroying yourself or other people. There's a grid of pain that you have to learn to operate within, and if you don't you get the shock—and it'll kill you if you get it often enough. So you have to avoid evil. The pain shows that the evil is there.

Is that alleviated by writing?

The pain? I think so. Anything that you do about pain alleviates it, and writing is half a dozen of the approaches. There are half a dozen different ways to go *at* the subject in writing—at least. Probably half a dozen hundred. You see, I'm assuming a connection—not perhaps a direct, one-to-one connection—between evil and pain. Like the same connection that you make between the presence of an electrical current and the experience of shock. Very often, though, that current, as I've been saying, is ambivalent; it can either light up your house or electrocute you. Destroy your mind.

13. DISTURBANCES

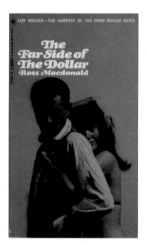

In the Sixties the covers of your paperback editions contained this blurb: LEW ARCHER – THE HARDEST OF THE HARD-BOILED DICKS. I don't think that was ever your intention—for him to be "The hardest of the hard-boiled dicks."

No, of course not. No, I think Archer is probably the *softest* of the hard-boiled dicks. [*laughs*] Well, very often books are described or advertised as being something a little different from what they are just in the hope that they'll sell. God knows, there's enough violence in my books. The central character—or the narrator, Archer—is not particularly hard. He barely survives many times.

It's not ever the kind of gratuitous, break-knuckles Spillane violence. Archer rarely fights.

Some of the earlier books, though, have quite a lot of violence. I don't think any of it is entirely gratuitous. After all, hard-boiled detective stories are supposed to be about violence. That's the basic subject matter, and I write them because that subject matter attracts me and is important to me. The causes and consequences of violence are sort of the subject.

You seem an unviolent man.

Well, I don't have to be violent—my books are. It's a violent world and I've been aware of that since I was a small child. I've probably seen more violence than some other people have, although I don't mean that I have a corner on it. But I've seen quite a lot of it. I've been protected in the second half of my life from the things that I saw in the first half of my life.

Were you a fighter as a kid?

Oh, not so much. I was a wrestler in college. That's a form of well-controlled violence, of course.

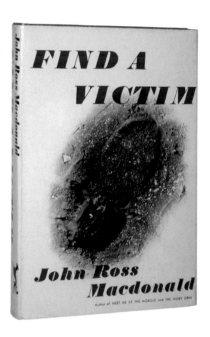 

I'm thinking of the crime-on-the-streets delinquent violence.

We're talking about two different things. You're thinking about fisticuffs or something, and I'm thinking about the kind of psychological violence that is visited on everyone—and particularly on children—in a society that doesn't look after people adequately. I suppose compared with the kind of violence that children are brought up in and exposed to in the ghettos at the present time, my experiences were fairly minimal. But they were of the same order.

They weren't minimal in the effect they had, so I guess they couldn't have been minimal.

No, I said by comparison with. Yes, they are minimal in their effect even when you compare my writings with those of a contemporary black writer, for example. *If Beale Street Could Talk* [by James Baldwin] or something like that.

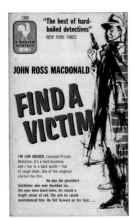

Clockwise from left: Inscription with "J. R. M." initials to John Ball by Ken Millar in the 1954 Knopf US edition; condensed version of Find a Victim *in* Manhunt, *July 1954; Cassell UK edition from 1955.*

They seem to be about mercy also.

I was just going to say that. But it is pity as well as terror. I'm afraid they go together.

Some of the characters can't help themselves.

You know, a schizoid person does have insights that go far beyond very, very often what completely sane people know and see around them. That's one reason why they're sick: they see too much and they experience too much.

That's what the psychiatrist R. D. Laing said they do.

Yeah, but I thought of it long before I read him. It's a pretty obvious thing. So much of good art in all forms has been produced by schizoid people. We do have schizoid consultants available. They experience what we all experience, but more profoundly. I'm not speaking of intellectual profundity, I'm talking about the thing itself. They really *see* more and *feel* more, so much more that they can't stand it. Some of it is true and some of it is visionary completely. You know, by shutting out so many of our mentally ill and emotionally disturbed people and keeping them away from society for so many years as we have tended to do in the past—although the process is changing now—we cut ourselves from a lot of sources of knowledge. In the old days when every large family had at least one somewhat disturbed member, it was very good for everybody, I think. Although painful.

In large cities, because of the pressures, it seems like the craziness becomes equated with violence.

It isn't generally the truly disturbed people who go in for violence. They all tend to be fairly gentle. I don't know what kind of violence we're talking about exactly, but the obvious thing would be to examine who gets killed and who kills this and this. That would be one way of examining the violence and its sources. But most violence leading to death in this country is caused by people who just happen to have a gun. In other words, what causes the violence is the gun. In most cases the people who commit murders are not disturbed.

I'm missing a connection there somewhere.

Well, you're regarding disturbance as a source of violence so important that it's *a* or *the* social threat; but statistically it's the people who have guns that commit

There was another question implied in what you just said. It had to do with what you might call my over-response in the books, my over-response to violence. But that response, as in the case of other writers, is not necessarily a *personal* response. It's a response in terms of the function of a writer. He reports what happens. If there's an earthquake he doesn't disregard it. Everybody knows and can see around him that we're inundated by violence. The whole society is assaulted. The particular biography of the individual is not the only source of experience in this matter. All you have to do is look around you.

It's true, though, that my early life, which was somewhat exposed, made me more sensitive of course to violence and its consequences. Very much so.

It can be looked at in two ways: The books are about violence, but they're also about the methods of control—psychological and moral, or however you want to put it.

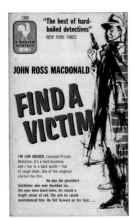

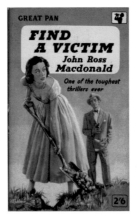

    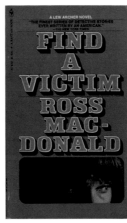 

murders, it isn't people who are mentally ill. The differentia is the gun rather than the mental illness.

It seems to me it's possible to be both. Why would someone who wasn't disturbed and who had a gun shoot somebody?

You mean disturbed at the moment. We're talking about mental illness. Mental illness is not a main source of homicide. It really isn't. I know that it's something that people are afraid it may be, but I'm speaking from experience and also from some knowledge of what has caused murders here year by year in town. The availability of the gun seems to be the essential thing.

A brief disturbance, not a long-term illness?

Oh well, everybody has periods of brief disturbances. I was distinguishing between mentally ill people and other people.

And armed frustration or armed anger or rage?

Well, that's another matter. I was talking about people who are certifiable. We were talking about insane people. Most murders are not committed by insane people, although naturally a percentage of them are. God knows that a good share of murders are committed by mentally disturbed people. I can think of two that have turned up in the parts here in recent years. One man thought he

was God, told the judge that he better shape up. The judge of course quickly got him out of there and didn't put him on trial. Another case, there's an Armenian who had lived here for many years and was a novelist as well as a real estate operator. In his seventies—he was as I said an Armenian and had been mistreated in Turkey when he was a small boy—he concocted a plan to murder two Turkish diplomats. He got them up from Los Angeles through a false story and killed them both.

I would be surprised if the murder rate is any higher in California than it is in the Eastern cities even though one can buy guns easier out here.

There's been a gradual tightening up, but just more or less on a local basis. Anyone who really wants a gun can go and get one. Of course, there's a lot of shootings still going on, even now.

There was one example of an accidental shooting. It really pleased me, but don't quote me in print. The head of the local society for the promotion of guns—he actually is the head of the group that feels that everybody should have a gun—accidentally shot himself in the leg. [*laughs*] Then, to add insult to injury, they put him on trial for possessing a weapon—he had this concealed weapon in the trunk of his car—but they didn't convict him. The DA, who's a close friend of his, stood up and got him off.

Is Santa Barbara's crime rate high? Low?

    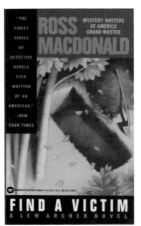 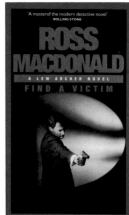

We have a lot of murders. A very active police force that do not hesitate to draw their guns. Occasionally somebody gets shot that way, too.

Have there been gun control efforts out here?[1]

Yeah, but they've been pretty well foiled by the efforts of gun users and gun sellers. There isn't really much control. For example, a young cousin of mine—not a first cousin, thank God—came to town to visit us from Canada, where gun control is pretty strict. He was seventeen or eighteen at the time. The first thing he did when he got to town was to go down to a sporting goods store and buy a revolver and the ammunition for it, brought it home, and started waving it around my house. I had to take it away from him—he threatened me with it. This came as quite a surprise to me. I hadn't seen him for a couple of years. I guess he was going through some sort of psychological growing pains. Anyway, I got it away from him and took it back to where he bought it. There wasn't any harm done, but it was an example of how easy it is to get a gun, you know, in our society. Well, anyway, he ended up teaching college. I don't know whether that's a happy ending or not.

    That's one of five times that I've been threatened with a gun in civilized situations. They're all where the gun is irrelevant. And in none of those cases was the person who did the threatening crazy, although they were acting strangely. In a couple of cases it was just a matter of disturbed young people pulling guns and

having to be talked out of them. And then there was a case of a policeman pointing a gun at me for no reason. It was a high-powered rifle.

Was it a case where he thought you were trespassing, or was it a mistake on his part?

You'd have to ask him what he had in mind. They're the dangerous ones because they think they can shoot and be scot-free. There's no danger to them. Anyway, it happened.

What were you doing at the time?

Nothing. Absolutely nothing. I was just there. There may have been some kind of alarm on or something, I don't know what. Nobody explained to me or apologized.

    And there was another case of my being down on the beach here. There were three teenagers shooting rifles at wild birds, which is illegal, and I told them that. They pointed their guns at me. I retreated.

What does it feel like to look down the barrel of a gun?

I guess there's a certain amount of fear involved, but it's more anger than fear I think. Also, the anger is controlled by the realization that your life could be at stake, and you behave carefully. I did. I didn't try to rush the young man who came into our house with a gun, for example, and I didn't argue with the boys on the beach either.

1 Paul didn't mention that he himself owned three handguns back in New York: a .357 Magnum, a snub-nosed .38, and a .22, all of which he had acquired so that he could know how it felt to hold them in his hand for the detective novels he was planning to write.

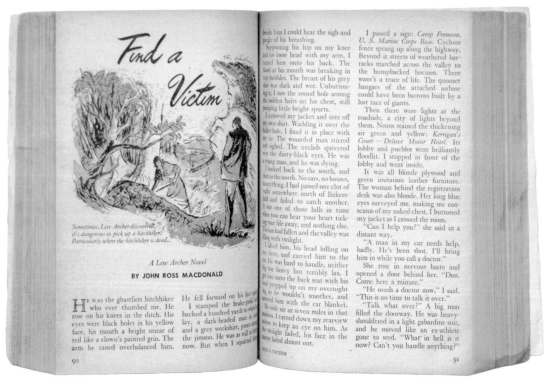

Giant Manhunt *No. 7 (1956) collected four regular issues of* Manhunt, *one of which was the July 1954 issue containing the condensed version of* Find a Victim.

14. STUDENTS AND TEACHERS

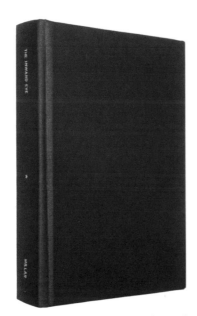

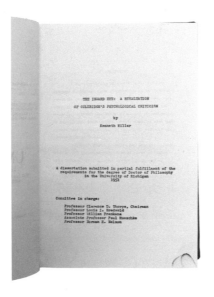

Alfred A. Knopf promotional cards for The Way Some People Die *(1951) with art by Bill English.*

Did you go all the way through graduate school at the University of Michigan to get your PhD in literature?

Sure. I didn't do it without a break. It took me something like fourteen years from the time I graduated from college to getting the doctorate. But in the meantime I had written a number of books, too, and done other things. I spent a couple of years in the Navy.[1]

Did Margaret get a PhD also?

No, she wasn't in graduate school. She was a novelist. She was a novelist before we ever moved to Ann Arbor. But as I was saying, it was really her being a writer that made it possible.

1 Millar graduated from the University of Western Ontario in 1938, but didn't receive his PhD from the University of Michigan in Ann Arbor until 1952—the year after *The Way Some People Die*, his seventh book, was published. He'd already completed his eighth, *The Ivory Grin*, which would be published in April of 1952.

Did Margaret know for sure in her teens that she wanted to be a writer?

She was writing in her teens, but she had other interests which divided her attention and really took her main attention. She was a musician, you see. A serious pianist. Then she became a classicist, which is a very demanding discipline, particularly at the University of Toronto. There's only one way to be a classicist really and that is to study Latin and Greek, and that's what she studied at the University of Toronto.

I have a recurrent nightmare that I never finished and I never got my degree.

Me, too. I still occasionally have that nightmare. You did get your degree, didn't you?

Yeah. As far as I know, the degree itself didn't ever help or hinder me later in what I did.

Of course, you came later, twenty years behind me, and the economic situation had changed. The period that I was going through college was in the Thirties and it was Depression right on through. In Canada particularly. Gosh, the idea of becoming a high school teacher and earning to start fourteen-fifty a year seemed very, very good indeed compared with the other things that were available. Just the ordinary working guy was getting five dollars a week.

A week?

That's right. And some of them were working for three-fifty in Canada during the Depression. So it was very valuable. I could have gotten a job probably since I had an aunt who was a department head in a big insurance firm. I could have got an office job there, but I didn't want it. They paid only ten dollars a week, and that was the best job available.

Speaking of students, what does the University of Santa Barbara contribute to the local population?

The university has 15,000.

How big of a town is Santa Barbara?

Oh, it's less than a hundred thousand, but the metropolitan area is two hundred thousand. So it's a fairly sizable town. But there is a student village called Isla Vista.

Where the Bank of America riots took place. What was the cause of the unrest?

There were all kinds of reasons for the riots, most of which cast the students as victims in one way or another. I'm not just talking off the top of my head. A group of us, self-appointed, wrote a report on the riots afterwards, making

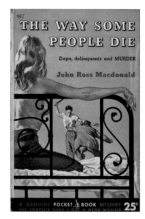

recommendations to the university and the local governments. Most of our recommendations have been put into effect over these last few years. But those riots were really pretty bad. They were generally associated with the Vietnamese War and those troubles, though there were other problems than that, of course. That's just where everything came to a head. There were simply crowds in the streets objecting to a number of serious problems. The Vietnamese War of course was an overriding concern, but also there was the business of people being busted for minor drug violations. There was also a situation which has not been entirely eased: Isla Vista is one of the two or three most crowded municipal areas in the United States. Its population density is comparable with some of the Oriental cities like Singapore. Incredibly dense. What it goes back to is simply profiteering on the part of certain real estate men.

Was it student housing or what?

So-called student housing. It was huge apartment buildings and nothing else. The housing problem was one of the things that caused the riots. It was probably the primary thing. Too many people on too small an area. Really slum-like living conditions for a large part of the student body. A slum is any inhabited area that has too many people. It really constituted an educated ghetto. That's what it was, and the students reacted to it as if it was. They rioted in opposition, and one of them was killed by a police officer. He claimed that he had fired his gun accidentally, so nothing was ever done to him. Last year he killed somebody else.

I presume Isla Vista was the model for Academia Village in The Blue Hammer. From the description in the book, it didn't seem that you liked it very much.

Sometimes, you know, you write about a place without intending to be describing a particular place. Very often in a book when I just have a chapter or two about

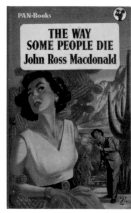
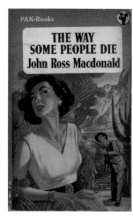

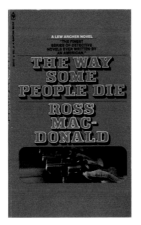    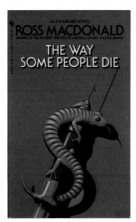 

a place, I don't try to go into it in any depth and I don't try to do it justice either. I just write it the way it falls. I certainly did that in the book that we're talking about. I wasn't trying to do anything with the university area at all.

I imagine that when describing a place you also have to keep in mind what the character is going through and what the dramatic circumstances are.

Yes. Thinking about it, well, just very generally in the last minute or two, I think in general my young people *are* worried and in many cases disturbed. That would be true to say that they tend to be that way. It doesn't really have to do with the universities, it has to do with the fact that these are university-age people who are in trouble, which is not really supposed to reflect the influence of the university.

I really am a very strong supporter of universities and other educational enterprises. We've got more people in colleges and universities now in this country than has ever before occurred in the history of the world, and I'm sure there are too many going. The result has been an unfortunate decline in the quality of education. Not in the good universities and colleges, but in the enormous numbers of others that have sprung up to meet the need.

I get letters from college students that I wouldn't have accepted from a high school student when I was a high school teacher. I've got one on my desk: this boy's in a writing course and he can't even spell. So there's a lot of phony or contentless education going around in this country, unfortunately.

Do you get a lot of manuscripts from young writers?

Yes. I wouldn't say a lot, but they add up to a lot of reading. There again, I'm not able to do justice to all of them, but every now and then I get a real honey

through the mail. For example, earlier this year I got a letter from a junior in a Canadian university, Trent University in Peterborough, a young man named Linwood Barclay. He informed me that he was writing in my field, and I replied in a friendly way. He wrote a short novel right in the middle of the school year. I think one of his professors gave him credit for two essays for writing his short novel. Well, it's a mystery novel. This boy has immense vitality. He's apparently a very good student and is interested in other things, too. He also is in business with his mother in the tourist industry in Peterborough, which is a great place for lakes and streams and woods. Well, anyway, this short novel that he sent me is just about good enough for publication and certainly immensely promising, so I suggested that he make it somewhat less short and submit it for publication. I think it's a mistake to submit a short novel for your first time around. You should do the standard length and then do short ones afterwards if you feel like it.

Anyway, by a nice coincidence Margaret and I went to Peterborough when we were in Canada this spring. We had reason to go there because Margaret's cousin, who is almost like more a sister to her, lives in Peterborough. In fact, her late husband was Peterborough's leading citizen *and* the main founder of the university that Linwood attends. So when we were there, she invited Linwood Barclay to have a meal with us, and he took me over to the university and showed me around, introduced me to some of his friends. For a former Canadian college student, it was altogether a very rewarding and fulfilling experience. Really one of the high points of my life in its quiet way, and I think it was a high point or a really good point for Linwood, too. I hope that the whole thing will give him a big shove in the direction of professional work. I'm sure it will.

It's a private detective novel?

Yes, based on an actual private detective whom he knows. He's rewriting it. He just finished his junior year in college. He's got lots of time. *The Open Eye* by Linwood Barclay. Imagine writing a short novel in the middle of all his other classwork. And it turned out quite well. I think if he'll revise it and fatten it out a bit, he should be able to get it published.[2]

Where is it set?

UK Fontana paperbacks from 1973, 1974, and 1979 that remained virtually identical over the years. The 1973 edition is priced for the UK domestic market; the 1974 and 1979 are export copies marked with multiple prices.

2 Despite Millar's encouragement, Barclay, now an internationally bestselling author who has published more than a dozen books, never published *The Open Eye*. "I recall him saying the book needed a subplot, and a rewrite. I did that. *The Open Eye* was very much influenced, of course, by his work generally and *The Instant Enemy* in particular, I think."

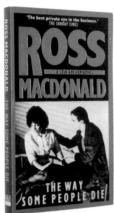
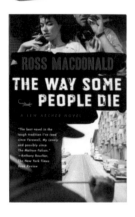

It's set where he lives, in Peterborough, Ontario. It has produced two of Canada's leading writers: one of them is Robertson Davies and the other one is Hugh Kenner. Kenner's a really good critic. He's more than a critic, but not in the direction of prose. He's a philosopher, he's philosophical. He was the most important single factor in my first university education here in Santa Barbara. He taught here at the university for about ten years or more. He's in Baltimore now at Johns Hopkins. They offered him a very good salary. He's a great critical mind. He and I were very close for about ten years in Santa Barbara. I got to know him as soon as he came out because I was connected with other people in the English department. I learned an enormous amount from him—more than I ever had from any other single person. Just being with him is like taking advance courses in a lot of things, you know, because he really is a fairly universal talent and he understands a lot of different areas. He really is a great teacher. Though I wasn't his student, I was just his friend, I automatically picked up a lot.

What did you learn from him?

I learned a great deal about modern literature in depth. It's difficult to pick out any one thing because in the course of our conversations we covered just about everything. When I open up the material that I read under the influence of Kenner, all with the new understanding that I got from talking to him, it really covers almost the whole range of modern literature—not specifically American literature but French, English, Irish. Two of the people that were very important to him and became more important to me under his influence were Flaubert and of course Joyce. He's written books about both of them.

Did that affect your writing also?

I'm sure it did. Not so much to write them, but as through the writers that I read or read with new eyes.

There's another college around here. I see signs for it every once in a while.

There's a denominational college out in Montecito here.[3] It has is merits. As I said, it's denominational, which limits it intellectually. I've known a lot of the kids. I used to live in the area of this college, and they're nice kids but they're not getting the same education that they're getting out at the university.

I went to a denominational college the first year and a half.

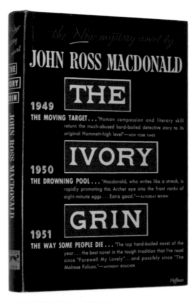
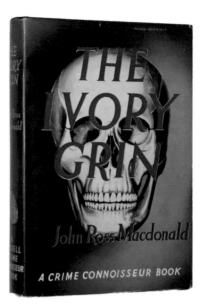
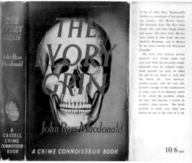
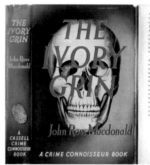

The US Knopf edition of The Ivory Grin *from 1952, the UK Cassell edition from 1953, and the domestic and export variants of the UK dust jacket.*

I did, too. Waterloo College.[4] Actually it was a branch of the University of Western Ontario, which is not denominational but which includes denominational colleges. After the first year I switched over to the main university. I really didn't lose anything. The freshman year doesn't require any really high-powered teachers anyway.

I was lucky. The English teacher I had in my freshman year, Carl Klinck, had a doctorate in English from Columbia. He was a local boy who went down to Columbia and came back. Later on he became one of Canada's leading scholarly authorities in the field, the editor of an enormous book by many hands. I think you would describe it as a history of Canadian literature.[5]

But that was just good luck. I was just darn lucky to get to college. It's what I needed and it made a big difference in my life. The difference between taking a ten-dollar-a-week job in an insurance office and staying there for thirty or thirty-five years, doing nothing of any importance, and on the other hand having an opportunity to learn as much as I was capable of learning and go right on up through the educational system. But you have to start out by becoming a freshman at any kind of a college. There are no shortcuts.

3 Westmont College, a Christian, liberal arts school.

4 The name of the college was changed to Waterloo Lutheran University in 1960, then to Wilfrid Laurier University in 1973.
5 Carl F. Klinck edited *Literary History of Canada: Canadian Literature in English.*

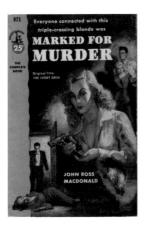    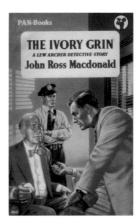 

Do you think that kids necessarily feel that way today?

No, they don't. College hasn't become the only way in, so to speak. There are other ways. I don't think they're as solid.

I really wish I had not gone to college right after high school. It was just too much like a continuation of the same thing.

It's true. I think kids should take a year or two off. Not necessarily between twelfth and thirteenth grade, but at some point. And I did, too. It was very, very valuable. You do need time to grow as well as learn. See, I didn't go to college right out of high school. I worked on a farm for a year, and then I took another year off. In the middle of my junior year I took a year off and went to Europe. I didn't exactly *plan it*, if you know what I mean. That's just the way it went. I was pretty young when I got into college.

How old were you?

Well, if I'd gone right out of high school into college I would have been just sixteen. I did some skipping, I think I skipped about three grades.

The fact that the small local college was affiliated with the University of Western Ontario was a piece of luck because I could go there and then switch to the university at the end of a year without any loss at all. I'd taken all the right courses.

Was going to a university for you a cultural shock compared to your upbringing?

Not at all. I'd been reading on the university level long before I got to a university.

Some of the people you stayed with encouraged this?

Did it on my own. Nobody *discouraged* me. I used to spend my evenings in the public library, as well as the pool halls. That's my mixture. This was something we did on our own. I and a few friends were reading stuff that was just as educational, just as important—more so—than what we read in our first year in college. Several of my best friends were budding writers like me. We read philosophy and poetry, and I was writing poetry. Gosh, I was reading the major European writers long before I ever got to college. The same with philosophers, too. My last two years of high school were in Kitchener, Ontario, where a good library existed. During my year on the farm I did a lot of reading. In between school, I was a great frequenter of the library. Our public librarian was herself a novelist. She's still in print. Mabel B. Dunham [her name was actually B. Mabel Dunham]. And she ran a good library [the Kitchener Public Library]. It's one of the best small libraries in Canada. A really good library can make all the difference to young people in a town.

I practically lived at the library. They not only had all the books that I needed but they subscribed to good magazines. I used to go in every weekend to read the magazines right after they came in. *The New Yorker*, for example. For a young person trying to learn about writing and so on, you couldn't find a better guide than *The New Yorker*. Just as good as a college education, up to a point. *The New Republic* is the magazine I have read longest and most continuously, starting when I was in my teens. It holds up, and it keeps finding new things to do with itself.

B. M. DUNHAM, B.A.
Instructor in Library Science

Bertha Mabel Dunham in
The Occidentalia 1936.

What about Esquire?

Esquire isn't going to be around. It's thrashing frantically at the moment, I gather. It's too bad. Over the years it's been the magazine I liked best. After *The New Republic*.

To some extent Esquire's had to take on a narrower identity. Either that or go the route of pinups, which they chose not to do.

And you can't outdo *Playboy* or its competitors, which do outdo it. You can't outdo *Gallery*.[6] You know, I read one of them—I'm not sure which one it was, but it doesn't matter—in the barbershop the other day when I was getting a haircut, and it featured a lot of so-called letters up front in which people described their sexual experiences, and the emphasis was all on trios. You know? That seems rather—well, it's rather strange in the front of what purports to be a men's magazine. You know, two men making out with the same girl at the same time and that sort of thing.[7]

6 The men's magazine ran two articles about Millar in less than two years: "The 'Secret' Success of Ross Macdonald" by Jeff Sweet in the August 1974 issue, and, in March 1976, "Ross MacDonald," an interview by Trevor Meldal-Johnsen.
7 Coincidentally, the cover of the magazine featuring Millar's second appearance in *Gallery*, in addition to touting him as "GREATEST MYSTERY WRITER," also advertised, in larger font, an article about "THE JOY OF THREESOME SEX."

  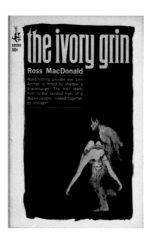   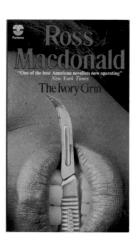

The classified ads in most of the fairly respectable counterculture weekly newspapers are just this incredible horror show of swinging couples, this, that, and the other thing. Page after page after page of them. You can apparently pick up the phone and have a girl sent over.

Are we reliving the Weimar Republic or what?

I don't know. That's what's wrong—it seems like that question doesn't even come up, you know?

I don't have any judgment to make. I just want to watch and see what happens. See, there are so many forces working in the other direction, too. As Dickens says, "It's the best of times and the worst of times." What I see is infinite possibility in either direction. We could simultaneously be the best civilization and the worst civilization. This has been true about high periods in other countries. France, for example. You could take a man like Proust and make an argument for the utter decadence of French civilization as depicted and exemplified by Proust; and simultaneously you could regard it as the highest flight that civilization has taken in modern times. Which is right?

I *think* myself that a great civilization is all-inclusive. That is, a great modern civilization. Certainly the Roman civilization was not.

I just find it really curious that things that would have been so scandalous five years ago don't rate so much as a nod of the head anymore.

Now the people who ten years ago worried that their kids might be smoking cigarettes are now grateful if they smoke marijuana instead of something worse.[8] I don't think I'm exaggerating the situation. It's happened very rapidly.

Well, it will be interesting to see who and what can pull this civilization together. It is done by writers like Proust, but the effect is not immediate, it's always posthumous. For example, we're learning *now* the lessons that Fitzgerald was teaching a generation ago. Two generations ago almost. We're only now catching up with him and understanding what he was talking about.

Do you think there's a danger in being a deliberate social novelist? It seems to me that, in retrospect, the people who became the symbols for their age weren't necessarily trying to be.

8 It's easy to surmise that Millar had his daughter Linda in mind when he spoke these words. She had, according to a source, died from an overdose just six years earlier.

Think of what Hammett would have been without the detective story. He would have been another Albert Halper or something like that perhaps. He wouldn't always have been a stylist. But he needed that particular slant, that additional new slant, and that extra material to take the message and put a new spin on it.

I guess I'm thinking of a filmmaker like Stanley Kramer, who makes films like **The Defiant Ones** *and* **Judgment at Nuremberg,** *which seem very timely for their particular year, but, twenty years later, those aren't the films audiences tend to go back to. They tend to go back to things like* **Casablanca** *and* **The Big Sleep,** *which at the time of their release weren't considered important at all.*

Yeah, well, somebody like Stanley Kramer thinks that history is spelled with a capital *H*, whereas a true historical force is immersed in the thing itself. He's not

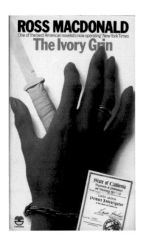 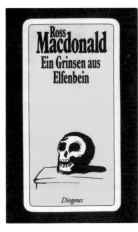 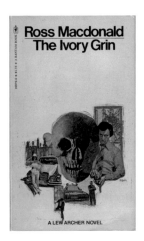   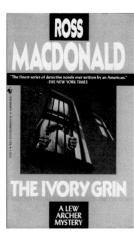

standing off to one side writing headlines about it, so to speak. In fact, the very best of us put themselves on the line and become themselves test cases in the history of history.

Do you think Mailer is an example of that?

I think he's trying to be, but I don't know whether he's naturally self-sacrificial enough to accomplish what he's trying to accomplish. The broad comic keeps breaking in.

It seems to me Mailer's writing tragicomedy.

Yes, but he's not doing it within the confines of a style. Not in the sense that Hammett was. I mean, Hammett was deliberately walking a stylistic tightrope and Mailer really isn't. Mailer is expanding the style to include everything—or at least everything that his experience is requiring his style to comprehend.

Do you respond to his prose style at all?

Let's say that I'm a great admirer of Mailer but not every time. The one about the march on Washington [*The Armies of the Night*] is the supreme example, I think, of what he's trying to do. But it's not at all the same thing that Hammett was trying

to do, and it's probably a mistake to try to compare the two figures because Mailer keeps expanding and Hammett followed a narrow, rather precise course.

Mailer seems to be trying to take in practically the universe.

He's constantly expanding his intellectual interests and his style to go with them. He's creating a style that will absorb anything that he wants to tell it or anything that happens to him. At least that's been true in his last decade. That probably won't continue to go on forever. He'll pull back and write another novel, I trust.

But Hammett's style is terribly exclusive. He very seldom includes language that wouldn't be available to a fairly uneducated though literate person. Whereas Mailer requires more and more of his style and of his reader as he goes along.

You said you started reading The New Republic in your teens.

Yeah, and also some of the good English journals. See, Canada is fortunate in being in between the two cultures, in a sense. It draws heavily on England—or it did then—and also heavily on the United States. It's very good for people to be subjected to more than one influence. I think that's one reason why in some ways Canada is so very highly civilized. It has learned from both of these societies.

How do you mean, "highly civilized"?

 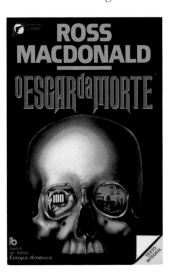 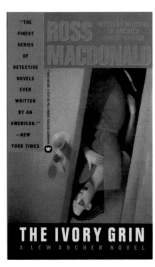  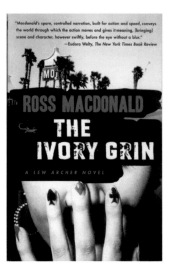

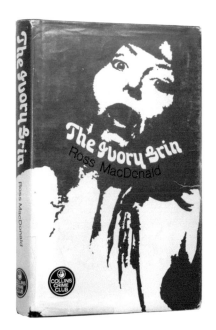

1975 UK Collins Crime Club edition of The Ivory Grin.

I mean that the Canadian schools, for example, are better than anything I've seen in the United States. The access to a good college education is much freer than it is in the United States. In the United States, to be sure now of getting a good education you practically have to go to a name school. This is not true in Canada. I know by experience. I went to the smallest, least well-known college that you could find and it didn't impair my opportunity.

What do I mean by *civilized*? Well, I mean the adjustment of means to needs in all fields of society. For example, Toronto I believe has the lowest crime rate of major cities on the North American continent. You can actually walk down the street anywhere in Toronto safely. That's the ultimate in civilization. Of course, that doesn't relate directly to what you learn out of books, but it's connected.

Do you agree with Marshall McLuhan that the machines and the computers will essentially free a lot of our time so that our main job in the future will be to learn?

I think that's already happening. If you'll just take a look at the people who are studying now that in a previous generation would have been working. The number of people in our universities and in our other advanced courses, adult education and so on, has just been multiplying enormously. I regard learning as an end in itself, and that's historical, too, you know. Learning, a life of learning, traditionally has been regarded as a desirable life and a useful life. Going back through the Middle Ages into the Dark Ages that's been true.

Marshall McLuhan is an acquaintance and a friend, isn't he?

He came out here to teach one summer and I got to know him through my academic friends. He's a long-time admiration of mine. I'd been following his work long before I ever met him, and also he's been reading me for a long time. He's interested, you know, in popular culture of all kinds. We became friends. I've seen him since in Toronto. He taught a summer class, which I was allowed to audit. That's the last course I ever took from anybody and one of the most useful. He was talking about the whole development of the modern world and its technological civilization, and the influences and counterinfluences between the technology and other branches of civilization, on which he is a great authority. His class was to me just very brilliant and eye-opening.

The book I read of his is Understanding Media, which I thought was just stunning. Some of them after that seemed more gimmicky.

He's had a long migration, culturally and biographically speaking, from—I don't suppose he was ever old-fashioned—a more or less of a standard English professor

and critic. Throughout his life he's been moving *beyond*, and then further beyond, the disciplines that he started out in, towards, well, territory that can be seized intellectually and historically. He does seize it that way, but he also seizes it imaginatively. Some of his vision, while it isn't the same as Bradbury's, has the same far-reaching aspect; is trying to understand the future and prepare for it by ameliorating the present. Or at least understanding the present.

He seemed to be very widely read for a while and is less so now.

He was a major discovery. Once he was discovered, he stepped back into the landscape again. But he's continuing his work.

Did you like teaching?

Obviously I did because I've gone on doing it for nothing. I really enjoy it. It's intoxicating, you know, if you're not only a born teacher but a trained one. It's a lot of fun.

Are you still teaching?

No. Except in the one-to-one situation. People, like this kid in Peterborough, send me things or bring them over to the house. I'm not teaching in any school.

What kind of courses did you teach?

When I taught high school I taught just about all the English courses and all the history courses and also geography. Of course, in the university I taught freshman English primarily.

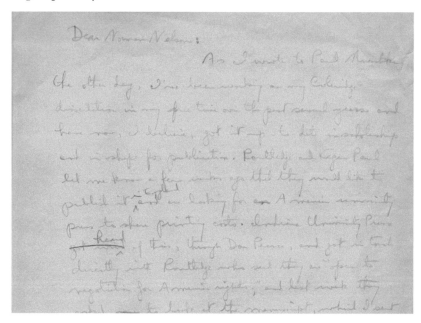

Detail of a draft of a letter (circa 1960) to Norman Nelson (who taught at the University of Michigan from 1928 to 1969) discussing the shortened version of Ken Millar's dissertation "The Inward Eye: A Revaluation of Coleridge's Psychological Criticism" (retitled as "Coleridge and the Inward Eye: The Historical Background and Critical Use of His Psychology") for potential publication by Routledge & Kegan Paul.

When you were teaching freshman English, what books and what writers did you assign?

The two things that I remember first off as using were Lincoln Steffens's autobiography and some of Shaw's plays. Both heavily tendentious. But that really wasn't why I used them. It's because they were so good. And *clear*, you know. They laid things out about the modern world that a freshman ought to know.

Do you ever get the urge to teach a college course again?

Oh, I don't think I want to teach a college course. It would seem to me, as long as I could be writing, it would be a misuse of my time. I'm talking now about a

full-time college course, where I'd have to change my life pattern entirely for a year. I sometimes do some teaching at a college level, but not for any length of time. Just a one-time sort of thing.

A lot of my friendships are set up on a pupil-teacher relationship—either I'm one or the other.

And so am I. That's where I do what I consider my best teaching; people who become my friends and who are interested in learning to write.[9]

9 In the case of his relationship with Millar, Paul was comfortable in the role of the pupil. "You sort of come away like talking to a great teacher. You want to go out and do something good or something right afterwards. He does have that uplifting, serious quality."

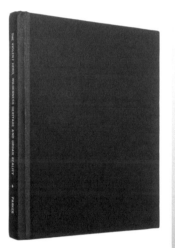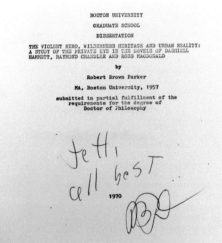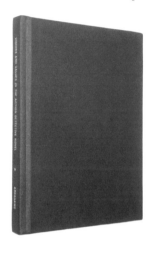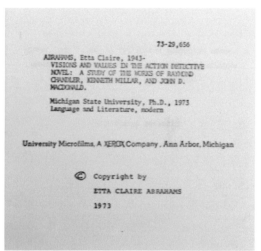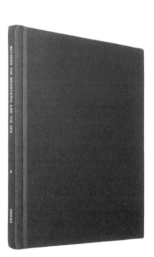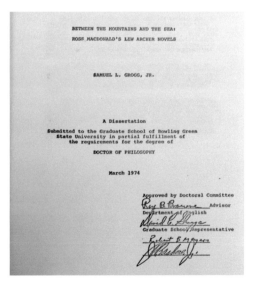

Top: Robert B. Parker's dissertation "The Violent Hero, Wilderness Heritage and Urban Reality: A Study of the Private Eye in the novels of Dashiell Hammett, Raymond Chandler and Ross Macdonald" (1970).
Bottom: Samuel L. Grogg Jr.'s dissertation "Between the Mountains and the Sea: Ross Macdonald's Lew Archer Novels" (1974).

Top: Etta Claire Abraham's dissertation "Visions and Values in the Action Detective Novel: A Study of the Works of Raymond Chandler, Kenneth Millar and John D. MacDonald" (1973).
Bottom: John D. Sutcliffe's dissertation "Lew Archer, Private Investigator: A Biography" (1974). Sutcliffe's thesis gleans details from the Archer novels to reconstruct Lew Archer's life, much the way Tom Nolan did in his foreword "Archer in Memory: A Biographical Sketch" for The Archer Files *in 2007.*

Above: Two carbon typescripts of the same page from a chapter from The Birds and the Beasts Were There (1967) *by Margaret Millar, and a first edition of the book. What is notable is that the holograph emendations to each of these pages from the sixteenth chapter, "Fire on the Mountain," are in Ken's handwriting. This represents final text that appears on page 215 of the Random House trade edition of the memoir, and suggests that Ken had a hand in writing or editing the book. His handwritten additions appear on other typescript pages from other chapters in the book, but this page has the lengthiest addition by Ken of the pages in this particular archive.*

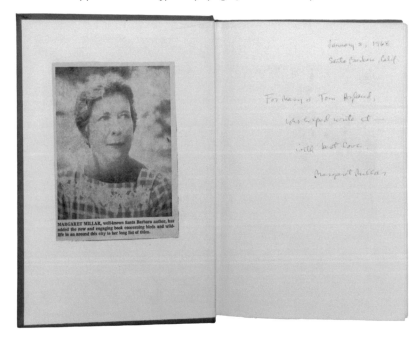

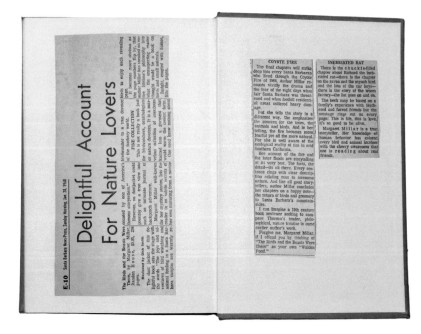

Above: Tom and Mary Hyland's copy of The Birds and the Beasts Were There, *inscribed to them on January 2, 1968: "For Mary & Tom Hyland, Who helped write it—with best love, Margaret Millar." The Hylands were fellow ornithophiles, and pasted clippings from a January 28, 1968,* Santa Barbara News-Press *review of the book on the back endpapers—they are featured prominently in the fifth chapter, "Morgan," beginning on page 52 of the book.*

May 31, 1974   Jill Krementz

May 31, 1974   Jill Krementz

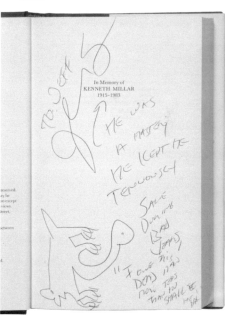

Above: Mysterious Press published Blood on the Moon *by crime novelist James Ellroy in 1984. The novel was dedicated to Kenneth Millar who died the year before. In the above inscription Ellroy has drawn an arrow pointing to the dedication to Millar and written: "He was a master: / he kept me tenuously sane during bad years / 'I owe this dead man more tears than you shall see me dry.'"*

THE LEGEND OF
OGDEN JENKS
ROBERT EMMITT

"A deeply imagined novel of western life in the last
century... one of the finds of the year."
—Ross Macdonald, *San Francisco Chronicle*

Above left: A letter from October 1970 to lawyer Bob Samsell: "It's thoughtful of you to offer to ask your doctor about my dog Brandy. I have talked it over with my wife and we have decided, however, to do nothing about it now. Brandy's condition has been stable for several years, after a bad period of a year or more. He has all the vision he needs for his appointed rounds, entirely with us, and can do all that doth become a dog. Actually he's become so murderous to other dogs that his loss of vision is a blessing ... My time is full these days catching up with a year's correspondence, and doing little jobs—a review of 'Ogden Jenks' for the S. F. Chronicle ..." Samsell helped Matt Bruccoli with California research for The O'Hara Concern: A Biography of John O'Hara *(Ken's copy of the proof is shown in Chapter Three). Above right: Photos of Ken and Maggie with Brandy, and Ken's blurb on the 1971 paperback edition of* The Legend of Ogden Jenks *by Robert Emmitt.*

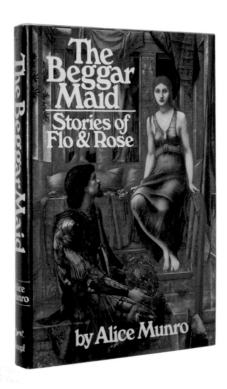

THE BEGGAR MAID

"Miss Munro is a writer of great imaginative power, deeply caught in life. She has a wonderful knowledge of our time, and the times just before our time. I think she is becoming, or has become, one of our tragicomic masters."

—Ross Macdonald

Above: Draft of a letter to Canadian short story writer Alice Munro from August 1977 and the US Knopf edition of The Beggar Maid *(1979) with Ken's blurb on the back panel of the dust jacket.* The Beggar Maid *was originally published in Canada in 1978 as* Who Do You Think You Are? *and won the 1978 Governor General's Award for Fiction, one of Canada's most prestigious literary prizes. From the letter: "The pleasure of receiving your note was followed almost immediately by a greater pleasure. A woman I know in Toronto, Beverly [sic] Slopen [then a book columnist for the* Toronto Star, *now a literary agent], without foreknowledge of my desire to read more of you, sent me your short stories that same week. I won't attempt to tell you how good I think they are, nor with what pressing interest and admiration I watched your memory-vision grow. You must know how original they are, because one of the elements is your pride and pleasure in doing something never done before—a deep and honest portrait of Ontario. I'm so glad that difficult place has at last produced an imagination strong and deep enough to submit to it then master it as you have. Congratulations from me and my long-dead grandmothers and their nineteen children, one of whom, my father, became a harbor pilot off Vancouver."*

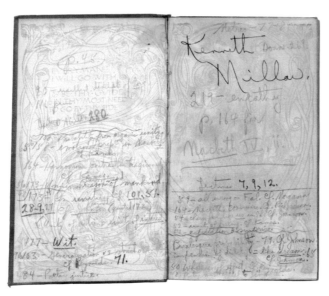
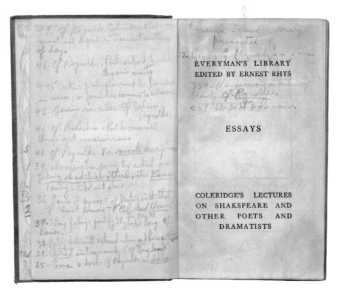

Above: Ken Millar's copy of the Everyman Library edition of Coleridge's Essays and Lectures on Shakspeare [sic] and Some Other Poets and Dramatists *(1919) with his unusually large ownership signature and copious annotations. Not surprisingly, this book is listed in the bibliography of Ken's Coleridge dissertation.*

The endpapers of Kenneth Millar/Ross Macdonald: A Checklist *(1971) from Gale Research Company, compiled by Matthew J. Bruccoli, featuring all of Ken Millar's published books up until that point. The photograph was taken by Bill Bridges, mentioned in Chapter Six.*

15. THE BOOKS

may 3, 1974

Alfred A. Knopf, Ashbel Green, and Ken Millar at Random House.

Alfred A. Knopf has published all of your novels since Blue City. How would you describe your editorial relationship with both Knopf and editor Ash Green? Have they improved your writing at all or taught you things?

The answer is no. What they've done is, so far as I can recall, caught fairly minor errors, that's all. There hasn't been any reconstruction of books or of me as a writer at all. It's all my own work.

There are all sorts of things that an editor can do: working closely with a blue pencil, providing a kind of wall to bounce ideas off of, or providing a psychological space purely because he wants you to write for him.

I don't think any of that process has actually gone into the making of any of my books. I just sit down and write. Of course, I send them in and they're subject to criticism and correction, but that has been of a minor nature. [W]hen I sent in *Blue City*, Alfred wrote back that he would publish it if I would rewrite the last chapter. So far as I can remember, as far as an editorial suggestion—of a major kind, as opposed to minor things, you know, words and sentences—that's the largest suggestion that was ever made to me. They've certainly helped me to *improve* certain books in what I would consider secondary ways. There hasn't been any rebuilding, nobody has ever rebuilt a book for me or with me. In fact, I couldn't work that way.

What do you mean by "secondary ways"?

Well, one makes errors in writing a book. You know, you misspell or something like that. In revising or rereading my books right after writing them, I've always found errors, and I just assume that I haven't found them all. Maybe there are some there that I should be bothered about, but I'm not. I don't think I make errors in diction—that is, using the wrong word—but I know occasionally, particularly in this last book, which was extremely complicated in detail, there were discrepancies between the details, and some of them had to be pointed out to me. One or two I found for myself *after* the book was in print. Nobody has pointed them out. There's one obvious error than anyone should be able to spot, but nobody really has.

It can't be that obvious or you would have spotted it also, right, when you were writing it?

No. After you've worked through a book several times, you get a little blasé, you know. You don't see errors and it's in front of you. Anyway, the answer is that, apart from minor editorial points, and so far as I can remember, everything that's in those books originated with me. They certainly did not originate with anybody else. I may have had some good suggestions on how to improve a structure occasionally, but it's so occasionally that I can't even remember an example. Generally, what we're talking about is minor errors and discrepancies which slip into a complex book, and some of them you just don't see yourself. I've always had very good editorial treatment, including catching errors, at Knopf. But still some of them persist. There are a couple of errors in the new book—which nobody has pointed out.

```
                              New York City
                              30 May 1976

Alfred A. Knopf, Inc.
201 East 50th Street        RE: The Blue Hammer, by Ross Macdonald
New York City  10022

Gentlemen:

I have seen no reviews of Ross Macdonald's latest Lew Archer story;
I suppose the official publication date has not arrived yet.  Very poss-
ibly, when the reviews do come out, you will hear from many sources
what I am going to say in this letter.

To indicate that I am writing from the viewpoint of a friendly follower
of Ross Macdonal, I add that I have read 24 of his books, and own 22 of
them.  What I have discovered in The Blue Hammer has disappointed me some-
what, even though I enjoyed the book.  Perhaps I should direct my
remarks to Macdonald himself, but you are closer, and surely, someone
at Knopf should have noted the little problems I am about to point out.

An error in the time sequence does not destroy a book -- such lapses
occur in Shakespeare, after all -- but Macdonald writes mysteries.  I
don't think it will do to say that a mystery writer may "rise above"
considerations of accuracy in his plotting.

The first problem is one of those little lapses The New Yorker satirizes
as "Our Forgetful Authors".  This one may appear there, but not because
I have sent it to them.

I believe The Blue Hammer's action covers five days.  The third day is
the trouble spot: on that day, Archer flies back from Arizona with
Doris Biemeyer and Fred Johnson.  When they arrive in Santa Teresa, Fred
is arrested.  Later that day, Archer looks for Betty Jo Siddon in her
office; it is just before 7:30PM (page 155.)  Then, on page 157:

    I walked down the block to the Tea Kettle's red neon sign
    and went in under it.  It was nearly eight o'clock . . . I re-
    membered that I hadn't eaten since morning.  I picked up a plate,
    had it filled with roast been and vegetables, and carried it to
    a table from which I could watch the whole place.

As in all of the Macdonald books, the action is continuous.  After a
conversation with Mrs. Brighton over dinner, Archer visits the Biemeyers,
observes the activity in the Chantry greenhouse, follows Rico to the pier,
captures him and takes him to Captain Mackendrick, pays additional visits
to the Johnsons, and then to Mrs. Chantry.  My estimate of the time required
for these activities suggests that we are now up to about midnight or
later, on page 203.  And here is where Macdonald slips:

    I passed a hamburger stand that reminded me that I hadn't
    eaten since breakfast.  I had a couple of hamburgers and some
    French fries.

After several more visits here and there, Archer arrives at Mackendrick's
```

Photocopies of Joseph Gisler's letter to Alfred A. Knopf, Inc. that prompted changes to the text of The Blue Hammer.

Would you care to point them out?

No, I'll let you find them for yourself.[1]

Which books of yours do you like best?

To me, the books I like are the ones that seem to me to represent a step in development, from of course a subjective point of view. I thought *The Ivory Grin*, after the first three [Lew Archer novels], was my first attempt to go into some slightly more psychologically realistic territory.[2] I thought *The Doomsters* was the next attempt to get in deeper.

I think quite well of *The Doomsters*. By comparison with all the books that preceded it, it seemed to me my most serious book up to that time. And it prepared the way for *The Galton Case*, which I consider the breakthrough book into my mature interests—or a more mature way of handling the interests, including the autobiographical. Also, what's very important in mystery writing, I thought *The Galton Case*, for the first time really, succeeded in inventing a plot form, a plot development, that matched the material in the book—or at least for a good deal of the book anyway. That's really from then on what I've been aiming at: trying in each book to find the form that expresses the material better.

I think The Galton Case has one of your best plots.

As I've made clear by now, I think, it's an autobiographical book. But my books are never literal autobiography, they're imaginative autobiography. Any one thing may or may not have happened, but the overriding central events of *Galton*—Notice that *Galton* has the first two letters as *Gatsby*, by the way?

No, I didn't. I did notice one thing: that a lot of the women characters' names in your books begin with the letter M. Mildred, Maude …

I call your attention to the fact that the first two letters of the name Mildred are also the first two letters of my surname.[3] I notice these things after the fact. This is done unconsciously, of course. I don't set out to do this as a plan. I leave clues like that all the time—not always consciously.[4]

---

1 On May 30, 1976—almost two months before this conversation took place—a New York high school teacher named Joseph Gisler wrote a three-page letter to Millar's publisher, Alfred A. Knopf, Inc., listing the errors he had spotted while reading *The Blue Hammer*. According to Ross Macdonald archivist and historian Jeff Wong, "Millar was known for airtight plotting, but I think the Alzheimer's was beginning to kick in." Knopf forwarded the letter to Millar, who replied to Gisler, thanking him for being such a good reader and asking if he would consider reading any of Millar's future books. "As a result of Gisler's letter," Wong says, "Millar altered the text to the novel. He wrote to Elizabeth M. Walter [his editor at Collins in the UK, where the book was about to be published in September], detailing the changes, keyed to the US text, he wanted to make to the book. These changes were incorporated into the first UK printing—but not until the fourth printing of the US Knopf edition. The 1977 Bantam paperback edition uses the new definitive text, as do all subsequent editions, as far as I can tell."

2 Warren Zevon told Millar: "Somebody gave us a copy of *The Ivory Grin* in Spain, and it had been read so many times the print had almost disappeared from the pages."

3 Actually it's the first three letters of his surname.

4 Jeff Wong, when asked to name a few additional clues that Millar planted in his books, replies: "There are so many layers to his books, you could do a book alone on 'clues.' Some are obvious and probably deliberate, others would be speculation and fall under his 'not always consciously.' *Mildred* and *Millicent* appear multiple times in the short stories and novels. *Hugh* was used and probably was a nod to his

That certainly doesn't mean that my wife, whose name is Margaret, is the model for my books. I'm putting this on the record. Certainly she's the woman that I know best. A really complete woman contains innumerable potential characters for a novelist. I've learned a great deal about women actually living with Margaret for nearly forty years.

I started to say something about the overriding events in *The Galton Case*. For example, the split between Canada and the United States, the crossing of the border, is sort of the central thing in *The Galton Case* for me. But none of the circumstances are autobiographical. I crossed the border to go on to graduate school, you see. But I know what crossing the border feels like, particularly when I was crossing the border really for the first time in a sense of rejoining the American life, where I had been brought up to think I belonged. See, I was a native American who spent many, many years in Canada and of course had the advantages Canadians have in some respects. I'm, let's say, culturally a Canadian more than I am an American. But I'm politically an American—and by choice. And that's the essential thing. I had dual citizenship. I could've been either. Ultimately and not too late I chose to be an American.

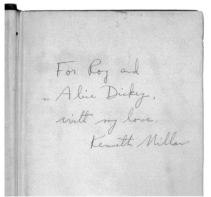

Knopf Blue City *warmly inscribed to Roy and Alice Dickey.*

You said there were advantages of being Canadian.

Yes. Canadians, for example, get better educations than Americans. We really do. See, I can say *we* about a Canadian education because that's where I was educated. Canadian high school education, in my time at least as both a student and a teacher in the system, was just about as good as anything in the world. And my friend Ford, whom I mentioned to you before was the Canadian ambassador to Moscow, he had been through both the Russian schools and the Canadian schools and of course schools in many other countries where he had been in the diplomatic service. He compared the Canadian and the Russian schools as being the best in the world and places where the students were really working hard.

I think there's a certain simplicity about Canadian life, at least when I grew up. But of course many of the important things were hidden and are only coming out now, and that's a disadvantage. Well, it's not a disadvantage for my kind of a writer perhaps, to have hidden forces always bubbling under the surface. On the whole it's good to have an intimate knowledge of two countries and even more. Perhaps not

friend, Hugh Kenner, or W. H. [Wystan Hugh] Auden. *Roy* was used more than once, possibly as a nod to Roy Dickey, the husband of Alice Dickey, who ran the Midwestern Writers Conference that Ken Millar attended in 1948. There's a character named Tony in *The Drowning Pool*, which is dedicated to Tony White (aka Anthony Boucher). Then there's Alexandria 'Sandy' Sebastian in *The Instant Enemy* and a Captain Mackendrick in *The Blue Hammer*, which in my mind are no doubt references to the director Alexander 'Sandy' Mackendrick, who worked on a Seven Arts movie project in the Sixties with Ken. In *The Galton Case*, which has some poetry tied into the plot, there's a character Culotti that might be a nod to Henri 'Hank' Coulette, whom a later book, *The Goodbye Look*, is dedicated to and whose poem provided the title for *The Blue Hammer*. Also in *The Instant Enemy* there's Henry Langston and Henry Langston Jr.—that's got to tie in with Coulette and Langston Hughes, no? There's got to be several *Annies*. At least one, Annie Meyer in *Find a Victim*, sounds like his mom's name: Annie Moyer. There's a Clarence Bassett in *The Barbarous Coast* whose name must be inspired by Millar's brother-in-law, Clarence Schlagel. There's a Dotty in *The Ferguson Affair* that is probably a nod to Clarence's wife, Margaret's sister Dorothy …" And, of course, right from the start, Lew Archer and Los Angeles shared the same initials.

too many, though. And when they're closely related, like Canada and the United States, it becomes even more interesting. So I always see the United States in a Canadian perspective, of course. That's probably one of the things that makes my books different from those of other American writers. I wouldn't be able to pick out the differences, though. It's more a matter of perspective and tone than anything else.

How about language?

Yes, language of course. The English language is somewhat more precisely used in Canada than it is in the United States. I'm just speaking generally. It's closer to the source and stays closer to the source. Precision itself is an advantage for a writer. At the same time, as you know, I jumped over the fence and chose to write what purports to be colloquial language. At least it's aerated by the colloquial to a certain extent and it relies on the colloquial being there. It's the undersong in a sense of the style.

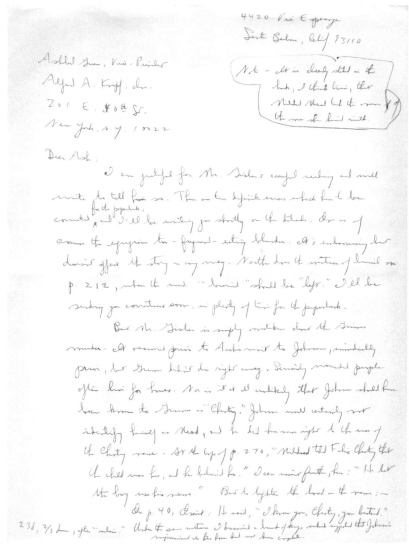

Draft of a letter to Ash Green in response to Joseph Gisler's letter. Millar wholeheartedly agrees with some of the mistakes that need to be fixed, but gets defensive with regard to the Grimes murder.

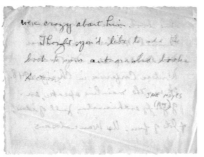

Wauwatosa, Wisconsin, native Jane Noyes was only fifteen when she attended the Midwestern Writers Conference in 1948 and got Ken Millar to sign her copy of The Three Roads.

That's really Archer's main function, to tell the stories in the proper language mix, which tries to combine, as I think all fiction writers in this society try to combine, the classical with the popular. Certainly, coming back to Fitzgerald again, that was what he accomplished supremely well in his best work.

In the introduction to Archer at Large, you write that the boy in The Galton Case and you "shared a sense of displacement, a feeling that, no matter where we were, we were on the alien side of some border." This sounds like a description also of a national problem. That's the way a lot of us feel.

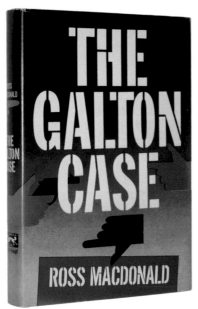

US Knopf The Galton Case *(1959) with a late Seventies period signature and a review copy with notes on the review slip in an unknown hand.*

Sure. It's more of an opportunity than it is a problem. Of course, a problem *is* an opportunity almost by definition: it's an opportunity to solve it itself or to be solved. A society without problems is a static society, which is probably in a state of decay.

One of the things that I found moving in The Galton Case was the way you had fashioned the plot with the boy coming from Canada as sort of a pauper. That you should come from your fifty houses in Canada and troubled childhood there and cross the border and indeed become a prince. It was a really nice, imaginative way to do it.

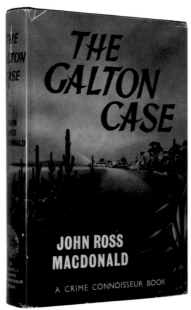

Yes. Well, it has to be true in a symbolic sense in order to come off. I'm sure it had to do with my entering into my estate as an American citizen. That's what carries the book. If you have a success of that sort, it's not really a success of plotting, it's a success of life itself. That is, the fact I made the transition and that it worked out is what caused the book to be able to work out, don't you think? For once, don't you think that it was almost the record of a mental action, however changed from the original? The terms were quite different. My life in Canada of course wasn't that bad, and the estate I entered into in the United States wasn't that good. But actually it was better.

You asked if I agreed "for once?" What did the "for once" mean?

For once I was writing what could be called autobiography at one remove. Ordinarily the autobiographical elements—I wouldn't call them hidden, because I put them there—but they're pretty well immersed. But this actually follows some of the main movements of my life. For once I was writing something that could be called autobiographical to the same degree perhaps that *Gatsby* is autobiographical. There's no doubt that it was, in my mind.

Was that a conscious act?

UK Cassell The Galton Case *(1960) and a UK edition inscribed to Tom and Mary Hyland.*

Sure. Just about everything I do, especially in structure, is conscious because I try out all the possibilities and make choices long before I start to write the book. Of course, other things occur to me as I go. I don't mean to say that everything in the books is conscious, but overt structure like that is certainly so. Of course, I'm not aware of all its echoes.

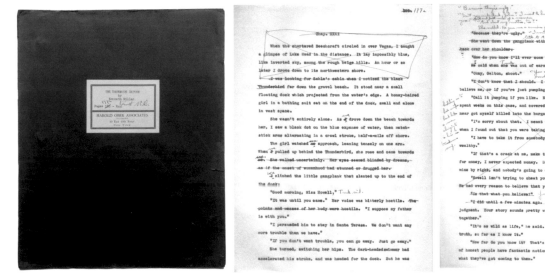
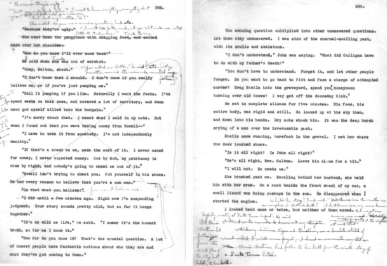

Corrected carbon typescript of an unpublished alternate final chapter of The Enormous Detour *(early working title of* The Galton Case*).*

You said that with each book you try "to find the form that expresses the material better." Can you explain that a little more in connection with The Galton Case?

I'm just talking about the individual form of each book over against the idea of just writing another mystery in the traditional mystery pattern. All these later books, starting with *The Galton Case* in 1959, they aim at combining the mystery form with a novelistic form also which expresses the specific material that they're dealing with. I thought *The Galton Case* was the first one that did that. You might put it another way: even if it weren't a mystery, the material would have a shape. Even without the mystery it has a developmental shape which can interest the mind by itself—as a novel should.

Then after that I thought *The Zebra-Striped Hearse* was the next step. A lot of people think that's my best book. I don't really have an opinion, but I think it worked. I think it's well-constructed. I take for granted some of the things that I value, like style and so on, but to me structure is the really difficult thing. It involves a great deal of mental effort to take this kind of material in its complexity and not just impose a structure on it but find the structure that's inherent in the material, and at the same time obey the rules of a mystery with your beginning in your first sentence and your conclusion in your last sentence. The serious novelist has a great deal more freedom. Obviously, I like to work within difficult and specific limitations.

What is The Zebra-Striped Hearse about?

Why don't you ask me a less general question?

What is the theme of The Zebra-Striped Hearse? Is that too specific a question?

Well, the story of *The Zebra-Striped Hearse* is constantly returning and recurring to the ambivalence of the central figure, the artist, and his relationships with other people. Of course, the theme changes as the story goes and the meaning changes as it goes, so you can't say the meaning of the story is what comes out at the end because the whole book carries the meaning. But it's about the powers and dangers of being an artist. There are many other themes, too.

You said you'd recently reread that book.

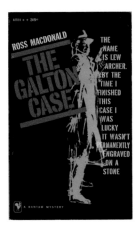

 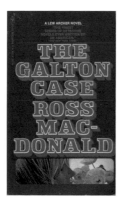  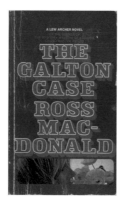   

It's so long since I've read it that I was interested to see how I did handle these things. I think it's one of my best books. It goes on a little too long and is perhaps a little overly complex, but on the whole it moves simply and sweetly. And it's moving, I hope. It's moving to me. Of course, it was just a lucky book, the book I had been working towards.

After that I had what I consider three good books in a row: *The Chill*, *Far Side of the Dollar*, and *Black Money*. But what set them up was *The Zebra-Striped Hearse*. I think *The Zebra-Striped Hearse* would probably be described as, well, my first book that really comes off in the various ways that I wanted a book to come off. Then it was followed by several other books that did, too.

I think my least favorite book of yours is probably The Drowning Pool. The pool seemed sort of a James Bond device that bothered me for some reason. It just seemed a more sensationalistic device than you'd ever used.

Of course, it was written a long time before Bond cut his teeth.[5] I should provide footnotes. [*laughs*] I don't carry any torch for it. You might say it was almost my first attempt in the Archer series—well, it was just the second in there—to do anything subjective at all. Of course, it didn't work too well. *But* it was a step ahead of the one that preceded it, *The Moving Target*. That's the only claim I make for it.

Oh, I quite agree that the whole business about the hydrotherapist is pretty hard to swallow. I made the mistake of drawing on life. It was based on a Santa Barbara hydrotherapist who had that kind of a room. Of course, it's not good at all. You're quite right, it's in the James Bond tradition. I learned to suffer for my sin there, too; they made that into a movie and they made that the central episode. I was sorry I did.[6]

I could never figure out why they moved the setting of The Drowning Pool to the South.

Well, they thought it would be easy, but it turned out to be very difficult. They thought they could do it just by having a couple of guys pretend to have Southern accents, and that wasn't enough. But from Hollywood everything looks easy, I guess.

The Far Side of the Dollar, The Underground Man, and The Chill are often mentioned as readers' favorites of your books.

Of the three I think *The Chill* is the best, don't you?

No. Of the three I think The Underground Man is the best.

I've also had it described to me as my worst book. It may be that a lot of people saw it on television and are responding to the television play or something like that.[7] Fortunately I don't have to make a choice.

I'm really surprised The Underground Man has as many detractors as you say it did. Sleeping Beauty I found has detractors. I haven't run into that many people who dislike the other one, though.

Well, I don't mean to say that there's a hue and cry after those particular books or anything like that. You get negative responses from some people. I think people have very, very positive or negative responses to the whole environmental movement.

I think The Underground Man may be another sort of breakthrough book in a way.

Oh, it was intended to be. It's a subject matter book, and it differs from all the other books in that respect. The obvious subject matter is a fire, which actually occurred and which is realistically shown. Then *Sleeping Beauty* is another one, of the same nature. They're both subject matter books.[8]

The fire in The Underground Man and the oil spill in Sleeping Beauty are natural metaphors. Which doesn't make them simply subject matter books, I wouldn't think.

All I meant to say was each one had a particular subject matter, which is not true of the others. I get the most varying reactions on those. Of course, environmentalism in general gets extremely varying reactions from people.

---

5 Ian Fleming published the first Bond book, *Casino Royale*, three years later, in 1953.
6 The 1975 film version of *The Drowning Pool* was Paul Newman's second appearance as private eye Lew Harper, the first being *Harper*, an adaptation of *The Moving Target*, in 1966. The studio, Warner Bros., was unwilling to pay Millar's $50,000 asking price for exclusive rights to Archer, which resulted in the character's name change.

7 A made-for-television movie of *The Underground Man*, starring a post-*Mission: Impossible* Peter Graves, also served as a pilot in 1974 for an Archer TV series that was never picked up. Another series, *Archer*, starring Brian Keith, debuted the following year, but only lasted six episodes.
8 A spark from an automobile exhaust pipe started the 1964 Coyote Fire, which raged for ten days in the Santa Barbara foothills and left 67,000 acres blackened. It killed one person, injured over 200, destroyed almost 100 homes, and inspired *The Underground Man*.

In 1969, an offshore blowout on Union Oil's platform A resulted in 80,000 to 100,000 barrels of crude oil spilling into the Santa Barbara Channel over a ten-day period. Inspiring Millar to write *Sleeping Beauty*, it still ranks as California's largest oil spill and the third largest in US waters.

  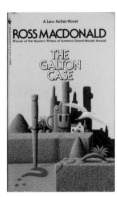   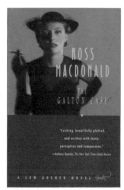 

Are they to be taken as a pair, those two books? **The Underground Man** ***and*** **Sleeping Beauty***?***

They certainly were written as a pair. You know, there's a hell of a lot more in the oil spill book than the oil spill, and there's a hell of a lot more in the fire book than the fire. In both cases I've done what I've always done: writing from life. A writer writes from his experiences, directly from his experiences, as well as from the deep past.

Was **The Underground Man** *a difficult book to write?*

No, it practically wrote itself. A very rapid novel, I wrote with ease. It really did go very fast. Of course it's not burdened by this enormous family structure that most of my books have to explore in order to come out at the other end. More of a book of action. The mystery plot is not particularly heavy or strong.

That seems to be a magical book in my opinion. The fire just seemed to be the absolutely perfect symbol.

Of course, I had the good fortune to experience the fire and not be burned by it. I think the little boy helped a good deal. He was drawn to some extent from my grandson who was some years younger then, of course.[9] It moves easily. I will say, it's not burdened by some of the other preoccupations that make the other books superior.

I think it's also logical that the second book should have possibly been less well received than the first because the fire was a brand-new thing and an almost perfect symbol, it seemed like.

Also, an oil spill was an awful lot harder to handle because it'd never been done in fiction, whereas there are fires all over in fiction.

This is a good place to talk about your concerns with the environment.

Where we're sitting. Yes, because it overlooks the ocean and is surrounded by a tree-planted area around the hotel and the club. Everything's natural here except what you can see that's man-made between here and the ocean: the pool and the deck and the diving tower. And, of course, the beach is interesting in its own way as regards birds. It has its own birdlife. So, where we're sitting, in my cabana overlooking the Pacific, it naturally brings up the subject of environment. In fact, the whole of Santa Barbara—you might say the whole of California—immediately involves you in environmental ideas and problems when you look around.

When the oil spill came in 1969, how big was it?

I flew along the coast for fifty miles and saw no area of unblackened beach in that distance. Of course, it originated a way out in the ocean, several miles out. It was caused by a complication of factors which released a lot of raw oil into the ocean. Essentially a break—a break in the ocean floor. The eruption wouldn't have occurred, or wouldn't have occurred with such intensity, unless there had been drilling done out here. However, we have had natural oil spills going back historically. So it wasn't anything new, it was just worse than it had been. Much, much worse.

How does one get rid of that?

Well, a lot of it just naturally dissipates over a long period of time. But in a case like this, which was so dangerous to birdlife and also repugnant to human life, it was necessary to clean it up, particularly down along the harbor where it was a ghastly mess. One of the techniques is to spread a lot of straw on the beach and rake it up and get rid of it and burn it, or get rid of it in some other way. But it's difficult. It's a nasty problem. It killed thousands and thousands of birds.

Also fish?

Yes. Birds were the worst victims, though, because they get a little oil and tar on their wing feathers and they're no longer able to fly. Also, raw oil is toxic. It kills them. It was a very sad sight around here for a while. The diving birds suffered particularly.

The first cleanup wasn't entirely effective and a lot of it was just left to time and the elements. Of course, right now if you walk on the beach today in your bare feet you'll pick up oil. The spill is a continuing thing on a smaller scale. Part of it is probably humanly caused by the tars out here and part of it is natural, like the traditional natural spills. Of course, I lived here for many years during the period

9 Millar's grandson, Jimmie Pagnusat, son of the late Linda Millar, was thirteen and spending the summer with his grandparents. He wandered in and out of a few of the interview sessions. Thirteen years later, in 1989, he died of a drug overdose.

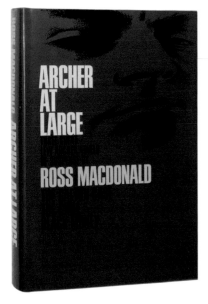

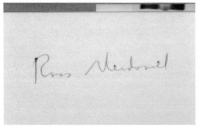

*Paul Nelson's signed copy
of* Archer at Large *(1970).*

of natural spills, before they put in the oil wells, and it wasn't anywhere near as serious at any time as it is now. The oil wells have made an enormous difference in the situation—and will continue to. They're dotted along up and down the coast. And many more are planned. They keep putting them in. They just put in off here within the last month the largest oil platform in the world. Nearly a thousand feet tall. Literally the largest in the world, it's right offshore here. It means that it will get worse rather than better. There just doesn't seem to be any way to do offshore drilling without spilling.

Is the community trying to stop further drilling? Or is that pretty impossible to do?

No, it's not impossible. Trouble is, the community is divided. The community, you see, also represents people who have financial and vocational interests in oil. Of course, people are honestly divided on the question of whether it's desirable to have these oil wells off here. Some of us feel that it's a misuse of this particular area. Others feel that oil is so necessary and in such short supply that we have to sacrifice everything, including our own environment. Including the place that we live. That seems to me a little crazy, morally a little turned around.

Do you think you have a chance to block further wells?

Well, we can slow them down. You know, our real hope—by "our" I mean environmentalists' real hope—would be to preserve at least some parts of the continent in a fairly unspoiled condition so that people can enjoy them. There's no really good reason, in our opinion, why all of the coastal United States should ultimately resemble New Jersey, which is a terrible mess. It looks like a real urban hell. It could happen here, too. I'm not exaggerating. You should take a look at some of the inland abandoned oilfields in California, within a very, very short drive from here. There are wastelands such as you wouldn't imagine human skill could produce. There's a lot of oil lying around in pools and a lot of the metal of the derricks and so on is still there. It's just a complete horrible mess.

Is California the state most concerned with looking out for the land and the future and the environment?

I don't think it would be fair to say that. California is the most obvious example because in a way it has the most to lose. It's got such a great variety of birdlife

and other advantageous environmental aspects, you know. It's got this wonderful ocean, which is so easily damaged and destroyed, as we've seen in other places. Also, of course, it's the most populous state. It's the state where environmental destruction affects the most people. And it's a forward-looking state, educationally advanced and culturally advanced, so that these things are more noticed and more talked about than they are in some of the other states. So there are various reasons why California is kind of the bellwether. In a way it's got the most to lose because it hasn't been destroyed the way the New Jersey coast has been. It's also got the most people who care.

Environment is becoming a major political issue. It will determine who gets elected in many places nowadays, particularly in California. Gradually [we will] realize that we only have the one world and that if we lose it it's gone. But from what we've seen of the surface of Mars in recent days, it's not

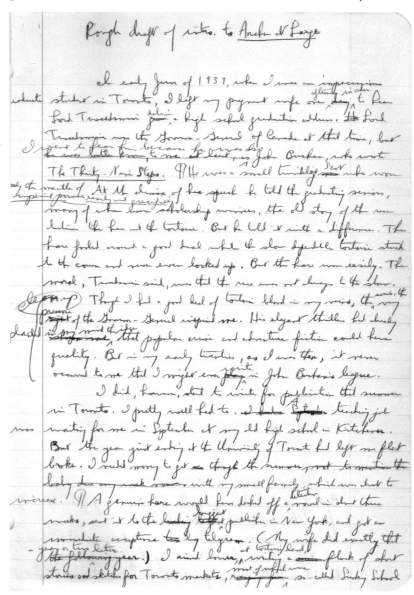

A rough draft of the introduction to Archer at Large.

a very promising place to transmigrate to if we wreck this world. I wouldn't choose to go and live on Mars. I'd rather stand and fight here.[10]

Is there an environmental organization you belong to?

I support various environmental groups, but I haven't been active in them as I was for a while.[11] I haven't been writing environmental material and that sort of thing as I did for a while because I have my own work to do. I did combine my work with the environmental movement in a couple of books…. Then I decided that it was a mistake to attempt to be an environmental novelist—or let's say primarily or distinctly an environmental novelist. The environment continues to play its part, of course, in my books.

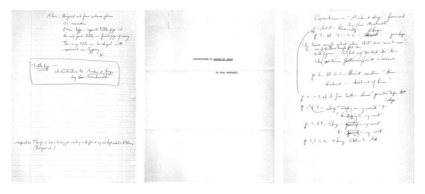

Note to Alice Kladnik (Millar's longtime typist) requesting the title page of the introduction be separate to allow for flexibility in case the title of the collection changed; the requested title page and a list of corrections to the manuscript.

You don't regard Sleeping Beauty **and** The Underground Man **successful as environmental novels?**

Oh sure. It's just that I didn't want to limit myself to environmental fiction. Having written two books in that field, I then went on to something else. I don't think a novelist should ever limit himself to a particular sociopolitical attitude or subject matter. I'm not in any way rejecting those books or regretting them. I'm glad I wrote them, and in fact they did carry the message around on a fairly wide scale.[12]

Did the plot of The Underground Man **always involve the fire?**

I don't think so. In fact, it couldn't have been. I worked on that plot for years off and on. In fact, I was working on the plot before the forest fire occurred—the forest fire that sort of pulled the whole thing together. I generally go back, when I start a new book, to a plot that I've been developing for years. I just open up the notebooks and go through them. Of course, obviously something like that

10 Viking 1 landed on Mars on July 20, 1976.
11 Kenneth and Margaret helped found the Santa Barbara chapter of the National Audubon Society.
12 Regarding how much influence *Sleeping Beauty* had, Robert Easton told Paul: "I really can't say how much I think it had politically, but I'm sure it added to the general impact that the oil spill and the books about it have had. Because it was on the bestseller list and received wide publicity, it was what Ken intended it to be partly: a blow in favor of the environment. I think it really was that. Not only just our environment but all environment; and to enhance environmental concern everywhere and perhaps reach a lot of people that weren't being reached by environmental books."

A draft of the introduction to Archer at Large *(1970) that has notations of the different residences in which the novels selected were written.*

forest fire, which was a recent event, didn't go back far, but the basic structure of the story did. The forest fire became the central symbol that pulled the old plot together. Really the thing chose me, I didn't choose it.

The fire almost burned my house down. That night, at the height of the fire, the city was about at least two-thirds ringed by fire. Most of it, of course, was fortunately in uninhabited areas. That's the basic reason why we don't allow building on the mountain slopes: the fire hazard. It got into the area behind the Riviera and burned some houses and threatened others. It was all started by a woman burning a little trash in her yard. I had been warned by the president of the local Audubon Society that a fire had started in our area. I was out swimming here and I could see the first smoke. It went on for better than a week. After that I moved to the far side of the highway, figuring that a mountain fire would never get across US 101.

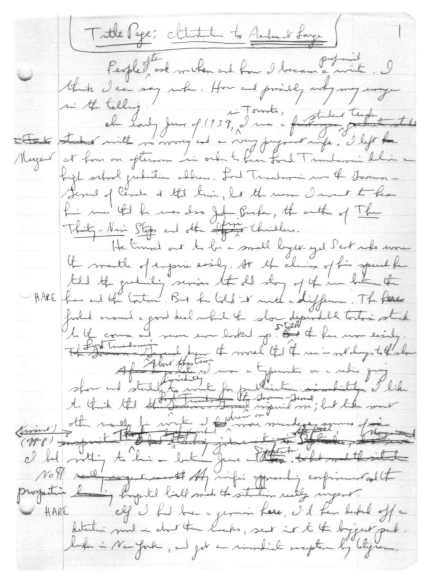

Another draft of the introduction to Archer at Large.

You got an oil spill on that side of it.

Yeah. I hadn't figured on that.

Of all the books you've written, which ones were the most difficult?

The most difficult to write? *The Doomsters* caused an effort. *The Galton Case* wasn't difficult in the same sense, but I did have to go back and rework the structure at some point in order to handle it properly. I wrote about that in that little essay ["Writing *The Galton Case*"]. The first time around I got tired and just sort of ended it before it reached its peak. I had to go back and reconstruct the ending. I gave it to a friend of mine to read and he told me that it wasn't complete. He was so right. That's the only time that ever happened. The only other difficult one was *The Blue Hammer*.

And it's one of your best, I think.

I didn't say that I thought it was one of the best.

Well, I get the feeling you like it.

Well, I managed to finish it. [*laughs*] I'm glad I finished it.

I think there might be a little correlation between books that were harder to do and books that were more successful.

Oh, I think it's a valid point. I mean, I think there has to be a struggle, and the more of a struggle, provided that you can conclude it successfully, the better. This is true not only of my books and detective stories in general but it's true of all fiction. *All* novels come out of a struggle. You can trace the struggle quite explicitly in some writers. Some writers who talk and write about what they're writing, they speak in these terms—of the struggle. It's particularly overt in crime fiction because there you have a naked struggle between good and evil.

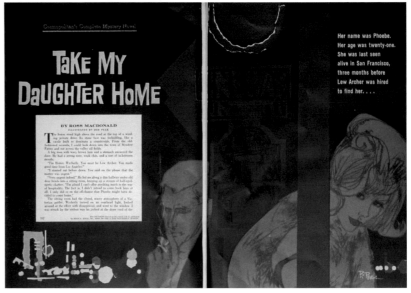

Condensed version of The Wycherly Woman
as Take My Daughter Home, *April 1961.*

The Wycherly Woman *is very unusual.*

I regarded that as taking a step, in the sense of the moral interest of the subject matter. I thought I got into more important moral material there than I had previously and also closer to *me*. But I didn't think the book was wholly successful. That should have been rewritten even.

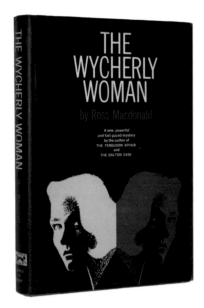

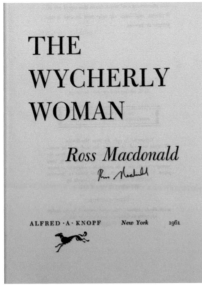

US Knopf edition of The Wycherly Woman *(1961)*
with a late Seventies signature.

The Chill is one of the books that you tend to talk about very fondly, as a favorite, particularly plot-wise.

Yes, well, I think it was just a very fortunate plot. I got the seed of it from life. It's simple and it has fairly important emotional and cultural reverberations, I think, and is strong.

It's based on something that actually happened.

I went through so many sea changes before I wrote it, and then before the book was finished, that it was actually only a fading resemblance. But of course there

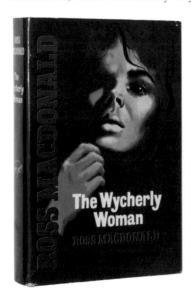

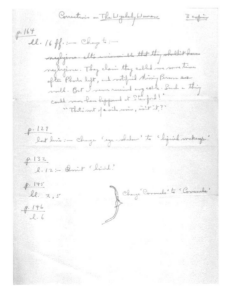

UK Collins edition of The Wycherly Woman *(1962) and a short list of corrections for the manuscript.*

was the basic structural resemblance. The essence of *The Chill* is a particular family structure, the particular structure of a marriage, to be exact. There was an imbalanced structure, and that was the source of the tragedy: a lack of balance in the structure of the marriage.

You once said that in real life it had a happier ending. In real life the couple got divorced and remarried other people.

I based it on an actual couple, both of whom are now dead. It wasn't a tragic ending. I wouldn't call it happy either. So I just got the basic idea from life. That's usually the case.

These are people that you knew.

Yeah, people I knew. The pattern of their relationship was something that I knew in other people.

German Scherz edition of The Wycherly Woman *(1964) about the size of a mass market paperback with a stiff paper dust jacket.*

You mentioned in one of your interviews that "There's no way I could have written The Chill except in terms of that complex plot. There's just no other way to tell the story."

Yes. But I wasn't talking about just the one central thing. I meant that the whole book formed a single structure which was interdependent within itself and formed a whole, according to my way of looking at it. Until I completed that whole, then the book wasn't there. Without the completion it wouldn't have existed as, well, a final book. It would've been a *try*. Follow-through is very important, I think, in this kind of writing. It involves a great deal of structural work. You actually explore the implications of what your material is and then find the means and the structure to carry all those implications. The verbal means and the structural means. You have to follow it all the way through. I think that's the rule that governs the novel, that you should pursue everything to its end and then tie it. But I probably learned that idea partly from practicing the detective form, you know.

That's very hard to do.

Yeah, but also, of course, it's work that tends to do itself in a sense. The mind is a naturally completing instrument, you know. It doesn't like to leave things unfinished or unexplored.[13]

13 In a different conversation, Millar told Paul: "You always have to assume that the mind knows what it's doing."

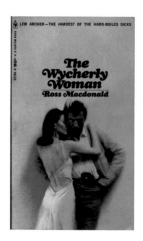

Don't you find that when you follow the implications they almost never stop?

That's right. Yet you have to do it. At least that's my method of working. You follow the implications right through to the end, the implications for all the people involved, as many as twenty people. When you get in a book as complex and with as many central characters as this latest, *The Blue Hammer*, you run out of steam almost before you run out of book. It's a demanding kind of work, you know, and it takes a long time to learn it and a long time to practice it. It *can* fill a life.

Was The Chill the first book where you felt that way about a plot in a mystery novel? That it was a personal story that you wanted to tell and there was no other way to tell it?

Yeah, I really think that's when those things came together most successfully. Or most successfully up to that time. The plot has a certain strength because of the various forces that go into it; you know, social, psychological and so on. Also, in some degree it's autobiographical.

In what ways?

It reflects what I've referred to before as one of the central structures of my life: the oedipal. I suppose the essence of that is my very strong relationship with my mother. You see, I was raised for the most part by my mother and other woman relatives. Then there are other aspects of the oedipal myth that seemed to me at the time to reflect my life in various ways. You know, the exile in return and that sort of thing. It's just a way to channel one's experience. It doesn't necessarily aim at detailed correspondences between one's life and legend, but the two aspects of experience support each other and they meld, they come together and fuse in fiction. The whole thing comes together in fiction. Words are so wonderfully malleable and suggestive. You take a whole lifetime of various kinds of experiences, including literary experiences, and put them all together in fictional statement which is so simple that young people can read it.

Is this sort of reworking out of your life very satisfying psychologically to you as well?

What do you mean by the reworking out of my life?

The autobiographical elements of your life that you use in fiction, what effect does this have on you as a person? Do you feel better when you do that?

Well, yes, because in a way it justifies what one has gone through. I think that's one of the prime motivations of writers, to make sense of the whole business and pass it on. Not just pass it on but make references backwards so it connects up with the history of other people and other writers, so that you join the human race as completely as possible. Isn't that one of our basic motivations, to become

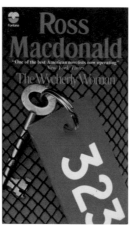

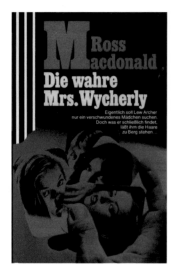 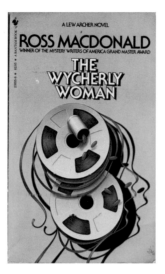  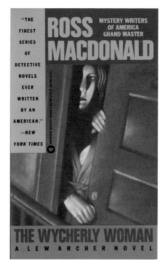 

a complete member of the human race and help to perpetuate it? That's going to take some doing, too, in my opinion. The human race is more gravely threatened than it has ever been.

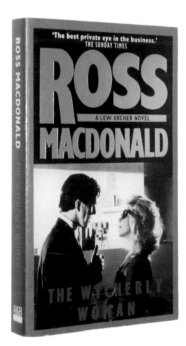

Something that recurs frequently in the books—in The Chill, *for instance*, and The Instant Enemy—*is the wife who is several years older than the husband. There are quite a few relationships like that in the novels. Is that an oedipal symbolism at all?*

I wouldn't call it a symbolism; it would be an oedipal actuality, and I am interested in that actuality.

What are the main themes of The Chill?

Well, the most obvious of course is the oedipal. It actually was a new way to handle the Oedipus theme, and quite different because in this case, in my handling of it, the criminal is the older woman involved. The Oedipus theme is one of the themes I've recurred to in a number of stories, books, and that seems to be my best handling of it. And I did it with a little help from reality.

What interests you about the wife who's ten, fifteen, twenty years older than the man?

I think my own nature is somewhat oedipal and I write out of it. Oedipal, and Freudian in other senses. The basic thing the writer does is to leave his own imprint. What's most desired of us is to leave that imprint as clear as possible and as unique as a signature.

You think that's one of your signatures?

It's one of the central things that I know about myself: my oedipal nature. I've often mentioned it in writing. I wouldn't go so far as to make myself emblematic of writers in general, but I see an awful lot of the same thing in other writers, too. I think my experience as a patient of good psychiatrists from time to time has made some of these things more available to me than they have been to some other writers of my generation. Although I think younger people are more self-aware than I was when I was young. I mean, the smart ones, the ones who are writing.

Draft of a letter from mid-February 1966 to film director Alexander "Sandy" Mackendrick regarding a Seven Arts film project that was to star George Segal. "I and my notebooks now are loaded with the ideas, multiple interesting ideas, for a great film play which I love. Let me write it, I think, Sandy." It appears that Millar was competing with a script by Seven Arts staff writer Francis Ford Coppola. Millar would write to Mackendrick and producer Stanley Rubin over the next several days complaining about the Coppola script, signing some of the letters as "Oedipus."

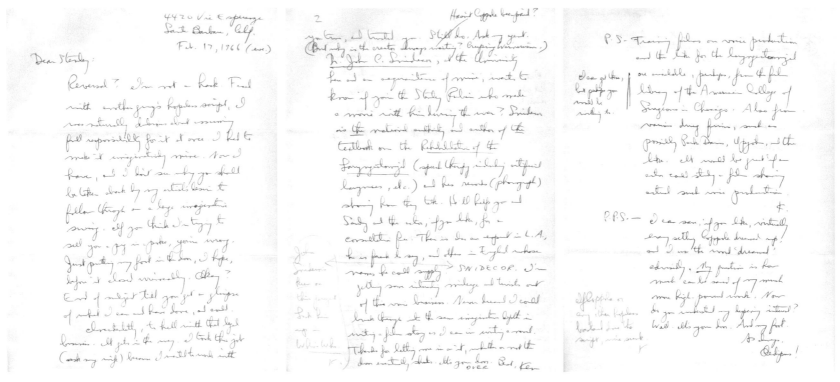

Draft of a letter from the evening of February 17, 1966, to Stanley Rubin that opens with "Reversal? I'm not a hack. Faced with another guy's hopeless script, I was naturally dubious about assuming full responsibility for it at once. I had to make it imaginatively mine." In his P. P. S. on the third page, Millar confidently tells Rubin: "I can save, if you like, virtually every setting Coppola dreamed up, and I use the word 'dreamed' advisedly." He has added a penciled note, "If Coppola or any other hopeless bastard does the script, we're sunk."

I'm not quite sure what the Oedipus complex actually means. Only in the broadest definition, but I'm certainly not talking about that.

You're not talking about what?

The Oedipus complex is that the son wants to have sex with the mother, right?

Oh no. Let's just put it in structural terms. I'm talking about the whole oedipal myth. Oedipus killed his father and married his mother, and those are the structural facts. That's what I'm talking about. In infinite variations you get that structure. You don't get it in its obvious sense. If, for example, a four-year-old boy no longer sees his father and spends all his time with his mother, he's living in an oedipal situation. Isn't that true? I think the variations are whatever an imaginative writer can make them and get readers to recognize themselves in.

What I value above all is a structure that is at the same time new and rather completely realized. In my terms, *The Chill* has a new structure. It's the Oedipus structure but with a difference: it's shaped by my own actual experience and knowledge of specific people, and it reflects in a kind of poetic way my own experience. When a fiction writer manages to combine what is a form of autobiography, so to speak—I'm speaking quite loosely—with a large classic theme and find an exact form for it that works, it's a happy accident. Those are some of the reasons why I like that book particularly. It's sort of what I was aiming at, a combination of the popular form and the psychological experience and the large cultural tradition behind the whole myth. They all meld into one thing. That's

truly what one aims at. That's what popular culture in general aims at, I think: to be both popular and culture.

Is the relationship of the couple in The Chill some sort of representation of the one between Raymond Chandler and his older wife?

I think probably that Chandler's life history has reinforced my understanding of my own. Let me hastily add that I am not married to an older wife. [*laughs*] We're talking about imaginative life and moral meanings. You see, this oedipal structure fits into *many* circumstances of life and *many* kinds of relationships. That's what I'm trying to say. Of course the most obvious example would be a situation like Chandler's where he marries a woman who actually *is* old enough to be his mother. That's an oedipal situation most obviously.

So did you have Chandler in mind at all when you wrote The Chill?

No. Naturally, obvious examples like that are useful in reinforcing one's understanding of what goes on. I don't pretend to understand Chandler, though. *But* if the Oedipus legend had not existed, it would have been necessary to invent it in order to explain Chandler, let's say.

Anyway, I go on inventing legends or variations on the old legends in the expectation that they'll *fit* various people and maybe the whole human race. It was Freud who regarded the oedipal myth as absolutely central. Among all my many masters, Freud is the leading one.

Was that true even before you went and saw a psychiatrist?

Oh sure. It was true from the age of twenty-one. When I first read him in quantity.

A William McPherson review in The Washington Post compared you with Nathaniel Hawthorne in that you're both obsessed with guilt and retribution.

Yeah, I saw it. I feel I'm being overpraised even to be mentioned in the same hemisphere. I'm afraid that's about the only substance there is in the comparison, although Hawthorne is a great admiration of mine and has been ever since I was a boy. I'm still reading him. He was the main influence or a central influence on Flannery O'Connor.

Could you talk about Black Money a little bit?

Well, it's been described, including by me, as "Gatsby South of the Border." It is a novel with the stronghold of the Gatsby myth running through it. As you've seen from what I've been telling you about my life, the Gatsby myth and the experience that went into it, Fitzgerald's own experience, is not so terribly different from my own experience. What I was trying to do was to extend my territory, which is also the territory of the American imagination, south of the border.

Were you consciously using Gatsby?

Oh sure, of course. *Gatsby* is my bible.

I was starting to tell you about my meager relationships with the people south of the border. They're really not so terribly meager if you live in a city like Santa Barbara, which was founded by the Spanish and of which thirty percent of the population is Spanish. You eventually come to know the Spanish and to value them. Something at least representing them has to come into your books, as it did for me in *The Ferguson Affair*, for example. There's quite a lot about our Spanish population in that. I think I carried this further in the book that we're talking about [*Black Money*].

One of the central insights I got into that south-of-the-border civilization came from the wife of a friend of mine who was a diplomat and married a Brazilian woman. In conversation she mentioned that every morning when she got up she read Descartes. Now, somebody who is oriented in that direction, that illuminates a whole civilization really. It indicates that, well, the cultivated people of Brazil live in France, so to speak, intellectually. They're French in the way that we're Anglo.

Anyway, I think that that single fact made it possible for me to sort of imagine myself into a south-of-the-border Gatsby, and I wrote about him. In a way it completed what I was trying to do in writing about California. Of course, it was considerably more of a book than that. It also deals with the role of the universities, which are just well known to me, of course. But most of all, I think, for

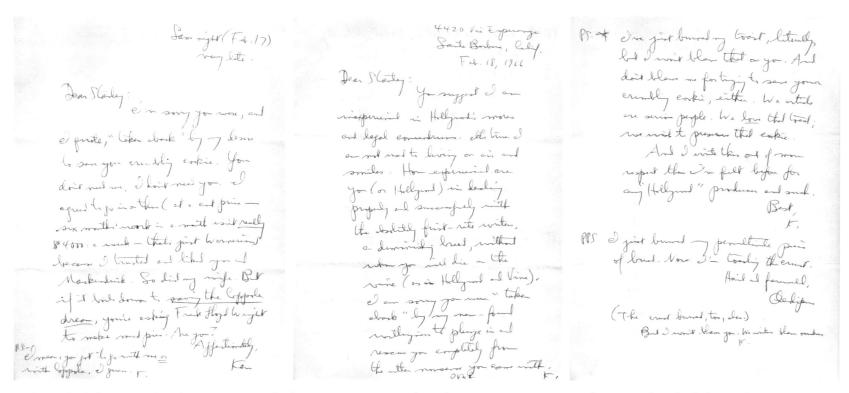

Left: Draft of a letter very late the same evening of February 17, 1966, to Stanley Rubin. "I'm sorry you were, and I quote 'taken aback' by my desire to save your crumbling cookie. You don't need me, I don't need you…. But if it boils down to saving the Coppola dream, you're asking Frank Lloyd Wright to make mud pies. Are you?" Middle and right: Draft to Rubin from the next day. "I've just burned my toast, literally, but I won't blame that on you. And don't blame me for trying to save your crumbling cookie, either. We artists are serious people. We love that toast; we wish to preserve that cookie…. I just burned my penultimate piece of bread. Now I'm toasting the crust. Hail and farewell, Oedipus. (The crust burned, too, alas.) But I won't blame you. We writers blame ourselves. K."

the first time I was able to get a peculiar semi-tragic atmosphere off of a kind of contemporary love affair, which was fated, not really tragic. I mean the love affair between the professor and the girl. I was the witness of a love affair which resembled it in some ways, had been privy to what went on, and while I'm not writing about actual people I tried to get the feeling of a fated and ultimately tragic contemporary love affair into my book. It became the center of the book.

It seems to me to be the broadest expression of whatever sensibility I have that I've written. Sensibility is something I value and I'm not always good at conveying. I felt the book came off in a kind of original way and had quite an original plot in spite of its broad comparability in *Gatsby*. Of course, it learned a lot from *Gatsby*, but there's more to it than that.

Could The Galton Case be called "Gatsby North of the Border"?

Yes, both the books owe a good deal to *Gatsby*. Both reflect my own experience and views, too. It's just that it's very difficult to write in the territory that *Gatsby* made Fitzgerald's own without following in his footsteps to some extent. For me *Gatsby* is the most important fictional breakthrough in the twentieth century in the United States. He made the breakthrough on behalf of all of us, of course, and we follow in his large footprints. Not all writers do, but I'm the kind of a writer who does follow in other writers' footprints to a considerable extent and then make of them what I can for myself.

The Ferguson Affair *came right on the heels of two breakthrough books,* The Doomsters *and* The Galton Case. *It was only your second non-Archer book since starting the series. Did you feel that Archer was somewhat used up at that time?*

No. Archer had hardly been used really. I suppose I wanted to try something a little different, and it meant a change in style, too. I just got the idea of this

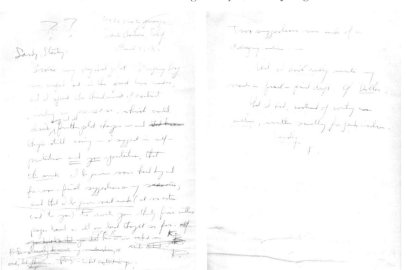

Draft of a letter from March 2, 1966, to Mackendrick and Rubin. Millar mentions the rejection of his plot, apparently based on his short story "Sleeping Dog," and that he be given a week to write "thirty-five outline pages based on all our best thought so far." He states that "Two suggestions were made of a damaging nature: that I don't really write my novels in first-final draft. cf. Dollar" and "that I had, instead of writing an outline, written something for publication." Hardly."

Draft of a letter from April 9, 1967, to Harris W. Seed that was not sent. Millar expresses concern about the "cessation or diminution of communications between us and Hollywood" and hopes that lawyer Robert Myers "will look into it this week" and also check on the status of The Chill *movie project.*

lawyer, and I think it came primarily from my knowing a young lawyer and going to trials and that sort of thing. The story just sort of came to me in that form. And now he's still my lawyer. He put together my movie deals. But he was just a young lawyer then, just out of law school.[14]

Is there some of him in Gunnarson, the character of the lawyer?

I think so. I don't remember him as being a very distinct character. I like the book. I think it's a good story.

I'll tell you one thing about writing about a new central character or a new narrator or whatever you want to call it: it frees you to introduce material that wouldn't be appropriate in the Archer cycle. I would say there's a freer treatment of the people in the town than you get in Archer. There seemed to me to be less exclusive control over what went into the book. It's a looser plot, too. It's not terribly loose, but it's looser.

You never felt the need to do another book with that character?

I never wrote another, not with him, but I did write one [*Meet Me at the Morgue*] about the probation officer. That, too, came out of my actual knowing a probation officer.

And you never wanted to do another book about him either?

No. That's an essential point about both these characters: they don't represent me in the sense that Archer does. Archer in a very broad sense is an autobiographical figure. That is, I haven't had his experiences, but if I had had I would have thought about them in the way that he does perhaps. You know what I mean: autobiographical in the broad sense. He sort of represents my view. These other guys do, too, but not to nearly the same extent. I wouldn't identify with them to the same extent. And they're in other professions than Archer. The specific thing about Archer is that he's a private detective. A lawyer and a probation officer are both servants of the community, pretty well controlled by the community. They're servants of the community in a broader sense, by training and what their job is. While this is true in the legal sense about private detectives, private detectives tend to be loners much more than lawyers do. Men who make their own decisions.

Would it be correct or incorrect to say that you consider the two non-Archer books entertainments in the way Greene considered some of his books entertainments and some of his books more serious?

14 Kenneth and Margaret met Harris W. Seed in 1951.

Well, I consider all my books to be entertainments. I really don't distinguish between entertainments and what you call "more serious" books, although I recognize that some of the books *are* more serious than others. *The Ferguson Affair*, being an effort in a slightly different direction, may not come off to the extent that some of the Archer books do, but the intent is serious. There are things in *The Ferguson Affair* that are very serious indeed for me, although I realize that the overall structure is not as "serious" as in some of the Archer books. As for the other book that you mentioned, was it *Meet Me at the Morgue*?

Yeah.

I don't think that's as good or important or serious a book as some of the others. I don't remember why I wrote it without Archer, but it may have been that I didn't feel the material was Archer material. I may have made a distinction between that and the other books deliberately. One does experiment, too, you know, with different personalities. There I have two different kinds of hero or two different kinds of central figure, and sometimes by taking a book off from your regular work you can expand the other work when you go back to it. I think that may have happened. I think *The Ferguson Affair* did introduce some new elements into my work. *The Ferguson Affair* has some new things in it, particularly the character of the mother and her relationship with her son. It seems to me that that gets into some psychological material that I hadn't done much with before that time. I haven't reread it for a while, I don't know.

At what point did your books move from stories to themes, if there was such a point?

I started right out with theme novels. Fairly obvious social and historical and moral themes, which became less obvious and more complex as I went on. *The Dark Tunnel* really did have a theme. It was, God knows, a simple and broad

Draft of a letter from November 29, 1967, to lawyer Tom Greene wishing to terminate the services of the Adams-Rosenberg agency, and retain Robert Myers, who "served us well initially, and seems to have become discouraged only under the influence of the televison-oriented agents." He adds: "I have no desire to toss Archer into the television series arena." A notation on the back reads: "draft of letter to Tom:—goodbye, agents!" Myers worked for game show advertiser Procter & Gamble in the 1930s and was an assistant general attorney for NBC in the 1940s.

enough theme. It had to do with the Nazis and the greatest kinds of political and moral threats that they presented. Also, the race problem came up particularly strongly in my second book [*Trouble Follows Me*]. I think in general my books tend to have themes, moral themes and psychological themes. The theme and the shape tend to come together and to remold each other. I generally seem to start a book with an idea; but if I think about it, the idea also has a shape … the essential shape of what happens. For example, in most of the books that I write there's at least one major reversal—that's a shape and it's also an event. It really combines shape, event, and idea, doesn't it? A real reversal. You can't distinguish really, you have to start talking in terms of actual stories and how they move and so on.

Why do you think reversals are such an important part of your plot armory?

I just think that's one of the basic bones in my inherited skeleton. By that I mean the basic structure of the detective story or the suspense story or the gothic tale in general. They all depend structurally on surprises, and that generally means some kind of reversal. A storyline is laid down and then it's turned back on itself and changed meaningfully.

Are there reversals in your own life?

My life has been a series of reversals. It certainly has. I'll say the reversals, like the waves in the sea, tend to propel me generally in the one direction.

Which is toward the light, I would think.

Whatever the direction is, it's a single direction. In other words, these reversals don't mean that one is bouncing back and forth in various directions. As in walking or running, which involves a lift and then a fall, the movement nevertheless proceeds in a single direction.

No, I wouldn't say that the movement is essentially one towards the light. Although the light is there, it's the atmosphere in which the movements occur. I don't think that it's simple enough so that the meaning can be isolated and simply called the light. The *light*, I repeat, is the medium in which good fiction occurs. It's what makes fiction possible. The whole purpose of fiction is to, in a way, celebrate its own increasing knowledge.

Are you in a way less or more personally involved in some books than you are in others?

Oh, I certainly have increased my capacity to get involved. Yes, my involvement is as deep as I can handle, and I can tell by the degree of difficulty how much the involvement is. You can't tell by looking at something really as you're writing it.

If I may change my image again, it's the kind of difficulty that uses you up for a moment, the same way that lifting the heaviest weights you can lift uses you up. I was just watching some weightlifting on television in the Olympics last night, and that's why the image comes up. Those guys, the weightlifters, do the ultimate, what's ultimate for them. That's what a fiction writer aims at, too. Although, of course, not in quite the same sense. But he does aim to lift as great a weight as he's capable of lifting.

Is that what you were doing in The Galton Case and The Doomsters, say, or was there a more personal stake in them?

Well, the personal stake is part of the weight that you're dealing with. But, of course, *weight* is not the proper image for degree of understanding; the correct image again is *light*.

It seems to me that you were grappling with issues at the time of those books where the fiction is about you ostensibly one way or the other for the first time or to a higher degree.

Yes, to a higher degree.

You were exorcising some demons at that point. Possibly you were not exorcising those demons later in fiction but struggling with some different kind of demon.

Exactly. What the thing is that you're struggling with reveals itself in structure and plot, and you learn how, so to speak, to *internalize* these problems, these forces, and these struggles in terms of the book that you're writing. It's at the same time a life movement, a development in your own life, and an artistic effort. It's both personal and quite impersonal. So's working out on the high bar.

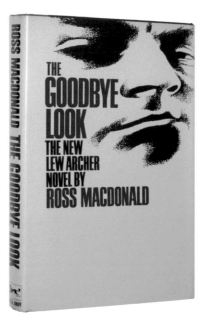
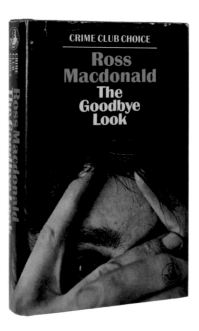

Left: First printing of the US Knopf edition of The Goodbye Look *(1969) in the correct dust jacket without the William Goldman blurb. The blurb appeared on the jackets of the second through eighth printings of the book. Right: UK Collins edition of* The Goodbye Look *(1969). Below: Fourth printing of US Knopf edition with the Goldman blurb, generically inscribed.*

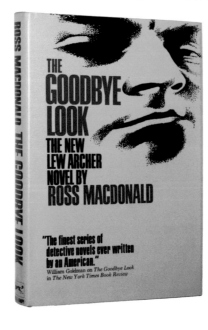
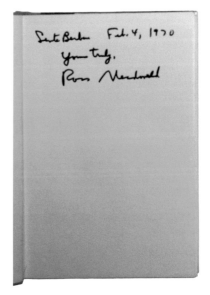

Draft of a letter from July 2, 1970, to lawyer Robert Myers, explaining that he has answered a letter from Myers through Harris Seed. Millar asks about his character, Reno detective Arnie Walters, who appears in The Chill. *"Can and should something done to reserve to me series rights to the Walters character, while recognizing that Warners have the right to use him in a movie?"*

It seems to me I read somewhere that you're only planning one more Archer novel. Is that true?

Well, of course, I often think about what I can do to finish out the series, but I haven't made up my mind as to what I'm going to do. I don't think it's finished now, although this last book could stand as an ending, if necessary. I spend about half my time—I mean half my whole time—making notes in prospect of future books. Among those notes, I have extensive notes for a concluding Archer novel. I'm a little dubious about the idea of sitting down to write a concluding anything based on elaborate notes. It seems to me these things should better happen than be planned too much. That's the way the books have come along, they've just sort of happened. They reflect my whatever you want to call it, my imaginative or emotional life at the time, and, with a time lag of a year or two, they reflect what's happening in the world, too, to a certain extent. You know, while they're not a chronicle, they're a contemporary series covering twenty-five years. God knows, the country changes, and the books do somewhat more slowly than the country. The country changes with breathtaking rapidity and the books change gradually, far in the wake of what's happening in real life.

Left: Rough draft (October 25, 1969) of a letter to Ash Green that was sent on October 27 concerning unpaid royalties for a year or two prior, for The Goodbye Look. *Millar indicated that he'd like to receive payment before the end of 1969 if possible. Right: Draft of a letter from July 18, 1970, to Ash Green that begins: "I'm delighted that you are pleased with* The Underground Man. *I'm too old at the genre, and have suffered too many disappointments, ever to count my chickens before they're hatched, but I think it may get me some readers. The nature of the action—fire and flight—brought much of its energy up to the surface and made the effects, I believe, more readily available to the ordinary reader than* Goodbye Look *did. While the latter was unquestionably my breakthrough book (as you predicted a year ago last spring) it was the series that broke through, don't you agree? Having said as much, I'm now inclined to write my first non-series book in ten years. But of that anon, very anon." He concludes: "I enclose an* Archer at Large *review." That non-series book never came to be.*

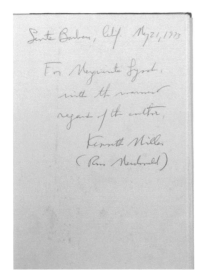
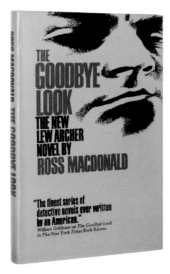
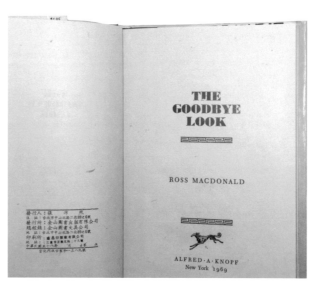
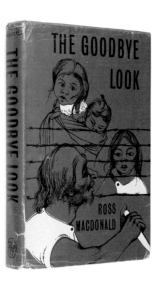

Left: Fourth printing of the US Knopf edition of The Goodbye Look *(1969) inscribed to friend of both Ken and Maggie, Marguerite Lynch. Middle: Taiwanese pirated edition of the second printing of the US Knopf edition with the Goldman blurb on the dust jacket and Chinese characters on the copyright page. Right: UK Thriller Book Club edition of* The Goodbye Look *from 1970 with completely different graphics than the trade edition. UK book club graphics seem to deviate from the trade edition designs more than their US counterparts.*

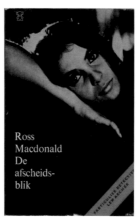

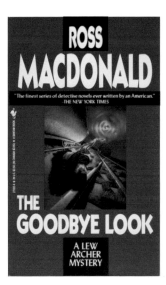
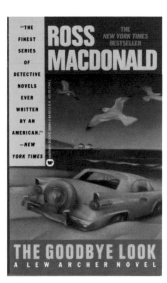

Norman Mailer said that one of the problems with the contemporary novelist was trying to keep up. By the time he had his book written and published, it was already out of date.

For him maybe. You don't have to keep up. There are enough readers, you know, who are behind you, let alone Mailer. What he's talking about is the difficulty of keeping up with his own interests in his writing. His most successful recent writing has been factual.

Any thoughts on any books we haven't mentioned?

The Goodbye Look I didn't set any particular store by when it was written, but it's had good responses from people. As for the last book [*The Blue Hammer*], I'm too close to it to really have an opinion. It cost me a lot of effort and it goes back a long way. If this is a progression, it doesn't belong in a progression, because I started it fourteen years ago and the full-phase plot actually goes back at least a decade. So it's a different kind of a book in a sense. It's not, so to speak, one of the annual books, it's more of a summing up perhaps of the last decade for me.

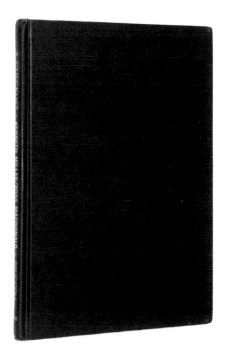

Corrected carbon typescript for the introduction to Kenneth Millar/Ross Macdonald: A Checklist *(1971) and first edition of the book.*

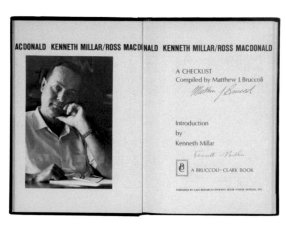
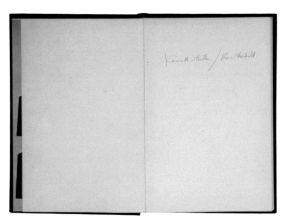

Above: Press release for Kenneth Millar/Ross Macdonald: A Checklist; a copy signed by both Matthew J. Bruccoli and Millar; a copy signed as both Millar and Macdonald (a scan of which was used for the limitation page of The Archer Files*); and a bookmark with a six-line poem by Millar and a facsimile signature in blue ink (often mistaken for a genuine signature) that came with some copies of the book. Below: Millar's invoice for five copies of the book from 1972; sports writer Al Abrams's copy inscribed by Millar in 1974; and poet Diane Wakoski's copy with her ownership signature on the left front pastedown. Wakoski contributed a poem to the Ross Macdonald tribute book* Inward Journey.

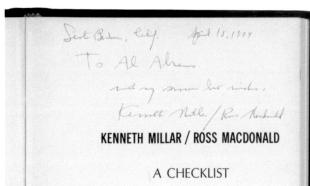
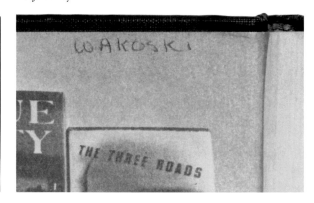

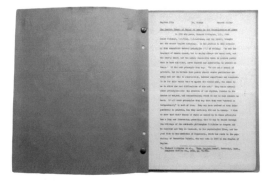

Page 12 of Kenneth Millar/Ross Macdonald: A Checklist *reproduces the opening page of Millar's 1938 term paper, "The Imagist Theory of Style," for Dr. C. D. Thorpe's class at the University of Michigan. Shown above is a carbon typescript of the paper and a thermal photocopy of the version in the book signed as both Millar and Macdonald in pen. Right: September 21, 1971, letter to Bill Bridges, who took the photograph for the endpapers of the book: "Your R. Macd. book should be along almost any time—I hope before I leave for France in two weeks. It was supposed to be published early this month, but there was a delay in binding. Anyway, what do you care, now that you've discovered John Macdonald, a much superior writer? (A great choice for a pseudonym, wasn't it, the same year John D. MacD. published his first book? His mother bought eight copies of mine, he claims.) Sorry for the long delay. Hope you like the design. There is, of course, no content."*

     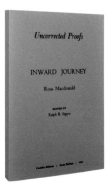 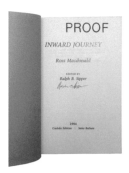

Above: Announcement, on the last page and inside back cover of Joseph the Provider: Catalogue Twenty-Six, *of the publication of Ralph Sipper's* Inward Journey *(1984) from Cordelia Editions. First version of the uncorrected proof in plain yellow wraps with a proof dust jacket with a plain white background; second version of the uncorrected proof in printed green wraps with a proof dust jacket with the blue background used for the trade edition signed by Ralph Sipper. According to him, the white background dust jacket is the only known existing example. Middle: Trade edition in dust jacket; Paul Nelson's contribution in the book; front and inside of a promotional mailer for* Inward Journey, *printed on the same paper stock as Ralph and Carol Sipper's* Kenneth Millar 1915–1983, *a hand sewn pamphlet from 1983; softcover edition published by Mysterious Press in 1987. Contributors included: Thomas Berger, Matthew J. Bruccoli, Jerome Charyn, Donald Davie, Robert Easton, William Goldman, Hugh Kenner, Richard Layman, Michael Z. Lewin, John D. MacDonald, David Madden, Margaret Millar, Paul Nelson, Robert B. Parker, Otto Penzler, Reynolds Price, George Sims, Ralph B. Sipper, Gilbert Sorrentino, Jerry Speir, Julian Symons, Diane Wakoski, Eudora Welty, Collin Wilcox, and Noel Young.*

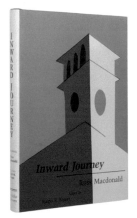   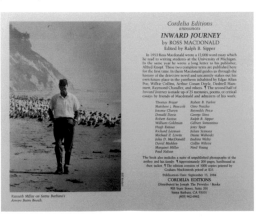 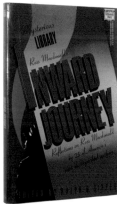

Below: Uncorrected proof—with photocopies of the images to be used and bearing the original title, Ross Macdonald/Kenneth Millar: The Poorhouse Prince—*of Matthew J. Bruccoli's Harcourt Brace Jovanovich biography,* Ross Macdonald *(1984); a hardcover trade edition (and review copy) signed by Bruccoli and Jill Krementz (who provided a number of photos for the volume); and art director Hal Siegel's copy with his mailing label clipped from the HBJ shipping carton. Siegel designed the Knopf dust jackets of the last three Archer novels,* The Underground Man, Sleeping Beauty, *and* The Blue Hammer.

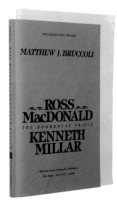  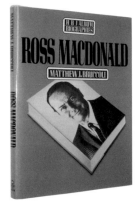  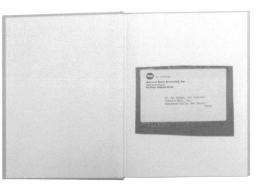

Above: Two letters that were sent by Ken Millar to the author of Little Big Man, *Thomas Berger, providing blurbs for* Sneaky People *and* Who Is Teddy Villanova?
Below left: Ken Millar's rough draft of his blurb for the first book. On March 6, 1975, Berger wrote a letter to Millar; he wondered whether there was anything more satisfying than receiving praise from a respected fellow author. He explained he'd been reading Ross Macdonald's novels for more than ten years and confessed that he wasn't really a fan of the plots, which often eluded him. What appealed to him was Millar's fiction and its humanity. On March 11, 1975, Millar replied: "No, nothing could be more gratifying, so you know the joyous effect your letter produced in me. The last thing we expect is to reach our contemporaries and peers, though I must add that I don't consider myself your peer. You are one of the great pioneers, and I read your new book with the kind of pleasure and satisfaction that seldom comes. It's a powerful and joyful book which took me by the hands and dipped me profoundly in the past, in the eden [sic] of that first rutting season." Millar continued: "I wrote a short statement praising your book as it deserves but then thought that my name might be a hindrance rather than a help. Not everyone is happy to see a detective story writer accepted as a regular kind of novelist. It is not considered good form for a detective story writer to fall seriously in love with his work. Still I'd like to praise your book as it deserves and enclose a short statement which you or your publisher are more than welcome to use as you wish. Your letter conveys the impression that you are willing to risk the association."

Thomas Berger is a master of the American vernacular language and experience. *Sneaky People* is a daringly outspoken and original sexual comedy set in the Middle West before the war. . . . At its heart is a tender and unsparing portrait of a home-grown harlot whose sins deserve to be remembered in our orisons along with the sins of that other saint of earthly love, Molly Bloom.   —Ross Macdonald

On March 20, 1975, Berger replied with a quote from James Boswell's Life of Johnson: *"I can by no means join in the censure bestowed by Johnson on his Lordship, whom he calls 'poor Lyttelton,' for returning thanks to the Critical Reviewers, for having 'kindly commended' his 'Dialogues of the Dead.' Such 'acknowledgements (says my friend) never can be proper, since they must be paid either for flattery or for justice.' In my opinion, the most upright man, who has been tried on a false accusation, may, when he is acquitted, make a bow to his jury. And when those, who are so much the arbiters of literary merit, as in a considerable degree to influence the publick opinion, review an authour's works, placido lumine, when I am afraid mankind in general are better pleased with severity, he may surely express a grateful sense of their civility." Berger concluded that Boswell had the better argument and that Millar was a very civil man. On March 30, 1977, Millar sent a letter to Berger apologizing for not doing anything for* Who Is Teddy Villanova? *He explained he got "bogged down in other problems," referring to Maggie having a lobe of a lung removed four weeks prior. He attached the blurb (top right) on the off chance Berger could use it even though the book had already been published.*

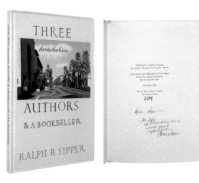

Above: Three Santa Barbara Authors & a Bookseller (1982), *a holiday keepsake for friends of Joseph the Provider Books with essays about Ross Macdonald, John Sanford, and Robert Easton, and a history of the rare book firm (signed by Ralph and Carol Sipper);* Kenneth Millar 1915–1983 (1983) *signed by Ralph Sipper;* The Faulkner Investigation (1985) *paired Ken's foreword to William Faulkner's story "The Hound," which originally appeared in the mystery anthology,* Murder by Experts, *with Eudora Welty's review of* Intruder in the Dust, *which originally appeared in* The Hudson Review, *signed by Sipper;* Larry Moskowitz: Man of Esprit (1986) *from Cordelia Editions, a keepsake celebrating the birthday of Moskowitz, childhood friend of Sipper and partner in Joseph the Provider Books (inscribed by Sipper and Moskowitz). The title comes from a Ken Millar inscription (in one of his novels, and according to Ralph Sipper "the only book that Larry owns which was inscribed to him by a writer"): "To Larry Moskowitz, a man of esprit."*

Middle: Ken Millar's copy of the uncorrected proof of Matthew J. Bruccoli's Ross Macdonald/Kenneth Millar: A Descriptive Bibliography (1982), *published by University of Pittsburgh Press with Bruccoli's letter to Ken bound in and inscribed on the title page; a binder containing a master proof set of the bibliography from the archive of John J. Walsdorf (Julian Symons's bibliographer); and a review copy of the published edition. Below: The first version of the uncorrected proof of Tom Nolan's Macdonald biography with the original subtitle intact; an inscribed copy of the second version with the sticker bearing the new subtitle on the cover and title page; the trade and softcover editions.*

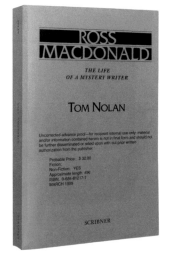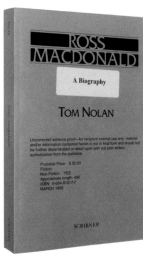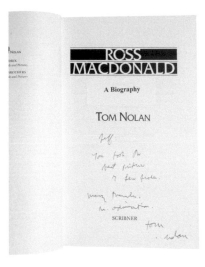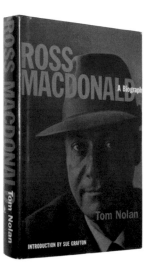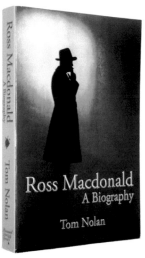

May 31, 1974

16. CHARACTERS

May 31. 1974   Jill Krementz

Do you ever start your books with only characters in mind? I know that in your notebooks sometimes you develop characters without any notion of who they're going to be.

Yeah, I never know completely what they're going to be or where they're going to go. Ideas come to me usually in the form of plot, quite simple plot ideas, but then as I work on them of course their latent factors emerge. The things that drew me to those ideas in the first place.

As the progression of novels goes on, do the latent factors tend to get more and more complex?

I suppose. They also become more explicit and not so latent. I suppose the whole thing is a long, long process of discovering what one's material is and then realizing it and doing everything that you can do with it. Period.

How do you tend to develop a character?

They generally start with a perception of some human being or some human characteristic. They just spring out unsought and unheralded. I suppose I've been granted four or five hundred characters, and there's no strain involved. They come when they're needed. I think that's one advantage of having lived in a great many places and known a great many people under different circumstances of life: the people are there in my memory. Some of them could be related to actual people, but the majority of them not. Although they would belong to classifications of people that I have known, but not actual people. Even when I write about something that has actually happened, the people are not the same as the people who took part in that in real life.

*Other than **The Chill**, did other novels come to you from real-life events?*

Well, I get plot ideas from various sources, including court cases.[1] From observation of other people's lives. Of course, a lot of these ideas are shaped by prior literary work by other people.

---

1 Kenneth and Margaret became a regular fixture at the Santa Barbara Courthouse, sitting in on criminal trials and getting to know the judges and lawyers. At the first murder trial Ken attended, a witness dropped dead from a heart attack after testifying.

May 31, 1974　　Jill Krementz

Do you have characters that keep coming back to you?

Yes, I think so, but I generally change their names and use them over again. Characters and their lives do recur in my books, with sometimes major and sometimes less important alterations. One of the things that runs through my books is a recurrence not of the same character but of a variation on the possibilities of a character that I've used before. My books are in many respects made up of further variations on themes that I've already touched on.

Do you have specific favorite characters, or at least a type of character, that you really feel drawn to?

I don't really have much of a reaction. You see, my relationship with my characters is not one of like or dislike, because I don't regard them as people. I regard them as characters in a story. In writing the story, of course, I'm not standing outside having feelings about the characters. I'm creating as I go.

You don't feel possessed by them every once in a while?

I don't really feel possessed by the characters, no. I feel that I possess them. Of course, I am possessed in the sense that I'm their mouthpiece. I suppose that's the traditional sense in which a person *can* be possessed. If you're possessed by a devil, the devil speaks through you. Isn't that what possession means in the old, diabolical sense?

I'm just wondering if sometimes the characters threaten to get away from you.

No, they threaten to fade out, which is the opposite of getting away from me. The danger would be that I lose my sense of a character rather than that he will take over too completely. You see, my work is so traditional—not only in the sense that I'm working in a tradition but that my training and preparation has been so traditional—that everything is almost too much under control in my books. Everything is controlled by the structure of the book really. But the structure of the book is created to a great extent by the sense of character. The sense of character is one of the basic drives, one of the basic energies, that makes the structure of a book.

I suppose sometimes a book will start with an inkling or a conception of a character and then I have to find out what the book about the character is. Generally, though, I don't start out with a character, I start out with an idea, which is generally a moral situation. And the characters arise from the idea, or let's say the idea takes shape in the characters. I don't regard the characters as *detached* from the material that they are possessed by or possess. It's the book that makes the meaning, and the characters are just notations which together form the book. They do represent energies of course, various kinds of imaginative energy going in different directions, and all that has to be orchestrated and unified. That's what really is so difficult: to get it all in a proper balance so that each of these energies represented by the twenty or so characters in a book gets its proper place, its proper presentation, and its final place in the structure.

You don't think this necessarily precludes creating memorable characters, though.

No, it's just that that isn't the way I see them. I don't give a hoot for a memorable character as such. What I care about is a memorable book.

I would think that it would be fairly impossible to create a memorable book without some memorable characters.

I suppose that's so. But I don't go at it directly through the idea of creating memorable characters. I never have. If memorable characters get created that's just a piece of good fortune—*or* because I've touched on something significant in my imaginative preparation for writing the book. Then that something significant is represented by a character or by a group of characters and their relationships. Not one of my books depends on a single central character in the way that we're talking about.

Yet I think Archer is a memorable character in a lot of them.

Yeah, but he's something different. He is also the voice of the books. If he weren't the voice of the books, he wouldn't be a particularly memorable character. We get to know him through what he says.

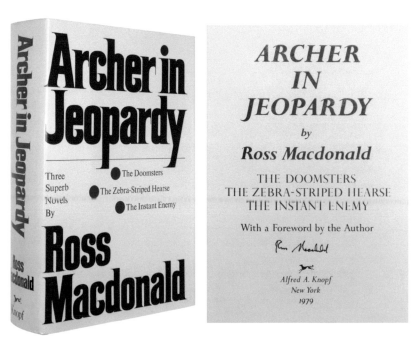

one of the main conflicts of the books. What we have, you see, throughout the structure of any one of my books is a conflict between the rawest forces of life and a very stringent, intellectual control.

Is that also true of your own life?

I suspect so. I wouldn't be surprised at all if it reflected my own life.

I was sort of surprised earlier when you said that you weren't too interested in memorable characters in your books.

The truth is, it's to me the most inexplicable part of writing.

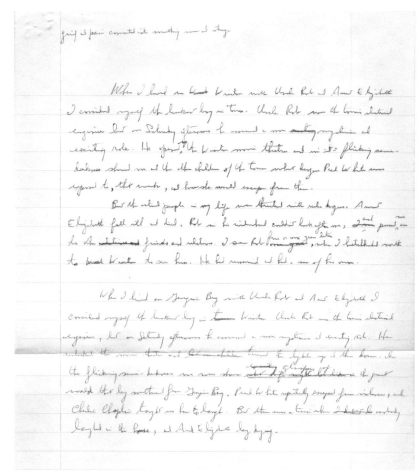

Manuscript for the introduction to Archer in Jeopardy *with two variations of a paragraph about Uncle Rob, Aunt Elizabeth, and Pearl White.*

Above left and right: Paul Nelson's signed review copy of Archer in Jeopardy.
Below left: Special advance review slip in Paul Nelson's copy.
Below right: A standard Knopf review slip.

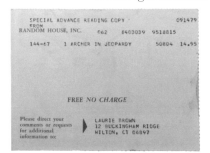 

In a sense that's saying that the books are not about the people, they're about ideas, isn't it?

It just means that that's the way I go at them. Of course they're about people. The approach, though, is by way of structure. I don't paint people directly from life as so many novelists do.

It's by way of intellect also, I would say.

Yes, it's a semi-intellectual approach. But, you see, symbol is the marriage of an intellectual idea with a more or less concrete image or character. What I do is symbolism. That's what I've been saying from the first.

You said that "everything is almost too much under control" in your books. Would it be possible for the books to become too much under control if you weren't aware of it?

Yes. That's the danger in the kind of semi-intellectual writing that I do. I suppose the various energies of my imagination are fighting against it all the time. That's

Because you don't know where they come from?

Well, I know where they come from. They come from experience. The characters are based on people that one has known or read about or whatever. All the various possible sources are valid sources. To me the business of writing a novel is not equivalent to inventing a character and putting him through his motions and then putting him to rest. In other words, for me the writing of a novel, the

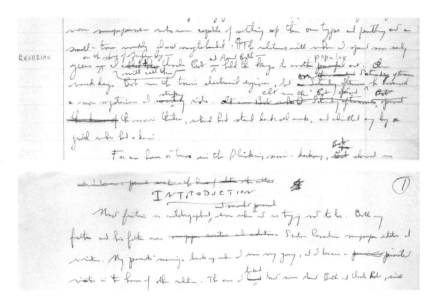

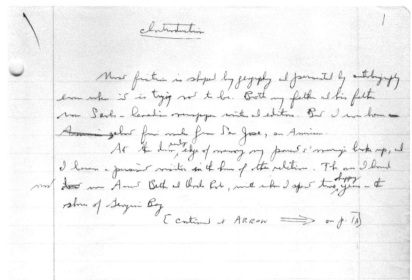

Details from two manuscripts for the introduction to Archer in Jeopardy *where Uncle Rob and Aunt Elizabeth are referred to as Uncle Bob and Aunt Beth.*

An older version of the introduction to Archer in Jeopardy.

substance of it is so inextricably made up of various elements—including characterization—that as I write I don't see myself, for example, as a painter who stands in front of a subject and paints that subject. The novel *is* the painter *and* the subject *and* the painted canvas *and* the room *and* the street outside *and* the person who is going to arrive in thirty-seven minutes from another planet. To me the controls of narrative include all the complexities of the controls of style and a lot more. Style is just one example of the complexities that a writer copes with as he writes, and character is another. I really don't think of these elements separately. I don't work at them separately. I'm not interested in characterization *as such*, standing by itself. I have no interest whatever in sitting down to describe a memorable character that I have known or haven't known.

But at the same time you do not want people in your books to be wooden stick figures or just symbols for something. Maybe I'm putting words into your mouth.

You sure are.

I assume you take a craftsman's pride in creating believable characters. The way it more or less came out was, "I don't care about characters," period, and I doubt whether that statement is true.

I don't care about character as an element considered in itself. I'm saying exactly the same thing really.

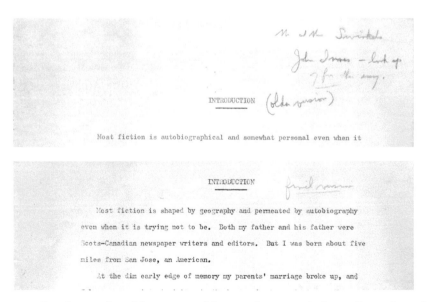

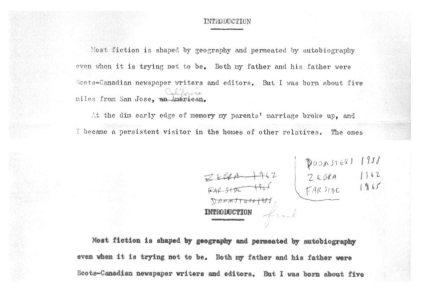

Typed copy of an older version of the introduction to Archer in Jeopardy, *and three copies of the final version with some minor changes and notes in pencil.*

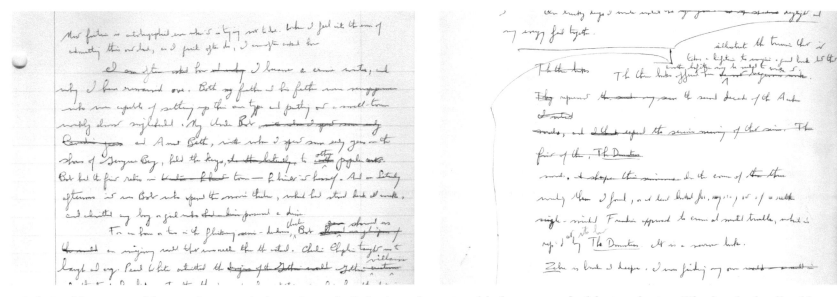

Left: An older version of the introduction to Archer in Jeopardy. *Right: An early version of the last paragraph of the introduction. "The three books offered here illustrate the truism that it takes a lifetime to imagine a good book but that another lifetime may be needed to write it."*

Well, it came out different last time.

Okay, but what was your question? What was your original question that I was responding to?

I don't know what the specific one was. I just wanted to talk about characterization more, on a broader level. More or less in the hope that you were more interested in character than you seemed to be initially, I guess.

You mean more interested in talking about it. We're just arguing about which end we're going to go at a subject. I don't think it's a good way to go at the subject, to look at character as a fictional element by itself. To me that isn't appropriate because fictional characters don't get created like that, apart from the structure of the book, the structure of the style. The style determines what kind of a character you can write about, you know. You can't write in a contemporary style about a character who belongs in a milieu or a culture that is a hundred years or two hundred years old. There's just no way to write it, though attempts have been made.

You want your characters to be believable without standing out. Is that a correct statement?

I just don't go at the business of writing from the standpoint of the creation of characters…. [I]t's part of the total act of making fiction, but it isn't something that I do consciously separately from telling a story. Just speaking from my own practices, it seems to me sort of an old-fashioned idea to get an idea for a good character and then find something for him to do in a story. It's always the story in a sense that calls for the character. Naturally the two of them come together. I always see the character that I'm writing about under the aspect of whatever story I'm telling. I'm afraid that the story is what determines what the character will do—not necessarily what he will *think* or what his motives may be—because that

has to be invented appropriately to fit in with the other elements in the story. I'm not one of those writers who gets an idea for a character and says, "Gee whiz, that will make a hell of a good story if I can only find the right story to tell it." I always start with the story idea or some kind of a perception that can be translated into storyline.

I think characters generally are interesting. Not so much for what they are, because we can only know that through what they do and what they say. So if what they say is interesting and what happens to them and the actions that they originate are interesting, the character tends to be interesting. I know there are much better writers than I who have concentrated on character portraits. Dickens is the supreme example of a man who undoubtedly painted from life and in many cases.

Is there a danger point at this, do you think?

The danger point of my approach is that of reducing everything to the same level in a sense. The danger point of Dickens is that the characters are more memorable than the stories in which they take part. This is true in some of Dickens's less successful books like *Oliver Twist*. You remember the characters, but what happens is not really very significant as fiction. It's significant, but it's not as significant as, say, *Great Expectations*, where the characters are subsumed in the fiction, in the story. Although, God knows, it's got great characters in it, too.

There is a tendency to a somewhat quieter approach to character in contemporary fiction. Another way of putting that would be that the author's voice becomes a character which in a sense speaks for all the others. Not exclusively, but the author's voice is always there kind of modulating and mediating among the characters.

In a first-person story that's almost literally true.

In a first-person story it's kind of unavoidable.

Original painting for the cover of The Archer Files *(2007) by Jeff Wong (after Mitchell Hooks's* The Name Is Archer *cover illustration).*

17. SHORT WORKS

A signed copy of Ed McBain's Mystery Book *featuring "Midnight Blue."*

You started out writing short stories.

All fiction writers start out writing short stories. I published some very short things in *Toronto Saturday Night*. I wrote all sorts of things for *Toronto Saturday Night* over a period of several years. It used to be a weekly, now it's a monthly. It's Canada's leading magazine. It's concerned with art, literature, politics. I used to review a lot of books for them. I started writing for them because I very much needed the money. Eventually I became an anonymous columnist in *Toronto Saturday Night* for several years.

Why an anonymous columnist?

Because the column wasn't all mine and the editor wanted to keep it anonymous so that he could make contributions to it and also assume more credit for it than he would have gotten if his contributions had been realized. But I was the main columnist. See, this is a column of short one- and two-sentence commentary. You know the sort of thing, one thing after another. The column was the most quoted column in Canada at that time. Of course, this was enormously important to me to have this outlet in *Saturday Night*.

This was in the early Forties?

I started writing it when I was teaching high school in Canada and I carried it on when I went down to the University of Michigan when I was in graduate school. Every Saturday afternoon I wrote that column. Started in the late Thirties and went on into the Forties. That was one of my main sources of support when I was in graduate school, though they didn't pay me much, I must say. Two dollars and a half a week. This was just my Saturday afternoons, but it explains why I never saw a University of Michigan football game; they were always on Saturday afternoon.

Also they published some short stories?

Yeah, and all sorts of things: book reviews and light stuff, poetry. There isn't anything of any particular interest or value. There's one very short story called "The Yellow Dusters" that I attach importance to. It's an important story for me because it's about myself and my mother. It was the first thing I wrote out of my own life.

Were some of the early Archer short stories in effect written for money, too?

I can't think of any other reason for writing. I don't regard myself as a particularly good short-story writer. All the stories were written to make a living. I realized that books were my strong point, so I didn't really spend too much time writing stories. I'm not primarily a story writer at all. I don't even get going in less than a hundred pages.

Do you think that's related to your emphasis and fascination with plot?

Probably. And I'm constitutionally long-winded. You can't do much with plot in a short story. And if you do, it makes not for a very good short story.

You don't seem to like some of your short fiction very well.

I don't think that any of my short mystery stories are first-rate. Maybe one or two of them are, I don't know. I think that since I wrote the stories I've learned quite a lot about writing. I have been a late developer, so they don't represent what I would call my mature view. On the other hand, I don't object to them. I wrote

Above: The June 1946 issue of Ellery Queen's Mystery Magazine *with the first appearance of "Find the Woman," a Joe Rogers story, later rewritten as a Lew Archer tale. Below: Ken's copy of* Best Detective Stories of the Year: 17th Annual Collection *(1962) with an Anthony Boucher review provided by Millar's clipping service; and Millar's erased notation that "Midnight Blue" appeared on pages 76–114 (its first book publication).*

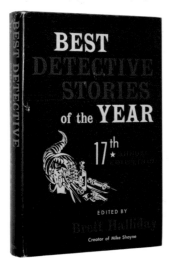 

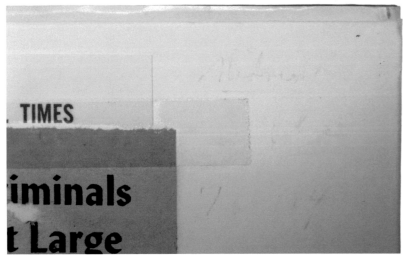

  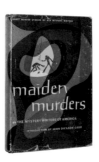 

Above: US edition of The Queen's Awards 1946 *with the first book appearance of "Find the Woman"; the UK edition (1948); US (1952) and UK (1953) editions of* Maiden Murders. *Below: The original typescript of the introduction to "Find the Woman," written especially for* Maiden Murders, *with Millar's contemporary printed name and signed at a later date.*

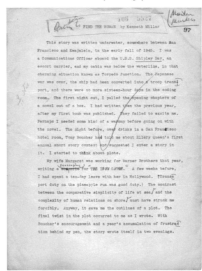 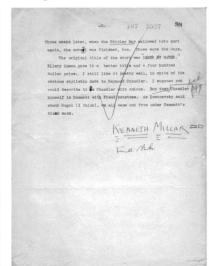

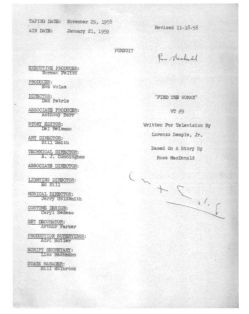 

Teleplay of "Find the Woman" (broadcast as "Epitaph for a Golden Girl," an episode of the 1958 show Pursuit*) written by Lorenzo Semple Jr. (signed by Semple and Millar); a note by producer Eva Wolas presenting the script to Millar.*

them and sold them and I'm glad I did. They got me started in the field. Most of those short stories were written very rapidly, under pressure and need for money. In fact, one of them was written right in the middle of a novel.

What story was that?

"Midnight Blue." Actually it's not the worst of the stories. [It] seems to work pretty well emotionally, but that's an exception.

I would think that would wreak havoc to both the story and the novel.

Well, it didn't. It just wreaked havoc with me. It's the sort of thing you shouldn't do. Actually, I was sort of conned into it in a way. I was in the closing pages of a novel [*The Wycherly Woman*] when *Ed McBain's Mystery* [*Book*], which was a new publication at that time [1960], called me up and asked me if I would write something for them. I said I might when I was finished with my book. Well, a short time after that I got an anguished further call from them saying that they had put me on the cover and left space in the book for me—this was their first number, I think—and I'd better write something fast. So I put my novel aside—as I said, I was in the closing chapters of a novel and pretty tired—and I wrote in four or five days this novelette "Midnight Blue" under considerable pressure. I still don't know how it turned out. I realized afterwards that I'd been put under pressure a little bit just to get a story out of me, but fortunately the story was there. It's an old trick.

Did you have anything, any notes of any kind or any seed of a plot?

No, I just wrote it from the ground up in one working week, then I went and finished my book. Usually, though, I give a good deal of thought to something before I write it, but this was right off the top. I don't care how a story gets written, I'm just glad that it gets written under whatever circumstances. I've only written not more than ten short stories that were published altogether.[1]

When you published your collection of Lew Archer short stories in 1955, The Name Is Archer, the story "Find the Woman" had originally been published with a detective other than Archer.

I just rewrote it as an Archer story in order to have enough Archer stories for a little collection.

1 He actually published thirteen: seven Lew Archer stories and six others, two of which were ultimately rewritten as Archer stories.

Archer originally wasn't in another one of the stories, "The Bearded Lady."

"The Bearded Lady" was a novelette written for *American Magazine*. They made me a good offer, I think it was $5,000, which I could ill afford [to turn down]. That was what I made in a year out of my books. I think that was what they offered me, so I wrote it. That paid for a lot of groceries. Then, some years later, Bantam Books took over my books, as you know, and they wanted to do something to start out with, so they asked me if I had enough stories to make a collection. Well, I did have enough stories. But they weren't all Archer stories, and the one that we're talking about, as you know, wasn't originally an Archer story. So I rewrote that, "The Bearded Lady," as an Archer story.

In their original form, was the character of the detective, Joe Rogers, quite a bit different from Archer?

I wouldn't say it was quite a bit different, but the original stories were, oh, closer to the run-of-the-mill storyline and style that you would get in those days in magazines. Before I put them all together in a book, I polished some of them. I think the character of the detective has been somewhat polished and sharpened. I certainly can say that my private detective short stories are not up in quality to my private detective novels. Page by page they're not up to the same quality.

I don't think Hammett's are either.

Oh, I don't think they are either. I think the short story demands different material and a different approach to your material. There's something too cut-and-dried about a mystery short story. Everything has to be done so rapidly, and there's more detail than you can justify in an imaginative way. I think that's maybe the basic problem: there isn't enough flesh to cover all those bones, structural bones, in the mystery short story.

In Chandler's case, several of his stories ended up as the bases for his novels, more or less. You've never done that.

No. I don't go back to material. I prefer to invent new material. Of course, it very often covers somewhat the same ground as the old material, but it's fresh. To me it would be extremely dull and boring to try to construct novels out of already existent material. Of course, I'm not saying that that isn't a valid way to do it, it just isn't the way that I choose to do it. Very often, by going back over material you can find new things in it, develop it. Of course, I return to themes, too, but not to something previously written as such.

You know, part of the pleasure and part of the reason for writing a novel is exploratory: find out what's going to come next and how you're going to handle it. It's really a lot more fun—and writing should be fun, however arduous. It's like gymnastics: it's arduous but fun.

"Midnight Blue" was written after The Name Is Archer. There's another one, too: "Sleeping Dog."[2]

I don't consider that a good story. That was written on assignment for *Sports Illustrated*. They decided they wanted a story from me but it had to have

2 When the stories collected in *The Name Is Archer* were reprinted in 1977 as *Lew Archer: Private Investigator*, "Midnight Blue" and "Sleeping Dog" were added.

sports in it, and I can't write that way. So it just turned into a bit of a muddle. It never appeared in *Sports Illustrated*. I think I sold it to *Argosy*.

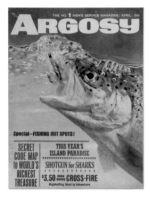 

You have a background in sports, though. Why did you have difficulty working that interest into a story?

Well, I just don't work that way. I start with an idea. I learned something from the effort. It's the first time I ever tried to do anything like that—and the last. I don't blame *Sports Illustrated*. Their intentions were honorable and friendly, and in fact I have written factual pieces for them. A couple of them. One was about the California condor and the other was about the Santa Barbara oil spill.[3]

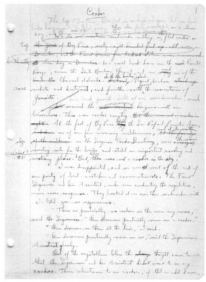

Manuscript for
"A Death Road for the Condor."

You also wrote a piece for The New York Times Magazine on the oil spill.

Yes, with Bob Easton.

Did you ask those magazines if you could write those pieces, or did they come to you?

They came to me. I never volunteer for that sort of thing.

I presume you found writing them different than writing fiction.

Yes, factual writing is much more difficult than fiction because everything you say has to be true. I spent months researching the oil spill. Easton spent years.

You've done quite a few reviews for The New York Times Book Review, haven't you?

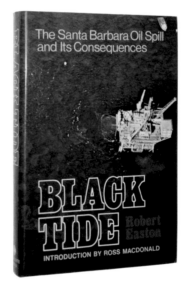 

Ken and Maggie's copy
of Black Tide *(1972) inscribed to them by Bob Easton.*

I guess half a dozen.[4] Reviewing takes, as you know, an awful lot of time. It just takes so much time that you can hardly afford it if you're writing a book at the same time. You can't take a week off and write a review, but that's what you would have to do if you wanted to go on and write. At least that's true of me; I may be a slower worker than some. And that kind of writing, of course, is more

3 "A Death Road for the Condor" appeared in the April 6, 1964, issue, while "Life with the Blob" was published in the April 21, 1969, issue. In addition to a piece that he cowrote with Robert Easton for *The New York Times Magazine* about the oil spill, "Santa Barbarans Cite an 11th Commandment: 'Thou Shalt Not Abuse the Earth,'" (October 12, 1969), Millar also wrote the introduction to Easton's 1972 book, *Black Tide: The Santa Barbara Oil Spill and Its Consequences*.

4 Millar wrote five.

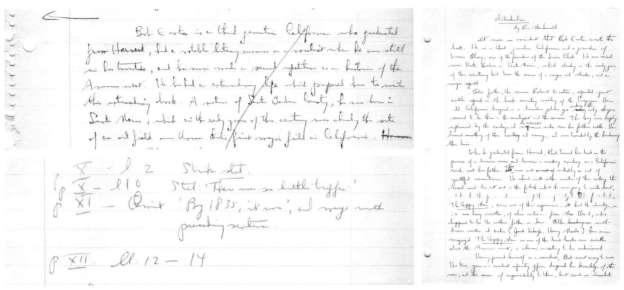

Manuscript material related to the Black Tide *introduction: a description of Bob Easton; a list of corrections; an early version; a corrected typescript; corrected carbon typescript of an early version; and the corrected original ribbon copy.*

Well, apart from the couple of essays that were published by Capra Press a couple of years ago, I don't think I've written enough critical material of a high enough quality to warrant a collection.[5] Unless it were to be just the kind of collection that exists because it's attached to a reputation in another field, you know what I mean? In which case it would be more or less of a special collector's item, that sort of stuff. That's the probability, I should think. A leading editor in the field, Otto Penzler, has already suggested the possibility. If he doesn't go ahead with it, maybe I'll do something about it myself.[6] There's a market now for that sort of thing, I notice. There didn't used to be. There's a general interest in mystery writing and mystery writers and in criticism in the field. Not that my reviews are limited to mystery fiction—most of them aren't. Most of them aren't about fiction at all, in fact.

I don't mean to downgrade my reviews, but most of them were written for newspapers and I wrote them just for the love of it. I wasn't paid for most of them. I have written a few reviews that I am proud of and that I would like to see preserved. One is my review of James M. Cain, which was really a general essay on his work. That was in *The New York Times Book Review* a few years ago. But for the most part, I wasn't ready particularly—even in the field of literature, which is my field.

I did this for fun, incidentally—I wasn't paid for it—over a period of several years. I was reviewing books for the *San Francisco Chronicle* merely because I wanted to do it. I wanted to learn my craft in all its phases, and I did, so when I had opportunities to review elsewhere I was ready. Bill Hogan, the editor of the book page, sent me books of all kinds. Books on psychiatry, for example, and books having to do with the history of literature, biography, all sorts of things, which I really loved doing. I worked on my own stuff all day and then turned to somebody else's work at night.

I've done half a dozen reviews for the *Times* that I put my best work into. Obviously, the ones I did for the *Chronicle* you'd expect to be up and down. I mean, some of them are good and some aren't, depending on how hard I had worked

difficult than writing fiction if you're a fiction writer. To get a review right is tougher really than getting a story right—I say if you're a fiction writer. When you go back to it, you have to learn it all over again.

I would much rather be a fiction writer than a reviewer, I think. It's not easy to be a good reviewer.

When I was speaking about reviewing, I was just thinking about my own relationship to reviewing, not yours, because I was bent on becoming a fiction writer. I didn't want to become basically a reviewer, although that's what my training was: literary criticism.

Would you ever consider publishing a book of some of the book reviews and essays you've written?

5 In 1973, Capra published "The Writer as Detective Hero" together with "Writing *The Galton Case*" as a chapbook, *On Crime Writing*.
6 Though that particular project never came to pass with Penzler, he did include Millar's essay "Lew Archer" in the 1978 book he edited, *The Great Detectives: The World's Most Celebrated Sleuths Unmasked by Their Authors*. In 1979, Lord John Press published Millar's book reviews as *A Collection of Reviews*.

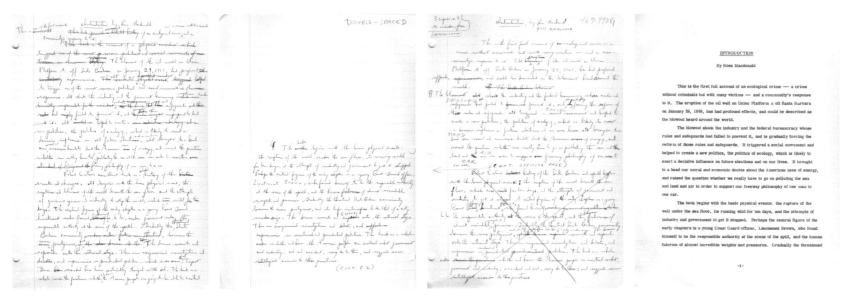

Above: Working manuscript for the final version of the Black Tide *introduction; revised draft with insertion page (see arrow); and carbon typescript of the final.*
Below left: A contract from May 21, 1976, reverting rights to the introduction to Ken Millar.

that day. I really did it as the exercise of a function that I value: the critical function. If you have it you should keep it alive. That's why I did it, and I wanted to learn how to do it properly. So, as it turned out, when the *Times* asked me to do Cain, I had some background as a reviewer. As you know better than I do, it takes a lot of practice to write that sort of thing.

I think it's real hard.

It's as hard as any kind of writing that there is. Line by line it's harder to write than fiction. I've done a lot of both and I certainly find the fiction writing easier than the factual. You can't get anything going that carries you along. It has to be minutely constructed, line by line. And, you know, fiction comes to you in whole pages at a time when you're going good. It just costs *enormous* effort to write critical prose. When you want to get something right, you have to write it six times. That's how many times I wrote my introduction to the suspense anthology. Not that it's any great prose, but it had to be right.

Getting back to your short fiction, were you thinking about The Snows of Kilimanjaro at all when you wrote the story about your father, "The Sky Hook," which appeared in The American Mercury in 1948?

I wasn't thinking about anything. That really wasn't about my father except in a sense. It did reflect my father's experience, but it was actually about another man who had the same illness, a stroke, and somewhat the same background in the Northwest. It was about a neighbor of mine in Santa Barbara who has since died. While I imagined his death, I imagined it in terms of his life. He actually had crossed the Great Pass. He had been in the Yukon in the gold rush days, you see. So it really wasn't fantasy, it was a remembering and a reenactment of his life.

Where was the Great Pass?

The Yukon. I think it was called the Chilkoot Pass. Anyway, it was the pass you had to cross in order to get into the gold country. And he had done it, he had walked up. I forget his name, but he lived just down the street from me on Bath Street and I got to know him well.

He was alive when you wrote the story?

I don't think so, but I can't remember. It's thirty years since I wrote it. I don't remember it very well. I just remember the ending. Also, a lot of my feeling about my father and his death went into it because my father, while he didn't cross the Chilkoot Pass, was a Northwest adventurer, so to speak.

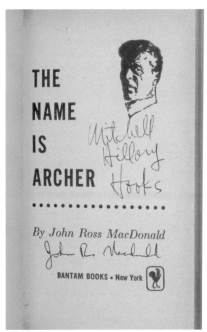
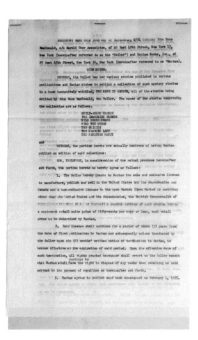

Above: The US Bantam short story collection, The Name Is Archer *(1955), signed by Ken Millar and cover artist Mitchell Hooks (using his middle name to match the John Ross Macdonald signature). This is almost certainly the only copy of this book signed by both the author and artist.*
Below: Ken's 1954 contract for The Name Is Archer, *mislabeled* His Name Is Archer *on the blue cover sheet.*

Left: First page of Millar's 1954 contract for The Name Is Archer, *listing the seven short stories to be included in the collection. Right: The UK edition, which wasn't published until 1976.*

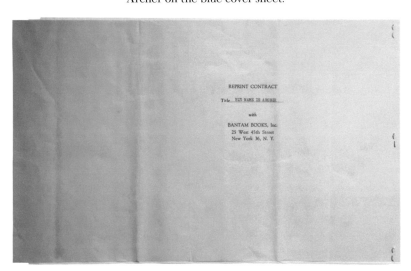

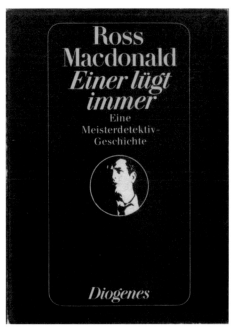

The separate 1983 German edition of the Lew Archer short story "The Suicide," published as a miniature book (shown close to actual size) and featuring a graphic of Paul Newman from the 1966 film Harper *(a.k.a.* The Moving Target *in most countries other than the US).*

I think it's a really good story. The ending is very moving.

Crossing the Great Pass to the promised land. And validating his life. It has religious meaning, too. Not for *me*, but for *him*. The Great Pass is also, you know, a passage into heaven or at least into another world. The skyhook is a piece of Western mythological, oh, let's say folk poetry. I didn't invent the idea of the skyhook. It exists in the corporate consciousness in the West. People refer to it.[7]

7 In folklore, a skyhook is exactly that: a hook suspended from the sky.

The ending sort of reminded me of Kilimanjaro.

Yes, it may well have been influenced by that. I imagine Hemingway was an influence on everything I wrote as I was becoming a writer. I think Hemingway was an all-pervasive influence on my generation of writers, particularly a stylistic influence. You must remember, too, as regards subject matter, it was Hemingway who really broke open what we call the hard-boiled crime story for literature. He was our first literary writer really to write the hard-boiled crime story.

Do you think this was the best short story you wrote?

Yeah, I think probably. I'm not a short-story writer.

It's a pretty good one.

You can't make a short-story writer out of one story. I never

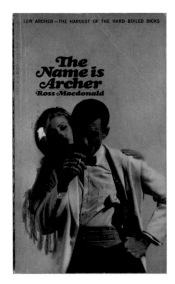
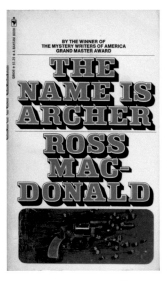

Below left: August 1967 issue of Adventure *that published the story "Sleeping Dog" as "One Brunette for Murder."*
Below right: 1982 Editions Campus omnibus of Thriller *that collects issues 1, 2, and 3 of* Thriller *and reprints "Sleeping Dog" (from issue 3) with an introduction that mentions the story being commissioned by* Sports Illustrated *but running in* Argosy.

really wanted to be a short-story writer particularly. Obviously. I've had lots of opportunity to write them if I'd wanted to. But it's the novel, the mystery novel in particular, that really has involved me all my life. See, I saw an opportunity to do something with the form that hadn't been done, and I keep seeing those opportunities. However correctly, it just seems to me that there was work to be done there.

But really on the whole I'm just delighted to have found a form that I could work in and at the same time make a living in. To do the two things at once is almost a miracle when you consider the background. I also have an idea that it's good for a writer to make a living out of his work and to write for publication, at least for the kind of writer that I want to be. You bet everything you have on the one thing. I think it's good for a man to do that. Bet your life on it.

Do you think it's good if you don't make it?

Well, if you're not going to make it, you can find out early enough to change your tactics, or hold enough back to be able to make a second bet.

Did you ever consider that it might have been the wrong choice at any time in your career?

You see, I've tried out the different choices. I tried out high school teaching, which I did with pleasure and successfully but didn't want to stay in, then I tried college teaching combined with scholarship. And scholarship was engrossing to me, but it didn't wholly satisfy my mind or my imagination. So ultimately I went right on to become a full-time fiction writer.

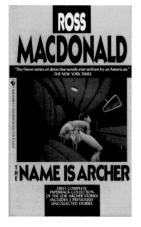

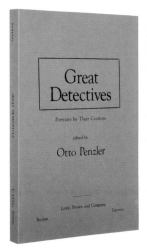
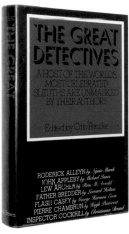
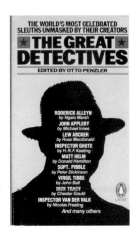

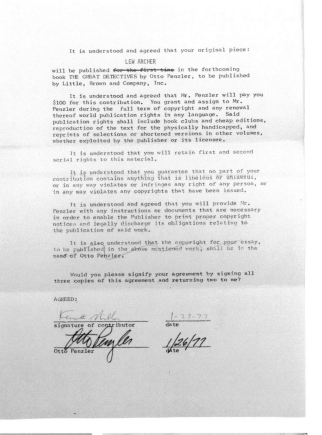

Above: The uncorrected proof and trade edition of The Great Detectives *(1978), edited by Otto Penzler, that reprints the introduction from* Lew Archer: Private Investigator *(1977); the 1979 Penguin paperback edition; and a promotional card requesting an opinion of* The Great Detectives *sent out with some review copies of the hardcover. The proof bears a different subtitle on the cover and title page than the one on the dust jacket of the trade edition (there's no subtitle in the book itself). Right: Ken Millar's January 1977 contract for the Lew Archer essay that would be published in* The Great Detectives, *signed by Millar and Otto Penzler. The words "for the first time" have been stricken from the contract since the essay would first appear later that year, in September, as a promotional pamphlet (200 copies not for sale) for* Lew Archer: Private Investigator, *published by Penzler's the Mysterious Press imprint. The trade edition (limited to 1,000 copies) including the introduction and the nine short stories would be released in October.*

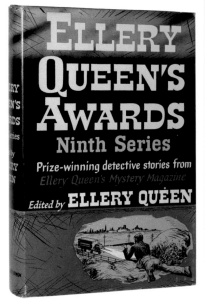
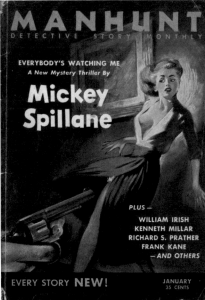

Above: Ellery Queen's Awards Ninth Series: Prize-winning detective stories from Ellery Queen's Mystery Magazine *(1954). This is the first book appearance of the Lew Archer short story "Wild Goose Chase" and precedes its publication in* The Name Is Archer *by one year; the first issue of* Manhunt *from January 1953 contains the only appearance of the Kenneth Millar short story "Shock Treatment" (this copy signed by him). The story was written aboard the* Shipley Bay *when Millar was in the Navy. The back cover of the digest has a wash portrait of Ken based on an author photo by Olga Cotton used on the dust jackets of* Blue City *and* The Three Roads.

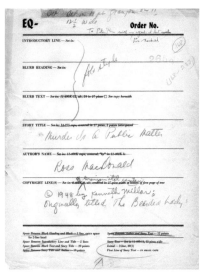
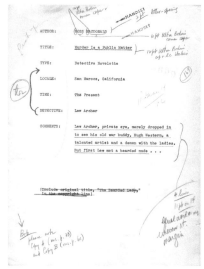
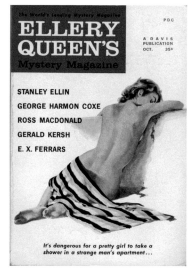
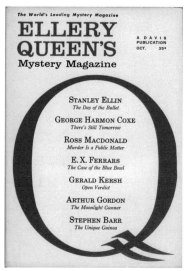

Above: Two cover variants of the October 1959 issue of Ellery Queen's Mystery Magazine—*one with girly art, the other typographic, probably to serve different regional markets. This issue reprinted "The Bearded Lady" as a Lew Archer novelette, "Murder Is a Public Matter." Top left: The first yellow sheet bears an inscription from Millar (as Ross Macdonald) in his miniscule later hand to the noted rare book dealer Peter Stern. The seventy-nine page carbon typescript has eighteen holograph corrections in ink by Millar and was probably one of several carbons that was prepared for* The Name Is Archer *collection as the story does have Archer in place instead of Sam Drake (who is the protagonist of* Trouble Follows Me *and the 1948 version of "The Bearded Lady"). Fred Dannay, editor of the magazine and one half of the writing team Ellery Queen, made editorial corrections throughout the entire typescript.*

THE BEARDED LADY

The unlatched door swung inward when I knocked. I walked into the studio, which was high and dim as a hayloft. The big north window in the opposite wall was hung with monkscloth drapes that shut out the morning light. I found the switch beside the door and snapped it on. Several fluorescent tubes suspended from the naked rafters flickered and burnt blue-white.

A strange woman faced me under the cruel light. She was only a charcoal sketch on an easel, but she gave me a chill. Her nude body, posed casually on a chair, was slim and round and pleasant to look at. But Her face wasn't pleasant at all. Bushy black eyebrows almost hid her eyes. A walrus moustache bracketed her mouth, and a thick black beard fanned down over her torso.

The door creaked behind me. The girl who appeared in the doorway wore a starched white uniform. Her face had a little starch in it, too, though not enough to spoil her good looks entirely. Her black hair was drawn back severely from her forehead. She said brusquely.

"May I ask what you're doing here?" she said brusquely.

"You may ask. I'm looking for Mr. Western."

"Really? Have you tried looking behind the pictures?"

"Does he spend much time there?"

"No, and another thing he doesn't do--he doesn't receive visitors in his studio when he isn't here himself."

"Sorry. The door was open, so I walked in."

"I guess I qualify. I used to be."

"When?" The question was sharp. I got the impression she didn't approve of Hugh's friends, or some of them.

"In the Philippines. He was attached to my group as a combat artist. My name is Archer, by the way, Lew Archer."

"Oh. Of course."

Her disapproval didn't extend to me, at least, not yet. She gave me her hand. It was cool and firm, and went with her steady gaze. I said.

"Hugh gave me the wrong impression of you," I said, "I thought

"You're lying, Archer."

"No. There's been a second murder, at Todd's."

He looked down at the girl at his feet. His eyes were bewildered. There was danger in his pain and confusion. I was the source of his pain, and he might strike out blindly at me. I watched the gun in his hand, waiting for a chance to move in on it. My arms were rigid, braced against the doorframe.

Mary Western ducked under my left arm and stepped into the room in front of me. She had no weapon, except her courage.

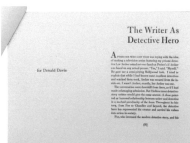

Above and right: Signed uncorrected page proofs for Capra Press's On Crime Writing (1973). Below left: An out-of-series, signed, unnumbered copy of the limited hardbound edition. Below middle and right: Two sequentially numbered copies (reunited after many years apart) of the signed, numbered hardbound edition.

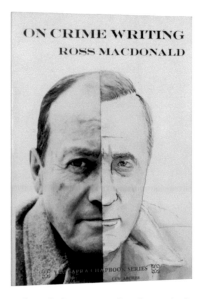
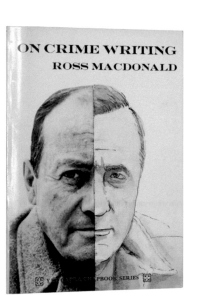

Above left: First trade edition (softcover) of On Crime Writing. *The cover is uncoated stock and the "Ross Macdonald" and "Lew Archer" lettering is printed with orange-red ink (unlike the gold ink of the hardcover edition). Above right: The second printing with coated cover stock lacks the "Ross Macdonald" and "Lew Archer" lettering altogether. Below left: First printing title page in red and black ink. Below middle: Second printing title page in black ink only. Below right: First printing price on back cover in black ink, second printing price in red ink.*

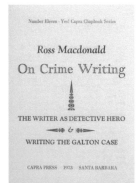
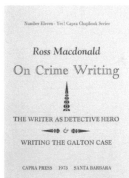

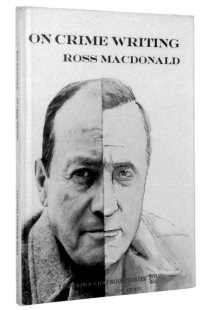

Left: the signed, limited edition with gold ink on the front cover. Above: A signed first trade edition (softcover) with first issue bright red pebbled stock endpapers, and an unsigned copy with the second issue cranberry laid stock endpapers. All of the hardcovers were issued with the bright red paper.

Above left: Second printing of On Crime Writing *with bright orange pebbled stock endpapers. Above right: An inscribed copy (just a couple of weeks after the Paul Nelson interviews in Santa Barbara concluded) of the first printing with the second issue cranberry endpapers; Ken Millar has signed an interesting abbreviated version of his pen name as "R. Macd."*

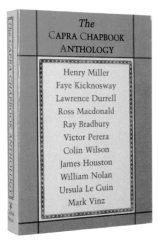

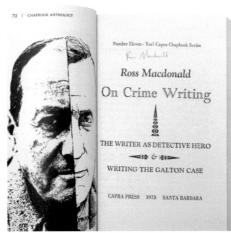

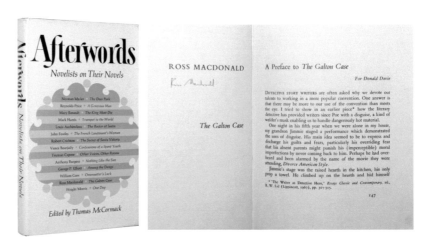

Above: A signed copy of The Capra Chapbook Anthology *(1979), which collected the first eleven Capra chapbooks in one volume.*

Above: A signed first edition of Afterwords: Novelists on Their Novels *(1969). This was the first appearance of the essay "A Preface to* The Galton Case."

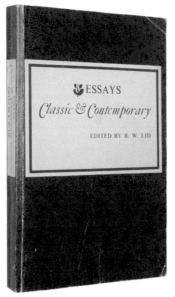

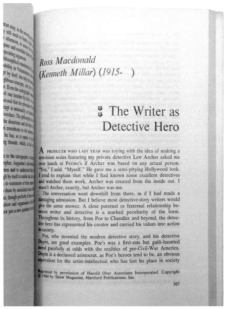

Above: Noel Young's foreword to On Crime Writing *with Ken Millar's holograph corrections on both pages. Below: Ken's 1967 contract for* Afterwords: Novelists on Their Novels.

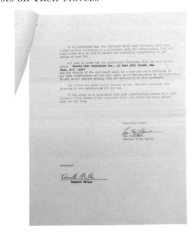

Above left and right:
Essays: Classic & Contemporary *(1967), edited by Ken Millar's friend Dick Lid, published by J. B. Lippincott Company as part of the Lippincott College English Series. This is the first book appearance of the essay "The Writer as Detective Hero," which was first published two years earlier in the magazine* Show *in January 1965. It was later paired with "Writing* The Galton Case" *in* On Crime Writing *in 1973.*
Left: Ken's set of long page proofs for the book Afterwords. *"A Preface to* The Galton Case" *was renamed "Writing* The Galton Case" *for* On Crime Writing.

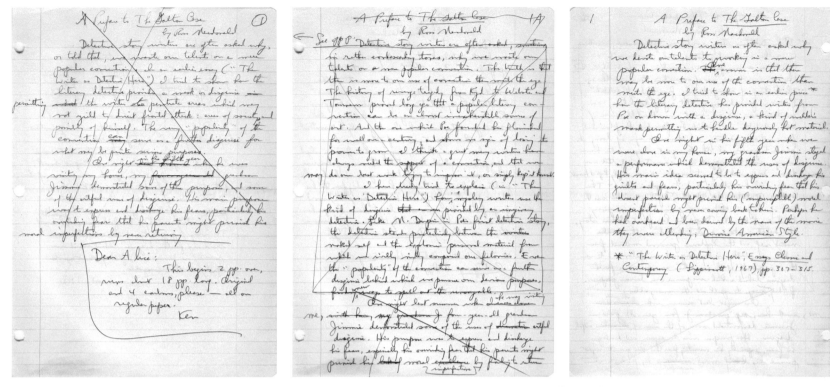

Above left: Manuscript for "A Preface to The Galton Case" with a note to typist Alice Kladnik. Above middle: An abandoned opening to the essay. Above right: Final version with a reference to "The Writer as Detective Hero." Below left: An early version with a slightly different towel scene with Millar's grandson Jimmie showing his foot. Below middle: An early version that leads off with Ford Madox Ford and follows up with Fitzgerald and Chandler. Below right: A later portion of an unused version of the essay that retains some of the ideas found on page 31 of On Crime Writing dealing with Oedipus, Sophocles, and Freud.

Above left: Carbon typescript for the final version of "A Preface to The Galton Case*" with Dick Lid's name added by hand by Millar. Above middle: Title page with a note: "This copy pencil-marked and cut for oral delivery to the N. Calif. Chapter of Mystery Writers of America, 25 May, 1968." Above right: Revised typescript with Dick Lid's name typed and the title of the essay altered to "The Galton Case and How It Grew." Below left: A working notebook for an early version of "A Preface to* The Galton Case*" from September to October 1967. Below right: A handwritten title page paperclipped to the final version of the essay.*

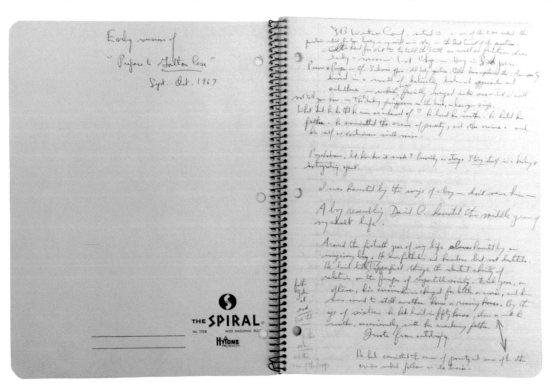

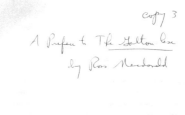

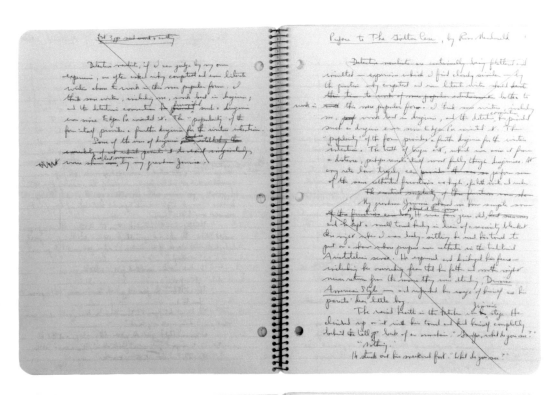

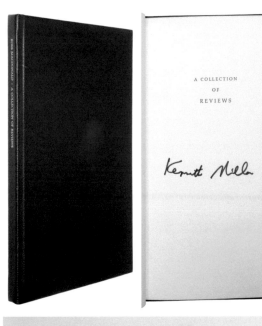

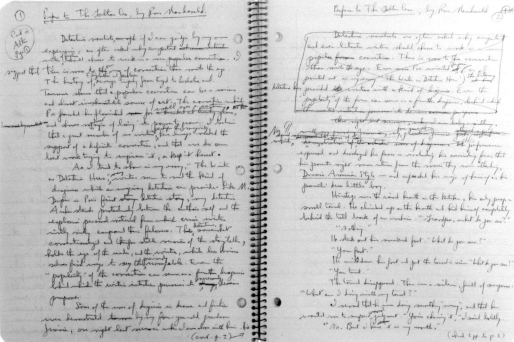

Above: The same working notebook with two other early versions of "A Preface to The Galton Case*"
from September to October 1967. "As I tried to show in my essay, 'The Writer as Detective Hero,' many
writers seem to need the kind of disguise which an imaginary detective can provide. Like M. Dupin
in Poe's first detective story, my detective Archer stands protectively between the author's self and the
explosive personal material from which crime writers willy nilly compound their felonies."*

Above: Ken Millar's personal copy of A Collection of
Reviews *(1979) bound in blue pigskin.
Below: Deluxe binding with marbled boards (one of
fifty copies), a deluxe out-of-series presentation copy,
and Alfred A. Knopf's deluxe copy.*

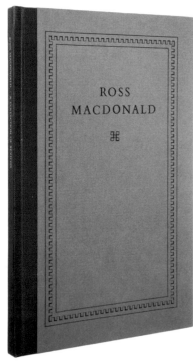

Above left and bottom right: The regular numbered edition (300 copies) in grey boards. Top right: Paul Nelson's copy of the deluxe binding with marbled boards.

Above left: Manuscript for the foreword of A Collection of Reviews *with a penciled note: "End of first sequence—that bard, as you doubtless guessed was my father." Above right: Manuscript with alternate titles of the essay: "A Vision of Childhood," "Two Steps towards Fiction," "Georgian Bay." "Jock and Nanny" was ultimately the working title of the essay. Right top and middle: Four different openings to the essay that explore the Robert Burns-style poem penned by John Millar, Ken's father. Right bottom: A photocopy of the typescript with a penned note for a scheduled interview; a carbon typescript.*

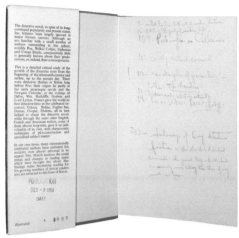

S F Chronicle

THE DETECTIVE IN FICTION

The Development of the Detective Novel. By A. E. Murch
Philosophical Library; 272 pp.; $6

Reviewed by Kenneth Millar

Readers, and critics, of mystery fiction seem to be divided into at least two main camps. There are those who feel that the English story of scientific detection à la Sherlock Holmes represents the mystery at its peak, and that everything since has been a falling-away. Dr. Jacques Barzun is the most vocal current laudator of crimes past. Then there are others who consider that the mystery novel is a form of the novel proper, subject like its other forms to the endless new developments which the word "novel" suggests. According to this second view, the contemporary movement of mystery fiction in a variety of directions--social, psychological, poetic, symbolic, philosophic--means that it is rejoining the literary mainstream where it belongs.

To say that the first is the English view would be to distort the opinions of many English writers from G. K. Chesterton to Dorothy L. Sayers and Josephine Tey. In the introductory chapter to her history, Mrs. Murch quotes Chesterton to the effect that "the detective story...is the earliest and only form of popular literature in which is expressed some sense of the poetry of modern life." But Mrs. Murch does nothing with this promising approach. She regards

Clockwise from top left: Ken Millar's copy of Alma Murch's The Development of the Detective Novel *(1958) with his penciled notes on the front free endpaper listing page references to Edgar Allan Poe, Wilkie Collins, and Charles Dickens. The handwritten manuscript for Millar's review of the Murch book, which differs slightly from the final version. It was written for the* San Francisco Chronicle. *The carbon typescript for the final version of the book review with a penned note, "S. F. Chronicle," at the top. This particular review opens the book* A Collection of Reviews. *Millar takes issue with Murch's book: "… Mrs. Murch allows her history to deteriorate towards mere bibliography, without virtue of completeness…. It is dangerous for a scholar, however diligent, to tackle an immense subject with hand-me-down critical tools. Mrs. Murch's limitations may be indicated by her opinion that 'criminal psychology' bears 'little relation to detection.' Her overall implication is, I fear, that crime fiction should stay away from the realities of modern life." He closes with this: "It grieves me to say this, because mystery writers are traditionally grateful for small scholarly mercies, and Mrs. Murch's book contains many good things, including a youthful likeness of the lady I love."*

Above: The hardcover (limited to about 1,000 copies) and softcover editions of The Private Lives of Private Eyes: Spies, Crimefighters, and Other Good Guys *(1977) by Otto Penzler. Penzler examines twenty-five of crime fiction's most famous sleuths in alphabetical order, leading off with none other than Lew Archer; the limited, numbered hardcover of* Strangers in Town *(2001) from Crippen & Landru, signed by editor Tom Nolan (facsimile Millar/Macdonald signature); an out-of-series hardcover; the pamphlet containing "Winnipeg, 1929" (issued with the limited hardcover); and the softcover edition.* Strangers in Town *featured three previously unpublished short stories by Millar (one Joe Rogers, two Lew Archer) that Nolan discovered while researching his Ross Macdonald biography.*

 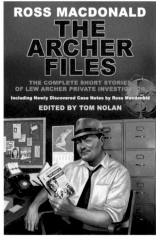  

Above: Rough ink sketch for The Archer Files *with Ken Millar as Lew Archer (reading the 1955 edition of* The Name Is Archer*); a finished cover comp of this idea that was ultimately too stiff and clumsy for use—a picture of Linda Millar and the covers for* Lew Archer: Private Investigator *and* Strangers in Town *can be seen on the corkboard; rough comp for the idea that would end up as the final cover; thumbnail ink sketch showing Ken Millar with a fountain pen in place of Archer's gun. Below: The limited, numbered hardcover of* The Archer Files *(2007) from Crippen & Landru, signed by Nolan and cover illustrator Jeff Wong (facsimile Millar/Macdonald signature); the pamphlet "We Went on from There," the twenty-ninth chapter of* The Far Side of the Dollar *that appeared in Matt Bruccoli's "Manuscript Edition" (issued with the limited hardcover); the first paperback edition; the third printing of the paperback with the price omitted from the front cover; and the 2015 Vintage edition. The Crippen & Landru edition contains the nine stories that were published in the Mysterious Press collection of Archer stories, plus the three from* Strangers in Town *(with the Joe Rogers story altered to Archer) and eleven previously unpublished Archer story fragments. Although the limited edition was intended to be 400 copies, a number of books, including the out-of-series overrun copies, were damaged during the binding process, shortening the print run. The Vintage release adds "Winnipeg, 1929," "We Went on from There," and, for the first time in print, a short piece called "Trial."*

18. WRITING

rate it thawed my autobiographical embarrassment and started a run of
somewhat more personal fiction which has, for better or worse, gone on
unabated ever since. Of my twenty-three books, so far, the three I have
just named are among my favorites. They have a certain intensity and
range.

But one writes on a curve, on the backs of torn-off calendar
sheets. A writer in his fifties will not recapture the blaze of youth,
or the steadier passion that comes like a second and saner youth in his
forties, if he's lucky. But he can lie in wait in his room -- it must
be at least the hundredth room by now -- and keep open his imagination
and the bowels of his compassion against the day when another book will
haunt him like a ghost rising out of both the past and the future.

Carbon typescript of the last page of the introduction to
Kenneth Millar/Ross Macdonald: A Checklist.

What are your general hours? Are you an early riser?

No. I stay up late and get up late. I generally go to bed between twelve and
twelve-thirty.

Do you watch television or read a lot at night?

I see a fair number of movies and I see a fair amount of television. Not an inordinate amount. Mostly I read.

But you work pretty constantly.

Yeah, about half the time. I work on the fiction about *half* the time, and the other half I'm in-between.

What do you do in-between?

Well, I swim half a mile a day. I talk to people. I read a lot, mostly journalism these days for some reason. It seems to be where it's at, at the moment.

How many hours a day do you spend writing?

About four hours.

Have your working habits remained the same through the years? Did you ever put in long, long stretches of fifteen or twenty hours sometimes?

No, I've never put in long stretches of writing like that. No more than just daylight.

Prior to The Chill you had a serious illness. What kind of an illness was that?

Oh, it was what could best be described as a near stroke. I put myself under too much pressure and didn't get enough exercise and so on. I was exhausted and had very high blood pressure and I was hospitalized for about a week. But it scared me. I hadn't been exercising properly or regularly. Since then I have. The day I got out of the hospital I came down and swam across the pool. That was the start of it. That was when I went back to my earlier habit of swimming every day, which I've kept up ever since. Also, I took off a good deal of weight. I used to be much heavier than I am. God knows, I'm heavy enough as is, but I used to weigh a lot more. I used to weigh up to 215 pounds when I was in my twenties.

That's the only instance where you've ever had a serious illness?

Well, I've had other illnesses. I've had a couple of operations, but I wouldn't call them terribly serious. I had a piece cut out of my thyroid, but it turned out not to be cancerous. I had some repair work done on my anal area.

Most of the books were written in that chair in your downstairs room. Would you describe that chair for me?

Well, it's an overstuffed, red imitation leather armchair. My wife bought it for me when I got out of the Navy, which was in 1946. That was thirty years ago and I've been sitting in it ever since to work. And it's wearing out.

But you wouldn't throw it out, I would imagine.

No. I figure it'll last me.

You have a pine writing board that you hold in your lap.

Yeah. The board is part of a house I used to live in.

My guess is that these aren't serious rituals, but that they're part of a nice, comforting routine. I don't think you would not be able to write a book, say, if you didn't have the chair.

No, I could write anyplace else. It's just that the chair is moderately comfortable and it's also in the right place. It's got a triple window on the left and it's right beside my bed, which I can use to keep my manuscript on. It's just plain handy.[1]

Actually, I do a lot of writing in my study, which has a rolltop desk. I do a lot of writing on the desk, but not book-writing. I write a lot of letters and other things.

You have quite a collection of notebooks that you work from. Do you keep all your various notebooks in that room also?

I keep the ones that are relevant on the table in front of me.

How would you describe them?

Notebooks full of material about characters and plot. The lives of the characters and so on. All the things that went into the book. But not necessarily in the right order. And, of course, not in any way set up in scenes or anything, just notebook after notebook.

A notebook for Ken Millar's The Instant Enemy *screenplay.*

Are you working on a notebook now for your next book?

The notebooks are perpetual. I mean, they're just there, and there are various ideas for stories in various stages of development. Occasionally I make a note when I think of something during my day. I think I made a note or two within the last week. But generally speaking, I take time between books. And I'm still taking time. See, since I wrote this new book, I have also written a movie, and I'm not ready to go back and do full-time work.

How many more books would you say your notebooks contain at this point?

I don't have any idea, but enough to last me the rest of this life and another life if I had one. The ideas tend, as I write the books, to coalesce, so I'll use up ideas

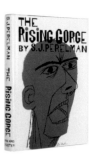

S. J. Perelman's comic sketch "Oh, I Am a Cook and a Houseboy Bland" first appeared in the February 18, 1961, issue of The New Yorker, *then later that year in his collection* The Rising Gorge. *The husband and wife writers and experts on the Civil War, the Fingerhoods, were inspired by a 1960 interview with the Millars done by Martha MacGregor for the New York Post where the couple discussed working in different parts of the house. A portion of the interview leads off the Perelman piece. Ken responded with the somewhat tongue-in-cheek, but slightly miffed, letter below to the editor of* The New Yorker.

840 Chelham Way
Santa Barbara
California

The Editor
The New Yorker

May I add a footnote to S. J. Perelman's report, in The New Yorker for February 18, on our split-level *modus vivendi*, which is as searching a contribution to contemporary anthropology as he has ever made. One difficulty in this all too human science, which even he has failed to overcome, is that the injection of an observer into the tribal or familial situation alters the very conditions he seeks to study. Now I have no doubt that Perelman was a model guest, according to his lights. My wife and I could see that he was doing his level best to adapt his eastern manners to the simple customs of our pueblo. The only really persistent annoyance was his strange need to have someone in the room, laughing with him, whenever he was writing. Of the various other annoyances which arose from time to time (the episode of the liquor cabinet, for instance) our western courtesy suggests that I not speak.

These mounting irritations had their effect on the sunny dispositions which Margaret and I share with the other members of the Santa Barbara commune. In Perelman's crucible, as it were, our native charm and gaiety evaporated. Margaret aged twenty years in as many days, so that, as he noted in his report, she looked all of fifty-eight; she dyed her hair blue in a desperate effort to keep her spirits up. I probably would have taken to drink if the pulque supply had not long since been exhausted, I will not say by whom. As it was, I developed a nervous habit of punching myself from time to time in the head, which did indeed take on the shape

---

1 Kenneth and Margaret kept separate bedrooms.

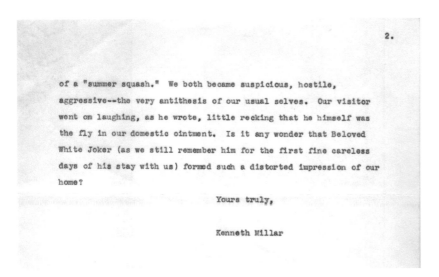

of a "summer squash." We both became suspicious, hostile, aggressive--the very antithesis of our usual selves. Our visitor went on laughing, as he wrote, little recking that he himself was the fly in our domestic ointment. Is it any wonder that Beloved White Joker (as we still remember him for the first fine careless days of his stay with us) formed such a distorted impression of our home?

Yours truly,

Kenneth Millar

for several books in one book. What I thought were ideas for several books will join together. That happened with this last book.

Does it reach a point where you start to get eager to work on a book again after a year, year and a half, not writing one?

Oh yeah. I'll probably start something late in the fall.

You'll go back to notebooks for at least part of it?

Yeah, I think it's a good idea to write something that you've already been thinking about for several years or longer. I fill notebooks before I write page one, because you have to know pretty well where you're going before you can write a final page one. After spending six months or a year filling notebooks with the plot, I generally have a fair idea of where I can start anyway—although I may not know where I'm going. I didn't used to work this way, of course—when I started writing, I just sat down and started—but after working this way for quite a few years, I think it's the only way for me now. I generally *attach* the old material to something that's suggested by something that's recently happened, as in the case of that fire. The plot really wasn't new; I'd been working on it for some time. The fire, as I said, pulled it together, gave it a central symbol.

Do you remember when you changed your method from writing without notebooks?

Oh, it just developed gradually over the years.

By The Galton Case you were writing from notebooks?

Yes, I think that would be an example of one of the first or maybe the first that I planned in great detail before I wrote it.

But when you wrote Blue City, for instance, a lot of it was improvised as you went along?

It all was. I wrote it all in one month. Without any preparation at all that I can remember.

Did you know where it was going when you started?

Oh sure, I knew what the general shape of the plot was.

But there were constant surprises, I imagine, as you were typing.

I don't type.

You wrote it all in handwriting.

Yeah. I got my fill of typing in the Navy.[2]

Do you think there's a correlation between the work of the private detective and the work of the writer?

Probably.

The Spring/Summer issue of Antæus *(1977) focused on genre fiction and included Ken's essay "Down These Streets a Mean Man Must Go." The title was an homage to Raymond Chandler's line from "The Simple Art of Murder": "But down these mean streets a man must go who is not himself mean, who is neither tarnished nor afraid." Millar's essay contains references to a wide range of authors: Edgar Allan Poe, Samuel Taylor Coleridge, Marshall McLuhan, Hugh Kenner, Malcolm Lowry, Dashiell Hammett, Raymond Chandler, T. S. Eliot, F. Scott Fitzgerald, and Millar's favorite librarian, B. Mabel Dunham.*

In The Moving Target Archer says he judges everybody he meets. That's in effect what a writer has to do with his work. Are you conscious sometimes that in addition to writing about a detective you're also writing about writing?

2 This work habit carried forth through Millar's entire career. Though in the early years Margaret would help him prepare his manifests, in Santa Barbara he eventually employed Alice Kladnik as his longtime typist.

Oh, I'm aware of it, but I think the answer to the question you just asked is no. Just writing a sentence involves so many decisions, it can involve your whole life. So my answer has to be yes, but also no.

How carefully do you plot things out before you can sit down and begin writing?

Oh, I generally work for years on a book, off and on, before I start to write.

Just on structure?

Well, other things come in, too. You really start with meaning before you have anything to structure.

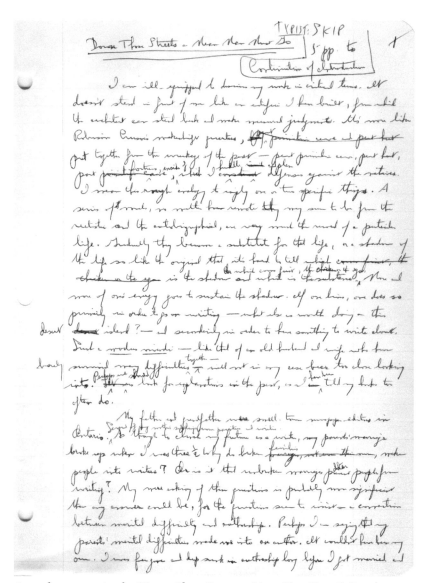

An early manuscript for "Down These Streets a Mean Man Must Go" with a note at the top for the typist to skip five pages to the continuation of the introduction.

Structure's the most difficult part?

No, it's my specialty. It's the one thing I can do better than my competition, so I spend a lot of time it.

Do you think that was one of the weaknesses of Chandler? That he almost neglected structure.

Yes, I really do. He didn't take the form as seriously as he should have.

Do you think because you were a teacher and because you've probably read more literature than Chandler and Hammett, say, that that's the reason—one of the reasons at least—you're more aware of structure and more drawn to it?

Well, I think there are things to be learned about mystery writing from non-mystery writers.

Who would you include among those people?

This may seem strange to say but I think I learned more about structure from Fitzgerald than I ever did from anybody else. I think anybody can learn a lot about it from him. He learned a lot in the course of his writing life. Structure and what goes along with it; the ability to say a very great deal in a very short space.

Such as Gatsby?

Yeah, and some of his other fiction, too. Some of his short stories.

Do you always know exactly what a book is about when you start?

Oh no. I know some of the kinds of things that go into making a book. They suggest subjects that are profoundly interesting to me. I know what they are—they're in books. I know the kind of structure I set up at the beginning, but then the structure needs to be far beyond what I would dream of at the beginning. *Always.*

Let's say I don't know what they are—even though I do. How would you describe the structures you set up in the books?

The essential structure of the books—I'm just speaking off the cuff now—is for the imagination of the writer and/or the reader to touch in at some point in a life and, before he's finished comprehending it, he's told a story that will fairly well cover not only that life of a central character but everybody involved with him. That's making a very exciting story into a dull one by abstract statement. Really it is a mix of emotional and imaginative excitement, then plunging back into the material of your life and trying to make sense of it. You understand it better and you feel it more.

You also change it.

Yes, and you change yourself. So writing a book is a process which is embodied in the book, a process that is very important. Either as a reader or a writer, you're not the same man that went in at the front end who came out at the other.

Is there a feeling of anxiety to do this? Or a feeling of some fear of doing it?

No. Perhaps I'm not smart enough to have been afraid. You see, the thing is, the book keeps opening up in its own terms, which are in a sense controlled by the form and by you. So it doesn't open up the whole thing to you suddenly and confront you with terror. It enables you to deal with terror—I'm just using *terror* as a word for a lot of things—it enables you to deal with it in artistic terms, which control it sufficiently that you can handle it. Also, these same artistic steps that you take lead you further into the terror—or the heart of darkness or whatever you want to call it.

I'm not talking about the terror that's implicit in the story you're telling. More the worry that it's not going to work, that it won't come out right.

That's not a worry, that's just a real sweat. That's the work, that's the work itself.

What's the difference between a worry and a real sweat?

A worry implies that you might not be doing it right or you might not be doing what you should be doing, or you might want to succeed. I really don't sit around in that fear. My books are of varying quality of course—it's human, varying quality—but I've almost never sat down to write a book that I didn't finish and that isn't in print now. The exceptions are very early in the game.

I think that's a rather rare, possibly unknown quality for a writer.

Yes, I think so. It's both an advantage and a disadvantage. It's an advantage always to be able to write publishable script, but it would be better if I were more terrified so that I worked harder. I could spend more time on a book than I do. Perhaps it's better not to be so blithe. It might make you work harder and better.

Have you ever gotten to a position where it was really difficult to write.

Not really. I know the kind of suffering that many writers do go through and I really haven't gone through it so much. Of course, I work hard and it's sometimes painful. This last book cost me a great deal of effort.

You mentioned in an interview that a fiction writer has to create difficulties for himself.

The detective in the detective story has to overcome a whole series of what are, for the writer, imaginary problems and difficulties. The purpose of presenting the reader with those difficulties and those problems is to get at further truth. In other words, the intricate process that you go through in reading any novel, and particularly the detective novel, is a way of learning. It's a learning process which is set up by the book and which takes you deeper into the subject of the book and what happened. In other words, you set up a structure which forces the imagination of both the writer and the reader to go further into the subject than he would just thinking about it straight. In a sense you're evading the direct reality which is in front of your nose, but your evasion takes the form of encircling it, incorporating it, and comprehending it.

Let's talk about your writing style. It seems to have elements of both Fitzgerald and Hammett, I would say.

I don't think it's very easy for a writer to explain or understand his own style unless he more or less sits down to examine it from a fairly critical point of view. I learned a hell of a lot from Hammett, but probably not enough. I mean, as far as influences go I belong more in the Fitzgerald group.

Your style doesn't have a lot that could date it by way of slang, by way of references.

That's true. But my objection to slang is not so much that it dates, as that it's imprecise. Also, slang is something that, because it's ephemeral, cannot be controlled by style nor can style rest on it permanently. Something that is really true stylistically never rings false, even if it ages. So you will find the falsity right here and now if it's ever going to be there, provided your ear is good enough. Otherwise how could anybody write a permanent style?

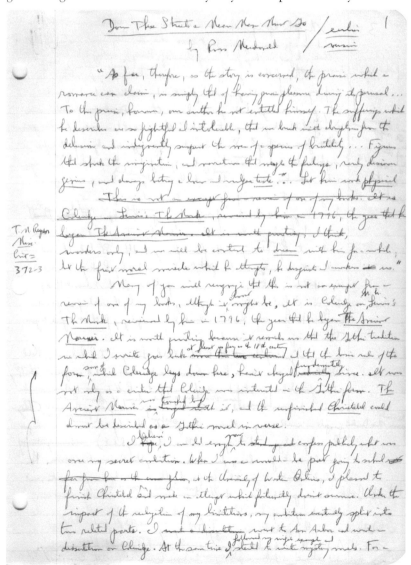

Another early version of "Down These Streets a Mean Man Must Go." This version, like the final, contains the section about Millar's ambition to complete Samuel Taylor Coleridge's unfinished narrative poem Christabel.

Hammett really hasn't dated all that much.

Not very much. No, and even where he does date, he *knew* he was writing something that was going to date and he inputs a little bit of a comic spin on it in general. I don't know whether my description is quite accurate, but he knows enough about what he's doing with style to be able to do things that the reader can share a critical attitude towards with the writer. He really was a good writer and he knew a hell of a lot about writing.

Fitzgerald of course is more classic in his work and in his intentions, but in his very late Hollywood stories about the run-down Hollywood writer who was supposed to represent himself—What was his name?

Pat Hobby.[3]

Yeah, Pat Hobby. They're much more freely colloquial than his earlier fiction. That doesn't prevent them from being classical provided that the writer knows exactly what he's doing and can find a means of sharing that knowledge with the reader so that the whole thing is intentional. What we object to is unintentional lapses in diction or ignorant lapses. Or failed attempts to bring things off. There's a lot of that.

Any good writer has to be able to and should be able to write a sentence that the reader can't improve on. Maybe another writer could improve on it, but the reader can't. He might think he can, but he wouldn't be able to do it. Maybe that's a pretty good definition of style. Because it includes all the good writing that's possible.

Can we go back to Gatsby a minute?

Anytime.

I was wondering what you thought of Fitzgerald's characterizations. I don't mean to separate them, but Gatsby and Daisy are memorable characters certainly.

Oh yes. But I think what makes them memorable, more than any other one thing, is their relationship. Their actual relationship, which becomes the structure of the novel. You can't really distinguish between their relationship and the structure of the novel, can you? Because each is *inched out* simultaneously and *pari passu* with the other. Apart from that structure, Gatsby doesn't exist in the same sense that we know him.

They are not three-dimensional characters at all.

But they do exist—they exist in the author's intention, and that intention is spelled out and very, very carefully laid out in the structure of the novel. The only way you can know the intention is in that step-by-step creation as you read. There's no place in the novel, for example, where either Gatsby or Daisy is described in a complete way. In a way complete enough to include her beginning, her middle, and her end. In other words, she is a character *of* the novel.

In a way it seems to me they are somewhat like Hammett's characters in that they also exist within the novel and aren't particularly naturalistic.

I think that's true.

They're not necessarily symbolic either. But Gatsby and Daisy are mythic, if that's the right word even.

No, they're not symbolic, they stand for themselves. Of course, anything that stands for itself can be mythologized, too. They're pared down and their basic strength is structural. By that I mean that if the novel were told in a different order it would destroy those characters. They are, so to speak, the skeleton of the novel. Skeleton isn't a good word. They are the *movement* of the novel. Their love is the movement of the novel.

Well, if I were smart enough to explain exactly what I mean about Fitzgerald's novel, I would know more about writing than I do. You can see how it works as you read it page by page, but it's very difficult to sum it up. But they're both ghosts in a sense, animating the body of the novel.

Have you tried for that quality in some of the characters that you've written about? Is Archer a ghost as well?

In certain ways he's intended to be a ghost, yes. He's a ghost in the sense of just being a tone of voice. But then of course he does *act* also. He not only speaks the words in the novel that are outside of quotation marks, but he speaks words that are inside of quotation marks. And you notice the difference, of course. They're two different voices, almost two different men in a sense, although I try to keep them within speaking distance of each other. The two Archers. But then there's my voice, too, you see, which is behind his and which speaks through what he says in quotes and also what he says outside of quotes. Also, it speaks through the other characters, both in what they do and in what they said. The whole thing has to be unified because he's the major element of unification, that single character.

Could you characterize Archer's words outside of quotation marks as opposed to his words in quotation marks?

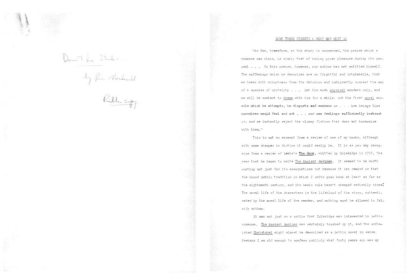

Left: Handwritten cover page denoting the typescript is the original ribbon copy and not a carbon. Right: First page of an earlier typed version.

---

3 Fitzgerald wrote seventeen Pat Hobby short stories, all of which were published in *Esquire* from 1940 (the year Fitzgerald died) to 1941. The stories were collected and published as *The Pat Hobby Stories* in 1962.

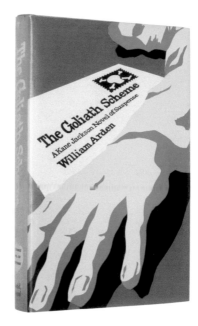
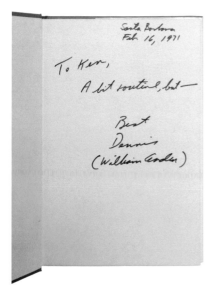
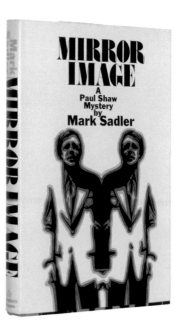

Ken Millar's copies of The Goliath Scheme *(1971) and* Mirror Image *(1972), inscribed to him by fellow Santa Barbara author, Dennis Lynds, who regularly attended a local writers luncheon with Ken. Lynds wrote under a variety of pseudonyms, including Maxwell Grant in the 1960s when he wrote a number of novels for Belmont Books featuring the pulp character the Shadow (created by Walter B. Gibson, who wrote under the Grant moniker in the 1930s).*

Let's put them in quotes first. His words in quotes are what could conceivably and would conceivably be said by an intelligent private eye on a case given the circumstance that he's in when he speaks. What he says outside of quotes as the voice of the novel *is* in fact the voice of the novel and of the novelist, but not *my* voice—the voice of me as novelist. There's a strong element of implied commentary, moral and so on, in this.

Which is your voice.

No, it's not my voice, it's the voice of the narrator. The narrator voice. Not Archer's voice and not my voice either, but the voice of the novel. The difference between it and the voice of Archer in quotes is that it's much more aware of what is happening than Archer is consciously. In fact, it's constantly making references and cross-references to other things past and present, such as other people's writing. There's an awful lot of echoing, for example. Literary echoing. And I don't mean imitation, I mean deliberate echoing in order to bring, well, another point of view to bear on what's being considered. Or to enlarge the significance of it by a reference to some classical event or something like that.

Can you think of any specific cases of literary echoing in The Blue Hammer?

I would have a hard time tracing down and saying, "This is an echo of that." I talked as if I was making specific literary allusions, but more often the echo is in the style and has to do with references and cross-references to other styles. For example, there's a lot of the modern French style in my writing, as I'm sure you were aware. That doesn't show up necessarily in one image but in an attitude, which is my own attitude. I'm using that style in order to express it. You find

Fitzgerald doing exactly the same thing in *Tender Is the Night*, I believe, and doing it much more extensively and more importantly.

Have you ever taken a line or a phrase from another writer's work and used it in your own as an allusion?

I don't recall anything offhand. As you get older as a writer you sometimes resist that kind of cross-reference. You want to purify your style in a sense of making it all your own. I don't know whether *purify* is the precise word.

Also, as I did in this book [*The Blue Hammer*], you resist writing anything of a great length. In spite of the length of this book, everything in it is told as briefly as possible and as simply as possible with the exception of the occasional image. Sometimes the imagery in this book, it doesn't take the simile or metaphor form. It's just a description of what's there, but heightened in intention so that it becomes imagery. For example, like the dead man's "massive hairy head and shrunken sex." That's the body, in the mortuary, of the drowned artist. That's an example of what I mean. That's just realism, but its intention goes beyond that, its intention is figurative. It's intended to be a fairly general comment. And so on.

You were quoted in The Observer as saying: "I find as I get older the romance keeps seeping back in."

What kind of romance am I referring to?

As opposed to realism, I believe.

Yeah, I think you're right: as opposed to typical hard-hitting American-style realism. We're getting back into the same subject matter that we've just been discussing really, and that is the poetic use of words and images. Of course, *poetic* means simply trying

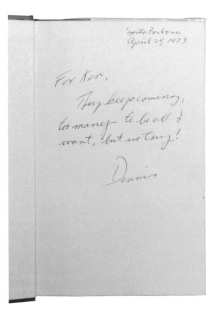

Another William Arden title, Deadly Legacy *(1973),
inscribed to Millar by Lynds.*

to get the most possible force and meaning and use out of the images that you're writing about. So the intention is poetic in a basic sense.

You were saying there's Archer's voice in quotes, which is more realistic, and then the narrator Archer voice, which is more poetic. Then you said there was also your voice. I don't think we quite got to your voice.

My voice is the unvarnished, unartistic, simple speaking voice that you're hearing at the moment. You have to distinguish between that and the mitigated and prepared voice that you get in any written work.

I thought you were talking about your voice in the books.

No, I'm just talking about this voice that you're listening to right now. There is my speaking voice, then there's the written voice outside of quotation marks, and then there's still a third *me* voice inside the quotation marks speaking as Archer.

And as some of the other characters in the books.

Oh sure, but that isn't so close to my own voice. The whole book is also in the voice of the author. I mean, that *has* to be the case, unless it's something that was just written down as somebody else dictated. No book has ever been produced that way really, except perhaps the *Sayings of Doctor Johnson.*

What do you think the best intellectual training is for a writer?

Whatever subject profoundly interests him. The diversity of writers is a blessing. Good writing can come out of any serious interest in the nature of reality. That's the only place it can come out of really. There has to be talent, too, of course. Specifically a verbal talent.

A March 1966 letter from Ken Millar to Henri Coulette requesting two copies of Coulette's first collection of poems The War of the Secret Agents—*one for Donald Davie and one for himself, since Millar had given his mimeographed copy to Marshall McLuhan. "After a brief bout with Hollywood—a draw—I'm going to Texas, but not to stay, just for the bird migrations." Millar is referring to his less than happy experience with Stanley Rubin, Alexander Mackendrick, and Francis Ford Coppola on the Seven Arts film project just one month prior.*

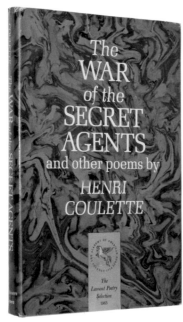

The War of the Secret Agents (1966) *and* The Family Goldschmitt (1971) *by Henri Coulette.* The War of the Secret Agents *contains the poem "The Blue-Eyed Precinct Worker." From the notes in the back of the volume: "The penultimate line of the penultimate stanza of 'The Blue-Eyed Precinct Worker' is from a mystery by Ross Macdonald." The title of Millar's final novel,* The Blue Hammer, *comes from the Henri Coulette poem "Confiteor" (an earlier working title,* The Silent Hammer, *comes from the same poem).*

You don't think this can be taught?

I think people can be taught what to avoid and led in the right direction and so on, but writing itself is something that the writer has to learn to do pretty much on his own. Another writer can help him, perhaps tell him what not to do. He can't tell him what *to* do, though. Another writer can tell him when he's pulled something off, too, before he knows it himself. He can encourage him in the right direction. Also, another writer can create an atmosphere that makes writing possible. For example, just taking a course from Auden was one of the main events in life that made me a writer. He inspired me. I'm not blaming him for my work. He took the whole thing so seriously and with such gusto, and also he was a very learned man.

Does it help that there are a lot of other writers that you see around Santa Barbara? You probably see them more often than that at your writers luncheon.[4]

Well, I see some few writers frequently. It certainly helps. A solution of writers is a pretty good liquid to swim in if you're another writer. I like working with other writers, too.

Let's talk a bit about the writers luncheon and how that originated. I understand that you had something to do with organizing it.

4 Paul had attended the luncheon with Millar that afternoon.

It really isn't organized. We're just a group of writers who have been meeting together for twenty-two or twenty-three years every second week on a Wednesday noon for lunch. We're there essentially for social purposes, not anything else. People just politely overlook anything good that happens to you [*laughs*], if you know what I mean. Paul Ellerbe and I were the people who got it started and kept it going. A short-story writer, he was the teacher of a class in writing. For a number of years, the sole structure that the group has really is that we're all interested in writing. Some one person has to phone everybody and remind them to come out for lunch, and after Ellerbe died I became that person. The organization aspect is minimal.

The nice thing about it, what makes it worthwhile, is that you form a group which has been meeting together for a long time. Of course, the group has gradually changed. Ellerbe died, for example. Other people have moved away. There are other people who have been in from the beginning or almost from the beginning, but offhand I can't think of anybody who was there today who also goes back to the beginning. Although there are a few.[5]

The name of the restaurant is El Cielito, or Josie's El Cielito. It used to belong to somebody else and she bought it. *Cielito* means "little [bit of] heaven." We haven't always been meeting there. At one time we met at a Chinese restaurant for a year or two. But for the last dozen years at least we've been meeting at Josie's place.

Is becoming a popular and critical success an entirely good point or does it have its bad qualities, too?

Well, from my personal standpoint it's desirable, of course. I like having a large audience and being able to speak to a lot of young people, for example. I can continue my teaching job in a sense by other means. There is that satisfaction.

Are there disadvantages?

Yeah, the disadvantage is that writing is essentially a private act, and if you lose your sense of privacy you might lose some of the, oh, sense of discovery perhaps in your life. I think it's very good for a writer to feel private and alone. He was "the first that ever burst / Into the silent sea," to quote "[The Rime of] the Ancient Mariner." You know what I mean. Good to have that feeling. If you have a large audience, you might eventually become its servant rather than its leader.

You find you don't necessarily write for that audience, though, is that correct?

No, I don't. It has never actually affected my writing, at least not consciously. The structural demands of the books are so pervasive, you don't really have much time to think about your audience. On the other hand, your knowledge of what your audience *is* might affect your choice of material, the kind of book that you choose to write. I'll give you an example—a simple but valid example: If you *know* you're being used in the schools, you would avoid some of the extreme statements that

5 The roster when Paul visited the group included (though not all of them were present) Willard Temple (author and *Saturday Evening Post* writer), Ted Clymer (textbook writer and children's book author), Ralph Sipper (seller of rare books), Dennis Lynds (author who also wrote under the name Michael Collins), William Downey (journalist), Barnaby Conrad (artist and author), Irving Townsend (record producer and author), Henri Coulette (poet), Robert Easton (writer), Don Freeman (painter, cartoonist, and children's book author), William Campbell Gault (writer), Chet Holcomb (business reporter), Bill McNally (publisher), Robert Kirsch (*Los Angeles Times* book critic), Herbert Harker (author), and Chet Opal (writer).

Ken Millar's May 1966 letter to Henri Coulette thanking him for the books. "You know, it only occurred to me afterwards that I could have gone downtown and bought them. I suppose I wanted them as a gift from your hand. (The Davie copy has been forwarded, of course.)" Millar goes on to say, "I'm having a difficult year, living in the world instead of writing, but not handling it too badly, and have made no moral mistakes except the initial late one of wanting success more than I dreamed I wanted it. Success, as no doubt you're learning, is no joke; it comes on like age and corrodes desire. Fortunately, both you and I have to go on working for a living, and I hope we both recover the keen edge of desire. Our hungry childhoods will not be denied, I think."

might be perfectly valid from another point of view in your novels. You know what I mean? Such thoughts can blunt your edge.

Have you done that?

No, I don't believe so. At least I don't consider that my books have been particularly extreme as regard to either sex or violence anyway. They *are* extreme, but the extremity is, let's say, psychological and moral rather than so overt.

Has it been more difficult to maintain a sense of privacy since your work gained popularity?

I haven't been aware of any difficulty. Except of course with each new book you're aware of the necessity to not necessarily top yourself but not fall too far short of what you've done before. But that's good for a writer. It's good for a writer to be *forced* in the direction of excellence and away from laziness. We lose some of our powers and perhaps gain others. But we do change.

So you haven't thought any more about a new book yet?

No, I haven't been working at all. I'm still cleaning up correspondence that I left unanswered during the past year and a half.

Do you get a lot of fan mail?

Yes. I hear from somebody nearly every day. I really enjoy it. Some of the letters are extremely feeling and intelligent and to me valuable. Of course, I've made a lot of personal friends that way. Correspond with somebody and eventually he turns up. I just had a beautiful letter from a young writer named Ed Gage. He lives near Tucson in Arizona. He came by the house and then went on and wrote me this letter afterwards.[6]

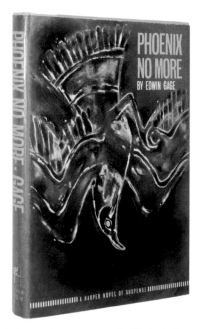

6 Two years later, in 1978, Millar blurbed Edwin Gage's novel *Phoenix No More*, comparing his writing to that of British thriller novelist Geoffrey Household.

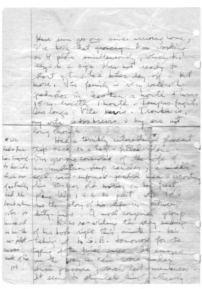
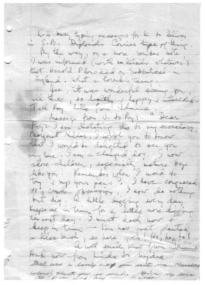

Letter from Margaret Millar to Don, Lydia, and Roy Freeman from May 1957 when the Millars were living in Menlo Park (where Ken underwent weekly psychiatric treatment). Don Freeman did the illustrated author portrait of Margaret Millar that appears on the back of her novels Wives and Lovers *(1954) and* Beast in View *(1955), winner of the Edgar® for Best Novel. Maggie explains that "K. is re-writing the very ending of his book right this minute—he's taking it to S.B. tomorrow for the typing of the final pages. It amazes me the way he can work under such pressure, such last-minuteness. It seems to stimulate him, actually." Ken sent the typed manuscript of* The Doomsters *air express to his agents at Harold Ober on May 27, 1957. On the third page of the letter is a note "from" the Millars' Scotty pup Johnnie (John Ross Macdonald Jr.) to the Freemans' son: "Dear Roy: I am dictating this to my secretary, Margaret Millar. I wish you to know that I would be delighted to see you any time. I am a changed dog. I now adore children, especially mature boys like you. Remember when I used to try + nip your paws? I have conquered this crude obsession. I now do nothing but dig. A little digging every day keeps me trim for a little more digging the next day. I must dash now + keep in trim—Ken has just planted a lilac bush, so here goes! Ho, ho, ho!" At the bottom of the same page, Linda Millar to Lydia Freeman: "That was a lovely scarf you sent me. Marvelous colors! Thank you so much. Give my love to Don and Roy—Linda." The Freemans lived in New York at the time but would eventually move to Santa Barbara, where Don Freeman would attend the Santa Barbara writers luncheons.*

Do you try to reply to most of them?

Yes. I can't, though. I can't answer them properly. Some I don't even try to answer. That's what takes up most of my free time: keeping in touch with friends and business associates. There's more of it in the later years. I get a lot more mail than I used to—at least of the kind that we're talking about. Potential friends, let's say.

Do you get a lot of interview requests and story requests?

Yes, and I've been giving quite a few interviews. Of course, I consider that part of the job. It's a part I enjoy. Interviews work both ways, you know. You learn something, too, as well as having a chance to express your own ideas.

John Leonard wrote in his piece in Esquire **that you and Eudora Welty have enjoyed a long series of letters to each other.**

Yes, we've been corresponding quite regularly for a number of years. Not a great many years, perhaps five or six. As a matter of fact, our friendship has subsisted mostly through letters, although we have spent time together four or five times.

Leonard suggested that your correspondence with her would make a wonderful book.

I don't see that it's a possibility. Eudora's letters are certainly worth collecting and I'm sure *will* be collected. She's one of the great letter writers of all time. I believe that seriously. There's no particular reason why mine should be. Hers will and should be collected altogether as a complete correspondence—*if she is willing, if she leaves permission.* And this should be done because, as I said, she writes very good and very beautiful and important letters. They're humanly important. Her letters shouldn't be chopped up and paired off with other correspondence and stuff like that. It should be a complete correspondence—her complete correspondence. Letters have been one of her major means of expression as an artist, in my opinion.[7]

7 Contrary to Millar's belief, *Meanwhile There Are Letters: The Correspondence of Eudora Welty and Ross Macdonald*, edited by Suzanne Marrs and Tom Nolan, was published in 2015.

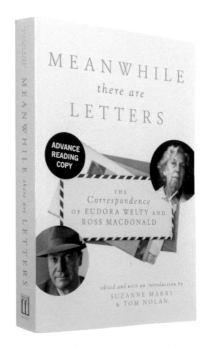

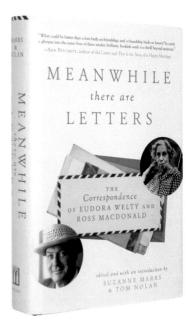

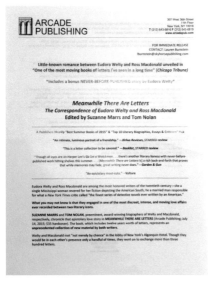

You don't have posterity in the back of your mind when you write letters?

I'm not that kind of a letter writer. I really have never taken myself that seriously as a literary personage, you know. In fact, the amount of interest that there is in me and my work now is a source of astonishment, and if somebody had predicted it when I was younger I wouldn't have believed it. At the same time, I did try to write up to a standard, but it wasn't any standard of the future, it was just the best standard I could set for myself at the time. Of course, it has shifted. I hope it's improved. Certainly it's moved on a curve anyway. One learns to write better through experience and it takes a long while for some people, and it did for me, to break through into your true subject matter, especially if you start rather far off from it and work towards it. It takes a long time.

I think the interest in you right now, it's like more or less the tip of the iceberg. I think there's going to be a lot more. I think that the question of collections of your letters and things like that will obviously come up, you know. Maybe you don't want to hear that, but I think it's true.

No, the whole idea makes me feel very good, but it isn't what I hang my hat on, so to speak. Naturally, any writer is delighted to be recognized, particularly by other writers and good readers. That's one of the main things that one works towards. And, of course, the interest of other people in one's work is enormously gratifying. Why shouldn't it be? It's the same pleasure that an athlete takes in accomplishing something and having it recognized, or anybody else who tries to do something more difficult than just living along.

You don't seem to feel any added pressure to keep topping your latest book.

No, actually there's been a release of pressure. The best formulation I ever stumbled across was simply that we write on a curve. Your curve, you see, can go anywhere you want it to, but you have to recognize that there are changes, and some are upward and some are downward. At what point you're on in that curve, you don't know. But you always have to operate as if you're on an ascending curve. And then even if you're *not* on an ascending curve you feel as if you might be. We really don't have to expect too much of ourselves, you know.

Still, a lot of people in your position would be worrying very much about consolidating their position and just jumping higher and higher up the ladder.

Yeah, but if that happens or *is* to happen, it won't happen by willing it. Or to put it in the old-fashioned way, you can't lift yourself by your own boostraps. You might just as well go ahead and do your best and enjoy it.

Bob Dylan I think is a good example of someone who everything he puts out was greeted as if it were the eighth miracle of the world. He was expected to be totally different the next time up than he was the last time. Better and completely different, which is a very hard thing for an artist to do. To be totally new every time out.

I know, I know. That's why I continually write the same thing over and over. It solves that problem anyway. You can call it variations on a theme.

19. VARIATIONS ON A THEME

There seems to be a need for you to keep exploring the same themes over and over.

Of course, I believe in continuing to explore things as long as they interest you, too. It's obviously a need, but it's also a strategy. You see, I don't really feel that a novelist necessarily has to cover a very wide range of human possibility. In other words, I think to explore very deeply one particular kind of a problem, and the lives involved in the problem, can be sufficient.

Most of your later novels move backward in time more than they move forward in time.

Yes. Of course, that's partly the result of my growing older, so that my look tends to be more backward than it was. You know, when you're young your look is *all* forward and when you're really old your look is *all* backward. Or nearly all. I'm talking about the extremes at both ends.

Some of the reviews of The Blue Hammer, ***I think in*** Time ***magazine and a couple of other publications, commented that if a reader has already read the other Archer books he could anticipate some of the action because he would already be familiar with the theme. Which is almost impossible to avoid, I would guess.***

That's right. Well, I'm not particularly concerned with it. It's the sort of thing that reviewers might comment on, but I don't really get any complaints. Leaving aside the question of the source of any particular thing, such as *Time* magazine and so on, very often a weekly reviewer is not the best source of opinion on how a book works or whether it's working. That's my feeling anyway.

I do think it's correct that anyone who has read all of the Archer books would anticipate things in The Blue Hammer.

Of course, but there would be other things that he wouldn't be anticipating. You know, the idea of variations on a theme is a perfectly valid one. Even if the theme is repeated over and over, it's a valid thing to do. It may lose some readers, but I really haven't had any complaints.

May 3, 1974

Alfred A. Knopf and Ken Millar outside Random House.

May 3, 1974   Jee Kherenke

Do you mind if I play devil's advocate for a while? Aren't you giving away suspense by doing that?

But suspense is only an element of fiction, it's not necessarily the be-all and end-all. In this last book I deliberately made clear what was happening because the book was so complex. I wanted to make things easier for the reader than they ordinarily might be in a shorter book. I deliberately gave away parts of my plot. But several of the reviewers who said that they understood the plot on the basis of finding out about the death of the son in Arizona, around page a hundred or so—you know what I'm referring to—couldn't possibly have guessed the plot at that point because there was a wholly different man and the point hadn't been made in the book. In other words, they were self-deluded in assuming that they had guessed the plot at that point. They may had felt that they had guessed the plot, but the plot that they guessed *wasn't* the plot. My point was to carry the readers over a long section of the novel in the certainty that they *had* guessed the plot, only to have that reversed again. You see, I really don't feel that that particular thing that I just referred to was a valid comment because it was impossible. How could they have guessed that so-and-so had done something who had not yet entered the story as such? It's not possible.

   Then along towards the end, of course, I laid the plot out. I had Archer sitting in his car for about a page or so and laying the plot out. It was more important to me that the whole thing should work and cohere and end properly and significantly in the reader's mind than that he should be kept guessing up to the last minute. In other words, you give something away in order to gain something else. Holding things until the last minute is not necessarily the only way to do a mystery—although I confess that's the way I've written most of my books. You know, trying to hold it to the last page. I didn't on this book. There's another form of suspense working in this novel, which is subserved by the reader knowing quite a lot, and that is the basic suspense as to what the fates will be of the people involved. That's more basic in fiction than suspense as to who killed who when, you know, and that sort of thing.

*It does seem to me that the books since **The Galton Case** primarily have dealt with crimes that have gone back twenty, twenty-five years, and that the*

philosophical impact of that is very great—if it's the first or the second or the third or the fourth time you read it. But don't you think that this lessens the impact somewhat if the reader knows you're going to do this? As a reader, you can't possibly have the same feeling of awe that you experienced the first few times. In that way I think the approach is somewhat predictable. The surprises and the wonders become less satisfying.

Yes. The basic structures of the books are too similar. Well, you start out aiming at a particular thing and later on you aim at something a little different. I'm still back on the idea that it isn't necessary, even in a novel of suspense, to maintain the suspense right up to the last. In other words, I'm just not accepting the rule that you have to maintain the mystery up to the end. Sometimes you have to give it away.
   A more basic question is very simple: should mystery novels attempt to cover a span of a generation? Well, if they do, what are they going to be about? If they're about crimes, which mystery novels are by definition, I suppose, you're *stuck* with more than one generation and crimes in those generations. I'm talking about the actual nature of the form. Now, it's quite true that there are many advantages and beauties in writing something that takes place in the here and now, period; and that's the alternative.

It's like doing the same card trick six times in a row. You're not going to have a sense of surprise—

That's right.

—which is necessary for a work of art sometimes to ignite. Is that an essential thing to give away?

Yeah, but half my books don't embody this theme.

I think they do.

Well, not to the extent that we're talking about. But all the good ones do.

The later ones do.

Yeah, but I'm talking about ones that don't.

I don't think they're bad books.

Well, I'm not ashamed of any of the books, but there are distinctions between them and some are better than others. I consider the first half of the production inferior to the second half, and I consider any one book in the second half to be better than any one book in the first half.
   You quote a *Time* magazine or some other reviewer, and I don't take that particular kind of thing seriously at all. I take seriously the idea that my books are repetitious, though. It doesn't cause me particular pain because I've always felt that if a writer produced one or two or three really good books in his life, he had succeeded in doing what he meant to do. I think my books *are* repetitious, but that is both a strength and a weakness. You can't quarrel with reality, you know. And I've written the books [*laughs*]—for whatever they are, there they are. I can't change them, you know?
   See, my theory of working is a little different from that of a reviewer for *Time* magazine. It really is. My basic aim is to write a few good books and, meanwhile,

May 3, 1974   Jill Krementz

in the times that I'm not writing those few good books, to accomplish work that's worth doing and that will be useful to me in writing the good books. Hell, if I can get one really good book out of my lifetime of work, I'll be content. How many really good books did Fitzgerald get out of his lifetime of work?

One and a half, I think.

Yeah, that's about it. Well, we could count his good short stories as a good volume, too. Anyway, two and a half, and he was a much better writer than I'll ever be. You see what I mean? The standard that I'm being judged by is a little artificial.

I have nothing against reviewers—I'm a reviewer myself—but a lot of these reviewers weren't following me twenty-five years or thirty years ago. So they've read all the books in the last two years, or the ones that they have read have been read in the last two years, and it gives the impression in their minds that, well, I'm just repeating myself rapidly, so to speak. At the same time, they miss the variations. They're all variations on a theme, of course. But you have to take all the variations into account. If you want to express *my* view, it's expressed by the whole thing; it's not expressed by any one statement that you can pick out and say, "This is what Millar thinks or says." The books are not written that way. Everything is in reference to its context. But on the whole, I've never had any letters from readers, including my teenage readers, asking me, "What on earth does this mean?" I think the books are pretty plain. That may be a fault, but I started out as a high school teacher and never got over it.

What are the dangers you see in your books that you have to watch out for when you're writing?

Well, I no doubt overdo the search for motive in the past. But you can't expect me to go on like this because, if this appears in print, a lot of reviewers will simply be echoing my own words and saying, "Oh, he *admits* that he makes all these mistakes!" In fact, I'll be telling them things that they wouldn't have noticed for themselves.

***Oh, I think there are great variations, but there are some repetitions. For instance, the fire in* The Underground Man *seems to me to be repeated by the oil spill in the very next book,* Sleeping Beauty.**

Oh sure. Although those books do stand a little aside. But while one repeats the other, they're quite different from the other books. In other words, they break the pattern of repetition. Take the two books together and they break that pattern. In any case, I was starting something a little new and I deliberately wrote two environmentalist books at that point. That's what I wanted to write, you see.

Ralph Sipper sees those two books and* The Blue Hammer *as being a trilogy. Do you feel that they are?

I don't know. I regard all the books as connected. To me it's essentially just all one.

But you paired up two of them,* Sleeping Beauty *and* The Underground Man, *in a deliberate way. Would you connect* The Blue Hammer *to them in the same overt way?

No, I don't see the obvious connections that I see between the two environmentalist books. All the books are just sentences in a paragraph, and the sentences come in a certain order and add up to a paragraph, I assume. The chief argument with my work that we've been talking about just now is the idea of repetition. Well, I accepted the fact of repetition in writing at an early stage. I've never hesitated to repeat a theme in the hope of doing it better. Or certainly in the hope of doing it differently. What may appear to be a weakness is also a strength.

You know, recurring to a subject or a form or a pattern or a plot can sometimes enable you to write something better than you've done before. I claim that I've done that with some of these books by repeating patterns. Remember, too, that the idea of variations in repeated patterns is another way of being original in relation to what you've done before. To find a new shape behind, or in, the old shape. Anyway, that's what I've done. I know there are writers who come up with a whole different world with each book, but I haven't been able to—or even sought to.

Speaking of variations on a theme, that's the ideal image in one sense for any artist. Jazz variations. I learned a lot, I think, about writing and attitudes to writing from the jazz musicians, you know. I'm not just dragging in the painters and the jazz musicians—they really spoke to me directly and they taught me things to do in writing that you couldn't learn from other writers. You had to learn it from musicians and painters. At least I did.

Ken Millar accepting his Grand Master Edgar® on May 3, 1974.

20. TRUTH IN FICTION

Do you think you fully understand your own books as you write them?

Oh no. But I understand them in a way that is central; I understand how they work. I have to understand the forces and counterforces in the structure as I write them, but I don't know what those forces and counterforces necessarily imply. I don't know all their implications by any means. Naturally, I try to write about things that are both very important to me and, at the same time, things that lead off from the personal in the direction of other people in the society. I'm certainly blind to all kinds of implications that go into the fiction as I write it. The main thing as I'm writing is to make it work.

Do you have enough inherent trust that, if it works on one level for you, the implications are pluses rather than minuses?

I'm certainly aware of everything I say, but I'm not aware of all its implications.

Let me rephrase it: It's not a bad thing to you that you don't understand fully everything that you write. Is that correct?

Right. I think it's better not to because it's a limitation to want to understand everything that you're doing. God knows, a high jumper doesn't. He doesn't get over the bar by virtue of understanding what he's doing, even though he may study what he's doing. Maybe that's not a very good example, but you know what I mean.

Do you think there could be several interpretations of one book?

Yes. In the case of a fairly complex novel approaching a hundred thousand words, I don't know how you could say of it that it had a unitary intention. It must be a multiple intention. One reader will see one aspect of it more clearly and another reader will see another aspect of it more clearly. While everything is intended by me, much of my intent is unconscious, too. And the truth is in the *structure* of the event, not in what you say one way or the other.

I don't follow.

Let's say that you have a picture: one hand holding the fist of the other hand, and they're pressing against each other. Now, here's somebody that says yes about some particular thing on the one hand, and here is somebody who says no about some particular thing. The truth of it is not in what this guy says or what this guy says but in the event of their contradiction. Because both are comprehended by reality. Does that explain what I mean? In other words, any particular statement is merely one thread in the web of reality. That's really what I implied by talking about the curled hand on the one side and the closed fist on the other side, coming together. They're pressing against each other in opposite directions, but between the two of them they constitute a reality. This is particularly true of fiction. Fiction is not by any means mono-linear *ever*. It's always multiple. In fact, dialogue, as far as my fiction is concerned, is sort of the essence of it. Dialogue implies people talking back and forth. You might say that my books are built on reversal of accepted ideas—by other accepted ideas, though.

You know, I don't mean to impose my opinion on readers, because obviously the weight I attach to some of these books is purely subjective. You know, we value things that have to do with ourselves, particularly in writing. I think we take great satisfaction in telling autobiographical truth. We take a particular pleasure. Obviously, it's one of the main motives of writing novels: to get the self or one's experiences on paper. So I value some of these books because they do that even though they may not satisfy me in other ways. The ones that work best sometimes, like *The Zebra-Striped Hearse*, are quite remote from my own experience. Sometimes the books that you break through in your own truth are not necessarily the ones that work out best. An excellent example is Fitzgerald's *Tender Is the Night*. There he certainly got more truth on the paper than he ever had elsewhere, but it was so much truth that he couldn't handle it. Or didn't, anyway. So truth isn't the only criterion.

There's one scene that recurs in some of your books: a young child witnessing a murder and not remembering it or remembering it only partially. What meaning does that scene have to you personally?

I'm sure that these repetitive themes of fear and violence on the part of a young child in a family relationship do go back to unremembered memory, you might say. I don't doubt it at all. I don't *think* I ever witnessed a murder when I was a young child, but I witnessed other things, including violent crime. I did see a man lying in an alley, from a hotel window when I was three, who I thought had been killed. But I don't believe he had been; that was just my initial thought. There were parental arguments, but so far as I know they didn't involve anything violent.

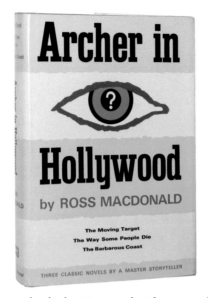

There actually is a scene in The Blue Hammer where Doris remembers hiding in the laundry hamper while her father and Mildred argue.

Oh yes. It's practically a transliteration of a scene of physical violence. In fact, there *is* some physical violence involved. He breaks down the door or something like that. But there again it's symbolically handled in a sense. But a thing like that, as you know, for children it can be just as significant as the most extreme event. The psychic reverberations can be even worse from something involving, oh, conflicts between people that you love or are trying to love.

I don't think there's any direct rendition of my own childhood experiences in my books, but I'm sure that the scenes that I have invented, the central scenes, *do* refer back to childhood experiences in relation with my family. And in relation to other people, too. The more important thing that refers back is the absence of the father. I would have much preferred, even if it involved violence, to have had a father rather than nobody there. I think the absent father is in a sense a more important recurrence in my books than what we've been talking about. Of course, when the father is absent a child is exposed to the possibilities of all the violences that a society can offer. A child is exposed by the loss of a father. That I think is a central theme, although perhaps not stated in just those terms, in the books: the extreme vulnerability of children and the significance of early events in their later lives. All of which of course is widely accepted psychological doctrine or derives from it.

What do you think it is that draws you so compulsively to the runaway theme, as well as the search for the father?

My original sin, so to speak, was to be left by my father when I was going on four, and there's no doubt at all that's why the subject is so personally important to me. But, you see, the personal importance when you work on it imaginatively over the years becomes what might be called a personal myth rather than a personal experience. In other words, you convert the pains and sorrows of your life into a structure of meaning, and I recur to that meaning and find new structures for it—I hope they're new anyway—different ways of handling the theme. Certainly the idea of the prodigal son reversed is old enough in fiction, it's a traditional theme. What any writer can hope to do with traditional themes which we all deal in is to find the personal shape and tone and feeling for it, and of course to explain it as profoundly as you can. Or explicate it—perhaps *explain* isn't quite the word. Fiction doesn't explain so much as present and trace out. It traces out causes and consequences.

Can you conceive of writing a book that wouldn't refer to this theme or explore it?

Sure, I have notes for books that don't go into that area at all.

Regardless, it's always there.

It's the central, original fact of my life, so to speak. You see, I'm not just talking about what happened when I was four, I'm talking about what happened throughout my childhood, and the theme and similar themes have been reinforced by my experiences as an adult. *And* as a father. And as a grandfather.

You said that your "attempts to write outside of genre haven't worked well." What would they be?

Oh, a couple of novels. They were early in my career as a novelist. One was a semiautobiographical novel, the sort of traditional going-into-manhood novel. It didn't turn out well enough so that I even showed it to anybody. And another was a novel that I collaborated on with a Jewish refugee [James Meisel] from Hitler's Germany, a subject which has interested me since I went there at the age of twenty and ever since. It was a pretty good novel. Most of the material in it came from my collaborator and most of the writing in it came from me. It was good enough to have been published if the timing had been right. Unfortunately, we submitted it for publication the same month that the Hitler Reich fell. Nineteen-forty-five. It was written in the preceding year or so. At that point there was a universal decision in publishing that nothing more about Hitler would ever sell again or nothing more about Nazi Germany would ever sell again.

That certainly hasn't proven true, has it?

No.

Where would these books come in at the timeline of your books? The autobiographical novel, when did you write that?

The autobiographical novel came later. It went on over a period of several years. It was something I would work on and go back to. Actually, I had written a number of detective stories before I finished it.

You pretty well have decided that you will not publish it?

I certainly wouldn't. I'd be ashamed to. It simply wasn't a publishable book. It was an experimental attempt, but that's not my medium at all.

I'm assuming that you're in effect telling somewhat personal stories through the Archer books. Did a lot of the strands from the autobiographical novel find their way into the Archer novels?

No, not really very much. Except in a very remote sense.

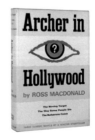 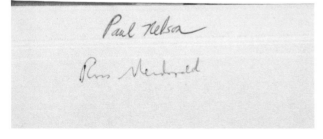

Paul Nelson's copy of Archer in Hollywood *(1967) with his ownership signature on the front free endpaper above Ken Millar's (as Ross Macdonald).*

Would you say there was no correlation between the two?

Correlation would be quite thin.

Emotionally, too?

Well, I don't know. I haven't even looked at these materials in twenty-five years or so. The Archer books are not intended to be autobiographical.

I don't mean that they're straight autobiography in any way, but, for example, there's certainly a lot of you in The Galton Case. *And in your foreword to* Archer in Hollywood *you make this statement: "We writers, as we work our way deeper into our craft, learn to drop more and more personal clues. Like burglars who secretly wish to be caught, we leave our fingerprints on the broken locks, our voiceprints in the bugged rooms, our footprints in the wet concrete and the blowing sand."*

Yes, but that wasn't the question that you asked. The question that you asked was the connection between the unpublished adolescent novel and my later books. That doesn't say anything about the unpublished adolescent novel.

I don't know what that was about other than it was apparently about your life.

About my adolescent self.

I'm missing a distinction.

Well, you just haven't asked the question that has the answer you want.

What's the question?

See, you're asking me to make a connection between an unpublished adolescent novel and something like *The Galton Case.*

I just assumed there would be overlapping events in both.

So far as I know there aren't. No, you see, I don't work from life the way a "serious" novelist does.

Why in that quote do you say that you do?

Just a minute. I work from life only in the restricted sense. I don't make any attempt in writing about a character or a family to paint a portrait of an actual character or an actual family. What I do is take out of my own life a felt and observed and lived, in many cases, structure, which is partly emotional and partly autobiographical and so on. But nothing that I write is a direct photograph or recording of something that actually happened to me or anybody else. Now, for example, *The Galton Case*, which I've written about in a short essay, which you're familiar with, *is* autobiographical in a kind of special sense. What I've

done is taken elements of my life which I consider important and put them into a pot, which doesn't already reflect anything that really happened in life directly. Now, you could by examining *The Galton Case* find many traces of my actual life, events in my life which gave me ideas and so on, but that isn't the same thing as asking me to point out in a fiction those elements which were drawn from actual life. If that's the question.

I don't think I asked you that.

No, I said, "If that's the question." I still don't know what the question is.

I'm not sure what the question is.

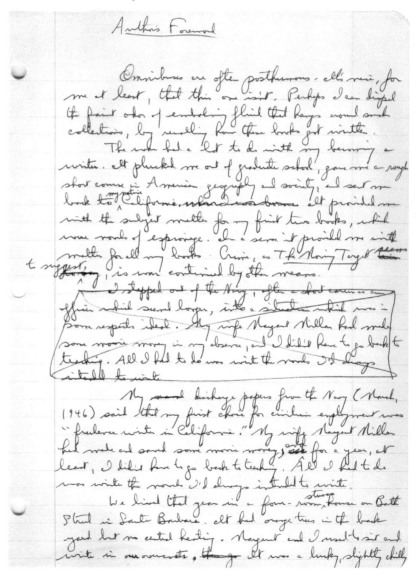

Manuscript for the foreword of Archer in Hollywood.
"We lived that year in a four-room stucco house on Bath Street in Santa Barbara. It had orange trees in the back yard but no central heating. Margaret and I used to sit and write in our overcoats."

Oh, what you said was it's strange that I should write a book which has autobiographical elements. But they're not the same elements.

Maybe I misunderstood, but I sort of thought that you were saying the emotional content was different also.

Did I? I certainly don't mean to say that. Let's put it this way: instead of trying to discover what I said or didn't say, let me just say it: *The Galton Case* is an imaginative reconstruction of certain aspects of my own life as a boy. Of course, this

Above left: Family snapshot of Ken Millar at 2124 Bath Street. Above right: Maggie Millar at Hendry's Beach in Santa Barbara. The Millars bought the Bath Street home in April of 1945. Maggie's 1950 novel Do Evil in Return *features several collies prominently. Below: Ken and Linda (probably at Hendry's Beach), January 1947.*

is obvious to anyone who knows even the most external events of my life, such as the family breakup in Canada and the move on my part from Canada to the United States. You see, those overall subject matters are autobiographical, but the actual events are imagined. Now do you understand how they can be both autobiographical and not? See, I actually didn't get to the United States that way. Even in the broadest sense my life is not reflected by the life of the boy in *The Galton Case* except in a most unexpected and totally non-autobiographical way. Now, for example, you may or may not remember that the boy in *The Galton Case* is befriended by a man in Ann Arbor, Michigan. Remember? Well, what happened to me in Ann Arbor, Michigan? I got my doctorate. There really isn't a hell of a lot of connection—except that in Ann Arbor, Michigan, I got a real lift from certain people, notably W. H. Auden.

Actually the books that I've written that come closest to being autobiographical are the early ones. *Trouble Follows Me* leans heavily on my experiences in the Navy, but it isn't autobiographical really. Thank God.

See, I'm not writing from life—except in the sense that the modal forces that drive the life, I try to reflect in the novels. They're the things that really fascinate me. My driving forces are reflected in the novels but only in a structural sense, not in any effort to give a picture of my life as it actually was.

But again I'm going to ask the question—but not in an emotional sense?

Oh, I don't deny the emotional whatever.

I thought at the beginning that it was coming out that it wasn't your emotional sense.

No. I would regard *The Galton Case*, within limits [as emotionally autobiographical], and the limits are that it's essentially an invented story. It really *is* essentially an invented story. I've left a record of how it got invented. Many of the notebooks show how it got invented. Within those limits, of course, it has elements of emotional autobiography. But all my books do, every one of them, of course. But I never work directly from life and I don't draw portraits, even self-portraits, from life. I think I'm different from most other writers in that respect.

Why don't you, do you think?

I think life as I've lived it is not interesting enough and not satisfying enough—

Do you stand on that quotation? [laughs]

Well, I haven't finished the sentence yet: —to be appropriate subject matter for the kind of fiction I write. To put it very bluntly: my life is not interesting, but I try to make my fiction interesting, dramatic, and so on. My life is extremely humdrum. Except when I have visitors from Los Angeles and New York.[1]

In most cases, though, my ideas for fiction come to me *as* ideas for fiction and not as an offshoot of some specific autobiographical thing. In other words, the notebooks are just full of ideas for fiction, not autobiography. But I've gradually developed a pattern and learned how to use my experiences and how to develop them into story ideas.

1 This was a nod to the fact that, for this particular interview session, Paul and Millar had been joined by Warren and Crystal Zevon, who had driven up from Los Angeles, and Kit Rachlis, who was in town from New York City.

There are a lot of bad doctors in your books, doctors who have gone wrong and who are central figures of evil. I'm just wondering if that means anything, whether that was coincidence or if you perhaps had a bad experience or two with doctors.

I don't know whether it means anything or not. Don't you think that fiction writers tend to write about the central figures in their society without necessarily aiming to define those central figures solely? In other words, we write about the power points. I know I do. Doctors are more than just characters, they're extremely central power figures in our society. You could make a case for their being the most important people in our society. God knows that there are cases where they don't fulfill their obligations, as people or as doctors.

You know, they're lightning rods also. They attract the lightning, they attract trouble—and I'm speaking now of both in fiction and in reality. You must accept the fact, as I do, that there's a sense in which my books, although I claim them for realism and still do, their basic structures are very often quite simple. They could almost be called fairytale structures. You know, it's possible to use a character in that sense, as an evil character, without pretending to yourself or to your reader that you're literally trying to describe a whole category of human beings, such as doctors. See, doctors are significant and therefore they can be used, turned either to good or to evil, as characters and also in real life. It's their significance that attracts the lightning, and this is particularly true of course in the kind of writing I do, which could almost be described as imaginative psychiatric writing. The doctor is very often a terribly central figure. Such writing doesn't reflect my judgments as a person. I can say with literal truth that some of my best friends are doctors and the people I admire most—I mean that literally—but I don't write about them.

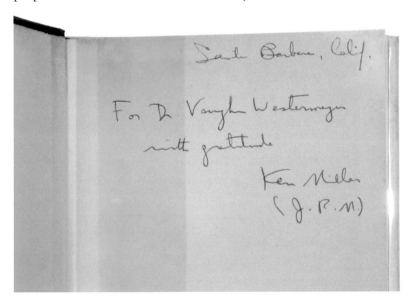

UK Cassell edition of The Doomsters *(1959), inscribed by Ken Millar to Vaughn W. Westermeyer, a doctor who was on the administrative staff of Santa Barbara City College as College Medical Consultant. Millar taught a night class at SBCC in the late 1950s.*

A near saint like my doctor—his name is Dr. Smith, who is I think the best doctor in town—doesn't make for good fiction of the kind that I write. He wouldn't even be believed.

I really did want to make a distinction there between what comes out in the books and one's personal experience as people in the same category. I'm really not damning *any* doctors. I'm writing about imaginative figures. God knows, as imaginative and symbolic figures they're terribly important in our culture. Of course, I'm aware of the fact that they're not all living saints like Dr. Smith.

Ken Millar, Paul Nelson, and Warren Zevon at the Coral Casino Beach and Cabana Club in 1976. Photo by Crystal Zevon.

On the whole I have reason to feel very grateful to doctors. And I do. But, you know, when you write this kind of book, which has a fairytale or a mythic aspect, you're not writing about the guy next door. You're writing about the *dreams* of the guy next door in a sense. You're writing about his interior experiences rather than his relationship with the neighbors. Now, all these of course are true facts about the guy next door, both the inner horrors and terrors and the outer pleasant relationships with the neighbors. I don't write about the pleasant relationships with the neighbors, although they're not completely absent from my writing. I'm writing about the nightmare aspects of modern life. That's my subject. I don't live in that nightmare myself. If I did I wouldn't be able to write it. But I *can* observe it. It exists, too, you know.

But at times you have been touched by that nightmare in your life.

Oh, of course. And everything I write is to some extent autobiographical. That's what we've been talking about all these days.

may 31, 1974   *Jill Krementz*

21. CRITICS AND CRITICISM

What has been your attitude towards reading reviews of your books?

I read all the book reviews that are available. I don't think any particular review has ever changed my pattern of writing, but certainly I've been encouraged by some reviewers and discouraged by others. In the early years when I was writing the first half dozen books, I was particularly encouraged by the support of *The New York Times* reviewer who called himself Anthony Boucher.[1] As a matter of fact, he started giving me good reviews when he was still writing reviews for the *San Francisco Chronicle*. We became friends when the Navy brought me out here to California and we remained friends for the rest of his life. Without encouragement from him, I really wouldn't have been able to go on in the certainty that what I was doing was worth doing. Because some of the other reviewers didn't like my work at all and said so.

Back in the days that we're talking about there wasn't much mystery reviewing as such. *The New York Times* review was practically it. Of course, there was the *Tribune*, but that wasn't as important nor was the reviewing as good.[2] There were just very few outlets for mystery reviewing. Now of course mysteries are actually being reviewed as novels, some of the particularly important ones anyway.

These were mainly short reviews we're talking about?

Sure. That's all that mysteries got in those days: just short, one-paragraph reviews. It was terribly important to a beginning mystery writer to meet with the approbation of Anthony Boucher because he was the reigning expert in the field. A position he earned. So that kind of support was just absolutely essential. I can't think of anybody offhand who ever became so important to me.

Did you like Boucher's fiction?

Well, it was consciously old-fashioned. It was the fiction of a critic and an antiquarian. Within those limitations I liked him. But that wasn't his strongest suit. It's as a critic that he's remembered. He was a learned man, too, probably the

most learned man in the field that there's ever been. Boucher was sort of the American expert on mysteries.

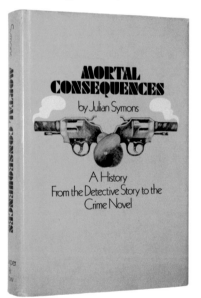

Ken Millar's copy of Julian Symons's Mortal Consequences (1972) *with his penciled notes on the front free endpaper. Millar's blurb for the book appears on the front flap of the dust jacket: "Julian Symons, the distinguished English crime novelist and critic, has given us the best history of the detective story and crime novel yet written. I found it wonderfully good reading!"*

Like Julian Symons in England?

Yeah. But a better critic than Symons, I think, or at least a more catholic critic. More catholic in two senses: he was also a devout Roman Catholic. He was the *Times* reviewer of mysteries for a good many years, but he made himself known in other vehicles, too. He wrote mysteries himself and he was a great scholar, not only of mysteries but he managed to learn an awful lot. He knew several languages well enough to translate from them. He was sort of a fine follower of the birthday culture. A very nice man, too. He also, for years, cowrote the *Ellery Queen* radio series.

---

1   Boucher's real name was William Anthony Parker White. Millar dedicated *The Drowning Pool* "to Tony."
2   Millar was most likely referring to the *New York Herald Tribune* and reviewers Will Cuppy and, especially, James Sandoe, to whom Raymond Chandler had issued his letter calling Ross Macdonald a "literary eunuch."

This page and next page: Three progressive drafts of a letter by Ken Millar to the Teacher Placement Office at the University of Wisconsin recommending Peter Wolfe, author of the Ross Macdonald study Dreamers Who Live Their Dreams: The World of Ross Macdonald's Novels, *for a teaching position. "Wolfe's book on Iris Murdoch was written as his doctoral dissertation and remains, ten years later, a brilliant study of that writer … I have read most of Peter Wolfe's books, and followed his reviews in* The New Republic *and other journals, have corresponded with Wolfe about his work, and had the pleasure of discussing it in person with him more than once. I am deeply impressed by his intelligence and seriousness, his unflagging devotion to the related arts of writing and teaching. Peter Wolfe is a wonderfully useful man, learned and serious, resourceful and dedicated. I consider him one of the finest teachers and critics of his generation." On the return address of the second draft, Millar wrote, "Kenneth Millar Ph. D. (Ross Macdonald)," presumably to lend academic weight to his recommendation of Wolfe. From the third draft: "His book on Graham Green's [sic] entertainments blazed new trails, as did his critical studies of Mary Renault and Rebecca West."*

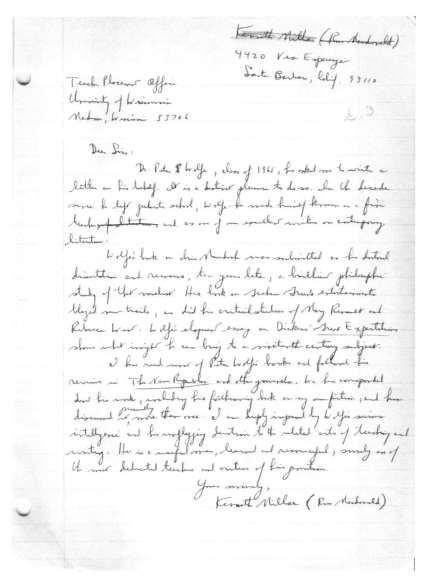

What are some of the other reviews you received that really were encouraging to you at the time?

Julian Symons is certainly an example. He was here incidentally a few weeks ago. He's, well, among other things a scholar, a real scholar, and he loves library work. One reason is I think that he never went to college. He's not exactly self-educated. Somebody who is a personal disciple of Wyndham Lewis could not be described as self-educated. He's a remarkable man, a really remarkable man. I don't know how he's gotten through all the work that he's done. He's a good poet, too, you know.

I met him in New York. I've known him for I should think ten or twelve years. Notice I have his picture up here. That's Julian and Auden. It's a fairly late picture of Auden. I think it was taken in Auden's last year [1973]. It was at a meeting of the Poetry Society [of America] or whatever you call it. They were two of the most benign influences on my life, those two British writers, Auden and Julian.

In recent years recognition of your work has moved from "Criminals at Large," Boucher's column inside the **Times,** *to front pages and into various doctoral theses—and an entire book, in fact. Peter Wolfe's book [***Dreamers Who Live Their Dreams: The World of Ross Macdonald's Novels***] is coming out. What kind of effect has that kind of criticism had on you?*

Well, it's had the effect of encouraging me and confirming me in what I'm doing. Of course, I feel that I've been treated enormously generously by various people. Eudora Welty, for example. She wrote a most generous review of … *The Underground Man.* That was probably the most important critical event in my life, in my writing life and also in my personal life, to be accepted by a really great writer.[3]

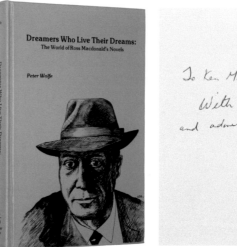

Ken Millar's copy of Dreamers Who Live Their Dreams: The World of Ross Macdonald's Novels *(1976), inscribed to him by Peter Wolfe in 1977.*

You hadn't met her at the time, or am I wrong?

I hadn't met her. Of course I've been reading her from the beginning. From her beginning.

I was surprised by the Eudora Welty connection with your work.

She's a mystery fan. She was sort of the most important figure in what you called "the conspiracy." I've since met her several times, and went to visit her in Mississippi. It was an interesting thing that happened down there a couple of years ago. The state of Mississippi proclaimed Eudora Welty Day [May 2, 1973]. So she invited her friends from all over the country to come down there. You know these marquees that they have out in front of modern motels? On one side the motel where I was staying had Eudora Welty Day and on the other side Welcome, Mr. Millar. [*laughs*] For one day and then the next day it was somebody else that was staying in the motel. Anyway, it lasted for several days and people did come from all over the country. It was a great occasion.

3 Welty's critical Valentine to Millar appeared in *The New York Times Book Review,* February 14, 1971. Two years later, he dedicated *Sleeping Beauty* to her.

May 1973 draft of a letter from Ken Millar to Ash Green telling of his visit to Mississippi: "I really enjoyed Mississippi much more than I expected to. Of course Eudora Welty naturally tended to bring together nice people from all over, including for example Joan Kahn and her sister, and Reynolds Price whose work I have long admired. I enjoyed meeting Diarmuid Russell, who is a great conversationalist in spite of his illness. And Eudora, who gave two parties and a reading, attended a production of "Ponder Heart" and a post-theater party that went on into the small hours, went on being indefatigably her sweet self. (Now she's in New York—just wrote from the Algonquin.)" Diarmuid Russell was Eudora Welty's longtime agent and died in December that year. Millar goes on to mention his upcoming extensive interview with Samuel L. Grogg Jr. in The Journal of Popular Culture *and* Sleeping Beauty *reviews from Matt Bruccoli and Gerald Walker, author of* Cruising, *a book for which Millar provided a blurb.*

Was she assigned that review?

She consented. The *Times* asked her to do it and she agreed. It came out of an interview that she gave to the *Times* in which she mentioned my work. That's what led to it. I guess John Leonard was the man who asked her to do it. I've been fortunate indeed in having fans in high places. John Leonard, of course, has been very nice to me. I hope I've been very nice to him. He's a Long Beach boy. I think the fact that Lew Archer is a Long Beach detective means something to him. There are other biographical details that I won't go into that led me to this.

Leonard was assistant editor of The New York Times Book Review when he and Ray Sokolov, Newsweek's critic, launched their so-called literary conspiracy.[4] Were you aware that the conspiracy was as conscious as Leonard alleges it was?

Yeah, I was aware of it at the time.

What was your reaction on this conspiracy as presented to you?

Joy.

Are you glad that you're not part of the East Coast media pressure cooker?

Yeah. I'm not part of any literary movement or coterie, and I'm glad. I suppose one reason why I write as I do is in order not to become [part of one]. There's a lot to be said for the writer as lone wolf. I don't mean to say that I don't have friends, but they're the friends I would probably have whether I were writing these books or not.

How have things like the front page of The New York Times Book Review increased those pressures, though?

4 In 1969, Leonard and Sokolov "conspired" to get Ross Macdonald recognized as, to use Leonard's words, "a major American novelist." In addition to Welty, they enlisted the critical prose of author William Goldman, who had adapted *The Moving Target* to the screen as *Harper*. The end results ended up on the front page of *The New York Times Book Review* and the cover of *Newsweek*, and brought Millar the critical and commercial success that had thus far eluded him. Goldman's *Times Book Review* called the Archer books "the finest series of detective novels ever written by an American."

Not very much.

Because you're geographically isolated from them?

That's right. I regard myself as a temporary front-page writer anyway. I never expected anything like a front-page review in *The New York Times Book Review*. I never envisaged it as a possibility. It really was a remarkable thing.

Now that the critics see you as an important American novelist, does each book have to be as good or better than the previous one?

Well, you do it as well as you can. I could have spent another year on this book [*The Blue Hammer*] and I didn't. I just felt that I had given it my best really and would rather put it out and get ready for something new. You know, I guess I don't have the kind of dedication that you mentioned, the kind of thing that would make you work for eight years on a project.

You don't particularly worry about the critical acclaim anymore?

I've had the kind of critical reception that I never even dreamed of, and it would be silly for me to sit around and worry about it. And if I don't get any more, well, I've had it.

And you got it without pursuing it.

That's true. I never made a move in that direction. Except with my pen.

What do you think would have happened if your first book had wound up on the front page of The New York Times Book Review?

I would have written fewer books.

Because you would have been in a position to?

Yeah, I think that economic pressure is a very good thing to have—if you're young. I think a deferred recognition or a deferred popularity is very desirable. Naturally, you want to be able to live and you don't want to be destroyed by melancholy, but in my case it worked out okay. It was enough to encourage me to

go on being a writer. My first book *did* go into a second printing and got a good review from *The New Republic*, so that's all I ever needed to go on with. Also, I didn't deserve any great recognition on the basis of my early books.

Before you achieved popular commercial success, was that important to you?

Yes, but it wasn't a primary goal. My main aim was to write good books. That really puts everything else in the shade as far as I'm concerned. Just being able to write something that nobody else has done.

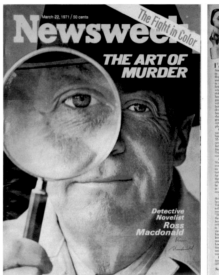

But also sharing that with several hundred thousand people.

That's less important than you might think. I mean, apart from the fact that I don't have to worry about money anymore. It's true, it's nice to have an audience, but I've always had enough of an audience to satisfy me after the first few books. A mass audience isn't really necessary, and I don't even know if it's good for a writer. I mean, you really shouldn't judge yourself by the number of people who buy your book and that sort of thing. I mean, you can judge yourself, but don't judge your book on those terms.

On the other hand, it's far better for that work to be widely read than for it not to be read at all, I would think.

Yeah. But it isn't an essential difference. Because much better writers than I, as you know, have not had an audience at all or any kind of large audience until long after they're dead.

Do you think there's anyone currently working who's unrecognized? Who ought to be?

I'm sure there are, but I don't know who they are. I generally am not very far in advance of popular judgment, although I went for people like Fitzgerald and Hammett and so on as early as I could have. Even though it's been beneficial to me—or at least I hope it has—I think it's unfortunate that fiction has become such a big deal. I mean, the whole publishing of fiction and what it can do for you and,

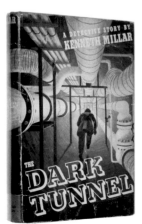

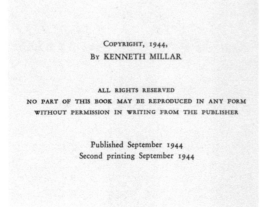

you know, suddenly you're a millionaire on one book and that sort of thing. It's sort of unfortunate for the proper conduct and ordering of a writer's life. It would be better if writers had more freedom from that kind of interruption even just in their own thoughts, you know? It deflects you from what should be your main goal.

Which is quality.

Which is quality, yeah.

With most writers, I guess, success comes later, so chances are they're a little more mature then.

That's true. Of course, if you're old enough you can't be ruined because you've already done your work. Very few writers are particularly successful much before middle age.

If at all.

If at all, right. And the longer you can put it off the better.

What about a public persona? Do you think that's a necessary role for the novelist—or an unattractive one or an untenable one—to be a public celebrity?

Well, I think it's a little unreal.

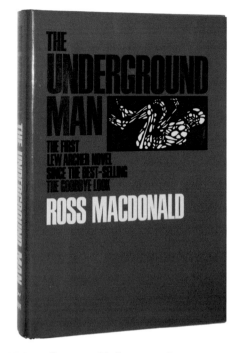

I mean, is it a choice you haven't made?

We all present a public persona to some extent, but I haven't worked at it. Maybe if I had been well-known like Mailer and also operating on the Eastern seaboard, where there is enormous pressure—of which he is terribly conscious for various reasons, including the fact that he's a small man who would've liked to be an athlete. I'm sort of disappointed in the way he's gone. But this is an old-fashioned attitude. At the same time I'm ready to admit, and do, that journalism is maybe our central medium right now in prose.

We've all seen All the President's Men. It's almost as if the journalist has become the new hero, and that part of the reason why he's become the new hero is that he's being identified more and more with being a detective.

Yes. Also, he combines two functions: he can both perform and celebrate his performance.

Which the detective only in fiction can do.

But the journalist can do it literally.

Have you read Hunter S. Thompson?

I've read some. I thought he was sort of disturbed. He seems to know that he is, too.

And celebrates it as well.

Yeah, he celebrates it. It's interesting to have people starting one-man movements all over the country, you know. Men who at one time would have been novelists and quite content to write a book and send it in and sell 5,000 copies, they've become rather enormous public figures. But you pay a price for that.

Creating a persona, then having to try to live up to it—for Hemingway the strain, I guess, became so much that he just cracked up.

Yeah. If he had maintained a more private life, it would have been better for him perhaps. You know, that business of feeding on publicity is something that everybody has to watch. It is dangerous. It's better not to believe what people say to your face, you know. If it's too good.

February 1971 issue of Cosmopolitan *featuring a condensed version of* The Underground Man. *This would be the last of Millar's novels to appear in the magazine. Like most condensed versions, this likely preceded the book publication.*

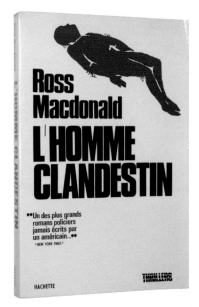
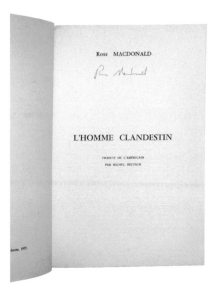

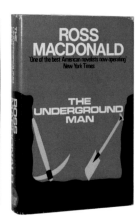

Above: Early (thicker) and later (thinner and tape-bound) uncorrected proofs along with trade hardcover of the UK Collins edition of The Underground Man *(1971). Below: Two inscribed copies of the US edition of* The Underground Man; *one as a gift inscription to someone's father, the other one more literary, with allusions to T. S. Eliot and Charles Baudelaire, to applied mathematician and aeronautical engineer Paco A. Lagerstrom: "mon* hypocrite lecteur *and oceangoing friend."*

Above: A signed copy of the French edition of The Underground Man, *which preceded the release of the UK edition by a little over a month. The French edition was published on September 25, 1971, and the British edition on November 1, 1971 (the US edition was published on February 19 the same year). Below: Two different Taiwanese pirated editions of* The Underground Man; *the one with the green binding has Chinese characters on the copyright page. The US editions of* The Goodbye Look, The Underground Man, Sleeping Beauty, *and* The Blue Hammer *all went into multiple hardcover printings and had Taiwanese pirated counterparts, presumably to take advantage of the demand for these* New York Times *bestsellers.*

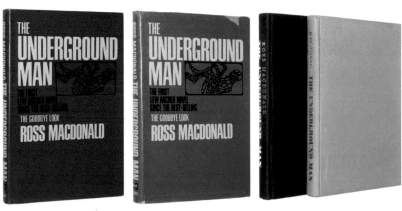

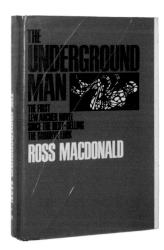
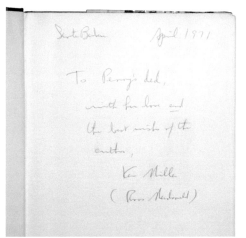

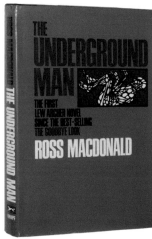
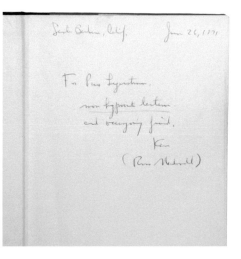

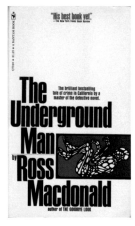

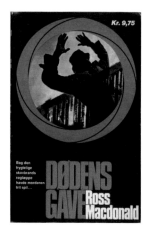

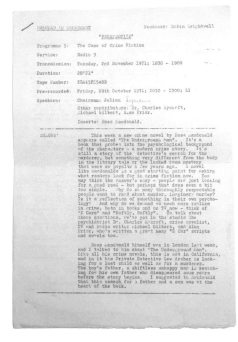
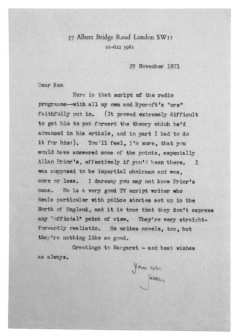

*BBC transcript (with Millar's penciled notation on the back) of a November 1971 UK radio broadcast featuring Ken,
and a letter from Julian Symons, who hosted the show, presenting him with the transcript.*

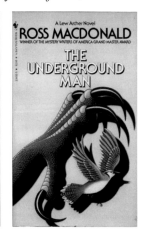
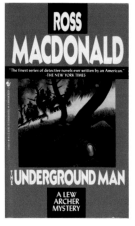

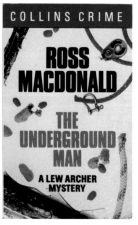

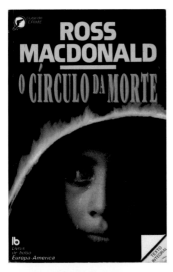
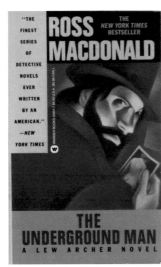
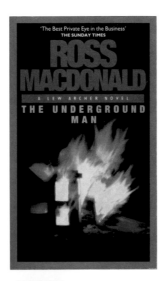
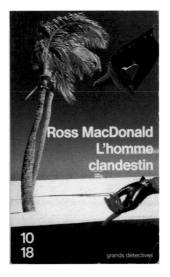
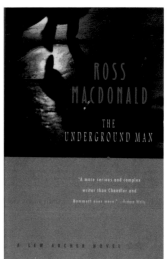

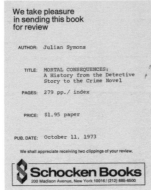

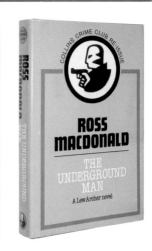

Above: Review copy of the US paperback edition of Julian Symons's Mortal Consequences *with Ken Millar's blurb on the back cover.*

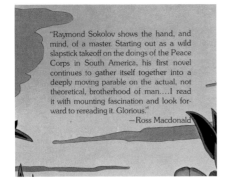

"Raymond Sokolov shows the hand, and mind, of a master. Starting out as a wild slapstick takeoff on the doings of the Peace Corps in South America, his first novel continues to gather itself together into a deeply moving parable on the actual, not theoretical, brotherhood of man....I read it with mounting fascination and look forward to rereading it. Glorious."
—Ross Macdonald

Above and left: Review copy of Raymond Sokolov's Native Intelligence *(1975) with press material and the 1983 paperback edition (above right). The rear panel of the hardcover's dust jacket features Millar's generous blurb for the book, which appears on the interior of the paperback. Sokolov wrote the 1971* Newsweek *Ken Millar cover story feature "The Art of Murder."*

Above left: US Knopf edition of The Underground Man *inscribed to American science fiction and fantasy author, and three-time winner of the Prometheus Award, Victor Koman. Koman met Millar at the Santa Barbara Writers Conference in 1974 and/or 1975. When Koman found out that Millar would be attending, he bought the novel in a used book store. At the conference, he mentioned that he lived in Los Gatos. Millar told him that he had been born in Los Gatos and asked how it was these days. Koman told him that you could still ride horses up University Avenue, that it still had a very small town feel to it, and that he thought it was the greatest place in which to be a boy. The topic of John D. MacDonald came up in conversation and they talked about his early science fiction novels,* Wine of the Dreamers *and* Ballroom of the Skies. *Millar said that he'd read them, too, and Koman asked if he didn't think the Level One, Two, and Three reminded him of E. E. "Doc" Smith's 1st, 2nd, and 3rd Stage Lensman. Millar agreed that they did, impressing Koman with his knowledge outside the mystery genre. The inscription in* The Underground Man *was based on the question raised in this conversation. Looking back, Koman felt Ken seemed to be suffering from the beginnings of Alzheimer's, and that he seemed nostalgic for Los Gatos and very sad.*

Above right: A later UK Collins edition of The Underground Man *from 1983.*

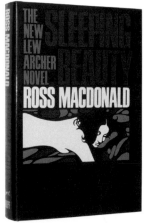
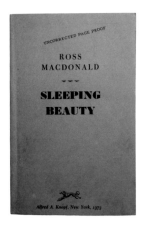

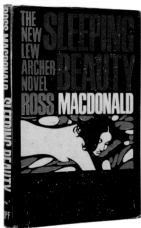
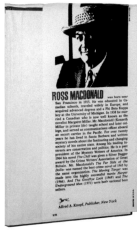

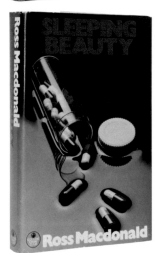

Top row: US Knopf edition of Sleeping Beauty *(1973); uncorrected proof; and US Knopf edition inscribed by Ken Millar to his typist Alice Kladnik, "without whom this book might never have seen the light of day." Middle row: Taiwanese pirated edition with black dust jacket instead of blue, author photo by Hal Boucher on the back flap showing multi-generational loss (appearing like a high-contrast image) and Chinese characters on the copyright page. Bottom row: UK Collins edition, early thick proof, later thinner proof. Right: Crawford Woods's scathing* New York Times *review that prompted Millar to publicly respond to the review and defend the book—the only time he did so in his career.*

Another case for Lew Archer

The Sleeping Beauty

By Ross Macdonald.
288 pp. New York:
Alfred A. Knopf. $6.95.

By CRAWFORD WOODS

This detective story carries a dedication to Eudora Welty —a gracious and appropriate gesture, but one that suggests, as the book suggests, that the author has fallen prey to the exuberance of his critics and is now writing in the shadow of a self-regard that tends to play his talent false.

I think it's fair to suppose that Welty's admiring review of an earlier novel, "The Underground Man," triggered the slew of assessments dedicated to demonstrating that Macdonald now had to be treated as a "serious" novelist—as though his intricate story-telling were not art enough. "I guess it's no longer a secret that he's one of our best novelists," another fan noted, in an opinion widely echoed.

All of which tends to force analysis of his latest book onto what I am convinced is an improper plane. For while Macdonald as a genre writer may be first-rate, as a novelist he is, at least in this new novel, so raw as to be nearly inedible; and I suspect the praise that's been showered on him is less a measure of his stature than a judgment on his competition. "Sleeping Beauty" is a book more built than written, a methodical account framed in language generally too dim to call for much praise.

On the plus side, the hero, Lew Archer, is appealing, perhaps because he has lived on thousands of previous pages and thus achieved an understood complexity even for a reader encountering him here for the first time. As a private eye, he's a thorough performer whose calm authority pulls the reader unprotesting into his world; as a man, he is long-suffering, essentially nonviolent, impressive in his self knowledge, strict in his ethics. Tempted to punch a punk, he forbears, reflecting, "There had to be a difference between the things that he might do and

the things that were possible for me." That is a long way from Mike Hammer.

But the people who form the sea Archer swims in are sheer spindrift, due largely to Macdonald's lazy reliance on a single surface aspect to suggest multiple depths: "His eyes kept moving, like water under wind"; "He looked at me with dark brown sorrowful eyes, the kind that faithful dogs are supposed to have." And so on and on. One might buy back the author's advance with a dollar for every character dragged in by the eyeballs.

Such careless detail work shreds the plot at every turn, as does the inevitable questionnaire form of the dialogue (a fault more likely inherent in the form than in the author). There are sharp observations that fix a mood with some originality: "The air in the room seemed to freeze into solid silence." But these are overpowered by fistfuls of phrases numbing in their void: "He was a tall dark man with a face that had known pain." Lew Archer would find that gross as a description of a suspect; why does the author settle for it as a portrait of a character?

None of this limps as badly as the dark-night-of the soul stuff. "Sleeping Beauty" crawls with spurious eschatology attached to un-fraught acts. When Archer takes an elevator ride, he feels "as if I were going down to the bottom of things." And he's soggy with half-chewed California Zen: "If you drew your spirit deep into yourself and out of sight, it couldn't be destroyed. But it might go blind in the internal darkness."

All this is a shame, because the story cracks along vividly enough when freed of its bad prose and ponderous philosophizing. Since it's foul play to say more of the plot of a detective novel than is said on the dust jacket, I'll note only that "Sleeping Beauty" absorbs the willing reader in complication upon convolution, adroitly flooding in false leads right to the end. If you care to play it like a chess game, it's a good one.

We have two books here: a professionally crafted and largely satisfying detective story, to which has been welded a tentative overlay of Larger Things—a literary pretension that somewhat vitiates a plausible fiction. That fact need not turn off the author's many admirers. But it should give his more thoughtful critics pause. ■

Crawford Woods is completing a collection of short fiction and a book of critical journalism.

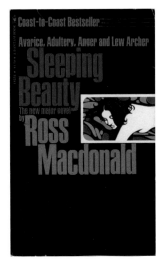

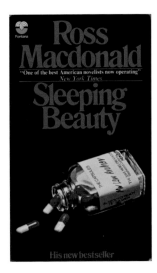

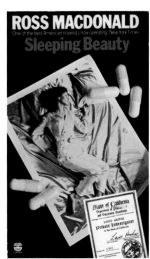

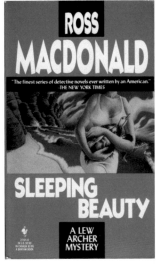

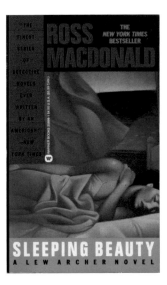

Several drafts of Ken Millar's letter to The New York Times *in response to Crawford Woods's review of Sleeping Beauty. Millar painstakingly revised the letter—there are over seventeen handwritten pages of material present in this particular archive, demonstrating how important and personal this was to the author. Above left: "Crawford Woods … does a masterly job of reviewing my three-word dedication. He may well have a future as a reviewer of dedications." Above middle: A false start that was an offshoot of the opening paragraph of the version on the left. Below left: The note at the top, "Ask Ash for Cheever's 'The World of Apples,'" suggests the story was being considered for inclusion in Great Stories of Suspense. Below middle and right: The "final" versions would change over two weeks' time.*

4420 Via Esperanza
Santa Barbara, Calif. 93110
July 4, 1973

The Editor
The New York Times Book Review
Times Square, New York, N.Y. 10036

Dear Sir:

Crawford Woods' review of <u>Sleeping Beauty</u> contains three misquotations and several other distortions of meaning or intention effected by suppression of my context. Woods quotes my sentence: "He was a tall dark man with a face that had known pain;" and comments: "Lew Archer would find that gross as a description of a suspect; why does the author settle for it as a portrait of a character?" But I don't. The sentence quoted is followed in the book by a more exact descriptive sentence, and then by an eight-page scene in which the dark man is the central character and his portrait physical, moral and biographical is continually added to (p. 186 ff.).

Mr. Woods writes: "<u>Sleeping Beauty</u> crawls with spurious eschatology attached to un-fraught acts. When Archer takes an elevator ride, he feels 'as if I were going down to the bottom of things;'" (p. 157) Mr. Woods corrects my narrator's grammar here, substituting "were" for "was." Also he delicately omits the fact that Archer's elevator ride is taking him down to the morgue where two dead men are waiting. A touch of the eschatological, which has to do with death and other final things, would seem not wholly out of place.

As evidence that my narrator is "soggy with half-chewed California Zen," Mr. Woods quotes, or rather misquotes, the following passage: "If you drew your spirit deep into yourself and out of sight, it couldn't be destroyed. But it might go blind in the internal darkness." Deprived of their original context and provided with Mr. Woods', these two sentences suggest that Archer is indulging in a self-centered philosophic solo. But in my version he is imagining the moral life of the woman he is interviewing: "Shock struck her face a glancing blow. I guessed that she had been struck in that way many times before, and had learned the tricks of moral evasion. If you withdrew your spirit deep into yourself and out of sight, it couldn't be completely destroyed. But it might go blind in the internal darkness." (p. 136)

I have quoted this twice-misquoted paragraph in full in order to show that it is Mr. Woods' phony "California Zen" gloss that makes it seem pretentious, and at the same time drains it of its meaning.

Yours sincerely,

ROSS MACDONALD

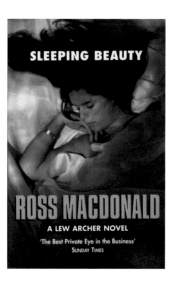

4420 Via Esperanza
Santa Barbara, Calif. 93110
May 20, 1973

Dear Ash:

Here is a review by Robert Finch of
the L A Times — part of the rundown of spring
novels. As I said it, its more of a corrective to the
N.Y. Times Book Review review, as indeed were the reviews you
sent me from all over the country. They make me feel a
certain confidence in my following in and out of the book
trade.

As always,

Ken

Above left: A carbon typescript of the final version that Millar sent to The New York Times that differs in tone compared to the earlier drafts. The earlier versions come across somewhat barbed and slightly more defensive, the final version more matter of fact. From an earlier draft: "I dwell on the word 'pretentious' because Mr. Woods finds me guilty at the end of 'a literary pretension that somewhat vitiates a plausible fiction.' What he seems to mean is that a detective novelist should not be presumptuous enough to dedicate a book to Eudora Welty. He also seems to mean that a detective story has no right to become an ecological crime novel about such a serious matter as a west coast oil spill, seen in its social and psychological causes and consequences, and not without symbolic overtones." Sleeping Beauty *was clearly a very personal book for Millar, almost an exercise in wish fulfillment, where Laurel Russo (the surrogate for his daughter Linda) lives at the end of the novel after taking Archer's sleeping pills. It's no wonder that he reacted so strongly to Woods's dismissal of the book. Above right: Draft of a letter to Ash Green that suggests that Robert Kirsch's review in the LA Times is "sort of a corrective to the N. Y. Time Book Review, as indeed were the reviews you sent me from all over the country."*

Above left: Ken Millar letter from September 28, 1978, to Paul Nelson: "Do be assured I'm in no hurry, although of course I'm looking forward to that saga of the past, my life. Indeed I'm very grateful to you for going to all this trouble, and only hope my life is worth such attention. I know I am not." He was glad Paul enjoyed Fred Zackel's novel, Cocaine and Blue Eyes *(but transposed the title), and recommended* Phoenix No More *by Ed Gage. He continued: "My own news is that I've just finished a movie script based on one of my books—*The Instant Enemy—*and Margaret just sent in a very funny (and sad) novel to Random House." He went on: "I was very grateful for the records. The Zevons as you know have lately moved to S. B. and in fact they're having a party—a housewarming—tonight. We were invited by [sic] unfortunately could not go. This is just the second night that a ten-week-old Newfoundland pup is spending in our house and we couldn't leave him to the mercies of the other dogs." In a postscript, he added: "I appreciate your making the cassettes." Above middle: Draft of a letter from July 18, 1976, to Fred Zackel, introducing him to Ash Green: "ASHBEL GREEN, vice-president of Knopf and my editor there, would like to see your book or what you have finished of it. If you don't feel it's ready to go, you should send him an appropraite letter. Knopf is the best publisher, at least for our purposes, that I know of. The next move is up to you." Right middle: Paul Nelson's review copy of Fred Zackel's novel.*

Above right: Draft of a letter to Ash Green from October 21, 1977: "It occurs to me after the event—as things often do occur to me—that I may have given the impression last week of trying to blitz you. I wasn't. Fred Zackel sent me a copy of his ms. at the same time as he sent you one, and my main concern was that your copy should not be lost or go unconnected with the young writer whom I had long before recommended to you. Although I am not a professional in the same sense as you, I do feel and assume a certain responsibility for younger writers, particularly those who come into my writing classes as Fred did at the S. B. Writers Conference…. To follow up on my rather awkward shepherding, I have talked to Dorothy Olding [Ken's agent] and she agreed to take care of Fred's manuscript if you reject it, or indeed if you accept it. I hope I may continue to recommend writers to you, and I hope I haven't overused that privilege…. I'm off to meet a train bearing Henri Coulette, a poet who has just been given, for his recent poems, a $7500 grant by the Nat'l Council for the Arts." Left: Draft of a 1978 letter to Joe Kanon, executive editor at Coward, McCann & Geoghegan (but incorrectly addressed in the salutation as "Mr. Geohegan"): "I don't mind the minor error in the spelling of my name ['MacDonald' on the Cocaine and Blue Eyes *cover blurb attribution] but I do appreciate your courtesy in writing. I hope Fred Zackel's book does well, and that there will be others."*

22. THE INSTANT ENEMY

Can we talk about **The Instant Enemy?**

The Instant Enemy is something new again. I don't know exactly how to explain what I mean by its newness, but it isn't part of that series: *The Chill*, *Far Side of the Dollar*, and *Black Money*. It's almost in some ways a step back into the material of *The Galton Case*. *The Galton Case* revisited. I didn't really value *The Instant Enemy* particularly, but a lot of other people have. I value the ones that take a step. I don't know where the steps are leading, of course.

When you say that it was "The Galton Case *revisited*," is that something *you decided at the time you wrote it or something that revealed itself later?*

Well, I went deeper into the lives of the kind of people that are in *The Galton Case* but are not perhaps so fully examined. Of course, a lot of these things, a lot of my relationships to these specific books, have to do with autobiographical elements, many of which are obscure to me, too. *The Instant Enemy*, while it doesn't reflect any actual events in my life, has—oh, how to put it—psychological autobiographical elements. Some of the people in the family are not pictures or photographs or anything like that of people in my own family but representations of family forces, so to speak. You can't take anything in any of my books literally because I don't write them that way. I don't imagine that I'm writing anything that ever actually happened.

What makes it different from The Galton Case?

Well, *The Galton Case* is pretty much of a romance by comparison with *The Instant Enemy*. *The Instant Enemy* is very much more realistic, closer to the kind of reality that I was trying to write about. *The Galton Case*, of course, has a more beautifully balanced plot and that sort of thing. It had the element of the Romantic in it that makes such things easier. It depended on previous models, but *The Instant Enemy* is very much its own book. Nobody else has ever written a book like it. Good or bad, or for better or for worse, that's my own book.

Do you like it better than The Galton Case?

I'd rather have written it. Oh, it doesn't have the obvious virtues and merits, and it isn't as easy reading either. I think the vision is closer to the vision that I'm

May 4, 1974

trying to get across, which is a rather grim vision. I'm just writing about the aspects of life that failed. You know, to show the tragic consequences of mistakes and human errors is a very positive thing to do. In writing a book like that you're not necessarily dwelling on evil but really showing the consequences of it and, by implication, how do we avoid it. In other words, I think it's a healthy book.

Even with the violence and murders?

But it wouldn't matter if half the people in the book died, provided rather that the thing made sense. I mean, you don't judge the lights of a book by what happens to the characters, God knows.

What is The Instant Enemy about?

It's about a boy who had a most unfortunate series of experiences with violence and so on when he was young and his attempt, unsuccessful, to save his soul and save his life. In other words, the element of violence eventually won out. That's the main theme. A book that complex can't be summed up just in terms of a single theme. I suppose one of its subjects is the sources of evil and the causes of evil in contemporary life.

Which are what in reference to that book?

Oh, various kinds of greed. And there are other sources of trouble: the refusal of people like the artist to become involved and so on. But mainly it's a tragedy of causality, I would say. When you get enough causes predisposing to further violence, you're going to have it. So the thing is to avoid the predetermining violence in our relations with young people particularly.

That book starts as this story of Davy Spanner, and when he gets killed by his high school counselor Henry Langston—I guess it's five-sixths of the way through the book—suddenly the emphasis shifts so radically that he almost becomes an afterthought. It's clear that Langston inherits the trouble. Do you feel that way at all?

Oh yes. I feel that there's more plot than I unraveled. I probably should have written a longer book. Or possibly a shorter one, I don't know. I'd have to go back into it, which I'm not going to do, in order to decide what could be done. Probably a longer book.

Do you see the violence continuing even after Davy's death because of the way that he does die?

Yes. I would say that Langston, while he shot Davy, was actually a further victim of this continual violence. He was a weak man and he fell victim to the violence by perpetrating it. Also, he was a victim of another kind of error: he offered and gave Davy a love that he Langston could not sustain. That's another thing we have to avoid: offering what we don't have or can't maintain.

Although Davy does some bad things, he doesn't actually kill anybody.

That's right. He's the one that people are afraid of when they should be afraid of themselves.

"Coincidences seldom happen in my work," Archer states in the book. But isn't the way Davy and Sandy Sebastian get together on the Strip something of a coincidence?

You're probably right. There are different ways to write a book. While I'm not defending the way I wrote this one, I will point out that it's possible to write a book with parallel events and characters that touch at various points without connecting them in a total causal net. In other words, it's perfectly valid to have one string of characters and then another string of characters not necessarily influencing each other in terms of from here to here to here to here to here, but in different directions and just touching at certain points. But the objection to that is that I use necessity and causal continuity in my books so persistently that when I do something else it's a fault.

I don't know if it's a fault, but to me this book is probably the most causally oriented. I mean, I literally couldn't keep track of all the switches at the end, there were so many. And I was writing them down even. This is the one book I think of all of them—and only towards the end of it—where the plot sometimes seemed to make the characters do things. There were simply so many people in this one that weren't characterized memorably that I couldn't remember who they were. They had made not enough of an impression as characters. It reminds me of Anatole Broyard's review of **The Blue Hammer,** *which I thought was a not very fair review, where he brought up that he didn't believe the characters.[1]*

I don't believe *him.*

He wrote that the story put precedence over the characters and he couldn't find any relationship to why they did what they did.

Yes, but, you know, writing a book where the plot makes the characters do things is a valid way to write a book. It isn't necessarily a destructive criticism, as he seems to think. That just happens to be my way of writing a book, and I doubt very much if he has read any of my books apart from that one. I don't take Broyard seriously, at least as a critic of me, because he simply dismissed my book. Nobody else did. He's alone in American reviewing in dismissing that book. To me that means he's probably wrong.

Really, though, to get into and read a complex book in a form that you don't much approve of, like the mystery form, takes a certain act of sympathy, and I don't think he was interested in performing any kind of act of imaginative sympathy. There's no sign of it. I admit that, especially for non-mystery readers,

1 "Books of The Times" by Anatole Broyard, *The New York Times Book Review,* June 11, 1976.

my books present problems. And to come on somebody's twentieth or twenty-fourth book for the first time can present problems. I don't know whether this is relevant to your question about Broyard. I don't know what the problem was, but he didn't seem to be reading the same book that the other reviewers were reading. Yet given the difficulty, kids in their early teens are able to read my books provided they've sort of built up to it. I hear from them. My youngest recorded reader that I've heard from is eleven, but he's a very brilliant boy.

I think you're also right that Broyard hasn't read any of the rest of your books.

He didn't show any signs of it anyway. You know, it not only takes time to learn to write books like that, it takes time to learn to read them. You can't just plunge in and read them as if you were reading, oh, you know, something that's dashed off in a hurry.

However, I would be the first to admit—and I know it better than you do because I've been working on scripts based on that book [*The Instant Enemy*]—that the complexity got out of hand. I don't know why. Probably because I was cutting very close to home in writing that book.

Close to home how?

Well, Davy is a self-portrait. Now, I don't mean an accurate portrait, but a symbolic portrait. The whole movement of the book is in a remote but true sense autobiographical.

Does the character of Davy equate to the runaway boy in The Galton Case?

Yes, and they both equate to me. Just in the obvious way: that there have always been kids who are at odds with the governing society and with the culture. Nevertheless, you're taking the boy in *The Instant Enemy* as a kind of representative of what we're talking about, and he was certainly based on something that goes quite a long way back in my experience. He's autobiographical to a certain extent. But of course Davy in *The Instant Enemy* is involved in a lot more than minor hooliganism. He's almost a total outlaw, although he really doesn't want to be.

An inordinate amount of the books are concerned with runaways.

For me a missing person is more interesting than a body, for one thing. But of course there are all sorts of reasons for that. I've never tried to conceal the fact that, in the broadest sense, the books are autobiographical. Very many of the things that I put in the books have happened to me, although not exactly in that way or to that degree. My life has been fortunate compared with that of most of the characters in my books.

Are the negative characters representative of you as well as the positive characters in some of them? The unlikable characters as well as the likable ones?

By all means. I would like to pick out the characters I'm going to identify with before I subscribe to this, but in general I think that I have a deeper understanding and feeling for the bad ones than I do for the good ones. But Archer is a kind of mediator between the two and he partakes of both worlds, both the dark and

the light. He knows he is a gray man in a gray world. That's sort of the essence of his style. He can move into either the dark or the light—and does.

An archive of nine binders and one notebook from January 1978 to January 1979 pertaining to the final version of Ken's The Instant Enemy *screenplay.*

He's also sort of between the city and the individual.

Yes, he's a mediator between the city and the individual. So the intent of the books *is* to make unities and meaningful human patterns. I don't want to sound as if I'm taking myself too seriously, but these are my intentions, however they've turned out. I'm just trying to do what fiction has traditionally done in all the various forms.

It seems to me that it's easier to tell—and this is a broad oversimplification—which characters represent you or your own story in earlier books, like The Galton Case, than it is in the later books. Where are you in the later books?

Well, that's it: there isn't such a distinction between what we might call the auc-torial alter egos and the other characters. There's more of a melding between the good and the evil characters, to put it that way, I think in the later books. There isn't such an imminent distinction between black and white.

I'm not sure I follow the "black and white" distinction.

What I mean to say is simply that I don't distinguish as openly or as blatantly between good people and bad people in my own thinking about the books. I'm not talking so much about the narrative but in what lies behind the books—the later books. There's a very narrow distance really in this last book [*The Blue Hammer*] between being a sympathetic character and being an unsympathetic character. I mean morally unsympathetic. Nearly all of the characters in the last book seem to me to have aspects of the sympathetic. That's been true perhaps of some of

the other books, too, but not perhaps to the same extent. I actually feel that no character in this last book is excluded from humanity, so to speak, including the central evildoer who committed the murders. At least from the standpoint of the book and of the person who wrote it—there's sympathy even for him.

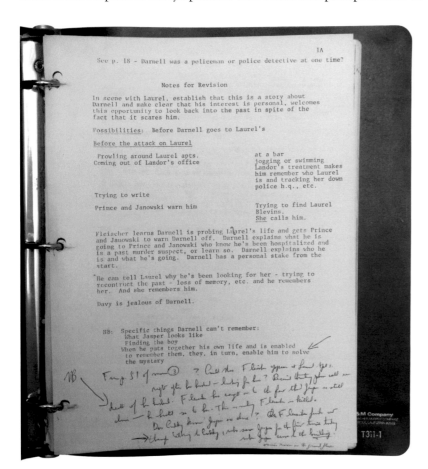

Above: Ken Millar's notes for revisions to The Instant Enemy *screenplay. "Could Mrs. Fleischer appear at Laurel Apts. right after her husband— looking for him? Received threatening phone call re death of her husband. Fleischer has caught on to the fact that Jasper is still alive—he hinted so to her." Top right: A scene where the detective, Ned Darnell (whose first name at the time of the interviews was Lou), drives through Santa Barbara and talks to a character named Doctor Landor. Middle right: A handwritten scene insertion. Bottom right: A scene with an exchange between Davy Spanner and Darnell with a handwritten insertion on the left page.*

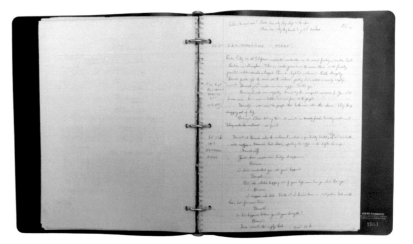

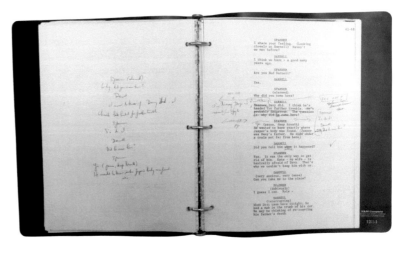

When the gun that's used for one of the murders is more or less literally passed along from father to daughter, was that intended as a symbol of the sins of the father being passed down?

Yes, and I happen to think that that's the way things operate in life. A gun is not just a symbol, it's death itself and the potentiality of violence and even training in violence. I'm making it sound like a highly moralistic document, but I'm just pointing out those aspects of the book which stand clear of what happens to the characters but have to do with the real meaning of the book. It's the symbol which is also the thing itself. Like the beheading of the father: that's the symbol which is also the thing itself. Those are the kind of symbols that are strongest.

Davy spending the night beside the beheaded body by the railroad tracks is an incredibly powerful image, I think.

Well, it's kind of a symbol. A lot could be said about it, but we don't have to say it.

[laughs] Well, let's say some of it.

You may remember that in a novel called *Resurrection* by Tolstoy somebody is killed by a train, it seems to me. Anyway, the train is used as a symbol of modern scientific causality and necessity. All that sort of thing. Let's say the causality of the naturalistic universe—naturalistic in the literary sense. I'm using the train in somewhat the same sense there. It's the overriding necessity, almost mechanistic necessity, that destroys people. And, of course, the beheaded father is a kind of central image. Almost any interpretation that you want to make of it is true because it's such a central figure.

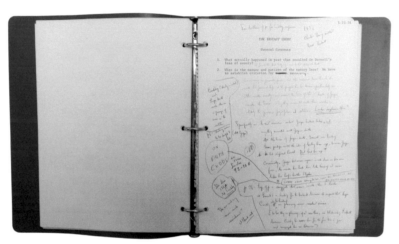

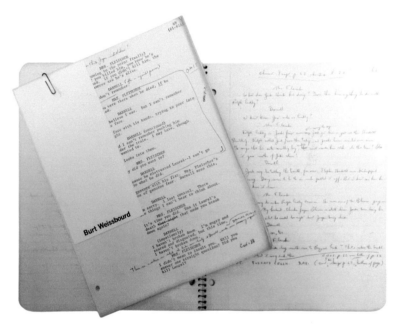

Above: Ken Millar's notes and general comments asking about Darnell's memory loss. "Specifically—he can't remember what Jasper looked like, and anything connected with Jasper's death." Below: One of Ken Millar's notebooks with scenes at the Hackett Estate that feature Davy, Sandy, Darnell, and Lupe.

Above: The same notebook with notes from producer Burt Weissbourd. Below: A binder of Weissbourd's notes to Ken Millar for changes to the screenplay from August to October 1978.

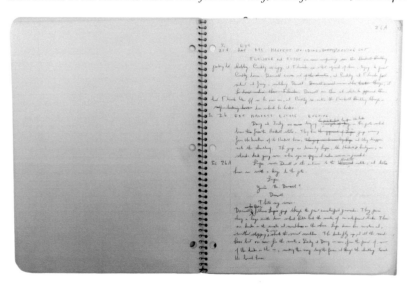

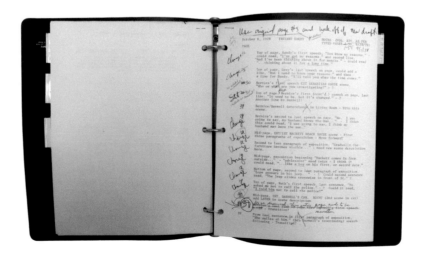

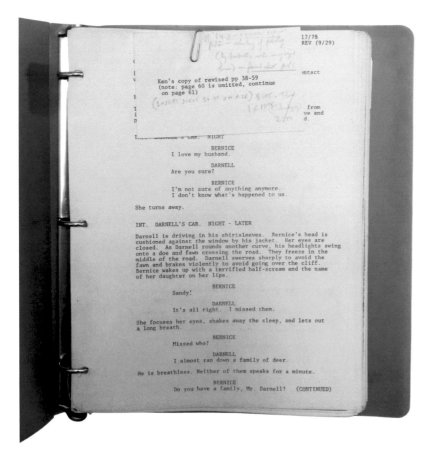

A binder from October 1978 with a paperclipped note changing a 2:00 PM Thursday (Thanksgiving) appointment with Burt Weissbourd to Friday.

It's Freudian, Jungian, whatever.

That's right. And Christian, too, or whatever you want to call it. Religious.

Do you remember what made you use that particular image?

No, except that I intended it to be sort of the central image of the book: a beheaded father. Everything in the book is related to the beheading or the instrument of beheading or whatever. That's what the book is all about. Everything that happens in the book is related either as cause or effect to the central idea of the killing of the father, in both its philosophic and narrative senses. See, the killing of the father is also the source of the main plot, the main trouble, in the book. It's central in more ways than one: structurally, naturalistically, narrative-wise, and so on.

Did you view each of the murders in the book as a variation on that one murder? Or do you mean everything is centralized around that one specific murder?

Those two questions are the same question really, and the answer is yes. Yes, I'm sure I meant that central beheading to be the archetypal shape of the book. It's not the plot, it's the central event going both ways. It's both a consequence and

a cause. It's the consequence of past troubles and the cause of future ones, but it's central.

There are a variety of father figures in this book. What do you think that reflects about you?

It reflects living in so many houses and families with so many surrogate fathers. And pseudo-fathers. And anti-fathers. That was the substance of my life. But one does make do. You know, the actual blood relationship is not so terribly significant.

There's a scene in The Instant Enemy with Archer encountering an open suitcase that has "a faint sour odor of time." It echoes another scene with a suitcase in The Galton Case.

It's Culligan's suitcase and it smells of saltwater and tobacco smoke and the smell of "masculine loneliness."

Right. I was wondering if you intended that parallel?

Well, I was aware of it, of course. In each case those are the key sentences in those books for me, just from the personal standpoint; I don't mean from the structural standpoint. They refer to my father. Sometimes, you know, you do put in what might be called a subjective and lyrical touch of reality.

There's a lot in The Instant Enemy about money. Art is almost always referred to in terms of money and psychiatric care is thought of in terms of money. Almost every reference, spiritual or aesthetic or medical, is translated into how much it's going to cost. In fact, money seems to be a theme in a lot of the books. Where does that come from?

Oh, I suppose once again a life in which money assumed almost supernatural importance, as it does when you don't have any at all. I mean, when you're absolutely stony-broke, money seems quite important.

But at the same time, I lived in contact with moneyed people. See, my childhood was terribly varied, depending on what relative I was living with. They varied from poor people to rich people. So I came to know quite a lot about money and the differences it made, and the differences between rich and poor. That's one of my subjects. Ultimately, of course, for many years now I've moved in contact with a lot of people with money. At the same time, I don't really blend in with the moneyed society. I'm an outsider and a critic. I try to write about the consequences of money, or the abuses of money, realistically and from observation. I think this moneyed society, to put it mildly, has some terrible problems going on in it.

Money is certainly a great part of The Instant Enemy.

You know, you make more references to *The Instant Enemy* than you have to any of the books. Is that just the impression I get from today?

I think so, yeah. I just reread it. I don't mean to make a federal case out of The Instant Enemy at all, no.

Oh, I didn't mean that. It's just that I've never regarded it as one of my best books. But I'm glad I wrote it. You know? It got me into, well, material that for me was

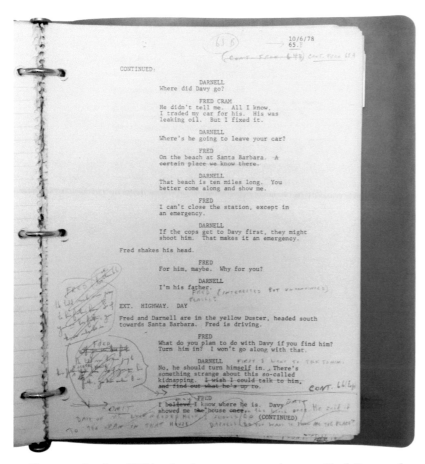

The same October 1978 binder depicting a scene between Fred Cram and Darnell with a number of handwritten changes by Millar.

fascinating and instructive. I suppose I pressed my research into this subject of money and its consequences further in that book than I did in any of the others.

You said that Black Money **and** The Galton Case **both owe a great deal to** The Great Gatsby, **but there seem to be** Gatsby **references in** The Instant Enemy, **too. Davy's list of ten "Don'ts," for instance.**

Yeah, I'm sure I borrowed that idea from *Gatsby*.[2]

Did you see Davy as a Gatsby figure at all?

No. He just stands for himself. Instead of giving watered-down renditions of other people's works, we try to avoid the very appearance of imitation. I don't hold back when I want to imitate something that will be valuable to me in a book. After all, how better to learn how to do it than from other writers? Fitzgerald, I think, can teach writers more than any other American writer, both through his successes and his failures. His failures are enormously instructive and valuable,

too. Or shall I say *his incompletions*? A writer doesn't really have failures as long as he's working as hard as he possibly can. I mean, the whole work hangs together. You can't say this part of it is a failure, this part of it is a success. The whole thing is what we have to understand and learn from.

That's sort of like the auteur ***theory of film criticism—which I definitely agree with—and which got Andrew Sarris into so much trouble. An author's whole work has to be considered to determine if he's a good author or not.***

Oh sure. And the failures are valuable, too. You can really learn from them. And not just learn what to avoid either. I mean, the idea that the only things worth publishing are successes is absurd. That would reduce American literature to a little five-foot shelf if we just put complete successes in.

Besides, who's to know what they are at the time?

That's right. Who's going to say that *Tender Is the Night* is a failure?

You mentioned that you've been working on a script. Would you relate the story about how the movie project for The Instant Enemy ***came about?***

Well, about eight years ago a young man named Burt Weissbourd, in his early twenties, came to visit me. He was living with his young wife in Chicago at that time. He's the son of one of the great Chicago builders, I believe. Burt came to visit me and expressed interest, in fact expressed the *intention*, of one day making a movie based on one of my books. He's going to produce it. I think even then he was thinking about *The Instant Enemy*. It's his favorite book among my books. I haven't gone into this with him much, but I guess he had grown up with the idea of becoming a movie producer and this was a story that he wanted to make the first time around. He came to me when this was just a gleam in his eye, so to speak.[3]

So we agreed to meet again on the subject and have periodically over the years. During those years certain developments have occurred. The movie based on *The Instant Enemy* has now reached the stage of a script, and just today as we were talking I heard from Burt Weissbourd and he told me that the treatments, which I had worked on earlier this year, had been attracting favorable attention among some pretty good Hollywood directors, whom I won't name now because nothing has jelled. It's very much in the air. Just the fact that this script should have been considered interesting and comparatively good by some fairly expert people in the movie industry is encouraging.[4] It's my first attempt to do a treatment. My original treatment is a hundred pages and the script is somewhat longer than that.

2 Late in the novel, Gatsby's father produces an old copy of the book *Hopalong Cassidy*, which belonged to his son. Written on the last flyleaf is a detailed daily to-do schedule as well as a list of daily resolves. Paul Nelson, too, had the habit of recording valuable personal notes to himself in the fronts and backs of treasured books.

3 Millar misremembered how long it had been since his first meeting with Weissbourd. It was not "about eight years ago," which would have been in 1968, but only a little over two years. Weissbourd's first call to Millar was on February 19, 1974; he then met with him a few weeks later, the second weekend in March, at the Coral Casino Beach Club.
Weissbourd's first choice was to adapt *The Chill*, but it had already been optioned, so he reread all of the Archer books. "I noticed that one of the books [*The Instant Enemy*] was dedicated to Ping Ferry." In Santa Barbara, Wilbur H. "Ping" Ferry, a self-styled gadfly and activist, and Weissbourd's father were both on the board of the Center for the Study of Democratic Institutions. "So I asked my dad to ask him how to get in touch with Ken. He said, 'Just call him up.' I did, and he couldn't have been more gracious."
4 Weissbourd fondly remembers in particular a lunch meeting about the project with director Alan J. Pakula, Millar, and himself. Among other notable directors to whom Weissbourd submitted the script were François Truffaut, Don Siegel, Sydney Pollack, John Frankenheimer, and Hal Ashby.

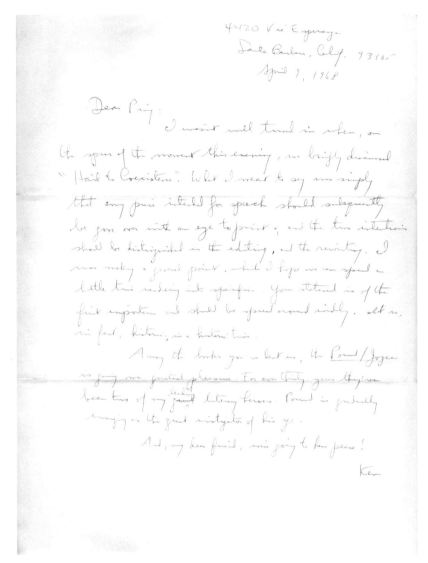

Draft of a letter to W. H. "Ping" Ferry (the dedicatee of The Instant Enemy) *explaining that "any piece intended for speech should subsequently be gone over with an eye to print, and the two intentions should be distinguished in the editing, and rewriting." He goes on to say that Ezra Pound "is gradually emerging as the great instigator of his age."*

You did both?

No. I wrote a treatment which was actually as long as a screenplay and that has had considerable improvement made in it by the writer who came along after me. But it's still basically my story and my treatment. He didn't make any basic changes in the story, with one exception, with which I agree. That exception was simply going back to the book instead of something that I had changed.

I noticed in your treatment that the detective is called Darnell. Why is that?

I probably got it from Linda Darnell. My daughter's name was Linda. I was asked to name him, and I can't call him Lew Archer because that name has

already been purchased and used. In one way or another, both parts of the name have been used.

Does the detective have a first name?

Lou. L-O-U.

Would there have been a legal problem had it been L-E-W?

The possibility of one. I didn't make these decisions myself about the name. I suggested the name Darnell, but I didn't decide to call him Lou. That was decided by lawyers from both sides, I guess.

When you started the treatment, though, you knew you couldn't call him Archer.

Oh, I knew that. Sold the name long ago.[5] I've been fortunate in this: that one of my closest friends [Harris Seed], from the beginning of his career and almost from the beginning of mine, has been one hell of a good lawyer. I didn't bring

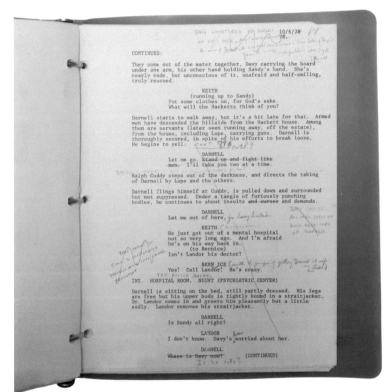

A scene in the October 1978 binder where Darnell fights with Ralph Cuddy and ends up in a straightjacket under Dr. Landor's care at the psychiatric center. Two instances of notes mentioning Davy Spanner masterminding getting Darnell into Landor's protection are crossed out.

5 According to Jeff Wong, at the time of these interviews "Paramount certainly had the rights to *The Underground Man, The Goodbye Look*, and options on some other Archer stories." As recently as 2011, *Variety.com* reported that Warner Bros. was developing *The Galton Case* into a film with an eye towards turning the series of Archer books into a movie franchise. In 2015 the studio announced that *Black Money* had been optioned for Joel and Ethan Coen to write and potentially direct.

him into my business affairs as soon as I should have, but soon enough so that there was no terrible mistake made.

You said that the only change the other writer made to your Instant Enemy treatment was going back to the book. Could you talk about that somewhat?

Well, the essential difference is that one of my novels would make at least two movies. Number of characters and the amount of action and reaction and so on, and the complexity of the plot, would take four hours instead of two hours to spell out probably. So one simply has to learn to foreshorten it—cut it down and simplify it to some extent. While I've never made a movie treatment before based on one of my books, I have had experience in cutting down the books. I've sold five or six of my novels to magazines when they were first written, and in the case of *Cosmopolitan*, which took most of them, I had to cut it down to a certain prescribed length, 25,000 words or something like that. But I got so I could do

it in a week. I could cut a novel down from 75,000 to 25,000 words in one week. I couldn't do it anymore. But they paid $5,000 apiece, which was more than I made out of the books. It would take a number of countries to add up to that much. So it was worthwhile doing, cutting them down.

Could you do it dispassionately and not feel bad about it?

There wasn't any reason to feel bad. The book was still there, and this was just a job that made it possible for me to stay in writing. Anyway, the process is somewhat similar in cutting a book down for a movie. You pick out the essential actions and the essential characters and put them in action in a simplified version of the plot. That's what I did here. But it's essentially the same plot. I did make a massive change in the plot, but that was changed back again by the second writer to what I had in the book.

What was your change?

Well, it's pretty complex to try to explain it. Let me see if I can. It had to do with the shooting of Davy. In this first version of the movie script I changed the killer of Davy to the same man who was responsible for the other murders, the central murderer, instead of an ancillary character as in the book. But in the second version the other writer went back to my original version in the book, and I'm glad he did. It works better, I believe. More psychologically interesting. I was overdoing the idea of unifying the plot for movie purposes perhaps in my version. I've changed the plot, too. There were too many intricacies at the end. Of course, those complexities have been just cut in half. Even so, it's probably still more complex than it should be.

Do you think there are great losses in doing this? The simplification down from the complexities of the book?

I think the movie is still sufficiently complex to represent the book in its complexity, but of course there are losses. There are things that you can't do in a movie that you do naturally in a book, having to do with development of character and also subtleties. All kinds of subtleties. On the other hand, there are, as everyone knows, things that you can do in a movie better than you can in a book.

Who is the other writer?

I can't name him offhand. I should be able to, but I can't. There'll be lots of time for me to be able to tell you. I don't retain names very well, as you're probably beginning to realize.[6]

An omitted scene in the October 1978 binder where Hackett is in an ambulance moving slowly through Santa Barbara and followed by the photographer. There is a note that says, "Hackett could be shown doing this shooting without revealing that he is Jasper."

6 Director/screenwriter Jim McBride (*The Big Easy, Great Balls of Fire!*) worked on the screenplay, which was sent to Millar on June 16, 1976. "It was a long time ago and I'm not sure I even finished the screenplay. I do remember going up to Santa Barbara with Burt to meet Mr. Millar. He was kind of aloof, or maybe it was me being intimidated, but we didn't interact much." In January 1978, Millar entered an agreement with Weissbourd to work on the screenplay himself. In 1979 and '80, screenwriter Jeremy Larner, who'd written *The Candidate* and *Drive, He Said*, worked on another version of the screenplay, which Universal Pictures elected not to produce.

Millar's inability to recall McBride's name, a key figure in the project and in his life at that time, was just one more instance during these interviews that suggested that Alzheimer's was already eating away at his memory.

23. HOLLYWOOD

I didn't feel personally responsible for what came out on the screen. I didn't feel particularly vulnerable to what came out on the screen either because for me the work exists in book form essentially.

***Would that be true also of* The Instant Enemy?**

Well, probably to some extent I'll have more personal feeling about this film, if it gets made. Sure, just having worked on something makes it more part of your living and feeling. But I don't know how I'm going to feel. This is my first time around.

Were you asked to write any of those other projects?

No, I was definitely not asked to do anything about *Harper* and I wasn't asked to do anything about *Drowning Pool* either.

Were you eager to see them as films?

No. You see, while I've seen a lot of movies and enjoy them, as far as my own work is concerned, *it* and I don't live in films. You know what I mean? I don't live in movies the way I live in books. I'm, of course, an ardent moviegoer, but that's another matter. Oh, naturally I was interested and I was pleased that *Harper* turned out as well as it did.

Do you have final script approval for* The Instant Enemy *project?

Yeah. Anything that I don't want, I can take out.

Why were you willing to abdicate that for the other pictures?

I didn't want the responsibility.

Let's say Alan J. Pakula calls your producer and says, "Let's go on* The Instant Enemy. *The script is pretty much in final form."

I wouldn't say that the script is in final form. It's in final form *before* the director gets a chance at it, but the director will certainly be having ideas and making

"UNDERGROUND MAN"

When we were talking in New York, about The Underground Man on television and the movies Harper and The Drowning Pool, you said that you didn't feel very personally involved in them once they were sold.

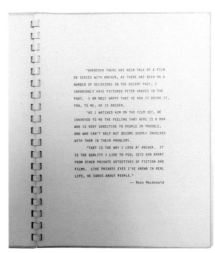
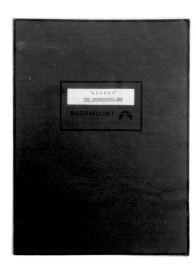
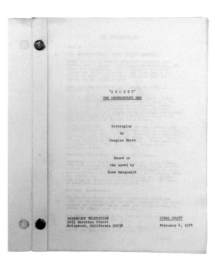

Spiralbound pressbook with quote from Ken Millar on Peter Graves as Lew Archer, and the final draft of the script for The Underground Man *(1974).*

changes. He's expected to. In fact, that's what lends its final form to the movie, it's what lends its final form to the script. His work will determine whether or not it's good or bad or whatever. The decisions he makes determine what the film is really about, too. And that's the way it should be. The script is just an implement in that direction; it has no artistic standing by itself, unlike the script of a play.

Well, I think it has some.

No, let's say it doesn't have *independent* artistic standing. It's subservient to something further and that is the making of the movie. So naturally we want the best possible director.

Do you plan on going to any of the shooting once it starts?

Well, I'm not going to plan on anything like that until the thing is actually in real process of production. Ordinarily I never have done it, but maybe I'm old enough now to break my rigorous training and go and actually see a movie, or part of it, being made. Certainly it would be fun.[1] I did get to go on the set, or rather one location, of *The Underground Man* when they were making that movie. In fact, I went to a couple of locations: one down in Los Angeles and one up here in the courthouse, and that was fun. The people were extremely pleasant.

1 Millar continued work on the screenplay for *The Instant Enemy* from 1977 to 1979. Even though Burt Weissbourd went on to produce two major motion pictures, *Raggedy Man* and *Ghost Story*, his and Kenneth Millar's version of *The Instant Enemy* never found its way to the screen. "You know, you can never say why one movie gets made and another one doesn't," Weissbourd says. "A lot of it is serendipity. The long and the short of it are movies are just very hard to get made and this is a very complicated story. I mean, toward the end there were issues around his memory as well. Clearly, I should take some of the responsibility myself. I was a young producer and I didn't have the clout that would just allow me to make whatever I wanted. But for whatever reason the stars never aligned quite right on this. Part of it is the screenplay wasn't far enough [along]. Part of it was just respect for Ken. I mean, I think a lot of directors were reluctant to, you know, try and make something of his into something of theirs. And part of it was just timing." Weissbourd also says that feedback regarding the script regularly cited "a sense it was too interior, too hard to realize as a movie." In short, "too much backstory." One studio executive wrote, "Too much of the action and storyline takes place before the movie begins …"

The last time Weissbourd saw Millar was in 1981 at the Coral Casino. Alzheimer's had already claimed much of the older man's memory. Weissbourd brought his one-year-old son along with him for the visit, and Millar played with the boy in the pool. "Ken recognized me," Weissbourd says, "which people were surprised by."

I didn't realize they'd shot in Santa Barbara.

The courthouse scenes were taken in the Santa Barbara Courthouse.

I didn't think it was very good.

Well, it didn't come together very well. That certainly was a fairly competent representation of the book, but it was rather poorly put together, I thought. I think it was poorly directed.

Peter Graves was a strange choice for Archer.

Well, I thought he was okay, but the movie didn't jell.

How are you feeling about the various treatments of Archer in film?

They've varied from pretty good to terrible. I'd like to see one good Archer movie.

Do you think Paul Newman is the man to play him?

No.

If you had a choice of anyone to play Archer, even dead actors, who would you conjure up?

I don't know. I don't have any image of Archer.[2]

Noel Young, the founder of Capra Press, told me he asked you once what Archer looked like and you said, "He looks just like me ten years younger."

2 To the contrary, in a March 19, 1974, *Los Angeles Times* article, "'Underground Man' to Surface on TV," Millar told Cecil Smith: "In thirty years of writing about Lew Archer, I never thought much about how he looked. Except that he was Californian, tanned, athletic. Then one night a few years ago, I saw Peter on *Mission: Impossible* and thought, 'That's Lew Archer; that's the way he looks.'"

I don't remember saying that, but it sounds reasonable. Archer does trail me by about ten years; and probably, if I write more Archer books, he'll get younger in relation to me rather than older. Although it would really be appropriate to write some kind of final story about him as an old man.[3]

 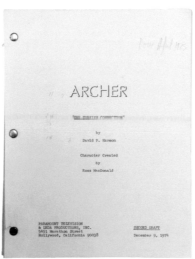

Above: Two versions of the second draft script of the pilot episode of the short-lived TV series Archer *(1975), starring Brian Keith. Right: Promotional NBC stills for* Archer. *Below: Station break card for* Archer.

3 In "The Last Testament of Ross Macdonald," Leonard Cassuto reported that Kenneth Millar had made extensive notes for such a final Lew Archer novel. The plot was to span Archer's career, and in it he discovers that he has a long-lost daughter. According to the article, "Macdonald planned for the young woman to come to Archer as a client searching for her unknown background. 'The unspoken irony,' Macdonald wrote in his notebook, is 'that she is talking to Archer, who *is* her background.' Macdonald planned for Archer to track down the truth, and this time the lost branch of the family tree would contain Archer himself."

He started out exactly the same age as you in The Moving Target. *As I make it now in* The Blue Hammer, *he's probably, what, a dozen years younger than you now?*

Ten. He's probably just under fifty, I'm under sixty-one. Yet, you know, I don't identify with him in any way outside of the books. He sort of carries my sensorium but not my mind. I was thinking, instead of *The Moving Target*, I should have called it *The Moving Sensorium*. [*laughs*]

Was the 1975 Archer TV series with Brian Keith a great disappointment to you?

Oh, I had nothing to do with that. All the material was just written from scratch. It really wasn't based on the books particularly. No, it's just that what happens to the books is very important to me, but what happens to something like television isn't important. I didn't feel it was the character anyway, particularly.

Earlier you mentioned your business affairs. Do you enjoy the business end of writing?

My contribution doesn't have to do much with the business end of it. I read the papers and try to understand those best I can. I trust my agent and my attorneys completely.[4] The one that I just mentioned [attorney Harris Seed] is one my oldest friends, whom I trust absolutely, and I don't mean just in the moral sense but also making the right decisions. Of course the decisions are referred to me, but I don't make them alone. It's all really quite simple the way it's handled.

You saw how little of my time was taken up today by major interest in a movie script. It took five minutes and then I forgot about it—except to the extent that you wanted to talk about it. Of course, I'm fortunate. Gut-wise, if I may express myself bluntly, I do not live in Hollywood. I long ago discovered and determined that no writer who wants to be a fiction writer should also have a basic allegiance to Hollywood and care terribly about what's done with his fiction in the movies. You've got to sort of care about one thing above all else, and if it's Hollywood and you're a fiction writer, you're in trouble. That's a source of a lot of the troubles of our American fiction writers, from bottom to top.

I'm not sure what it means, "from bottom to top."

Well, I meant from the lowest kind of writer to the very best. By the very best, I mean Fitzgerald and Faulkner, for example.

I'm wondering if you're talking about only writers who have worked in Hollywood.

No, there are writers who live in Long Island but who live spiritually in Hollywood. In other words, what is happening or might happen in Hollywood sort of sits on their shoulders as they write. That's the sort of thing that I mean. I don't have any particular person in mind. I just know enough from my own experience to know that a fiction writer had best stick to his own game for the most part. Of course, I broke that rule when I wrote that treatment.

There *are* writers who move easily from one form to the other and back again, but most of them don't do it without damage to their work. There are exceptions.

May 4, 1974

Agent Dorothy Olding (dedicatee of The Wycherly Woman) *and Ken Millar.*

Graham Greene is an exception, but he's had things under strict intellectual control. And don't forget that his being able to write excellent movies is not an accident; he was a movie critic for many years and a really good one. It's a natural part of his life by now.

Have you ever been offered an inordinate sum to be a screenwriter?

I've had offers, but it wasn't anything that I wanted to do. I don't really consider myself a screenwriter. If this new project turns out, I may consider myself a screenwriter. But not necessarily a good one.

Do you think that Hollywood damaged Faulkner as a novelist?

4 Millar's agent was Dorothy Olding of Harold Ober Associates. She also represented J. D. Salinger and, among others, Agatha Christie and Pearl S. Buck.

It damaged him, period, as a novelist and every other way. I mean, there's no direct connection between what he did in Hollywood and his novels getting bad or worse, but he himself was personally damaged by his life in Hollywood. Let's say it accelerated the damage that alcohol was already doing to him.

You think that could directly be attributed to Hollywood?

What happens in Hollywood is directly attributable to some extent to Hollywood. It just wasn't a good place for him to be. I know for a fact that Fitzgerald was damaged by Hollywood. He wrote about it extensively in both fiction and otherwise. While Faulkner didn't, you can see the change in his work. And we know, thanks to that massive biography, how he lived when he was in Hollywood.[5] He lived partly sober and partly so drunk that he had to be hospitalized. You might as well not quote me. I don't want to emphasize that aspect of Faulkner, because he was a great man.[6] But he really was just in the wrong place, and he knew that, too. He went there for the money. He had to go economically if he wanted to live the way he chose to live—and which a great novelist has the right to choose.

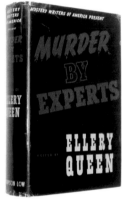

US Ziff-Davis edition of Murder by Experts *(1947) and UK Sampson Low edition (1950) signed by Fred Dannay as Barnaby Ross and Ellery Queen.*

Have you read Tom Dardis's book Some Time in the Sun? It takes a somewhat pro-Hollywood point of view, saying there were some good things that happened to these writers also in Hollywood.

Sure. I know that. It was useful to Fitzgerald, for example, in keeping him above water, not just financially but also with a certain degree of self-esteem. But we know how he felt about it; he's left it completely on record. Incidentally, Fitzgerald was not liked in Hollywood or understood. His own agent, after his death, wrote an article for *The Hollywood Reporter* saying that Fitzgerald never knew what Hollywood was all about and so on and so on. The point I'm trying to make is that it was an alien place for him. No matter how much work he did there, no matter how hard he worked, he would've been better off elsewhere. I don't doubt it for a minute. It was not the place for him. It's just the place where so many writers end up. I'm speaking now, you understand, about book writers. I'm not talking about

dramatists and I'm not talking about movie writers. Just about book writers, guys who should be writing books. Of course, my whole opinion is essentially a self-defensive one and a self-explanatory one. I'm explaining my own attitude. I'm not trying to tell other writers what to do; I *am* telling you how I feel about it. And some of the evidence.

Some of the less important younger writers have been able to turn their hand to novels on the one hand, screenplays on the other. I know a couple. Plays, too. It's really what your imagination is used to. It's hard for somebody whose whole life has been involved with books to turn around at a fairly late date and be able to think in a new medium. You know, there's another difficulty, too; I mentioned it before in this conversation. A screenplay is not a final anything, it's just a stage. And it's frustrating to write something that isn't a final something if you're a writer. Especially if you're a fiction writer. You tend to imagine the whole thing in its final form.

Ken Millar's notes for Filmways' payments for the Archer TV movie and series.

Even a director can have difficulty realizing his vision. Sam Peckinpah, for instance, has often had his movies taken away from him and recut.

He worked on one of my would-be never-was movies. I think it was *The Chill*. They weren't able to pull it off.

They couldn't get a screenplay?

That's what they couldn't get.[7]

That was at the time it came out, in 1964?

It was later, after the success of *Harper* [1966]. A year or two after that. *Harper* incidentally was a tremendous hit. It really was at the base of the current proliferation of detective stuff, both in movies and on television, which is what started the whole thing going again. That's when I started to sell enough to live on, let's say.

---

5 *Faulkner: A Biography* was published in 1974. Written by Joseph Blotner, the book consisted of two volumes, was 2,115 pages long, and weighed eight and a half pounds.
6 The Millars met Faulkner in 1945. Kenneth and Margaret cowrote an essay for the 1947 Mystery Writers of America anthology *Murder by Experts* that introduced Faulkner's short story "The Hound." A loving tribute, early in the essay they write: "The fact is he has made a more original and imaginative contribution to the mystery form than anyone since Poe …"

7 According to Tom Nolan in his book *Ross Macdonald: A Biography*, financing for the film fell through—perhaps due to the reason Millar gave Paul.

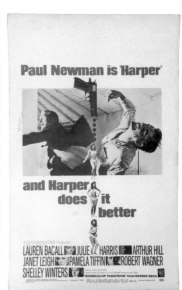

Top row: US one sheet, US insert, US half sheet, and US card stock window card for Harper *(1966). Left: US six sheet. Above: 10" Warner Bros. radio spot record and 10" Warner Bros. promotional record with Paul Newman interview by Dorothy Atlas. Below: Small promo sheet.*

Harper US lobby card set, US pressbook, 12" mono white label promo soundtrack and stereo LPs, two 16mm trailers, and a 35mm Technicolor IB (imbibition, a dye-transfer process) trailer.

This page: European one sheet poster for The Moving Target *(1966) with black lettering (the red lettering version next to it is possibly a post-1969 rerelease distributed by Kinekor for the South African market), front (red) and back (blue) covers of the Japanese pressbook, Warner Bros. European market six sheet (left), and Warner Bros. European market three sheet (above). Opposite page: European lobby card set (only has two images in common with the US lobby card set), UK Warner-Pathe pressbook and US Warner Bros. pressbook (probably for the European export market), and litho stone printed Australian daybill (similar in size to a US insert).*

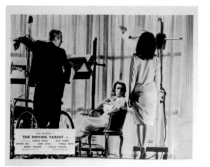

This page: French Détective Privé *one sheet and half sheet posters, linen mounted Danish poster, and small promotional pamphlet for* Harper: Privat-Detektiv, *Opposite page:* Argentinian *one sheet for* El Blanco Movil, *Yugoslavian* Privatni Detektiv *one sheet, German* Ein Fall Für Harper *one sheet and postcard sized promo, and Italian* Detective's Story *half sheets and inserts.*

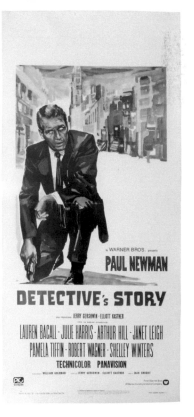

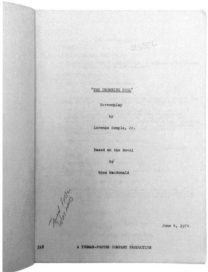

Top row: Screenplay for The Drowning Pool *(1975) by Lorenzo Semple Jr. with "David Foster" penciled on the first page (Foster produced* The Drowning Pool*), and US yellow and black half sheet. Middle row: US red and white one sheet, red and white card stock insert, US black and white one sheet, and Warner Bros. pressbook signed by Ken Millar next to the gun holster. Bottom row: Warner Bros. cardstock theater program, and Warner Bros. press kit containing promotional stills.*

Top: US lobby card set for The Drowning Pool. *Bottom: French lobby card set for* La Toile d'araignée.

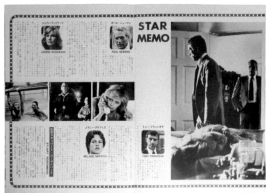

Top row: Japanese pressbook for The Drowning Pool. *Left: German one sheet for* Unter Wasser stirb man nicht. *Above: Front and back of Japanese "chirashi" promo sheet. Below: Australian daybill for* The Drowning Pool, *Italian one sheet and insert for* Detective Harper: Acqua All Gola.

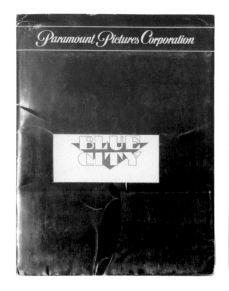  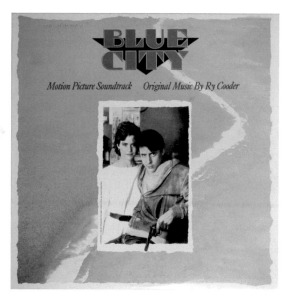

Press kit for Blue City *(1986) starring Judd Nelson and Ally Sheedy, and Ry Cooder soundtrack album.*

Do you think that contributed to making it possible for William Goldman's piece on The Goodbye Look to appear on the front page of The New York Times Book Review?

Literary criticism in this country does tend to follow movie exposure. Have you noticed? I don't say it's the only way—far from it—but very often the critics seem to come around after the movies have started showing interest, which is an upside-down version of how it should be.

The Beatles were really just Top Forty artists before the movie A Hard Day's Night. That's what legitimized them in America as serious artists, not the records. It was the same thing you're talking about with books.

A *Hard Day's Night*, by the way, is one of my favorite all-time movies. I think it's a masterpiece. I saw it just within the past month again for perhaps the sixth or seventh time. Margaret feels the same way about it. It's really a great movie, and done with great simplicity.

It almost seems like a French New Wave movie, like Truffaut might have directed it or something.

It's just as good as Truffaut, I think. It has the same light satiric comic vein. It's poignant, too. It's the one movie I can bear to see over and over and over for the rest of my life. At least the one of those that are available to me.[8]

There are an awful lot of good movies that it's very hard to get to see. Fortunately, here in Santa Barbara for some years we had a film society which showed

all the available good films from other countries. It helped to educate a lot of us. We used to fill our largest theater. Now, of course, a lot of these films are being shown at the university. They had a Truffaut festival. I got to see a number of them that I hadn't seen before.

You've kept up with interesting movies, it sounds like.

I go quite often. I enjoy movies. Of all kinds. I like all the good modern and contemporary moviemakers. I'm extremely *broad* in my tastes.[9]

Paramount Pictures filming sign for Blue City.

Do you feel that same way about B movies or C movies? There's something endearing about some of the bad ones.

Yes, I find them interesting. On television there isn't so much difference between the good ones and the bad ones. I mean, the difference is not so obvious. That's where I see most of the older and the less important movies, I see them on TV. Although I go out to theaters maybe every couple of weeks to see something.

8 "I'll tell you something very poignant about that film," Margaret Millar told Paul. "I always manage to bawl at the end of it. The day my daughter was buried that movie was on television." Margaret and Kenneth watched the movie with their son-in-law Joseph and grandson Jimmie. "We just didn't know what to do. I mean, it was just one of those *terrible* situations. Somehow it got us through one night, didn't it?"

"I've been grateful for that sort of thing," Kenneth said. "Every time they came up for the weekend, after Linda died, we would all watch *Mary Tyler Moore* together. I've often thought of writing to her and saying, 'God, you've no idea how much your program meant to four people.' You just have no idea sometimes."

9 Another of Millar's favorite films was 1967's *The Graduate*. "Gee, that's a whale of a good movie. It gets better. I've seen it several times now, and I really do appreciate it. I realize that it's a classic."

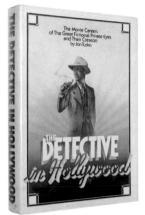

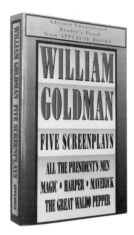
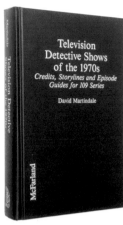

Jon Tuska's The Detective in Hollywood *(1978) contains a number of interesting snippets of conversation between Tuska and Millar. Tuska posited the question, "Can the company of one's fellows ever equal the solitary solace of being alone, watching sentences slowly form on a page?" Millar said not at all. "Writing is painfully lonely." After a pause: "But I make sure I'm not alone the rest of the time." William Goldman's* Adventures in the Screen Trade *(1983) devotes a chapter to working on* Harper *and* Five Screenplays *(1997) contains the script for it. David Martindale's* Television Detective Shows of the 1970s *provides plenty of minutiae for the TV detective fan, and includes brief storylines for the NBC* Archer *TV show starring Brian Keith.*

Did you see Taxi Driver? I felt sort of mixed. I like Scorsese, but his lack of control really bothers me. It seems to me he never quite knows where the material is going to go.

I felt the same way. The first half really got me and then gradually it lost its hold by, oh, becoming too extreme and not knowing where it was going. You know, one of the things that really worried me in it was, in the second half, it was impossible to tell whether the man who made it was on the side of the angels or the guy who was doing all the shooting. You can't have it both ways.

I think Travis Bickle is becoming a folk hero in a way now. In a way that movie is going to be important for creating a new type for the Seventies, I think.

It's good that we should be aware of them. Because there are a lot of them.[10]

Did you like The Passenger?

I haven't seen it. I've liked everything that Antonioni has done, though, one way or another. I think, of the ones I've seen much of, he's the best. But that's just a worthless personal opinion because there are so many that I haven't seen. I'm not a student of movies. It just seems to me he's a very striking talent. Very original. There's always something there. I haven't seen all of them, but, gee, I certainly love his touch. Even a movie like that one that he made in London which didn't have much of a binding story or intention had wonderful things in it.

Blow-Up?

Yeah. I thought *Red Desert* was a smash.

10 The week before, Millar had been on a movie-writing panel with Paul Schrader, who wrote the screenplay for *Taxi Driver*, and Peter Wollen, who cowrote Michelangelo Antonioni's *The Passenger*. Millar also had lunch with Schrader, who remembers the meeting this way: "I was—and am—a grand admirer of Macdonald's books and it was a treat to meet him. I'm sure I seemed starstruck."

I liked La Notte a lot, too.

Me, too. He really opened up the whole movie.

The only one that I had any difficulty with was L'Avventura, which a lot of people consider the great one.

I liked it at the time. Its rhythms are rather long, to put it mildly. It makes you wait and wait. Who was it that said, "Make 'em laugh, make 'em cry, make 'em wait"? Anyway, that's a good prescription for a lot of us, but perhaps not for a moviemaker. That's the trouble with Antonioni—he's a novelist. If he has any weakness, that's it.

You said in New York you once knew James Dean's best friend from his old days in Fairmount, Indiana. Did Dean's films make an emotional impact on you?

Rebel Without a Cause did. It's the only one I remember that had any real impact on me. That was quite a powerful film.

None of his other films?

They made an impact on me, but not to the extent that he could be regarded as a real force in my life. You see, even though he's long since dead, he came from a later generation. He certainly was an attractive figure to me.

It became fashionable for a time, it seems to me, to become a rebel without a cause whether you actually had a cause or not. He was so powerful and such a Romantic actor that everybody wanted to go out and get as screwed up as they possibly could, it seemed to me, because that is what Dean did on the screen, therefore it must be good. Half of it was sort of creative and the other half was destructive, but I couldn't always tell the difference.

You couldn't tell the difference because there is no difference. The creative and the destructive *do* go hand in hand.

Well, there is a difference to some extent, don't you think?

Yes, there is a difference. I said they go hand in hand, and this is particularly true in this present century. I'm talking about individual lives. Many of the writers that we've been talking about—people who created this century, like Dostoyevsky and Rimbaud and so on—in their lives the creative and destructive were inextricable.

Young people have to risk themselves and should risk themselves, but it should be for something worthwhile. That worthwhile something, though, can simply be a sense of personal development or freedom and finding a thing outside of you to show for it. People have to learn to take risks, and this is connected with what I said earlier about our having to be able to make decisions. And life forces decisions on you anyway. You might as well make a decision as let life make it for you. Your decision is likely to be perhaps not better but a little more your own.

During your days in Canada were there any popular culture figures that were an influence on you?

I go back a long way.

About twenty years back further than I. That's not a long way.

Well, it takes me back to the days of Pearl White, though. She was my first movie star I remember. And Tom Mix. Tony the Wonder Horse. These earlier representatives were intended to be presented as heroes, remember. Virtuous heroes. The good guys and the bad guys were always perfectly distinct.

As far as my movie heroes are concerned and early moviegoing, it was the comedians that I really loved. You know, a man I know [Osvaldo Soriano], an Argentine, came to Los Angeles. He's a writer and critic. He made two visits that I know about. He came to visit me, and he went to Stan Laurel's tomb. Gives

you some idea of Laurel's significance in a country like the Argentine. He was the benign wrecker and also the little man. Tremendous influence on me. My knowledge of him goes back to the age of three. I drew a picture of him when I was three.

There's a sense, you know, in which some of the great comedians—Charlie Chaplin, supreme example—do represent both sides. He's both virtuous and antisocial. He probably had more influence on a lot of us than anybody else. But also he's a good man and at the same time he thumbs his nose at authority. Most of the great comedians did. That's almost their trademark.

Could we talk a little bit about Hard Times and get some of that on tape? The Charles Bronson movie we were talking about. You said it reminded you of growing up in Canada.

Yes. Almost by definition, and by title, too, it was about hard times. Until quite recently, hard times are what Canada knew best. It just seemed to me that, while it wasn't specifically about the Depression—it was about an earlier stage in the economy, I think; I wouldn't try to put the date, but let's say it was 1900 or something like that—it reflected the kind of sparse and unwilling economic atmosphere that I grew up in and the kind of atmosphere in which a man might fight for a living with his bare fists. What was so good about that movie was, oh, the use of setting and color and, I think above all, the understatement. It had the understatement of an early Hemingway story like "The Battler," for example. But it was done in movie form. The understatement, it was indigenous, let's say. It wasn't borrowed from anybody.

Bronson had I'm sure not more than a hundred words in the entire movie probably.

Very little dialogue, yeah. It was done in action, pictorially. It illustrates the fact that movies are essentially pictures after all and they get their deepest effects through the pictures. Anyway, I thought it was a very, very well-made movie, and very original. It reminded me of early Dreiser or something like that.

Two 35mm Technicolor IB prints for the trailer of Harper *(1966), VHS cassette tapes of* The Drowning Pool *(1975),* Deadly Companion *(1980), and* Criminal Behavior *(1992). The Canadian-produced* Deadly Companion *was also released as* Double Negative *(which was the original working title in script form) and is based on* The Three Roads. *It starred Michael Sarrazin in the lead role, Anthony Perkins as a blackmailer, and John Candy and Eugene Levy of SCTV fame. The ABC TV movie* Criminal Behavior *starred Farrah Fawcett and is based on* The Ferguson Affair.

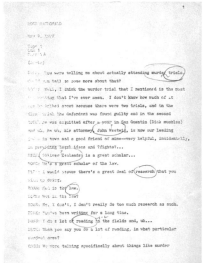

PBS promotional still for The Originals: The Writer in America *(1978), featuring Ken Millar and his grandson Jimmie Pagnusat. PTV Productions' Richard O. Moore conducted the interviews for this episode in the offices of Joseph the Provider Books in 1977. Shown here are some pages from the eighty-seven-page transcript of the unedited interviews: Ken Millar talks about Chandler on page 10, Coleridge on page 23, Freud on page 25, jazz pianist Marian McPartland on page 77 and, on the same page, Ken introduces Jimmie to Moore.*

Frank Norris and those guys.

Yeah. It was a naturalistic movie to some extent. It's just that the main theme is itself somewhat broad, let's put it that way. Somewhat simplistic. But that's true of a lot of naturalistic writing. It's almost a part of the form that it should simplify. It gives you broad strokes rather than subtleties. And this is true of Norris.

Pauline Kael wrote in The New Yorker *that* Hard Times *was "unusually effective pulp—perhaps even great pulp."[11] Would you agree with that?*

Yeah, but I don't know what she means by "pulp." It's pulpy in this sense: that one is asked to share with the hero's fistic triumphs. In other words, we're asked and expected to get a kick out of his beating people. We identify with him in a sense that could be described as *pulpish* or *Romantic*. I think pulp is just Romanticism left on the shelf too long.

11 "The Visceral Poetry of Pulp," October 6, 1975.

24. THE DOOMSTERS

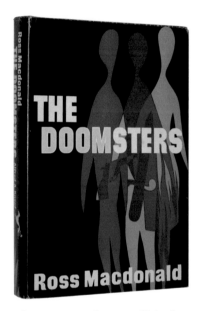

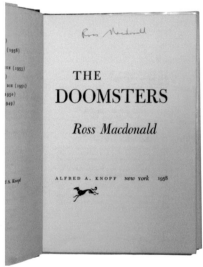

What are your best qualities?

Oh, intelligence and persistence.

What is the worst thing about you?

Anger. [*laughs*] Anger in all its forms.

What are all its forms?

Well, anger can strike out at other people, it can strike inward at the self, it can take various intellectual and emotional forms. It can pervade the whole atmosphere of a life if it's permitted to, unless you get it under control.

Have you gotten yours under control?

Well, I wouldn't claim the credit for it myself. My anger is under control, yeah. I'm no longer much motivated by it or much pressed by it. But I still have it.

You don't seem angry.

You don't see the anger itself because it no longer is terribly important in my life. It's not overtly important.

Was it readily apparent before?

I would think so. Particularly when I was under extreme pressure, I was very short-tempered.

When do you think this came under control? As the books became more what you wanted them to be?

It hadn't occurred to me that the books would have anything to do with it, but I suppose they did. I suppose getting the books under control and getting myself under control were parallel processes which influenced each other very much. You might even say that one of the main themes of the books is anger, which is gradually at least tinctured with intelligence—if not suffused with it.

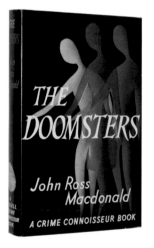
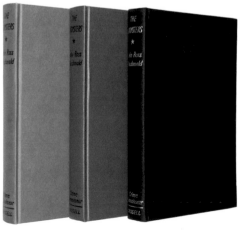

The UK Cassell edition of The Doomsters *(1959) was available in green, orange, and black bindings (no priority established).*

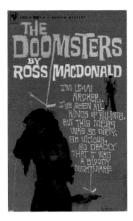 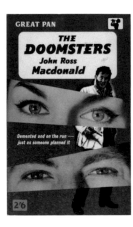 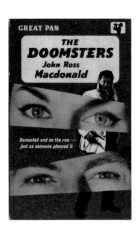

I'd like to talk about The Doomsters, but I'm going to have a problem with it I think.

But you don't know why.

Oh, I know why. At least I think I know why.

Okay, tell me why.

I don't know that we can talk about it, or that I can, because it seems to me that it just obviously comes from the situation with your daughter.

In what way?

Do you want me to talk about it?

Well, I want you to explain. Turn this off.

[when taping resumes, there is no further direct discussion of Linda Millar]

How would you describe what The Doomsters is about?

It seems to me that for me it represents a kind of an attempt to do an imaginative humanization of the strict laws of fatality. Because it's a psychologization of philosophic necessity. It takes necessity, and the process of necessity and causality, and psychologizes it to some extent, you see.

Necessity for what?

Necessity is simply the process by which one thing leads to another necessarily. That is, where if a certain thing happens, something else happens. That process of cause, from one thing to another, is what most of my books are about. This is a step into the psychological handling of that kind of necessity. Now do I make myself clear?

Yes.

It's a Freudian breakthrough. I'm using the word *Freudian* in a loose sense. I don't know whether Freud was directly connected with it or not at that time. I suspect he was, though, because now that I think of it the … year that I wrote

The Doomsters in [1956–1957] was also the year in which I was seeing a psychiatrist regularly—every week—and that experience opened up a good deal for me that had been closed before. I began to see the connections between my work and my life and my own psychological patterns and general *human* psychological patterns. That's what led to what I consider a breakthrough in my thinking, which *The Doomsters* represents. It's a first step in that breakthrough. For me it was a breakthrough to a somewhat different consciousness of how things worked in people and in the world. A more serious and an emotionally deeper feeling about crime and its sources. I still believed in necessity—*causality*, if you prefer that term—but somewhat humanized. The human consciousness enters into the process of cause.

How is this change of mental attitude reflected in Archer?

I think Archer becomes much deeper in his understanding of the processes that he's trying to deal with, and he becomes more humane in his attitudes. Let's say, by his contacts with psychoanalysis, he gets a little bit touched himself with the psychoanalytic and becomes to some extent not just a detective, and not a doctor either, but someone who understands the processes, or comes to his understanding of what has happened psychically to the people involved. He's sort of the upshot of the book. It's been a long time since I've read the book, but I think that is probably true. Is it true, do you think?

I think so, yeah.

February 1962 issue of Ellery Queen's Mystery Magazine, *featuring a condensed version of* The Doomsters *called* Bring the Killer to Justice.

It's not just an intellectual understanding either—it's a feeling, an emotional acceptance and sympathy. At least I felt some of those things when I was writing the book. And I think Archer represents a man who has genuinely got his anger under control. I accomplished it symbolically through him long before I accomplished it in my own life.

And psychiatry had a great deal to do with that?

Yes. It certainly was a watershed event in my life.

I know that a lot of your plot ideas came from notebooks that date from years back. Was this partially a result of going to psychiatry, where one's life comes together suddenly and a lot of ideas tend to coalesce?

I think I'd probably find that they did, in that general period, you know. But I'm stilling writing in those notebooks. Certainly there was a great upwelling in connection with my year of psychiatry, yeah. That's when what I consider my more serious work started. With *The Doomsters*.

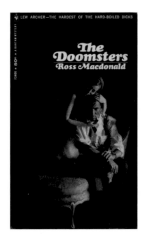   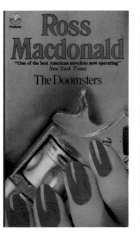  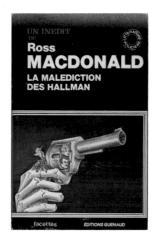

Do you think in any other books preceding The Doomsters ***that Archer was changed as dramatically as he was in that book?***

No, I don't think so. I think that's the place where the change occurred or is most evident. Of course, the other books were working up to it, the previous books, and the later books have the consequences of it.

I thought *The Doomsters* was my first serious and moderately successful attempt to reframe the situation in the detective novel. It's more serious in its intention and, as you put it, it depicts a gray world rather than a black-and-white world, more a battle between the good guys and the bad guys. *The Doomsters* was a more conscious attempt to go a little deeper into my subjects. It was the first of the books that I regarded as, let's say, a serious novel.

Is there in any of your other books a speech like at the end, which lasts several chapters?

No, that's unique in my books. And, according to the canons of the craft, it's a flaw. Up until that point, I was obeying the canons, you see. In *The Doomsters* I tried to, well, step over the limits of the form a little bit. The structure is much simpler in it than it is in most of my books. The structure of the novel, particularly the mystery novel, it tends to keep the reader at a certain distance from the characters. The structure, I

won't say it's in-between, but it's there and it's what holds the thing. In *The Doomsters*, which represents in a sense a breakdown of the detective story structure, it enables the reader to get closer to the characters, because the characters are, so to speak, just being themselves. They are not creatures of a structure.

It's your most openly emotional book, I think. It's certainly complex enough, but it's complex in a different way somehow.

Well, the causality is different. The causality is more emotional than anything else, it seems to me. As I remember the book, it's a book in which the main forces are emotions. This is not true of my books in general. They all have a lot of emotions in them, but the emotions are not the prime forces in the book. My books are somewhat intellectualized. That's what we're talking about really, isn't it? Intellectual structure as opposed to more free expression of emotion?

I think this has both.

The emotion is more directly expressed anyway.

Don't you think that Archer, certainly to a greater extent than he is in the other books, may be the main character in The Doomsters***?***

 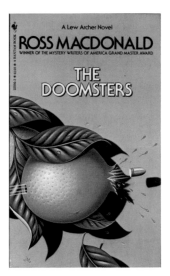 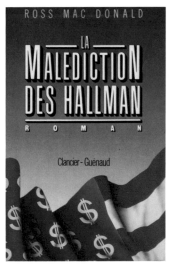 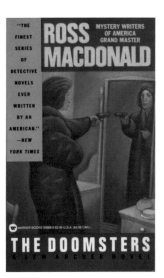 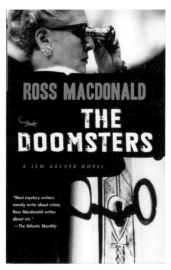

March 1956 issue of Cosmopolitan, *featuring a condensed version of* The Barbarous Coast *called* The Dying Animal.

Probably. He becomes more deeply involved emotionally with the people in *The Doomsters* than I can think of him being in any other book. As I say, I really have to reread the book before I can make a judgment about it.

Archer is literally embroiled in this case before it starts.

That's right. Either the book, or an earlier version of the book or the story out of which it came, starts with Carl Hallman coming to Archer's house. Is that the way the books starts?

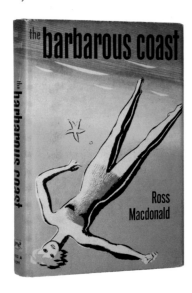

Yeah, Archer has this dream about somebody trying to get in, and it's Carl Hallman actually knocking on the door. He retains Archer, and Archer talks him into going back to the mental hospital.

Yes. Now, at that period of my life I had a close friend whose job it was to deal as, let's say, an outpatient adviser and therapist to patients who had left Camarillo State Hospital but who still needed some supervision. The friend I'm talking about, his name is Stanley T____—he's since dead—was an enormously gifted lay therapist, a man who really cared about sick people. I had the privilege of spending some time with him and also going around with him here and in other cities in the area that are served by Camarillo State Hospital, which is just down the

US Knopf edition of
The Barbarous Coast *(1956).*

hike here about forty or forty-five miles. I had become familiar with it through the fact that my daughter spent some time there as a patient. Of course, I've always been interested in psychiatric problems and people who have them, but this accelerated it and intensified it. Then my friendship with Stan T____ gave me access to a lot of experience and information.

Now, just for your own information, the saddest thing of all is that this gifted and humanitarian man, Stanley T____, ended up by shooting himself, because he himself was a former mental patient with severe problems.

You dedicated The Barbarous Coast to him in 1956.

I don't remember which one I dedicated to him. Perhaps it would be better not to use his name, because his widow is still living in town. They had children, too. You could just call him Stanley if you'd like to, if you wanted to refer to him. He was a wonderful man. Yet he was sick, too. Not all the time. He had his periods of sickness.

You see, I dipped fairly deep into that whole aspect of our civilization—through him, through my own experiences, through my daughter's experiences as a patient—and all of that certainly had a lot to do with that book [*The Doomsters*]. Also, during the year that I was writing that book, I was an outpatient myself. This was immediately after the business with my daughter's accident, which knocked her for a loop and affected all of us very strongly.[1] I left Santa Barbara on account of my daughter's trouble. The whole family moved. We sold out here and bought a house up north. We lived in Menlo Park, which is just south of San Francisco near Stanford. Linda took her last year of high school there and then she went on into the university. I spent nearly a year in therapy, seeing a doctor every week and talking to him. A very good psychiatrist. We lived for a year in Menlo Park. Then we moved back here. When I left there, I left him and I didn't pursue it with another doctor. Though I'm on good terms with a couple of local psychiatrists, I'm not their patient. But the process continued.

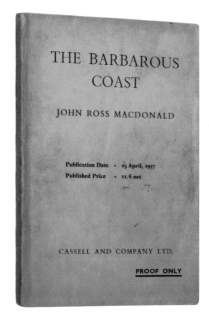
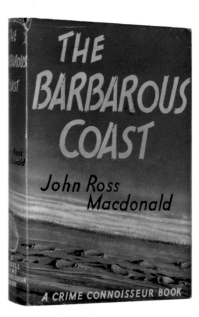

UK Cassell uncorrected proof and trade edtion of The Barbarous Coast *(1957) in black binding (there was also a blue binding).*

I didn't mean to bring that up in a problem way. I wasn't sure if it in any effect had anything to do at all with that. I didn't know.

Oh, I don't mind you bringing it up. All I'm concerned about is what gets printed, and that's not worrying me.

1 Driving drunk at the age of sixteen in 1956, Linda Millar struck three young boys, killing one of them. The family moved north for a year or so while the legal consequences and attendant social climate calmed down.

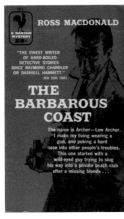

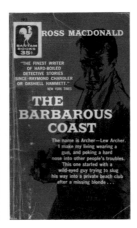

I'm just surprised that you went for only a year.

Well, that's just the way it worked out. Of course, I was psychiatrically-oriented long before I ever talked to a psychiatrist. Freud was one of my early and most important masters. And not just Freud. I've read a lot of psychiatry and been influenced by it. More than influenced by it—it's been quite central in my life. I think the perceptions of modern psychiatry are just central for us.

One advantage of being a rather subjective type is that you *can* pursue processes like that on your own. And you should if you can, if you're not too sick to do it. There are certain advantages in doing it on your own. The homemade is better than something you buy in the psychic realm. In other words, your own development is really the source of any health you're going to have. Doctors really only teach you this and open the way for you. When the way is open you can sometimes go on by yourself. I'm not recommending this for terribly sick people.

But the anger is under control.

Well, of course, anger is a response to facts, and the facts have altered, too. Perhaps in a personal sense I don't have so much to be angry about. And there has to be some benefit from getting older. Maybe that's one.

I don't know that there has to be a benefit from getting older.

I don't think there has to be either. I meant to put a little bit of a twist on that "has to be." I meant to put a little bit of an irony on it.

To a certain extent, the therapist that I worked with was an existentialist. He belonged to what's generally, I suppose, considered the Palo Alto school of existential psychology. Although he was more than that. I can't explain existentialism in a word. I don't understand it. But the idea is that you deal with the perceived reality at the time that it's perceived. In other words, what's important to you here and now. Naturally, you don't blot out the past or anything, but everything's, so to speak, of equal

significance. The remembered and the immediate now. This, of course, I think is true to the mind.

You mentioned necessity and causality. Do you see Archer as an agent who fights this?

We're all agents fighting causality, because causality is not absolute. We also are the instruments of causality and we can shape ourselves as instruments and sources of causality. That's the basic human struggle, and it's the struggle that all people with mental trouble are fighting: to make themselves masters of their own fate again instead of being mastered by what's essentially an external thing, an illness, and a consequence of external circumstances. Most illnesses are anyway.

Do you think psychiatry in its purest state, say, or most well-practiced state, could clear up most of that?

No. They can help to contain it, but not clear it up. The only thing that can clear it up would be, I *think*, a better culture. I think that what we're talking about are the illnesses of our culture, and there are a hell of a lot of them. Of course, there are worse things than illnesses.

Such as?

A slave culture, for example, is worse than a neurotic culture by a long shot. Yet it might not have much mental illness in it as such. The whole thing is an illness, and our illnesses are to a great extent the result of the chances we take in freedom. Too many of our kids, of course, are exposing themselves to unfortunate influences, which I won't go into. It would take all afternoon, and we all know what they are anyway.

*It seems like a lot of your books are based on this duality that we're talking about. Archer says in **The Blue Hammer** that "the place and the time and the family you're born into … are the things that fate most people." In **The Zebra-Striped Hearse** he says, "A man stops being an orphan at twenty-one." These two seemingly contradictory statements are different holes in the same personality basically.*

Yes, and they're both true. Each fact would be meaningless without the other. We all fight out that battle. It's the battle of maturation, it takes all your life. You never quite win the battle.

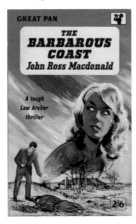

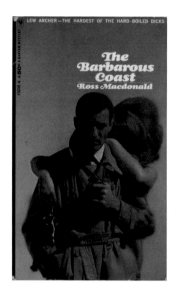
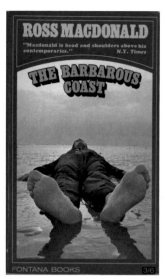
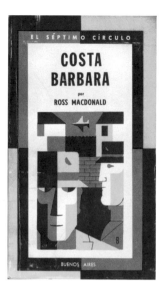
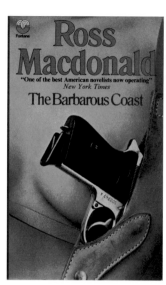
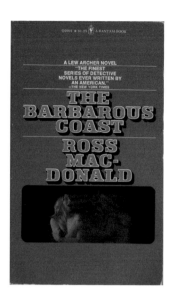

The characters in **The Doomsters** *are often described using childlike terms.*

Yes. In the world of psychoanalysis, of course, there isn't really much distinction between adults and children. Adults are simply children a little later in the process. The tendency of psychoanalysis, at least the kind that I was writing in and under the influence of, does see people as very much children of their own childhoods, offspring of their own pasts. Still, in the state of children in relation to the forces of the world, we're failing them.

Was the childlike imagery a conscious choice? Describing Jerry's dead body as "a defunct teddy bear"? Zinnie treating Martha "as if she were a doll"? When Mildred Hallman faints on the lawn, you provide this really lovely childhood image of this frail woman falling down rather languidly and a rubber ball rolling from her hand.

Well, I can't remember how I would make those choices. What you do is create a world or a fragment of a world which expresses your feelings in detail, and your feelings realize themselves in precise imagery and descriptions of people and so on.

This book came out of a period of stress in your life. Do you think writing from a period of stress tends to make the books better or worse, or no different?

I think there has to be some stress to produce a book. There has to be contending forces in the self, and the book represents their contention and the resolution— at least the temporary resolution—of those forces.

You said in New York that with **The Doomsters** *you began to realize that the books were about yourself.*

I think I always knew that. But you have degrees of knowledge and depth of knowledge, and it came upon me much more strongly in that year when I was writing *The Doomsters*. I've been an "autobiographical" novelist from the start. All my books have a personal reference. As you begin to understand more about

your life, you can put more of it into fiction. You begin to realize that *all* fiction is either consciously or unconsciously an expression of the author's life. It's other things, too, but it's centrally an expression of the author and his life.

I think psychiatry, in which I've always been interested, is another very useful art and/or science for opening up this dark side and making it useful, making it comprehensible, instead of something that we turn our backs on and are afraid of. It's really invigorating. This is one of the reasons why people love to read gothic fiction in general: it's invigorating to face the darkness. You begin to see forms and patterns and shapes of life in it. Because those shapes are our own shapes. We recognize our own shadows.

One doesn't necessarily make that choice by himself, however, to face those shadows. In my case, when I went to a psychiatrist I went out of sheer desperation.

Oh, I think we always go to psychiatrists out of some degree of desperation. People never do it for fun. It's a frightening prospect, although of course once you start it, from the very first day, it's no longer frightening. Not necessarily frightening, but things come up that are frightening. But there again, you're facing the things that frighten you or things that you're facing in your own life, which are there anyway. It's better to know something about them.

My own experience has been that the early life, which in my case was difficult—most of our early lives are—but mine presented some rather spectacular difficulties, which I mentioned to you. It helped me to accept that life and think about it without too much pain or hysteria. But at the same time it's still the hardest thing for me to accept. It's the hardest thing for me to think about rationally. Of all the things in my life, my childhood is the most difficult to face. It was not so very long after *The Doomsters* that I did try to face certain aspects of it in *The Galton Case*.

Miss Parish in **The Doomsters** *says that "when a person breaks down, he doesn't do it all by himself. It's something that happens to whole families. The terrible thing is when one member cracks up, the rest so often make a scapegoat out of him." Is that an auctorial statement or is that a statement of a character? Do you believe that that's true?*

   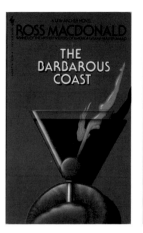  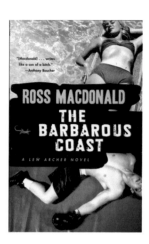

Yes, except that *scapegoat* is a loaded word. Let's put it this way: the breakdown of family life expresses itself in the sickest one most clearly. Which is exactly the same statement without the tendentious word *scapegoat* in there. Obviously, the family isn't deliberately trying to make a scapegoat of somebody—at least not the average family, though this may occur and does. Don't forget that scapegoat has two aspects, too: it's the one that inherits the guilt, but it's also the one that absolves.

Absolves who?

Well, in the ancient tradition the scapegoat is the figure which carries the guilt for the others and absolves them. *Scapegoat* means that.

Jesus Christ in effect is a scapegoat figure.

That's right. That's what *scapegoat* literally means. So, you see, there's a certain holiness involved in being a psychiatric scapegoat. I believe that literally. I believe that in many families the most interesting and the most valuable and the most *moral*, at least in the insight and feeling, is the really sick one. I'm not exactly alone in feeling that; I'm sure that's a Dostoyevskian concept.

It's becoming a concept of modern psychiatry now also, particularly with schizophrenia, I think.

Yes, that's true, but I wrote that before the development [of that concept].

R. D. Laing and all those people.

Right. Long before. And I was writing out of my own experience with sickness. You know, there's a sense in which sickness in the family is not all a curse. I mean that it can lead to elimination and even improvement, if you're terribly lucky. I mean, it can lead to insight, too, and change your behavior. And so on.

Do you see any connection at all between the conclusion of The Doomsters, with Archer brushing off Tom Rica and then recognizing his own guilt, and Spade's conclusion in The Maltese Falcon?

Offhand I don't make any connection, no. I certainly wasn't thinking about it when I was writing *The Doomsters*. I was thinking about how on earth to write the book and get it written, you know, and what was going to happen to the characters and so on. But, of course, the stratagems that we use, even in an emotional book like *The Doomsters*, are to a great extent laid down for us by what our predecessors have done. Especially if we're writing in this kind of a form, which has a structure. *The Doomsters*, though, violates almost all the rules—I hope. *The Doomsters* is one book in which there's a great deal of subjectivity and an awful lot of that subjectivity is expressed through Archer, I agree. That's true, *The Doomsters* becomes his story to a considerable extent. Not to the extent, though, that *The Maltese Falcon* is Spade's story.

I was wondering if, with Carl Hallman in The Doomsters and Anthony Galton later in The Galton Case, in effect you created your own father figure in Archer for these characters?

Could be. That's certainly one solution of the fatherlessness problem: create a father figure. Or become one.

may 31, 1974   Jill Krementz

25. THE BLUE HAMMER

 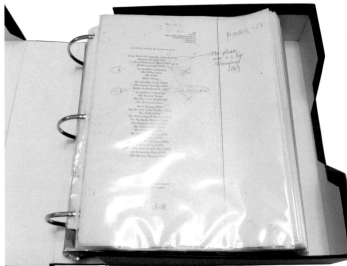 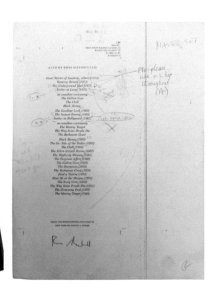

Master set of unbound page proofs used for typesetting the US Knopf edition of The Blue Hammer, *signed by Ken Millar.*

You told me in New York that George V. Higgins had called The Blue Hammer ***the blackest book of yours yet, or your darkest vision yet.***

I would take it as a compliment because it implies strength, a strength of the vision. It may be the most fully developed vision of darkness yet. I don't think the content is actually any darker than the other books, but there's more of it perhaps. It's a larger book. Also, it's quite concentrated. A great many characters and a great many events are all jammed together.

You don't feel more pessimistic as the years grow on?

No. In fact these emotions in the books don't necessarily reflect my current emotions. I lead a comparatively happy life. Much happier than Poe. And longer. I don't mean to compare myself with Poe except in that sense. He had a very miserable life, and he made a hell of a lot of good art out of it, I think.

The theme of *The Blue Hammer* really is making something out of nothing. The hero, in a sense, simply because he went on painting, is that poor, terrible man at the middle of the book.

At the middle of the book?

Well, at the center of the book. The one who did the killings. One reason why I made it a little bit of a puzzle in my statement is that even in an interview like this I don't believe in giving away the plot of a book. So I put it in a slightly concealed way.

The Blue Hammer *is a black book in many ways. Several of the characters in the book express wanting to be dead. One assumes that this was part of the pattern of the book.*

Everything in the books was intended, but not always consciously. Some of the most pervasive things in fiction are not intended consciously. Of course, these people are all caught in a tragic pattern, they're caught in a tragic event.

They're also caught by the society of this town.

I wouldn't say that the people are caught by the society of the town. There are unfortunate people and criminal people, murderers and murderers' victims in *every* town, every city in the country, and they don't represent the whole life of the town or what the town stands for. But they just happen to be my subject. Yes, there are pressures on them, but those pressures don't really originate in the town. The town is the place where the last act is played out. These pressures arise primarily from moral error culminating in crime in the lives of all these people. All these people have committed moral errors—and are suffering for them. It isn't the town that is punishing them. But the *real* hurt is inflicted by people on themselves, not always deliberately or consciously.

What about Captain Mackendrick who says he won't investigate Francine Chantry because the town won't let him? That's both a moral error and a pressure, it seems to me.

But he's just as much the town as anybody. I'm not saying that the town is spotless, but the fact that the town prevents a policeman from investigating one person, who represents the most famous figure the town has had in it, is a *long* way from saying that the town is the source of the unhappiness of the people in it. It would be true of any collection of people in a town, unfortunately. I'm afraid I regard these things as typical. Santa Barbara has murders quite frequently. So does every other city this size. As regards to such matters, this is a *clean* town compared with others that I've known. I mean, the police are much cleaner here than they are in certain other places. God knows that would include New York.

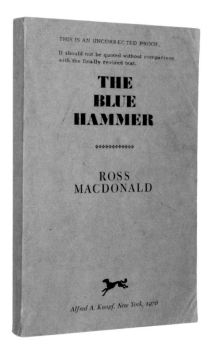
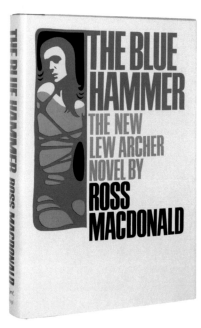

US Knopf uncorrected proof and signed review copy of the trade edition of The Blue Hammer (1976) *with promotional still signed by Jill Krementz.*

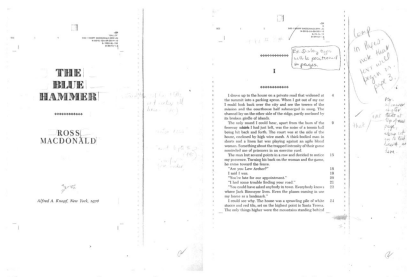

The master set title page with typesetting corrections and the first page of the first chapter of The Blue Hammer *with a change by Alfred A. Knopf marked in orange pencil—the proofs have markings, notes, and changes by several Knopf editors throughout the book.*

I'm not trying to blacken Santa Barbara.

Neither am I, neither am I. No, and in fact it isn't about Santa Barbara; but it's the closest to a natural physical description of Santa Barbara that I've written.[1]

1 Throughout the books, Millar repeatedly used the fictional town of Santa Teresa as a stand-in for Santa Barbara and thereabouts. As a nod to Millar and his influence on her work, author Sue Grafton also situated her female counterpart to Lew Archer, Kinsey Millhone, in Santa Teresa.

There's no question that one of the aspects of any city that I write about in a crime novel does have in it this aspect, too: I'm also writing about the city of hell, which is a traditional approach going back at least as far as Baudelaire. I mean, I don't want to deny that, but that isn't the same thing as saying that Santa Barbara is hell. No, it has to do with my imaginative use of Santa Barbara. That's one reason why I've never wanted to write directly about Santa Barbara as such, for the obvious reason that I'm *not*. I'm writing about the city as hell, too.

When Betty Jo tells Archer about her encounter with Mead in the attic—"He held a gun on me and made me take off my clothes. Then he tied me into the chair and painted my picture"—that's not a comic image, but it has its comic overtones.

Of course. A commentary on the action. Of course, that's exactly the way nutty people often tend to think. They just go from one extreme to another. They're not good at telling the difference between, well, areas of importance. Nutty people really are nutty, and nuttiness often takes just that form, of being unable to distinguish between levels of importance or relevance. They overreact or underreact, or react completely inappropriately.

It reminded me of Iris Murdoch's writing.

Yeah, well, her whole tragicomic mix is unique. It's what I love about her. I came to her rather late. I think the first book of hers that I read was *A Severed Head*. I actually haven't read all of her books or even most of them, but what I have read

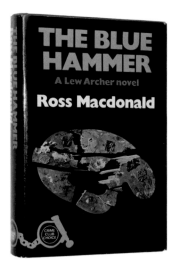

UK Collins uncorrected proof and trade edition of The Blue Hammer *(1976), and signed card: "with thanks for your interest."*

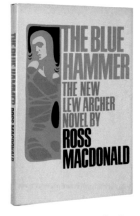

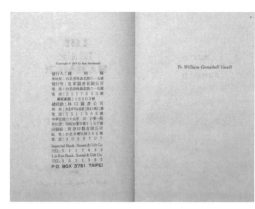

Taiwanese pirated edition of The Blue Hammer *(1976); and Paul Nelson's inscribed copy signed by William Campbell Gault, the book's dedicatee.*

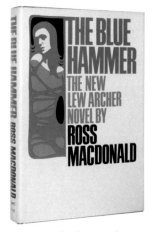

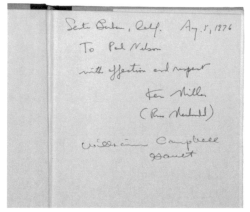

I've enjoyed. I hope I don't assume too much credit when I say that I think we're working at somewhat the same psychological and social territory. I consider her a much larger figure than I consider myself.[2]

Could you talk about the original title for The Blue Hammer?

It wasn't really the original title, it was just a bright idea I got after I finished the book. It didn't last very long and it's not inherent in the book. I wrote a little bit into the book to justify the title and then I took it out again. The title was *The Tarantula Hawk*. The tarantula hawk … is a kind of wasp that's found in California. The female finds a tarantula, paralyzes it with her poison, deposits her larvae on it, and leaves. Then when the baby wasp is born it has something to eat—the tarantula. If you think about it in connection with the book, you find it's a fairly exact description of what happens in the book as regards Mildred and the child. My editor thought it was a giveaway. I changed it because it was inherently obscure, and something that needs explanation isn't a good idea for a title. Also, it's hard to remember. Well, it was just an idea. Somebody told me about the tarantula hawk and it just gave me the idea.

Does the title come often first or last in the books? Do they change titles sometimes or do they frequently stay the same?

2 Murdoch, as did Millar before her, succumbed to Alzheimer's.

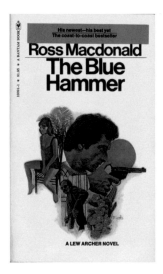

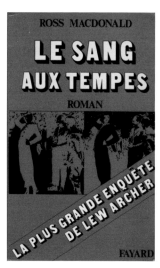

Half and half. Sometimes I have to try a number of different titles before one works. Other times I have the title before I have the book.

I would imagine that The Blue Hammer ***was a particularly difficult book to write.***

Well, the basic problem was that I'd been developing the plot over a period of a dozen or more years. I had this enormously detailed notebook material. When I decided to do this book I had to master the material, and then think with it, you know. I don't ordinarily spend so long a time developing a book as I did this one. Material tends to grow on you like potatoes underground when you keep it in your mind for so long. At the same time, it becomes more and more difficult to handle as it becomes denser and more complex. I wouldn't say it's the longest gestation period, but it may be the one I've returned to most often and most intensely. I have other books that it took a dozen years to get out, too.

Which ones?

Offhand I can't tell you because I don't keep the dates in my mind. There are much more complex books than this one, though. I think the detective

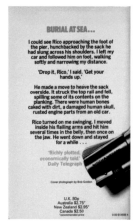

UK Fontana paperbacks of The Blue Hammer *from 1978 with export prices that changed within that year.*

form is what makes this book different from some of the other more complex novels, because it has to meet not only the regular standards of narrative but certain special standards that are set up by the detective form. That makes it difficult.

It makes it difficult from another standpoint, too: you have to do an awful lot of exposition in novels like this.

Of course, the ideal solution is to convert the exposition into pure narrative, and that's very difficult. It's very difficult to meet both requirements and keep on doing it. I'm frankly surprised that it turned out as well as it did. In particular on towards the end of the book it became quite difficult.

You said the notebook material was "enormously detailed." In what way?

In the way that the book is. The plot way, and just in terms of being in it. You know, putting the whole thing together, the people and what they do and what happens to them. Of course, that changes, too, as you work with it. But you have to master the basic material in order to think about it. It was tough just because it went on over such a long period of time. I don't mean to complain. It wasn't all that bad. It was more difficult than usual.

Because there was more of it?

Yes. It's my longest book, too. I think. I usually write a book … after I've spent months, or in this case years, developing the story, and then when I'm set to go I write the book right through from beginning to end. And that is the book. I haven't actually sat down and rewritten a book through in many years.

If The Blue Hammer ***were 150 pages longer, with all that complexity I don't think it would hold up.***

Well, I don't have to go on extending. That just happened. I didn't even plan a longer book. But by the time I finished covering my material it was a long book. Also, it would just simply be impossible for me to maintain the tension. Holding it up for as long as I did took everything I had. I was completely exhausted when I

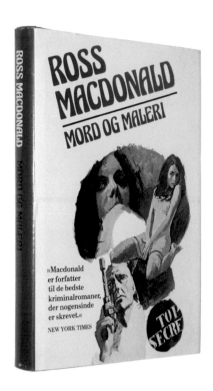

finished the book. It's very close to a hundred thousand words and I think that's about the limit for that kind of a book. For me, not necessarily for somebody else. In any case, there's no great advantage in writing something longer merely in order to make it longer if you've already covered your material. I do know, of course, that the longer a book is the more you *should* be able to get into it, but the question of form is the limiting factor. You have to find a form that will comprehend and contain and *hold up* all the material that you put into it. There's no point at all in material that is not aerated, so to speak, by the form.

We were talking about the key to Archer being that less is more. I think you caught this one just before it crossed over to more is less.

It could very well have broken down. You know, in order to finish a complex book, also somebody has to write the damn thing. [*laughs*] It isn't just a book happening, you know. You have to work it out, and it's difficult sometimes. But it's really rather fun.

I've never had to abandon a book on account of being unable to solve the complexities. Eventually they all work out. Now, I'm sure there are errors in them. I'm sure there are errors in this book. Not serious errors. I don't mean large errors, but small errors, discrepancies of time and place, stuff like that. Somebody perhaps being in the wrong place at the wrong time. That's generally true of fiction: you nearly always find errors in it. They sort of validate it in a way—as fiction.

Going back to what you wrote in the Archer in Hollywood *foreword: "We writers, as we work our way deeper into our craft, learn to drop more and more personal clues. Like burglars who secretly wish to be caught, we leave our fingerprints on the broken locks … ," etc. I'm just wondering, is this the same sort of statement that William Mead makes when he continues to paint his way into suspicion?*

No. In the first case I'm just making a comic comparison between a burglar and an artist. In the second case the comparison is not comic, it's for real. He really is a suspected murderer. There's a connection between them, but they're not equivalent. One is a burlesque of the other.

Both depend, of course, on the widespread popular position of the artist's suspicion when the artist-as-burglar, the artist-as-danger-to-society, concerns them.

I wasn't struck so much by the burglar metaphor as much as the sort of insistence on the self I guess by both statements.

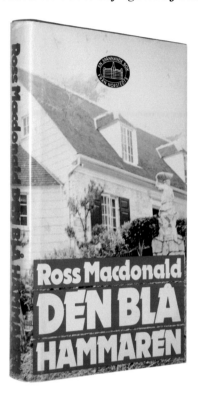

Oh, you mean the insistence of the writer self in the fiction? Is that what you mean? Oh sure. Now I understand you. Of course. We aim to put absolutely as much as we can of our personal traces in the work. But that's not egotism necessarily, it's just that the work is an image of man and the obvious source is self-portraiture. It's the only certain source. That's part of the initial structure of the book and it does have to do with self-revelation. But it's true of all of us, all of us who write: we do reveal ourselves. It sort of is *a* central idea of the book.

Speaking of self-portraiture, isn't really Joyce the absolute model for all of modern art? *A Portrait of the Artist as a Young Man* and *Ulysses*, they're the absolute models, and not just for novelists. Of course, every writer starts rather remote from the self and works towards it. Even Joyce did. His *Dubliners* is not about him, at least not for the most part.

Several of the characters consciously romanticize what Mead has done.

Well, he's negative in a sense, but he's positive in another sense. In one sense the most important thing a man can do or be is good at his work, and particularly if it's important work like art. This conflict between the artist and society is traditional.

Could another theme of The Blue Hammer *be the dangers of the false front of Romanticism? Dangers of over-Romanticism, say?*

I think that's *a* subject of practically everything I've ever written. I'm a Romantic writer who's concerned about the dangers of Romanticism. I'm writing in a Romantic form in a Romantic tradition, but I try to turn it around onto itself, to examine itself to some extent. All these things are tied together. You can't really disentangle the Romantic hero from the Romantic tradition; one produces the other, one expresses the other. In fact the Romantic tradition *is* the behavior of the Romantic hero.

Is the Tucson artist Simon Lashman based on an actual painter?

None of my characters has ever been based on an actual person. I'm using painting as a stand-in for any art, and my subject is the *poète maudit*, the cursed poet.

 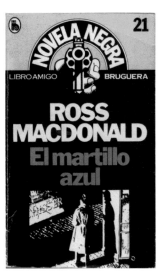   

Do you regard Lashman as a heroic figure in that book? And were you in any way making a personal statement when he says, "I've stayed here and kept at my work. I'm not as well-known as the disappearance artist. But I've outstayed him, by God, and my work will outstay his"? That sounds like it could be somewhat your personal philosophy of longevity and sticking with it.

Maybe so. If so, it wasn't meant to be a personal statement on my part. And I don't regard Lashman as a heroic figure. He does represent a heroic aspect of painters, though. They do keep on going and functioning no matter what. He represents writers, too. Artists in general. I have a kind of aesthetic admiration both for him and for Mildred. Simply by virtue of their longevity and their survival and their having done the things they wanted to do.

Mildred is a wonderful life force to many men in that book.

Lashman represents the same kind of life force—really on a higher level because he's a painter. She's just a model. But then, she's of course a much more important figure in the book. I'm glad you like her. I like her, too.

   I'm sure *The Blue Hammer* was intended to be among other things some kind of a statement about what it is to be an artist, and some of the complexities and the difficulties and so on. I was brought up in relation to those difficulties since quite a number of my relatives have been in the arts, as painters and writers and so on. My mother was a pretty good writer, too.

Can we talk about how Archer's drowning of Puddler in* The Moving Target, *which he immediately regrets, comes around full circle in* The Blue Hammer *when he saves Rico from a similar fate?

Well, what happened was that I wrote the second scene and then recognized the connection with the earlier scene, so I decided to have Archer remember it. Of course, the interesting question is why I repeated that scene before I remembered that it was similar to a previous scene. Then, of course, I obviously tied it in a way that, where *The Moving Target* was an opening, this would be a closing. I simply mean what I did was to handle it in such a way that it completed a movement that started in *The Moving Target*. I mean, it was a rescue instead of a drowning. So it pulled the first Archer novel and the last Archer novel, as of then, together.

Was it at all conscious?

It's the sort of thing that you can't really plan. If you planned it, it becomes awkward. It has to happen. I think there's something that holds together *all* the Archer books and is a sufficient coherence that you *can* say that one book leads to another and one book might help to complete another or look at the material in another from a different aspect.

   What we've been talking about—these two scenes on the wharfs, one of which was a killing and the other a rescue—is a very obvious and overt example of what I'm talking about. Actually, there's a web of meaning in life, imaginative life and imagined life and verbal linkage and so on, that runs through a whole bunch of the books and makes a unity which I've been careful, from beginning to end, not to violate. Even though I try to improve the books and broaden them and deepen their subject matter and so on, I've tried not to violate that essential web of meaning, which is expressed primarily in style and imagery but also in action and what people say. In other words, there's a unity of intention, even though the plots are diverse, and there's a relationship, as you point out, between one plot and another. Very often a plot will take the previous plot one step further. That sort of thing.

Throughout the book Jack Biemeyer is one of the most unsympathetic characters, yet he undergoes a sort of salvation at the end by going out of the house.

Yes. What he does, he undergoes the general fate and accepts it. That's what the meaning of the last sentence is: acceptance of his fate and even the ability to show love. Or at least a humane acceptance. The central overall movement of the book, or at least one of them, is that movement by Biemeyer from the beginning to the end towards the realization of his own life. In terms of a novel like this, self-realization and acceptance of the reality is about the most you can expect of anybody. These people are all tragically held by various kinds of fates. I don't mean anything large or terribly obscure by that either. What we do generally determines what we become. So what we do becomes our fate. But you can undo your fate by seeing what you've done and stopping doing it.

He's unsympathetically presented throughout the book and is an unsympathetic character. He's an angry character and an egotistic character and so on, but he isn't really presented as a bad man. Don't forget that in spite of, let's say, his victimization by his own fate, including that unfortunate early love affair—which can be quite damaging to a man, and it was to him—he still is not presented as a bad man, and he reaches out for his own salvation at the end when he reaches out towards his son.

It's a variation on the Oedipus theme—somewhat of a reversal, and I think a valid reversal—that somehow has more to do with our society than the Oedipus story does. Perhaps.

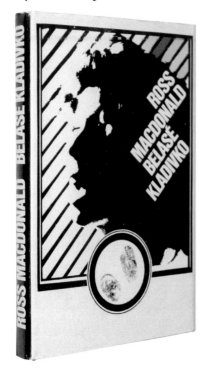

Could you explain that?

I'm sorry I said it if I have to explain it. [*laughs*] I'm not even going to try to answer it seriously or in detail, but let's say that instead of living in a paternal society we live in a maternal society. Is that sufficient? I'm just saying that the mother tends to provide the continuity rather than the father in families. And in many cases the father is no longer there. So that's why I think it's an appropriate myth for this society. The mother is very much there in the books. Unfortunately, unavoidably there.

The ending of the book—and by that I mean not just the last thing with Biemeyer but the preceding scenes, several of them, some pages at the end of the book, a dozen or so—didn't jell until I went back over the book as a whole and wrote them. It seems to me that I wrote the book, finished it, but it wasn't a finished finish. I was tired, very tired, when I finished, and then I waited a week or two and then redid the last chapter or so. That's why I was able to end on a stronger note.

My decision to end the book that way was the only basic change in structure. I can't even remember how I was going to end it previously, though I probably have it written someplace.

Is that unusual for you, to rewrite an ending?

No, that's pretty standard. By the time you get to the end of one of these books, you're not really ready to write the final ending. Usually, if I do any rewriting at all, it's at the ending and also at the beginning. It's hard to get started, too, properly.

You have some great endings and some great closing lines.

Oh, I think last lines are important. They're what the reader is most likely to remember.

Did rewriting the last chapter of Blue City *mean changing the outcome of the book or simply stylistically?*

No, it meant that I got tired before I got to it and it simply needed to be—

Stronger writing.

—stronger writing. Exactly.

Is that a danger in a book?

Only when you write a novel in a month, which is how long I took to write *Blue City.* No, I don't think it's really a danger. Because you can always take a little rest. There is a sense, though, in which by the time you get to the end of one of these books, with all its interlocking mechanisms, the ending is pretty well preordained. You don't have much choice. You can't suddenly change everything. You know, "Meanwhile back at the ranch" and so on.

Still, you did on The Blue Hammer.

That's true. While it comes at the end and is not unimportant, really it doesn't violate the structure in any way. In fact, it's an illustration of what I'm talking about. The structure of the book sort of determined that ending. I didn't recognize it until after I had sent the book in.

Wouldn't you agree that, if you *can* make a change of that significance at the end of a book, it's inherent in the structure of the book? You see, I didn't have to change anything in the book. All I did was add something on. I'm not claiming that it works perfectly, but it does illustrate the real point that I was making: that is, that what you put into the book gradually determines how it will end. And that's what happened in this case. The fact that there was a brief delay in *my* recognizing it is simply one of the accidents of writing. You don't always know exactly how a book should end—until you've tried it.

We're talking now, though, about gross structure. The detailed structure is made up as you go along. You never know for sure how a book is going to end. You may *think* you know, but, as in the case of this last book, the inevitability of that ending just occurred to me after I had already written *an* ending. Then I saw that the other was, well, almost unconsciously dictated, I would think.

How elaborately do you prepare your plots? You know, before you get down to writing chapter one?

Well, I spent a dozen years preparing the plot for this last one. Of course I was writing a lot of other books in between. That's typical. Nearly everything I write goes back some years.

Hitchcock said that by the time he's finished writing the script and has all the camera angles down and can see the film in his head, the actual making of the movie is something of an afterthought. Is there any similarity of feeling, after more than a decade of working on the ideas and creating a structure for the book, that the actual writing is anticlimactic?

No, that's the real thing; the other is just preparation. I've prepared a lot more books than I'll ever be able to write. Fortunately, I find that plot ideas tend to

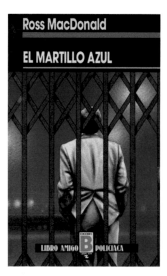
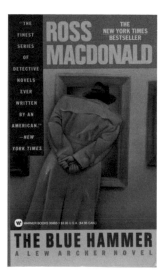
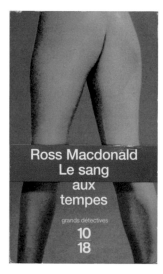
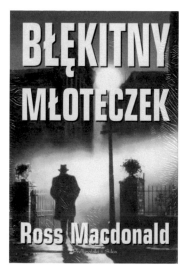

coalesce and collapse into each other, so that I get more into a book than I expect I'm going to.

Plot is always the starting point, though?

An idea, generally involving a reversal of some kind.

What do you mean "an idea"? How does it come to you?

Well, you tell me. What's the central idea of this last book? For me the central idea was the disappearance of a very well-known man into a garret and his living a submerged life in the same town that he had disappeared from. That for me was the central idea.

I saw the son as the focal point in my first reading of that book.

My memory over the various notes I made a long time ago, the son was there quite early on. I should say that the central idea coalesced into something like this: A young man is interested in an almost mythical artist, and he's living in the same house with him all the time and doesn't have any conception of it. That's really the central idea. That came early on.

You said your initial conception of The Blue Hammer was the artist disappearing in his own town more or less.

Yeah. Disappearing in his own life almost. Because he does tarry on and all his talent persists, and that's what leads to his discovery. As I've said to you before, it's a parable of the *poète maudit.*

All poets aren't cursed. Our society isn't *that* Romantic yet. We're all in the family of the descendants of Poe, who was our prime example.

Do you think this is highly accessible in reading the book? That that is the primary idea in it?

How could you avoid knowing that that was primary? Because that's the main discovery in the book. You couldn't read the book without going through the process of making that discovery. Now, you might not draw a generalization from it or an abstract conclusion, but that isn't necessary. You go through the imaginative experience of the book—that's the important thing. And that's what you experience.

Had you asked me that question, I wouldn't have given that answer. That the central idea of the book was that.

Well, that isn't exactly what I meant. Remember, this was in the context not of "what ideas would be drawn from the book by readers?" but what *I* started with. Two different things. That's what I started with, and the book doesn't abandon it.

Is that also what you ended with?

No, very often a book can outgrow its idea. I mean, there are a lot of other things in the book. I won't try to give you more than one illustration, but the first thing that occurs to me is that, in spite of the fact that we have this cursed artist, the book is an affirmation of the importance and value of art. Specifically plastic art. Wouldn't you say?

What do you mean by "plastic art"?

Painting and sculpture.

The man's paintings are good, but I don't think I would see the book that way.

Well, let's put it in the simplest possible terms: Let's say that I painted a picture of some object or some person. Wouldn't that picture inevitably be a statement of the value or importance of what I was painting? I'm not saying that's the only thing it would be. You don't write a whole book about a subject without affirming its importance.

That seems to me implicit: that in the act of writing one is affirming the importance of writing.

Yes, but I'm not talking about that. If the act of writing involved painting, you're affirming the importance of painting. Even if you're *attacking* it, and I'm not

It seems to me that one of the ideas that comes across in that book is that his art is far superior to the man.

Sure. And also his art plays a double-edged part in his life: it's his glory—it's the only glory he has—and it also destroys him. His persistence in it destroys him. Yet all this has nothing to do with the central idea: that by writing about art you confirm its importance. I mean, you don't have to say, "I think art is important." If you write a whole book about art and artists that's sort of basic. For me. I'm not saying that *important* means morally valuable or even desirable. Just important. However, that wasn't all of what I meant when I said that. There are spokesmen for art in the book who affirm its importance. There's another painter in the book, you remember.

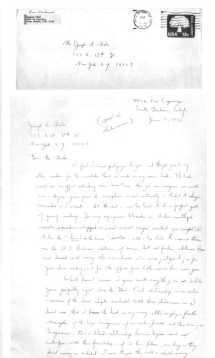

Above: Ken Millar's June 18, 1976, two-page letter to Joseph Gisler in response to the high school teacher's letter pointing out errors in The Blue Hammer *(shown on page 120). Top right: The original mailing envelope postmarked June 19. Middle right: First page of the earlier three-page draft to Gisler from June 11, with the penned notation of having sent the shorter version. Right: Ken Millar's note to send a missing page in Dorothy Olding's first carbon and a list of corrections for* The Blue Hammer *typescript.*

Lashman.

And he speaks for art. He speaks, well, more completely than the other man who's a divided personality. Lashman is a pure painter and he doesn't have to say much. The message I assume gets across that I am glorifying art.

He makes a very good speech: "In this work, you really need endurance." Does that sum up some of your views on being a writer?

Well, I was really just thinking about Lashman. I don't think you need endurance to be a writer to nearly the same extent as you do to be a painter. It's possible to sit down and write a damn good book in your twenties and stop. There are writers who have done that. Ordinarily, painting is a pretty consuming lifetime habit. Painters are generally more *persistent* than writers I think.

So you cannot do one great painting and then stop?

No, but there are innumerable cases of one great book. There are few cases of painters that have done rather few paintings. But for the most part painters work right through a lifetime.

See, I interpreted that endurance speech in terms of emotional endurance, the ability to wait things out. The ability to, in terms of Sam Spade, take a full accounting of oneself. An ability to see that through over a period of years. Tenacity. I think writers do need that, whether they write at the age of twenty-seven or at the age of fifty. An emotional endurance.

Sure. And the writers who fall by the wayside are the ones who lack it. I quite agree.

What are you going to do with Betty Jo? That's one of the few things that I think you have left unresolved in the books.

Archer's life has remained unresolved from book to book. It had to be left unresolved. Because I don't know what the next book will require, and it has to be determined by things more important than that.

In addition to the Puddler reference, there's another instance in the book that connects back to Archer's own past. Archer and Betty Jo go to Long Beach, back where Archer was born.

Yes, I was making a bit of a tie-up there, but I wasn't trying to do much with Archer. There were too many other things to be done. That's one reason why, as you say, I left the girl hanging. There wasn't a place in that final morning to do more with her than indicate some continuity between her and Archer. If I *had* tied it up more neatly, it wouldn't really have been effective in the context of all these other things being tied up. So I didn't really intend it to be left hanging, but rather open and positive. I did try to bring the girl into the ending movement and have her make a contribution or two, you know. Even leaving breakfast food is indicative of something, but it certainly is not what I would call a Romantic union.

Why did you put her in? You must have had some reason.

No, she just came in naturally, the way she came into the book. She simply was a girl that he met at a party. I didn't have any intentions of making her Archer's

Two-page draft of a letter from Ken Millar to Elizabeth M. Walter, editor at Collins in the UK, listing corrections keyed to the Knopf edition of The Blue Hammer *to be incorporated in the UK printing of the novel.*

girl when I brought her in. But it sort of happened. I liked the idea of the girl. I don't know whether I want to continue with her. That involves some of the problems we've just been discussing, and that's why I left it hanging. It wouldn't be natural anyway for that aspect of Archer's life to be tied up so rapidly at the end of a book like that. Certainly it represents an opening of his nature towards other people.

Aren't you running the risk of perhaps obscuring your central theme with deflecting readers like me who get very intrigued with Archer's relationship with Betty Jo?

Well, there can be certainly more than one thing in a book. It could be that the book would be cleaner and stronger without that side issue of the girl. I didn't plan to write about her at any length. The book found uses for her. I wouldn't say that *I* did particularly, but I started a train of narrative that just spread out a bit and then there came a point at which I had to determine whether this was going to go all the way. And by "all the way" I don't mean whether they would sleep together, I mean whether they would become lovers or affianced or whatever—partners, in any sense—or whether I should draw back at a certain point. Well, I left it open, and that's because I'm a series writer and I didn't feel, having gone only so far, that I should use the whole thing up. If I had, I think I would have run the danger of having a somewhat double book. This way I think I've managed to introduce Betty Jo into the book and use her and handle her, but not used her to the extent where she's finished and she is the end of the book. I haven't thought about this question except in terms of what I'm going to do. I haven't tried to explain it to myself until today. Let's say that the structure of this book is somewhat looser than that of some of the other books.

Her and Archer's future is left very much in the air.

Just exactly as it would be in life at that point. It would tend to be just very much in the air at that point. In any case, I didn't want to commit Archer to anything further in that direction.

Does this mean that you will have to answer that question or discuss that question in the next book? The question of Betty Jo?

If I still have the same readers, I'll have to. The chances are that she'll make an appearance, either in person or at least in memoriam, but I don't know how much further I want to go with her. I don't know how much further I want to go with the series either. That's always open to change.

Why wouldn't you have the same readers?

I can't guarantee to myself that I'll always have the same readers. I won't have the same readership. All I mean to say is that for people who are interested in the continuity from one book to another, it will have to be taken into account. Or I can simply drop the whole thing. That's the beauty of a loose structure, you know. I don't pretend to be writing Archer's whole life. These are just some of his cases.

One more book at least would you say is fairly certain?

Yes, I should round it off.

26. PAINTERS AND OTHER ARTISTS

Let's talk about the Henri Rousseau painting that you have hanging in your office.

Well, I found the print in a book and print shop downtown that was going out of business. I was lucky just to see it. It wasn't in very good shape. But it doesn't have to be—the picture's there.

Part of one corner's missing, but otherwise it's not in too bad of shape.

The margin doesn't matter. The picture we're talking about is *Une soirée au carnaval* [*A Carnival Evening*]. It's one of the most profoundly Romantic pictures I've ever seen. I can't describe it. It's just so full of feeling, feeling for the people and the place. Of course, also it's very highly stylized. It's got these deep human connections. I mean, there is a Pierrot there. We also know it's just a French peasant on the way to a party with his girl. On his way to a carnival party. It's a happy picture in spite of its somberness. Look at the whole sky; half the picture is sky, blue sky with a moon in it, and a couple of pretty clouds. It covers the whole spectrum of feeling and possibility, and does it so simply. Of course, those black skeletal trees are not exactly happy, but they're beautiful. They're not threatening them, they're just there.

How do we know it's a French peasant?

Well, that's just what *I* think it is. Also because the girl is dressed like a peasant. But of course she may be in costume, too.

It does have a really solid human quality.

Sure. The setting is both natural and, as I said, highly stylized. It keeps it from being too much of a landscape and it emphasizes the human. Otherwise the human figures would seem perhaps a little lost in the landscape.

  Anyway, I'm glad [Rousseau] existed. I take a great deal of pleasure in what I've seen of his work. I think he's a profound painter.

Painters pop up in many of your books.

There are actually more painters in my immediate background than there are anything else. My Uncle Stan [Moyer] painted all through his life, right up through

his seventies, and I have several cousins who are painters. And so on. My daughter also started painting. She made her first sale in an art gallery when she was twelve.

You literally led a life surrounded by artists, then, from the beginning.

I wouldn't say I was surrounded, but I was in intermittent contact with artists from the age of three and I was excited about art from that age. And I started drawing when I was three. It didn't last long.

So you knew your Uncle Stan from when you were three and four?

I knew him a little later. Maybe five and six. He was my mother's brother. He lived in Canada. Off and on over the years I spent a fair amount of time with him, in his house and in his studio. I was around him when he was painting people and so on. Enough, I think, to be profoundly impressed by his image. The image of what he was and did, not so much the person. It's very liberating for a would-be artist in any medium to have artists in the family. It makes all the difference, it makes it a lot easier for you. I think he had an awful lot to do with my forming an intention of becoming some kind of an artist. Although my father was a writer, too, you know. But Stan was let's say the most important continuing male influence in my family on me. You might say that, after my father's departure from the family, which occurred when I was about four, Stan was the most important man in my life.

More important than the "uncle" with the movie theater?

Oh sure, in a much more continuing sense. Right through from early childhood right into manhood, for a period of fifteen or twenty years. See, I only spent two years with the cousin who operated the movie theater. I wouldn't underestimate his importance to me, though, as a human being. He really saved my life in the emotional sense. He really treated me as a father. And this wasn't true of Stan; but what Stan did fascinated me. He was a real artist, and that's what I wanted to be.

Was he a recognized painter?

Yeah. Of course, there were lots better painters than he. Being a recognized painter, though, is a long way from making a living. He spent a lot of time

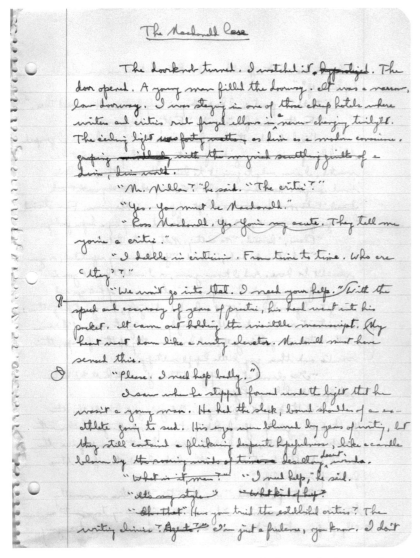

"The Macdonald Case" provides a fascinating look into a little seen side of Millar's humorous work and his writing methods. Written sometime between 1958 and 1964 in fountain pen in two different spiral-bound notebooks (the first, with smaller holes, as seen on the left), it's presented as a first-person piece written by Kenneth Millar. In the story mystery writer, Ross Macdonald brings his latest novel, The Galton Case, *to the literary critic Kenneth Millar for evaluation. The character Millar, is critical of Macdonald's use of similes, Macdonald quotes Aristotle as a defense of the use of similitudes, and the Mystery Writers of America factor into the story as "the Organization." The author Millar was clearly copying and revising from notebook to notebook, editing and honing the piece, finally resulting in six separate drafts of the story. It's a revealing and in-depth look at the author wrestling with himself and his work. The different drafts are a physical document of a celebrated writer's thinking and working process. Seeing the crossed-out words, their replacements, and the editorial choices made in each successive version until the piece is polished to three typed pages is something that will be seen less and less of in the digital age.*

teaching. He taught for a good many years at the Ontario College of Art.[1] He was a professor of art.

I was just thinking: probably one of the most important things that Stan did for me was to introduce me to the work of the modern school of painting. You know, the whole revolution that originated in France, I suppose.

Monet, Pissarro, and those people.

Yeah.

Was your Uncle Stan a model in some ways for the artists that you wrote about?

1 The school, which changed its name to the Ontario College of Art and Design, is now known as OCAD University.

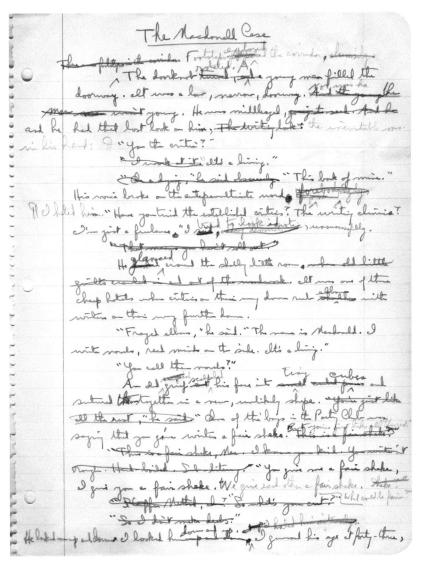
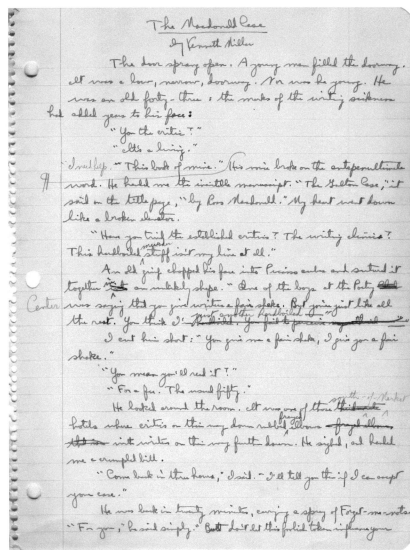

In the first and second versions, Ross Macdonald leaves and returns with a dozen roses for Kenneth Millar. In all subsequent versions, the flowers are changed to forget-me-nots. In the second version, Millar describes Macdonald: "An old grief scalpeled his face into tiny cubes and sutured them together in a new, unlikely shape." Perhaps not surprisingly, this description takes on a more artistic bent in the fourth draft and becomes "An old grief chopped his face into Picasso cubes and sutured it together in an unlikely shape."

None of the people in my books are intended to represent him.[2] I have often thought of writing about him and may yet, but I haven't. His life story is immensely interesting. It's so interesting I hesitate to tell it to you. I want to save it. It is fantastic! I'll tell it to you when the recorder is off. I'm not afraid to give it to *you*, I just don't want to give it to your reading audience. Somebody might just happen to use it, you know, and then I wouldn't be able to.

Is it the kind of story that you could fit into a detective plot?

Yes, or something that might take the place of a detective story. It's a psychological drama, somewhat Dostoyevskian, but with a happy ending. In real life it had a happy ending. An incredible story.

He was very ill. For a number of years, as a boy and young man, he was hospitalized. I'm not going to tell you any more because this is part of the story I don't want to tell. It's a beautiful story really. He ended up living to a ripe old age and being more or less surrounded with honors and pleasures of life even though he never made a financial killing. Artists don't usually, you know. They're just glad to accomplish what they set out to do. When he was in his seventies, he was still going to Mexico to paint every winter. In fact, he had a one-man show in Mexico City just a few years before he died. That would only be about a dozen years ago. Stan was a writer, too, by the way. So he led me in more than one sense.

2 Three days later Millar answered a similar question this way: "Yeah, I think he had quite a lot to do with Lashman. Also, his life story had elements of ambivalence such as appear in the book. I won't go into that in detail because he is my uncle."

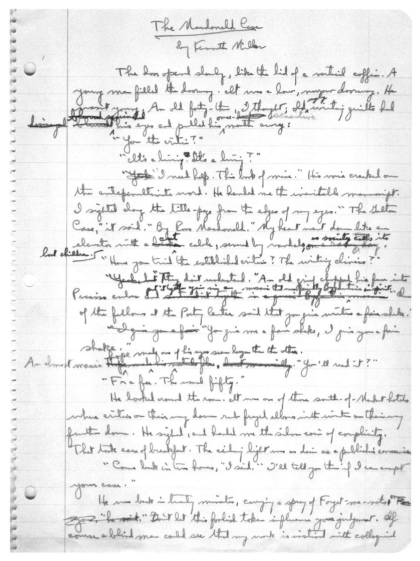

By the fifth version, the story has begun to tighten up and become more economical. The Picasso line evolves yet again with another artistic reference: "An old grief chopped his face into Picasso cubes and put it together again in a mosaic that was faintly Byzantine in spirit."

Is this a story that you have in notebook form?

Yeah. I'd tell you more, but I don't want to give it away. When you tell a story also and it goes into print, it sort of takes the pressure off the desire to tell it in your own form. I try to avoid talking about what I'm writing or what I intend to write. That's the only reason. It's not because I want to keep it a secret, it's just that I've learned over the years it's better to hold it back, let it build up your pressures. Build up your narrative pressures, whatever form they take.

But it was always writing with you, not painting?

That's right. I was word-oriented almost from the very beginning. It doesn't matter what kind of an artist you intend to be; to be introduced to modern art is absolutely basic. And to be introduced to pictorial art, plastic art, is absolutely basic. It was to me. I think I probably learned just as much from the painters as I did from the writers. Or let's say that I could have if I had been smart enough.

What kind of things are you talking about?

Oh, the nature of the reality that you're writing about. External reality, including people. You know, what those painters that we just mentioned in that great French school and pre-French [school accomplished]. It's the creation of the modern visual world. We've learned to see a completely different world than what the eighteenth century saw, and this is the world that writers write about.

When was Bruegel?

Oh, he goes back to an earlier period. And he didn't create a world, he notated it.

I think you could argue the man created one.

Well, but only in the visual sense. His work doesn't have philosophic implications. I'm not expressing myself too well, but there's an enormous difference between what he did and what Goya did. Goya was not only depicting a dramatic world but he was commenting on the people and the actions in profound psychological ways and with historical consciousness. And this is true of all the French painters. I mean, you'll find earlier writers who might accidentally sound like Flaubert, but they really aren't. Because Flaubert was writing out of a philosophy, a new interpretation of the world. I'm just using that as an analogy; it's not an exact comparison.

Don't you think, though, that some of those vast canvases, by Bruegel and Bosch, with crowds of people just doing all these garish things, represent some sort of philosophical vision of life?

Yes, but it's not the modern philosophical vision. That's what I'm saying. It's tied to the Middle Ages. You just mentioned Bosch, for example. I'm sure that he was giving a vision of heaven and hell—literally. Literally a vision of hell mainly. Now, what you get, you see, in the modern French painters is not only a vision but also a comment on it, a comment *so* subtle and *so* definite that just to change a line alters it. And that's the sort of thing that was new.

Hemingway always used to say that Cézanne showed him as much about writing as any writer.

And that's what I'm saying, too, and for the same reasons, just to take Cézanne as an example.

Do you think movies are serving this same purpose now?

Yes. I think they have right from the start. They've become just about our dominant visual art and they influence everything, particularly prose fiction. But they also influence life itself. They're changing our modes of life.

And television, too.

Yeah. Television has accelerated this process at such a pace that we're in danger of flying apart culturally. I mean that the image itself changes so rapidly that we don't know what's what. I'm not thinking about people your age or mine, I'm thinking about young people whose main source of information about the world is television. They're getting a pretty strange picture and it's essentially artificial in the bad sense. They think they're seeing people, but what they're really seeing is quickly whipped up travesties of human experience in many cases. I'm just talking about what I see on the screen and what the kids are seeing, too. I know the kids become quite sophisticated and they reject the false, but nevertheless they're subjected to an awful lot of it: the false and the superficial and the insipid and the foolish.[3]

It's almost science fiction-y. Nobody really looks like those television leading men. They don't really look real.

No, the whole thing has gradually lost its reality. It has sold out. Just sold out. It was a much more interesting medium ten years ago. It's a world of its own, a world of itself. A kid, when he shuts himself up in a room, he immures himself with this strange world. Of course, it has many relations to the actual world, but not enough. I'd be happy to see the whole thing just go down the drain. Commercial television. It practically *has* gone down the drain already.

Getting back to what we started to talk about: artists and the theme of art runs through many of your books.

Yes, they're the novels of a critic. I was trained as a critic and my mind tends to think in the terms that the critic is brought up in. Certainly I regard art as the most important activity that people can [do]. That's just how I feel about it. I don't really claim that as a universal truth, you know. One thing I'm trying to do on my own small scale is write art about the sources of art. That's almost one of my main subjects. My first book was a 400-page study of Coleridge's philosophical criticism and its sources. The psychological backgrounds of Coleridge's criticism. And by the psychological backgrounds I don't mean the personal but the history of psychology starting with Augustine and coming on down. Naturally, you work what you know and what you're interested in into your fiction. That's what it's for.

You wrote that while you were at the University of Michigan. Was it ever published?

No. It's a book, though. In fact, it's the longest book I ever wrote. It was a good thing for a writer, I think, to work on, but it was much too big a subject to do in a thesis. I could probably have gotten it published if I'd wanted to take the time to rework it and go through all the process, but I felt I had already given enough to the subject of Coleridge, several years of my life, and so I went back to my novels. See, I took time out to write that from my books, from my fiction, because it was an unfinished business in my life and I wanted to finish it.

Do you remember the title of it?

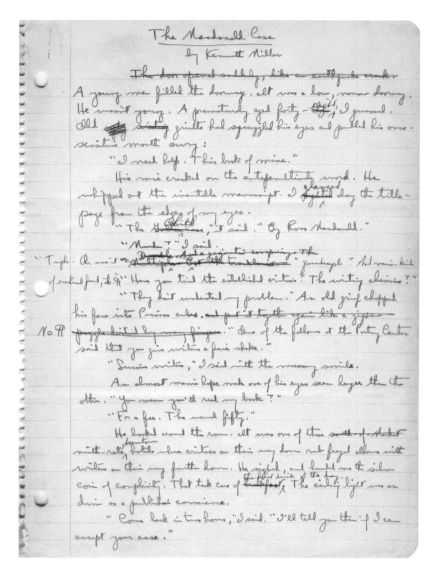

This sixth version of "The Macdonald Case" essentially represents what became the final typescript shown later in this chapter. However, this version contains revisions and emendations in ballpoint pen in what appears to be Millar's later microscopic hand, suggesting he might have worked on the piece well into the late 1970s.

There were so many possible titles. I can't remember offhand.[4]

Do you really think your books are the novels of a critic? I don't think so.

Whenever I make a statement, please surround it with objections and variations and so on. See, when I make a statement like that, I don't mean that to be the last word. It's just something that one might suddenly recognize and state.

Certainly they're the novels of an ex-critic. Nobody but an ex-critic could have written this last book, in my opinion. I'm not saying a good critic, either, just somebody who is fascinated by art and artists and various media.

---

3 One can't help but wonder what Millar would have made of the state of television today, with its "reality TV" boom, to say nothing of the Internet and its offerings. Coincidentally, he was involved in one of the very first reality television programs, PBS's 1971 documentary series *An American Family*. When creator Craig Gilbert was planning the show, he knew exactly what kind of family he was looking for: the one he had read about in *The Underground Man*. He reached out to Millar and, with the assistance of an acquaintance of his, an editor at the *Santa Barbara News-Press*, located the Loud family of Santa Barbara.

4 Millar named the thesis "The Inward Eye: A Revaluation of Coleridge's Psychological Criticism."

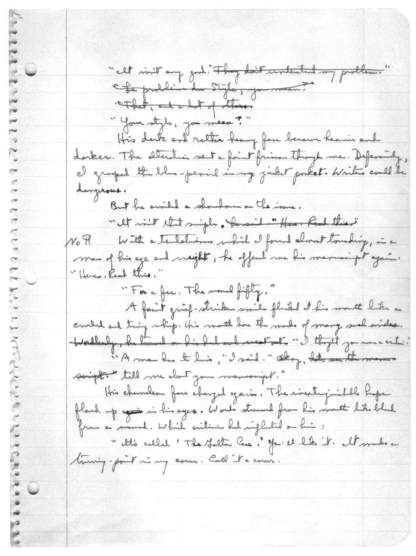

The original second page of the first version of "The Macdonald Case." This page follows the text at the bottom of the first page: "Have you tried the established critics? The writing clinics? Agents?" Millar abandoned this approach and began writing on the back of the first page with the new angle.

I can't jump to why "nobody but an ex-critic could have written this last book." I'm missing a link in there somewhere.

Well, who else would be interested in writing a whole book about art and artists? The central subject is a critical idea and it has to do with the making of a distinction between general human virtue and the specific virtue that enables a man to be a good painter. That's a critical idea.

It's a philosophical idea.

Criticism and philosophy merge and feed into each other. I would rather speak of myself as an ex-critic than as a philosopher. I don't claim to be a philosopher. That would expose me to a set of rules that I don't want to have to write or live by.

I'm trying to remember if you've ever had writers as characters in your books.

Not very much. Anyway, painters are more interesting to me than writers. Writers are hidden people except to the extent that they make themselves known in their writing. It's very difficult to write about people who don't do anything in the external world except put words down. That's why there are so few successful books about writers although so many of them written. Painters are very much out there in the three-dimension world, operating in it and creating things out of it. Visible artifacts. The work they do is something that you can hold up and show. Show and tell. To me that's a much more dramatic and interesting way to put yourself on record than to sit in a room writing with a ballpoint pen. There's something just inherently dramatic about it.

Don't forget that the arts were first known to me through painters. Not just the painters in my own family but John Innes, for example, who was my father's friend. In fact, the two of them researched the West Coast Indians in British Columbia. My father wrote about them and John Innes painted them. He made a powerful impression on me even when I was three.

Have you ever considered the idea of writing about critics in any of your books?

I don't think of critics as a specific kind of person really. There are so many different people who are critics. I think criticism is simply something that one can do or not, and many people can do it. In fact, most critics are something else, too. There are a few exceptions. But even Kenner, who so far as I know hasn't written any fiction, does do other things besides be a critic. For example, he teaches and he writes what might be called cultural history, which is something a little different from being a critic of specific works and so on.

You said that "it's quite an achievement to survive" in this civilization. Do you think it's particularly harder for painters and writers and musicians?

No, I don't really think it's particularly harder. I think this is a wide open civilization in which imaginative people can find themselves in ways that they couldn't when our society was apparently much simpler and less excitable.

You said in another interview that "Yearning for reality and the pleasure of it and a knowledge of it are the basis of art." That phrase "Yearning for reality" is a rather strong one.

Yes. But, you see, unless you have had that yearning *met* by art, you do indeed yearn for it. That's my opinion. I think the subject of art is reality. Whole civilizations, or whole parts of civilizations, live cut off from reality, by political, religious, psychological, whatever barriers. Or simply ignorance. I think the most extreme example would be Nazi Germany, but the United States under Nixon or Ford also has its elements of unreality which are rather hard to penetrate. It's true in varying degrees of every culture. Art exists, among other reasons, in order to penetrate or at least cast a new light on this unreality so that you can get some kind of answering glint from it that speaks to you. You know, there are many forces, money forces and others, which conspire to keep the truth from other people. This is not a conspiracy theory of history or anything, it's just a simple fact.

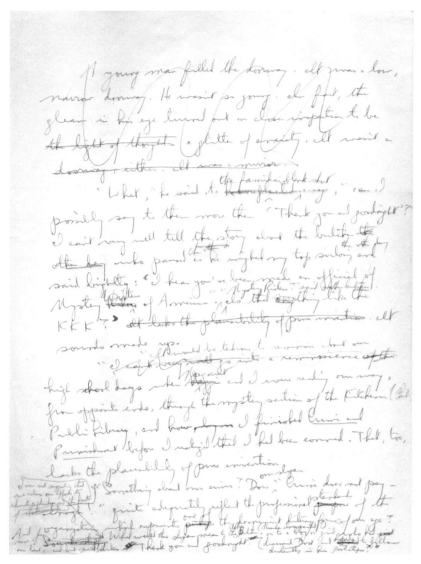

This manuscript starts off with elements from the opening of "The Macdonald Case" as previously mentioned in Chapter Four. It is a draft of a speech or essay on being elected president of the Mystery Writers of America in 1965.

This statement also suggests that there was a time in your life when reality wasn't that easily graspable.

Sure. I think we seize it as we grow up, if we're lucky. And we keep on growing up, again if we're lucky, until we get old. I know some old people who illustrate this. Reality isn't just something that you know, it's something that you enjoy. It's the native element of the human mind, and unless the human mind is in contact with this reality it lacks joy and it lacks meaning. This is a multifaceted reality that I'm talking about, of course. It comes to different people in different ways. To only connect is the watchword.

Your upbringing in Canada made reality a rather hard one to battle at times in your early life.

Yes. When you're exposed to multiple versions of reality, none of them very deep-reaching, as I was among various relatives and so on and even in school, I didn't feel I was rather fully in touch even in the intellectual sense with reality until I was about thirty—let alone the imaginative sense. It was the result of meeting the right people, both in the flesh and in books. A gradual revelation and also a finding of self in relation to that revelation. The self doesn't exist in a vacuum, you know; it has to grow in relation to other growing selves, which are part of the reality I'm talking about—the prize part of it.

Do you think that what you just talked about is one of the reasons why several of your characters have multiple names? There are various switches in identity in your books and no one is often who he seems to be.

Yes, I think that a lot of those elements in my fiction are overtly autobiographical. I mean, overtly to anybody who knows my life.

Because of the confusion of roles and various father figures.

Exactly. The confusion of cultures, too. I lived in more than one culture and more than one subculture. Of course, it's the best possible training for a fiction writer. If you survive. See, my experience, while extreme, is similar to the experiences of many millions of our population. We've all been going through rapid cultural changes and had to adapt to all the changes. Adaptation, I think, is one of the lessons that my books can teach. Or at least it can let the reader get some imaginative sense of all the problems of adaptation.

Do you think that a similar writer/artist could have gone through very bad times in his life and come out with a different definition of art than "Yearning for reality and the pleasure of it"? Someone who's gone through a lot of trouble may convert their art into quite the opposite, a need, a yearning, for fantasy or for something besides reality.

But his fantasy would be colored by reality.

It would be a heightened version of reality. Van Gogh I'm thinking of particularly.

He was working in reality. It was the reality that he saw and, once he saw it and put it on canvas, other people saw it, too. All of a sudden reality has changed.

Is it possible for art not to be reality?

Well, it just has varying degrees of success in representing reality, and there are of course many varying depths of reality. But it isn't what's depicted, it's the depiction itself that is the reality.

How does that jibe with the fact that your books on one level function as a form of escape? That one can enter into your books and escape into the world of Lew Archer and Southern California as depicted through your imagination for however many hours it takes to read them? How does that work with your idea of reality?

Even though the reader who reads them may not be fully conscious of this, my books, while they themselves mime the operations of reality—cause and effect,

Warren Zevon's Bad Luck Streak in Dancing School.

for example—force the mind of the reader to follow the same process of miming. That's what I think. Of course, this isn't a direct attack on reality; but for me reality is the complexity of counter forces that are at work in the mind or in the culture. However escapist the books may be in one sense, they don't let the reader escape from some of these things really.

I'm the first to admit that I'm not a profound, realistic novelist. I'm writing something different from the realistic novel and I can't define it exactly. It's an attempt to make something personal out of a particular genre. There are a lot of other serious attempts going on, too, on the part of dozens of other writers in the same genre. It's true it's not a genre that represents itself as being realistic, but I don't think people would be interested in reading the stories unless they touched on what the readers consider reality in *some* sense. But for me the structure itself of the books is perhaps the essential respect in which they relate to reality.

As opposed to characterization?

Yeah, but, you see, character is part of the cause and effect process in the books. You couldn't speak of the cause and effect in the books without referring constantly to character because that's what motivates so many of the events and actions. There is a sense in which my books are too much concerned with structure and not enough with the people who are espaliered on the structure perhaps.

Do you think that it's possible for writers and artists to creatively drift?

I think there has to be some overall current, and not just an objective current. I mean not just something external of itself. There has to be a life movement in itself and some sense of continuity and of having been at a certain place and of going to a certain place. Pieces of work are just episodes in that continuity, but the continuity has to be going on like the movement of a river.

Do you think there are periods in an artist's life where he might not know what he's going to do, but he can sort of soak up things?

Yeah. We spend half our time in that condition.

That he can almost make a conscious decision to create less? Is that a very dangerous thing to do?

I don't think it's dangerous at all. I think we frequently need a good long rest without the strain of writing.

Did you not have that in that period when you were producing, on the average, one book a year?

Well, I didn't have as much time off as I take now. I was writing shorter books then and somewhat less demanding books, too. And, of course, I was younger. It makes a difference.

Do you think those books suffer in any way for not having a period of creative rest?

I don't know whether I was capable of benefiting either [from] a lot of empty time. Rest is important, but what's even more important is the constant practice, especially if you're learning your craft. That's the most important thing of all: keep at it. I think it's only an older writer who should and *must* take time out to fill up. That's my experience. Of course, the great desideratum is to maintain a career without too much drift throughout a lifetime. I think that's the best way to fill out your life and the best way to get your books written. Anything that enables you to survive creatively and go on working is what you should do. It differs for different people.

I'd say that's one of Jackson Browne's thematic concerns.[5] At one point he says, "I haven't planned my life and I haven't done it deliberately because things seem to be working out this way, and I'm getting the work done maybe *through a sense of chaos.*" It seems a rather courageous, dangerous decision to make, but he has managed to pull it off. Other people perhaps couldn't.

Of course, the work of a novelist and particularly a crime novelist is not comparable with lyric song. I mean, it doesn't need the same kind of philosophic approach. In the course of writing a great many of my books I felt as if I was wrestling with enormous forces and trying to get them under control. What I'm saying is that there's a powerful element of structural effort that goes into the kind of book I write that doesn't go into song. Because you actually are dealing with the forces of the world—even though you're doing it metaphorically. You *are* struggling with your own life and with the world around it, and with specific things in that world. Each of my books has its own specific struggle with specific things. They could be identified and named.

Well, I think he sees his songs as struggling with himself and specific things. I would liken them more with short short stories, I guess, in dramatic structure.

Yes, but he's not struggling so overtly with the specific things in the outside world. The lyric impulse which he represents is more profoundly concerned just with the self and its immediate surroundings. I'm not making a comparison in favor of one or the other. It's just that the kind of books I write present themselves essentially as structural problems, and the structure isn't just the structure of the novel, it's the structure of the world that the novel is trying to relate to.

5 Paul had given Millar three record albums, including ones by Jackson Browne and Warren Zevon. In 1980 Zevon, in the liner notes on the back of his album *Bad Luck Streak in Dancing School*, wrote: "For Ken Millar / *il miglior fabbro*." T. S. Eliot, in his dedication to *The Waste Land*, used the same expression (quoting Dante from *Purgatorio*) to describe Ezra Pound: *the finer craftsman*.

When we were talking about movies in the car you said what interested you in a work of art, what attracted you, was the moral force of it.

Well, I don't think I was talking about plastic arts, was I? It would be very difficult to make that statement about the plastic arts. They just don't exist in terms of moral force. And they're the wrong words in which to discuss plastic arts. They're the wrong words in which to discuss the literary arts, too, but not so wrong. I think the verbal arts are inescapably moral in their effect because of the use of language, and language is pretty difficult to detach from life in general and its moral meanings. Very difficult to talk without using moral concepts and coming to moral conclusions—or even just having moral doubts.

I think what I've just been saying is peculiarly true of drama. Drama just exists in a moral world. You can almost not have it without the moral. And, of course, the movies, being a kind of simplification of drama, make that even truer, I think. We tend to judge them in moral terms. I don't mean the kind of moral terms that say sex has to be banished from the universe or something like that, but somewhat simpler moral terms. Having to do with life values, let's say. That's certainly what movies are about traditionally. It's what novels are about and, to some extent but in a subtler way, it's what poetry is about, too. Life values. What's good in human life, what isn't, and so on. I think perhaps my own attitude to those arts, dramatic arts and fiction arts and so on, is more moralistic than is quite fashionable.

Some of the best American directors to my mind, Hawks and Ford and Hitchcock, are really moral force directors.

Sure. Morality is what their movies are essentially about. It's the central balance in those movies, and that's almost inevitably true with the kind of thing that Hitchcock does—or the kind of thing that I do. You can't really write about crime or make a movie about crime without taking some kind of a moral position. There's no way to do it, and the attempts that have been made to treat the subject in a completely amoral way, strictly for laughs, don't turn out very well, is my feeling.

You said in an earlier conversation that a novelist's "best energy goes into describing the lives of other imaginary people." Is that true of artists in general as well?

There are ways in which art is an action, but it's hard to think of writing a novel as an action in the same sense that painting a picture is an action. I think a painter or a musician is closer to being a man of action than a novelist is, because he's operating on material objects in the real world and he's creating material things in the real world, such as paintings or symphonies or whatever.

The novel isn't a material thing in the real world?

You see, the book itself is not what we're talking about, but when we're talking about a painting that's what we're talking about.

I'm confused.

There's a difference in the order of substantiality and reality between a painting and a book. There's a sense in which painting a picture is an action in the real world whereas writing a book is not. You see, you can write a book without even writing it down. Now do you understand what I mean? I could write a whole book and not even make a mark with a pen. It could all go on in my head.

Couldn't a painter do that or a writer of music?

No. That's my point. There's a difference. There really is a difference.

Wait a minute. I don't see that, I'm sorry.

Let's put it this way: A composer or a painter *has* to have the substantial collaboration of the actual world and he has to change the actual world physically in order to perform his function.

Make sound or—

Make sound or a painting, yes. Now, you just can't deny that.

Why is making letters on a typewriter that much different than making paint make colors on a canvas?

I'm not even talking about writing with a typewriter. I'm talking about writing with a pen. I make marks on a piece of paper with a pen. That is really different from painting a picture because, well— A novel doesn't exist until it's been read.

A painting doesn't exist until it's been seen.

There's a difference.

Do you think it's a major difference or a superficial difference?

Well, it's important to me.

Is it possible you're romanticizing painting?

I doubt it. Perhaps I shouldn't present this as a philosophic difference having to do with realities, although there certainly is a distinction between a painting and a book. There's only one copy of a painting but there are innumerable copies of a book, for example. Now, you can say, "Sure, they can make copies of a painting," but that's not true. They can only make simulacra of a painting; they're not repetitions of the painting. Even the artist who painted the painting couldn't paint the same painting twice.

Again, it's a somewhat superficial difference, since the writer only writes the book once, just as the painter paints the picture once. I'm just not sure that these differences are major.

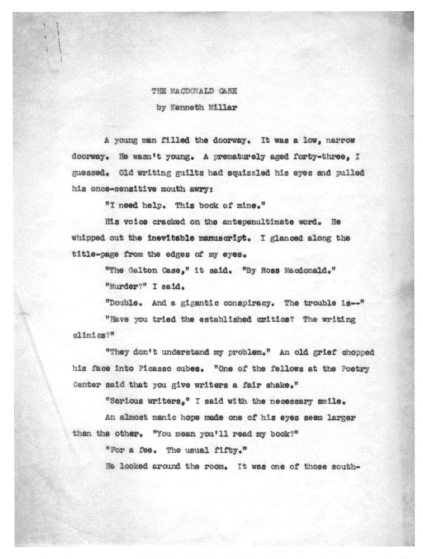

THE MACDONALD CASE
by Kenneth Millar

A young man filled the doorway. It was a low, narrow
doorway. He wasn't young. A prematurely aged forty-three, I
guessed. Old writing guilts had squizzled his eyes and pulled
his once-sensitive mouth awry:

"I need help. This book of mine."

His voice cracked on the antepenultimate word. He
whipped out the inevitable manuscript. I glanced along the
title-page from the edges of my eyes.

"The Galton Case," it said. "By Ross Macdonald."

"Murder?" I said.

"Double. And a gigantic conspiracy. The trouble is--"

"Have you tried the established critics? The writing
clinics?"

"They don't understand my problem." An old grief chopped
his face into Picasso cubes. "One of the fellows at the Poetry
Center said that you give writers a fair shake."

"Serious writers," I said with the necessary smile.

An almost manic hope made one of his eyes seem larger
than the other. "You mean you'll read my book?"

"For a fee. The usual fifty."

He looked around the room. It was one of those south-

*Final carbon typescript for "The Macdonald Case." The first handwritten draft
was about four and a half pages; the sixth and final, a little over two pages.*

I didn't say they were major, I just said they existed. See, you're denying their existence.

No, I'm not.

You started out denying the existence of them, and that's all I'm arguing about. I didn't say they were major. They're major, though, if you spend your life doing one or the other. It makes a hell of a difference which one you do. They're two entirely different approaches to art and to reproduction of reality.

All right, can you explain to me, for you as a novelist, why it's different and why it's important?

All I started out with was that painting and writing are two different kinds of act. You see, being a painter is much more being a man of action than being a writer

is. I mean, just considering the two activities. I'm not saying that writers can't be men of action, I'm just saying that the act itself—

You're denying Emerson, who said that "Man Thinking" is a man acting.

Well, that's just a play on words.

I don't think so. No, I think it's at the heart of what we're talking about.

But I'm not talking about that, and I'm the one that's answering the questions.

I know. I'm trying to bridge the gap between the questions and the answers.

No, you're trying to get me to say something different from what I already did say.

No, I'm trying to understand what you're saying.

Well, can't you see the difference between painting a picture and writing with a pen on paper?

Only that in a graphic sense one would be more interesting to watch or write about.

Why?

If I were making a movie, because painting is more visual and there's more action in it. But I'm not sure that that's what you're talking about. It sounds to me like you're talking about something that's a much bigger difference.

No, no. That *is* what we're talking about. I'm just claiming that the exact way that you spend your creative life is significant. It really makes a difference. Because you do wholly different things from other people, such as painters. You become a wholly different kind of person.

How?

How? You want me to tell you the difference between a painter and a writer? Between a mature painter and a mature writer? Okay, a mature painter looks out there and he sees design and color. I look out there and I see people and think in terms of, if I'm mentally active, how to describe it in words. We actually live in different worlds. You know, it isn't just one world out there. It's the world that we're prepared to observe and, if we're artists, reproduce or imitate. We *project*, especially if we're trained in an art, all that knowledge onto whatever we're looking at. So we move through a different world.

I agree that it's a different form of observation, it's a different form of thinking, it's a different form of creating. But the very act of taking that observation and trying to create, whether in words or with paint, a piece of art, whether it's a novel or a painting, is in fact an act. Writing is an act as well as painting is an act.

I'm not denying that it's an act. I'm talking about the nature of the act.

2.

of-Market-ninth-rate hotels where critics on their way down
rub frayed elbows with writers on their way further down. He
sighed, and handed me the silver coin of complicity. That took
care of breakfast. The ceiling light was as dim as a publisher's
conscience.

    "Come back in two hours," I said. "I'll tell you then
if I can accept your case.

    He was back in twenty minutes, carrying a spray of
Forget-me-nots:

    "Don't let this foolish token influence your judgment.
Of course, you're bound to like my fascinating variation on
the Hamlet-Oedipus--"

    "Shut up," I said. "I'm the critic."

    He held his breath while I finished reading, then let
it out in a gasp: " You like it. But how much? Tell me how
much."

    I hated him, and his wheedling charm. But I couldn't
hurt the man. I'd run with writers in my time, before a
kindly professor straightened me out. I knew their wild
vanities, their sad little hopeful desperations.

    "It has a certain crude power," I said. "And some rather
nice atmospherics in the San Mateo coast section. Quite nice
for a beginner."

    "But I'm not a beginner. This is my tenth book."

The difference only is in the kind of observation, the forms of observation.

No, the real difference is in what you do with it. We're not talking about the artist as passive observer.

It seems to me almost—and this is probably wrong—that you rank painters higher than writers.

I certainly don't. Far from it. I think writing is by far the most important art—in modern times. It hasn't always been. I don't mean to denigrate painters either. It just has to do with what's overall important.

You seemed to be saying that the painter's process is possibly better than the writer's.

Oh no. I said that the painter operates in the actual physical world in a sense that the writer does not—and this is what the argument is about. That's all I said. I

wasn't saying that the painter is closer to reality because he's operating directly on the physical world. So is the plumber. That doesn't make what he's doing more important.

Can we talk some more about the man of action? Specifically, your concept of Archer as a modest hero.

As far as the man of action goes, yes, my ideas are quite modest. I think the man of action should be modest also in his hopes and claims and his intents. You know, the devastation that's been wrought on the world in the last century and may destroy it in the next century will have been largely the work of men of action. These oil pipeworks that are right out on the sea here, and the oil that spills on our beaches and will ultimately destroy them completely in another half a century if the men of action have their way—this very beautiful blue coast will be as hideous as the worst shores of New Jersey—those are the actions of the men of action. I've grown a little suspicious of them.

There are people in this town, though, including yourself, that have been men of action fighting that. Bob Easton, for instance.

Well, it would be a mistake to describe either Bob or myself as men of action. We're capable of action, but we're both writers. Please be assured that my articles for *New York Times* and *Sports Illustrated* and his book *Black Tide* have had a lot more to do with interfering with the men of action in the oil business than anything we've done physically.

Was Thomas Paine a man of action?

Yes, he was, and his books were directed towards action. But, you see, I wasn't saying that Thomas Paine was or was not a man of action, I was pointing out that there's a distinction between *action* and what I do. You can't say that I'm a man of action because I perform actions. I'm saying that I'm not *defined* by the term "man of action." Anybody to whom you describe me as a man of action, who knows me, would just laugh in your face.

I think you can make an argument that a man who's written as many books as you have is a man of action also. You're not a man of inaction.

Yeah, but I'm talking about physical action.

Mental work, you know, is a different kind of action.

Oh sure. I regard mental action as more important.

I think it takes a lot more discipline to sit at that desk and write those books. It's certainly no easier than physical exercise.

It's very nice to burst out of the study and go and do something physical. You know, the combination of the two really are what gives pleasure to both sides of the picture.

Well, let's leave you out of this and talk about Bob Easton and the oil spill, then. Didn't he make some form of action that had a physical result on the actual environment in much the same way a painter would have?

```
                                                              3.


     "You didn't tell me you were a nine-time loser.  I
might have guessed from the literary touches.  That poetry-
to-jazz parody in--what was the name of the nightclub?"

     "The Listening Ear.  Any resemblance to actual--"

     I cut his gabbling short:  "Now don't get legalistic.
You claim you're serious, going straight.  How do you explain
the fact that your book has a reasonably happy ending?"

     "Quiet."  His ink-stained fingers bit into my arm.
"They probably have the place bugged.  They have enforcers
in every major city."

     "'They'?"  I said sardonically.  Clearly, the man had
written too many mystery novels.

     "The organization.  Mystery Writers of America.  You
don't know what they do to critics who give away plots.  And
writers who collaborate."

     "Nonsense."  But then I heard the footsteps in the
corridor.

     "I fought that ending all the way," he said.  "I
couldn't make it turn out badly enough.  The guilt was
terrible.  I came to you."

     "It's too late now, Macdonald."  It had always been too
late.  The doorknob was turning like a bursitic joint.

     "At least this isn't a happy ending."  He smiled.  And
they came in.
```

Yes, but you *do not* get an action confused with its consequences, and that's what you just did. See, his writing a book is *not* really the same thing.

It's not the same thing as making a painting, but it did—

No, but you didn't say it was the same thing as making painting. You were equating it with doing something about the oil out here in an active way, and it's not the same thing. Of course he does things that are active, and actually he's a very effective political leader. In that sense he is a man of action, but that isn't what we're talking about.

Well, I think it's what I meant to be talking about. Maybe I phrased it badly. It seemed to me that in calling the oilmen men of action it wouldn't be too farfetched to call the anti-oilmen men of action either. They try to stop the spills. That's all I'm saying.

My concern just has to do with the definition of words and with philosophy. You see, unless you make specific distinctions in the meanings of words, you can't

have a philosophic discussion of any kind. Or even a discussion of criticism, which is a branch of philosophy. I was just concerned with the meanings of the words. I'm not denying any facts or realities that we're talking about. I just want to go on insisting that for me there is to some degree a distinction between the kind of verbal action—and I'll call it *verbal action*, if you like—that goes into writing a book and the kind of *motor action* that goes into painting a painting or playing the piano. It seems to me that there's a difference.

Let me put the question again: Is Easton a man of action because he fought the oil spill—and indeed won to some extent?

Yes. Of course.

It didn't seem like the answer was yes before.

Well, you changed the question.

I don't think so. Did I?

Yeah.

I didn't mean to.

Now, you see, you're defining a man of action as anybody who performs actions. Everybody performs actions.

I'm getting lost in the philosophical apparatus here completely, I guess.

Do you know of any human being that doesn't perform actions?

No.

Okay, that means that every human being is a man of action according to your definition.

Which is a different one from yours, am I correct?

I certainly don't regard every human being as a man of action. A man of action is what is commonly meant by that phrase: that is, a man whose prime purpose or activity is action.

I mean, I don't know why this is even so important, but we seem to get embroiled in these things. I'm not quite sure why. I'm just wondering if, in your definition, Bob Easton is a man of action for trying to stop the oil companies.

Yes. I regard Easton as a man of action.

You seem, in The Blue Hammer and The Zebra-Striped Hearse, to be very critical of hangers-on in the art world.

Yes. [In] *Zebra-Striped Hearse*, it just happens that the society in Mexico that I was familiar with is like that. It's hard, you know, for expatriates to find decent values to hold onto in a form of society; and one of the things they can hold onto is what we were talking about: artistic values. They're not really true members of the society and it's very difficult for them just to exist. They have to use all kinds of life preservers, and art is one of them. Then, of course, there are a lot of artists who migrate to the sunnier climes. As a matter of fact, my uncle did. He used to go to Mexico to paint, on account of the sun, every winter for many years.

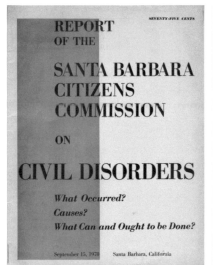 

Ken Millar on the Report of the Santa Barbara Citizens Commission on Civil Disorders *(1970), from Matt Bruccoli's bibliography: "I didn't write any of it, but I filtered nearly all of it." The purpose of this commission was to investigate local civil disorders in the Santa Barbara community and report the possible causes and solutions. Ken was one of the forty-six members of this commission. The report stresses the "importance of action": "We will persist in our determination to assure that appropriate action is taken." This contains the report on the Bank of America riots in Isla Vista mentioned on page 106.*

Frances Johnson . . . . . . President, Women Associates, University
Religious Conference.
Robert M. Jones . . . . Attorney.
Richard M. Look . . . . . Counseling psychologist.
Anita J. Mackey . . . . Field social worker (Veterans Administration Social Work Service).
Marc McGinnes . . . . Lawyer.
Kenneth Millar . . . . Writer.
Theodore L. Million . . . . Manufacturer.
Bruce D. O'Neal . . . . . . Merchant.
Bernard C. Parent . . . . . Stockbroker.

Am I reading too much into a kind of implied criticism of hangers-on and parasites?

Yes, I think you are reading a little too much into it. There are such people. One knows them, describes them, lives with them and so on, but I don't attach enormous importance to their existence. Even if I put them in a book, they're not the figures that I'm really concerned with. This is true in *Zebra*: the figures I'm really concerned with are the young artist and his girl or girls. A few like that. I know there are half a dozen Americans in the Ajijic chapters. They're really just window dressing to a considerable extent. I didn't spend enough time in Mexico to do it properly.

Do you agree that these two novels are similar examinations of the artist?

Yes. In the case of the earlier book, though, *Zebra*, the artist, while he presents this double face throughout the book, he doesn't turn out to be a predominately evil or dangerous man—although he's dangerous enough. He's not a criminal, he's just potentially one.

I'm not pretending to make a blanket indictment of artists—far from it. It's the other way around. I really regard this poor murderer in my last book as also in a sense a heroic figure because he does persist. He does persist in what he does best, even though it leads to his ultimately being caught out.

Now, most artists are not real good guys incidentally. Have you noticed? They're in internal conflict, I mean to say.

But you said also that some of these characters represent you. To me you're a real good guy basically.

You mean I've overcome my early propensity to violence?

If indeed the artist figure represents the novelist, I'm surprised you paint it so black.

No, the artist figure doesn't represent the novelist. All the figures represent the novelist. I'm not writing about myself. No, what the artist figure represents is the creative daemon.

Now, don't ask me what *daemon* means.

[laughs] No, I did that already.

May 31, 1974   Jill Krementz

27. CAUSE AND EFFECT

Would you describe yourself as a tragic writer?

Yes. I think some of my books are tragedy or at least aim at it. That's what I aim at, but I don't regard my central detective figure as the vehicle for tragedy. He's the narrator of them and to some extent he fills in and participates in the tragic events. But he is not himself a tragic figure. He's a comic figure by definition. A comic figure survives in a way that Sam Spade really didn't in *The Maltese Falcon.*

I don't know whether the word *tragedy*, though, is a word that can be used to apply to any contemporary fiction. We've lost some of the norms that tragedy is about. I don't know whether there is such a thing as Freudian tragedy. I just don't know.

It seems like your fiction is sort of balanced on the one hand by the cause and effect, which is I guess Freudian, and fatalism on the other hand.

Well, Freudian enters into it, I suppose. I get lost in long abstractions.

Do you think your books use both of those apparatus, cause and effect as well as fatalism?

Sure. All fiction uses cause and effect. I don't really savvy what you mean by *fatalism.* You mean fatalism as an attitude towards life? Or as an operating principle in life?

The sins of the fathers being passed on from generation to generation. Guilt being passed on. Is this fatalism or is this cause and effect?

No, fatalism is an attitude towards what happens, and cause and effect is a principle of relationship between two things that happen in order. Fatalism, I repeat, is an attitude. It's not the way things operate, it's how you feel about whether they operate. It's just one particular attitude that you can assume towards almost any important event. You can feel fatalistic about the death of your brother or the death of your dog.

Instead of using the word fatalism, perhaps you embrace two almost contradictory ideas in your books. One is psychological cause and effect. For example, the seeming disappearance of a father in The Blue Hammer, the

artist father, that has a specific psychological effect on the son. The other is a kind of inevitability that a generation passes the effect on. That as soon as an event occurred twenty-five years before, there was no way the son was going to avoid being affected by it.

Well, the first is *causation* and the second is *causality*. Causation is simply what actually happens in the physical world. One billiard ball hits another and the other billiard ball moves. That's causation. Causality is the belief that once the billiard player has hit the first ball, a cue ball, it's going to go and hit the other ball, and the other ball is going to go into the pocket—or not. In other words, there's a certain fatality that takes over once you've got one ball moving. In other words, if a series of causes operates, certain things will inevitably follow. There's a sense of the inevitable in the word *causality*.

Isn't is possible for somebody to be bad all by themselves, without having a sin handed down from father to son and so on?

Without reason for it? Well, we don't have to bring in more than three generations, if you don't mind. I usually just write about three generations, and my observation is that there's a definite connection from one generation to the next. I don't pretend to understand it. I only observe it and write about some aspects of it. And I don't really believe that if somebody's troubled, his children have to be troubled—although they usually are.

Can the converse of that be true? From a family in which the marriage is solid the child can emerge bad?

Sure. I think there are lot more sources of good and evil than heredity.

You choose not to write about those generally, though.

Well, you know, it's true that murder fiction is what I do. That's a choice, but having made that choice, well, I have certain constraints on me as a writer. If I were to write murder mysteries the point of which was that murder is okay or something to be taken lightly, I would be criticized for that—and correctly, I think. You see, I chose the form because it dealt with the kind of subjects that I wanted to write about. Probably, along with that subject matter, I inherited attitudes and ideas about causality that I don't necessarily regard as universally true. Their truth is within a context or within a form. I don't regard my murder mysteries as the last word on human life or human death or what causes crime.

You said that you inherited these attitudes and ideas. Inherited them from who?

Other writers for the most part. You know, the extent to which not only ideas and words but specific literary forms are handed down is something that we really have to recognize in order to discuss this stuff intelligently. Now, of course, one chooses a form because it deals with the subjects that one wants to write about, and *then* one takes the form and turns in his own direction as far as possible.

This very pervasive theme of cause and effect from generation to generation, I don't think it's insisted upon by the form, is it?

Well, I think the detective form is very much concerned with cause and effect.

But the detective form does not dictate that cause and effect is generational.

No. Of course, each writer interprets the nature of the causes I wouldn't say in his own way but in his own way plus the way of his contemporary culture. I mean, the vocabulary includes a vocabulary of motivations and causes as well as language. And unless you're writing in that language of both words and forms, unless you're writing in the language of your contemporaries, you're not doing what you should be doing. A contemporary writer should write in terms that are apprehensible to their audience, I think. This all has to do, though, with my theory of popular culture.

It has do with your theory of life.

Probably so.

Does this idea of causality have to do with your philosophy of life?

Well, I'm sure it does, yeah. In fact the books, to the extent that they have any philosophic serious purpose, I would say are an attempt to lay out in great detail how cause works in contemporary life. Of course, this is imaginative, it's not scientific, and whether you call it *causality* or not, I can't say. I don't believe that there's any overall force of a religious nature determining everything that happens, and that is one of the implications of the word *causality*.

The failure of one or two sets of parents runs through many of your books. That seems to reflect your idea of families.

It also directly reflects American society, what's actually happening there. This long generation that I've been writing in has been marked by an almost total breakdown of the family. I'm talking now about the traditional family. It's simply a matter of common record that the family is in trouble and that particularly the older form of the family, in which the family members of several generations lived in healthful contact with each other, has broken down.

Now, I tend to overstate. When I say something like the family structure has broken down, that doesn't mean that everything has gone to hell. The *accepted*

or *norm* family structure has broken down and we're getting new structures to take their place, new relationships between adults and children.

Is it the novelist's duty to go beyond pointing out failure and point to some sort of solution?

Oh, I think the solution is implicit. I think my books constantly celebrate a loving concern for other people. Or, even in its absence, to indicate that that's what's missing. I'm not saying that this is my main subject or anything like that, although it may be. The last person who knows what he's really writing is the guy that's writing it. He has to find out from his readers. But I know what goes into them.

It does seem that a sense of guilt pervades the books in general. With your parents not being together, I'm sure you must have felt that it was partially your fault.

Yes. Children blame themselves for what's wrong, no matter whether they have any control over it or not. In fact, the less control you have over it sometimes, the more you blame yourself, I think.

Could that be connected with the anger you got under control?

Yes, I think so. I just want to point out that the idea of the transference of guilt from one generation to another is practically implicit in our culture. It's stated in the Bible, for example. Just to paraphrase, "The good will of the Lord will be with those who keep my commandments even under the third and fourth generation of those that love me," and refers to the opposite case with people who don't.[1] In other words, this idea of the inheritance of guilt is pervasive in the Christian culture and the Hebrew culture.

But it's also pervasive in your writing, is that correct?

Yes. I think you'll find it perhaps not so overt in other people's fiction, but I think you'll find it in a lot of fiction. It's one of these strands of meaning that holds the whole thing together.

Is attempting to salve that guilt using psychology always a good thing?

No, I don't think it's always a good thing. I think if guilt is valid it shouldn't necessarily be salved, it should be understood. Understanding it alleviates it without getting rid of it.

Let's just switch it to another channel, so to speak. This country is going to *have to* realize and incorporate guilt about what we've done in Asia in the past couple of decades. That would be a saving grace for this country if we can do it. God knows, some of our good writers are working on it now. Not just writers but other people, too. But the realization of having done something wrong, or having had something done wrong *on your behalf* by a previous generation, is something that saves civilizations. It doesn't destroy them. It's a step in the direction of the light. This is true on the symbolic level, too, in fiction.

---

1 The exact quote, from the King James Version of Exodus 20:5, reads: "I the LORD thy God am a jealous God, visiting the iniquity of the fathers upon the children unto the third and fourth generation of them that hate me...."

May 31, 1974   Jill Krementz

I found this to be one of the weaknesses of psychology—maybe not theoretical psychology but medicinal psychology. There was one thing that I did do that I was, I think, pretty totally guilty of—and it's certainly the worst thing I've done in my life—and that was leave a wife and child for someone else. I went straight to a psychiatrist for years, who kept telling me that this is the way it is, and it takes two sides and all that, and I kept saying, "Yes and no. You're taking something away from me that you cannot take away from me. It isn't my fault that we grew apart, but it is my fault that I left. I will not relinquish that guilt."

We can turn that around, too. Your sense of guilt was important to you. It was in a sense the truth in your life. In a book, symbolically, not as writers but as readers, we accept the guilt, recognize it as ours, and it's refreshing. It's not a negative thing. It's not an evil necessarily to inherit guilt and recognize it and see that we own it. For some reason the facing of one's own guilt, even symbolically, is liberating. Or at least it points you in the direction of truth, which is the only liberation there is. So all this business about guilt in novels is not necessarily a negative thing at all. In fact, from reading good novels a reader can learn how to deal with guilt, both to recognize it and accept it and understand it and to some degree step free of it—although we're not meant to step entirely free of guilt. "In Adam's fall, we sin at all."[2]

2 The correct quote, from a rhyme in *The New England Primer*, used to teach colonial children their ABCs in the seventeenth century, is: "In Adam's fall / We sinned all."

It seems to me that in your books you've worked out your own guilt feelings.

Probably. Guilt feelings are one of the main things we have to work with. In life, too. They're the whole *anti*-structure of our lives. I'm not trying to set up a psychology. I'm not a psychologist. You have guilt on the one hand and desire on the other, so to speak, in the illustration you just gave me. You have to somehow weave your path between them. Well, the same thing could have happened to any of us. It would have been very easy, extremely easy, for me to marry in my late teens and then regret it a few years later and *have* to get out. I was hotly involved with a girl when I was sixteen and she was nineteen. All the circumstances sort of called for us to get married, but I didn't. If I *had*, though, I would've had to walk away a few years later.

It's the only time in my life, I think, where I have deliberately done something that I knew would—not kill somebody—but really possibly destroy somebody or maim them a great deal psychologically. And I still did it.

Well, of course, the thing is not to maim yourself and not to over-suffer over something like that. We have to learn to recognize that we've done wrong and then be able to turn our back on it. Not be trapped by it. Because, God knows, we all do wrong all the time without wanting to.

I didn't mean to go off on that track.

Well, I'm glad you did.

We were talking earlier about some of the French writers. Your books, like theirs, are very much about cause and effect, it seems to me. Some of their books explore Gide's theory of the "gratuitous act." The acte gratuit, *which deals with the unmotivated deed. Do you believe there is such a thing?*

I haven't seen many. No, I really think that most people do whatever they do for reasons that are traceable—or could be traceable. Let us say, for example, if the person who performs the act could be subjected to psychiatric disciplining and questioning—by *disciplining* I mean intellectual disciplining—so that he would understand his own intentions.

I really do see the human life as a sequence in which cause plays an important part all the time. Of course, it's infinitely complex. You could spend your whole life just examining the causality involving one person's actions. And in fact Freud did, and the life was his own.

But you do think that a person could understand a lot of what they do through psychology?

Yeah. I don't mean necessarily just formal psychology, but the kind of psychology that everyone practices when he knows himself. Everybody knows what he's doing and why, what he's thinking and so on to a degree. I suppose one of my main disciplines was psychology and the history of psychology, though I didn't take many courses relating to it. My book about Coleridge is really about the history of psychology on which he drew. That's really the subject matter of the book, and I'm using psychology there as both a scientific discipline and a philosophic discipline. I should add that my book is not nearly as good as it should be—and I know it. But nevertheless that was its subject matter and it led me to do extensive reading not only in the history of psychology but in the psychologists themselves, from Aristotle and Augustine right on

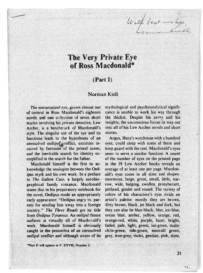

Left: Stapled photocopy of both parts of Norman Kiell's article (signed by him) "The Very Private Eye of Ross Macdonald," which appeared in the journal Literature and Psychology *in 1977. Late that year or in early 1978, Kiell, who had written and edited books on psychology and psychiatry, sent his two-part article to Ken Millar. The article focused on Millar's heavy use of eye imagery throughout his novels, and connects this with Oedipal themes, Freud, and psychoanalysis. Opposite page: Millar's reply to Kiell: "You are perfectly correct, as you must know, in tying my work to Freudian influences. I became a conscious disciple of Freud when I was twenty, and still regard him as my master. I had of course, other masters, the most important of whom, Coleridge and Poe, were precursors of modern psychology and symbolism."*

down. All the great Western philosophers were psychologists, incidentally—among other things they were psychologists—right on down to Kierkegaard.

Is a psychologist also a philosopher?

Western philosophy has found itself very often in terms of psychology, let's put it that way. That is, the study of the operations of the mind. It's not the only philosophy by any means. It isn't the kind of philosophy that you get from Bertrand Russell, for example. His ultimate source is the nature and the behavior of the physical world. That's the science in which he grounds his philosophy, so to speak. That's his specialty.

What I said about Western philosophy in general is true. Even Descartes is primarily a philosophic psychologist. His work is based on self-examination, in my opinion. This is my own fundamental background that we're talking about now: psychology and philosophy. Apart from what one does in school and graduate school and so on, it's what I've been pursuing all my life, including in fiction. I don't know that I can say I've done it successfully, but it's what I've been after.

The troubled people in your books, what would you say is their relationship to cause and effect? Are they troubled **because of it**, *or is it because they don't understand it and are trying to?*

Well, I wouldn't want to make a general statement—I've got so many troubled people to think about. Yes, I think to some extent they're trying to understand it, but mostly they're just living out the consequences. When they do they come to some understanding, that's a red-letter day for them. My interest as a fiction writer is not in their coming to some understanding so much as having the reader come to some understanding. In other words, I'm not writing about salvations. Almost by definition I'm writing about people who have failed their salvation. I'm writing crime novels.

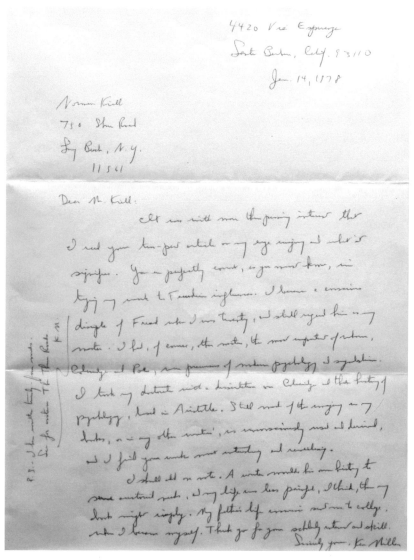

Toward the end of The Zebra-Striped Hearse, Archer almost suggests that Dolly Stone was a prepared victim. Do you believe some people are prepared victims?

Yes. There are certain people who are psychological setups. They not only expose themselves to violence but they *attract* violent people.

This in effect could be called a meeting of cause and effect and fate, then, is that correct?

I suppose you could call it fate, but I wouldn't put it quite in such lofty terms. It's accident really. Somebody who is a natural victim runs into somebody who is a natural victimizer. This is a very common situation in life. You don't see it always leading to murder.

That could be defined as fate, couldn't it?

Fate involves a philosophic theory of what makes the world work, and I don't think there is any overall force that moves us around like chessmen on a board. That's what the word *fate* sort of implies. But that's not what I'm saying now. I'm not saying that people are prepared victims, although they are. *Prepared* involves a subject for the verb *prepare*. I want to talk about it in terms of *preparation*, but not necessarily by a fate. People are prepared by people who mistreat them to become the victims of other people. Isn't that true? I just wanted to leave fate out of it because I don't believe in fate. I actually think that people are able to change their lives by themselves with help.

Do you think, though, that they have to struggle against this prepared victimization to do that?

Yes. One of the terrible things is that inability to struggle is one of the things they've been infected with, and that's what makes them victims. There are an awful lot of them, particularly among women. And among homosexuals.

Why would it be more women than men?

Who are prepared victims? It's just a historic fact.

Do you think we are all victims?

No, I don't really think we are all victims. Actually we're subject to certain fates. That doesn't mean we're victims of any external force or any intelligent malignancy. We're all victims in the sense that we ultimately can't control our own destinies and we don't live forever. We have to learn to live in what is and always will be a rather dangerous world. I think it's well to be aware of that. I think women, now, have been victims in a special sense. They've been victims of men and victims of a lopsided social and judicial structure. That's what I mean about women being victims. We all die, but that doesn't mean we're the victims of death—except in the end process of life.

You said that people can change with help. Can they change without help?

Oh sure. Most of us do. You change whether you want to or not, that's the human story. What you change into is to a considerable extent under your own influence—if you're able to exert any. Learning how to exert influence on your life is a very important problem. It's almost central: how to really exercise your will intelligently so as to improve your life. The best most of us can hope for is simply *not* to exercise the will in directions that are outright deleterious.

Do you think generally in today's world that the various pressures are making cause and effect harder to find, harder to break down?

Oh yes. When society fragments as our society is in process of doing—it fragments and regroups—all causality goes through underground alterations and they have to be traced out again. That's one reason why fiction, philosophy, and psychology have to be rewritten in every generation in a changing civilization. This wasn't true in the classical civilizations. They remained very much the same for centuries. Not this one. Every decade is something quite new. Of course, I try to, at least as a secondary thing, keep up with some of the things that are occurring. I'm not a writer whose main strength is depicting the contemporary as it happens. I write about it in a backward view, and that's one reason I think why I let my novels stretch over such long periods of time. Fifty years in the last book.

What is one reason for doing that?

It isn't my strength to write about the immediately contemporary as it happens. Some other writers do and can. There's a certain retrospective element in my books, which is shown in their structure and their content. The story starts fifty years ago. I'm interested, you see, in the whole process of causality through several generations. Social and psychological and so on. I'm also interested in trying to tell a good story. That's one of the basic things. I don't want to give the impression that my interests are primarily scholarly. They were at one time, but they're not now.

Places in your books are given an awful lot of power to change people's lives. Houses are almost described as characters and are given great power to ruin things.

Yes, but it's generally in connection with a causality that stems from what happened there. It isn't the place that does it to somebody there—the place is merely the place where it happened before and then happens again as a consequence of what happened before. In other words, the places serve as partial determinants of what happens. People go back to places because something happened there that they want to have happen again or that they want to undo, or whatever their motive may be. Then something else happens at the same place. It's not really the place that does it, it's the people going back to the place, either in physical fact or in their minds. Places are really just symbols of the human past or the human intention we're talking about. It's the place as known in the mind and the people involved. It becomes part of the chain of causality. Of course, there is a sense, too, in which known places can cause you to do over again what you have done before. You go back to a ruined farmhouse where there's been a murder that you've been involved in and thoughts turn to murder, just to put it very bluntly. We are creatures of place very, very strongly. Place is one of the major determinants in our lives.

What you say is certainly the logical explanation, but the way it's stated in the books is almost—I don't want to use the word supernatural—

But it almost *is* supernatural. This wave of causality almost is supernatural. It's only when you trace it very, very carefully, looking into all the things that go into it, that you realize it is part of the natural web. It's not supernatural. There are certainly things that are supernatural, though, in a sense that they're beyond our understanding. The physical world itself is beyond our understanding. We're still trying to understand it.

It's not only the characters in turmoil in the books who feel that way; Archer says that frequently, too, without the philosophical underpinnings.

Sure. But the truth is poetic. It's not intended to be taken quite literally.

What places in your own life have had that "supernatural" effect on you?

Well, I suppose any of the places that formed me as a child. But, of course, when you become a man—particularly if you've had the benefit of a little psychiatric treatment and a lot of study in that and related fields—you *can* gradually cut yourself loose from the web, at least to a certain extent. That's not all good, though.

I think if you went back to Kitchener and felt nothing that wouldn't be good at all.

I go back to Kitchener and I always feel a good deal. I feel both the good and the bad. And I keep going back. I was there four months ago and I'm going to be there in another couple of weeks. Of course, I have family reasons for going back, but that's part of the thing we're talking about. Family reasons are very closely connected to the place, *always*.

Speaking of places, what connotation does the ocean have to your work?

My earliest and happiest memories have to do with being in the Pacific. Early on in Vancouver. My father was a seaman. He had his captain's papers in Canada. At the time that I'm talking about he was a harbor pilot in Vancouver Harbor. He took me out on his boat, I remember that. That was a wonderful experience, going out with him like that. What I remember even better is swimming at Stanley Park. My first memory was age three. I was playing in the water at English Bay outside of Vancouver with a black lifeguard. That's my first memory of the city that I have— all good. I know how old I was because I know when we left Vancouver, you see. I remembered it so well that when I went back there I could walk right to the place. I also found the hotel where we lived at that time, in downtown Vancouver. It's an old folks' hotel now.

Despite these fond memories of the sea, it's hardly ever mentioned in a non-ominous way in your books.

Strange, isn't it? You just have to draw a distinction between the writer and the person. I'm the most persistent ocean-swimmer in Santa Barbara—that I know of. Because I swim summer and winter and every day, and nearly always in the sea. I certainly don't do it because I dislike it. And all of my connections with it have been fortunate. I just plain love it. Of course, it's dangerous and it's un-limitable and uncontrollable. It's like life itself: you can say anything about it and be telling the truth.

In The Moving Target you wrote: "The sea was cold and dangerous. It held dead men." And in the very first Archer story, "Find the Woman," Archer looks down on the beach and sees a very unreal, unsettling image of a man walking out of the sea.

Well, of course, both those things that you refer to were written immediately after my war experience, which involved the sea. That I'm sure colored the sea for me a good deal, while I was never in any particular danger or anything like that. But sea warfare had become part of my experience. In the Navy nothing really bad happened. None of it was bad or even frightening. So you just have to assume that in these books I'm using the sea as a particular image, but not the whole thing. They're not intended to be realistic and they don't necessarily reflect my own feelings. At the same time, I'm obviously obsessed with the sea. I love it and I feel deprived if I don't get down to it every day. So anything that you're obsessed with I'm sure has its ambivalent qualities.

Or at least magical qualities.

Yes, *magical* is perhaps a better word. The sea is certainly, among all inert physical things, the major thing in my life.

28. POPULAR CULTURE

I think the last ten years have shown a remarkable breakdown of the old concept of high art/low art. Dwight Macdonald used to be sort of everybody's favorite very sophisticated critic who put down all the pop things and saw pop culture as a threat to high culture. I think he went from being sort of the last-gasp heroic figure into being a ridiculous figure within about two years.

He was the last defender of the ruined castle. Actually, what you do with the ruined castle is not defend it but get inside of it and understand it, but that takes a lot of knowledge.

He chose to fight until his position became so patently absurd that nobody paid any attention. Stanley Kauffmann does that occasionally.

Kauffmann was once my editor at Knopf.

I would guess his grasp on the mystery novel would be pretty tenuous at best.

Yes. He wasn't really interested in it. Well, he didn't understand exactly what I was trying to do. He thought I was failing in attempting to do something that he might want me to do, if you know what I mean.

I think he's pretty much a failed novelist himself, isn't he, amongst six or seven books?

Well, he's a novelist. I don't know how you define a failed novelist. Most novelists in terms of sales *are* failed novelists, but in the long run that doesn't seem to count. I don't even know his work as a novelist. Anyway, I like the man.

You said yesterday that you have a theory of popular culture. Can you expand on that?

A popular culture is a culture with water. I mean to say that the mythology that lies behind high culture is somewhat watered down, and that's really part of the beauty of it because it makes it more amenable to the kind of use that one tries to put it to. I'll put it bluntly: You don't want to write the Oedipus plays over again; they have to embody current experience. That's what they're for. That's really what

they were for when they were written originally, too. I just think that a writer *can*, if he writes in a popular culture form, sort of take up his stance right in the middle of the arena, so to speak, and use all of it if he gets the right tones. This is where a narrator like Archer comes in. If [the writer] gets the right tone and the right meld between what everybody knows and what only educated people know, he can enrich what's popular in his work with ideas that come from the other realm: the realm of high culture. If he is concerned with his audience and really cares about speaking to them, he can introduce these images and facts and characters and so on with archetypes, in terms that a teenage boy can understand. I know that because I hear from teenage boys who understand what they're reading. Obviously, they're not going to read books like this unless they do understand them. There would be nothing to make them go on.

So on the one hand is the opportunity to use the large forms, but not use them to the hilt the way that major writers do and high-culture writers perhaps; and then on the other hand you're able to draw on life itself and your own experience and your own perceptions in a way that any novelist can. When you put the whole thing together you have, if you're lucky, achieved what I consider the whole purpose of popular culture—popular culture writing at least: to create something that's accessible to everybody in the culture. That's my aim.

It really is a reaction against the idea of the intellectual class system. I don't believe in it. It's dangerous. There's really no good reason, in a period of universal literacy, why writers shouldn't speak to the whole constituency. I just feel this very strongly obviously. Because in spite of my own "high-culture" background I prefer to write for everybody.

Does that make you a renegade scholar with a lot of scholars?

I don't think I'm a renegade. I'm not treated by other scholars as a renegade. I just found something different to do. There's, as you know, a large and growing movement in scholarship itself in the direction that I've just been talking about. Not all of the results are happy, of course, but it's there and on the whole I think it's a valuable movement. But I'm talking about something different, that's related. The fact books like mine are now being used in schools and colleges is certainly related to what I've been saying, and it's part of the intention. I mean to say it's an outcome of the intention. It's not anything that I expected or intended.

I think that the gradual self-democratization of America is served by this kind of writing. I'm not, of course, ruling out the importance and the value of other kinds of writing, and the *higher* value of some other kinds of writing, such as first-rate poetry, first-rate imaginative novels, and so on.

Was this a factor at the very beginning? I know you picked the detective novel for your form for a lot of reasons, but was one of them to reach a potentially large audience? Not in a commercial sense, but just to say what you had to say to a larger audience?

I didn't think in terms of a large audience. In fact, when I started writing detective stories, for the most part they didn't have a large audience—but a larger audience than your students sitting in a classroom. A few thousand is a large audience, actually, when you think in terms of reaching people. Of course, when a writer starts out, especially if he's doing something slightly different from his contemporaries, he doesn't know where it's going to lead or he doesn't really know what his intentions are. They haven't been formulated. The books themselves constitute the formulation of the intent. And, of course, he gradually improves. When you start writing you don't ordinarily succeed in accomplishing what you ultimately will. It took me about a dozen books to get into the league that I wanted to be in.

So you did not start writing books with a full-blown theory of popular culture.

No. The idea of popular culture didn't exist in its present forms when I started writing. Obviously, what I above all needed—and I think what any writer needs, novelists anyway, fiction writers in general—is some sense of belonging to a total community. The larger the better.

You see, I was stretched in different ways. Here on the one hand I was a scholar and good at my work and going places in scholarship; on the other hand I wanted to write, but I didn't want to write fiction, so to speak, for scholars. I think I have a very strong proletarian or equalitarian bias built into me by, well, the experiences of my early life and also family tradition and so on. I never really felt at home as a high-culture scholar. It really turned out to be not really what I wanted to do. So I quit it. I mean, I quit it as far as my main career was concerned. But I think one or two people have pointed out that these complex novels are the work of a former scholar. [*laughs*] The difference is that the footnotes are embedded in the text.

And Archer's function in some ways is to find the footnotes.

Yeah.

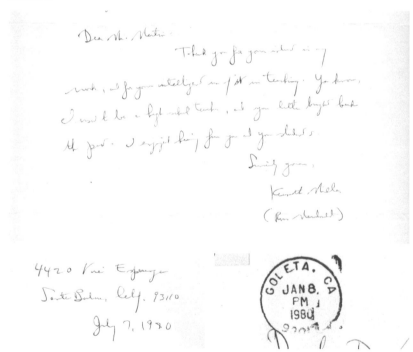

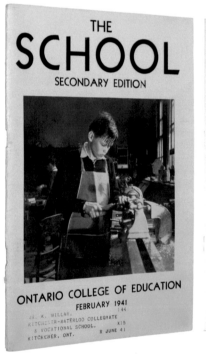

A 1980 letter from Ken Millar to teacher Douglas D. Martin: "Thank you for your interest in my work, and for your intelligent use of it in teaching. You know, I used to be a high school teacher, and your letter brought back the past. I enjoyed hearing from you and your students." Millar dated the letter "July 7, 1980"—sadly, the postmark shows it was January, evidence of Millar's fading powers due to Alzheimer's.

Ken Millar's copy of The School (Secondary Edition) *from Februry 1941, with his mailing address printed on the front cover. It contains his article "Thought and English," which begins: "My chief justification for presuming to write an article about the teaching of English is that I distinctly remember what it feels like to be a high school student. I remember believing when I left high school that literary creation was esoteric if not inspired, and that sonority of sesquipedalian phrase was the noblest grace a writer could aspire to."*

29. CALIFORNIA

California is not the sort of place that Nathanael West pictured it: you know, the end for the old and dispirited and the crazy.

Well, I don't like any big city really. I prefer a more spread-out kind of place where you don't feel so confined. The thing about California is that there are choices. I'm a child of California, too. I was born here and couldn't wait to get back. You know, probably the majority of people who work in Los Angeles live *outside* of Los Angeles or outside of the metropolitan city area. They live up in the Valley and so on. Many of the places are extremely pleasant, as you know.

Did you have any particular reason for having Archer come from Long Beach?

We had relatives in Long Beach and stayed there for a few days when we first came out to the coast. It was in effect our first home on the Pacific Coast, however briefly.

And you lived for a short time before that in San Diego.

Yes. Of course, San Diego is a place that my parents lived. They had two children before I was born that died in San Diego and are buried there. There are certain parts of San Diego that I particularly love, particularly La Jolla. That's where Raymond Chandler spent his last years, by the way. Max Miller, who wrote *I Cover the Waterfront*, also spent his last years in La Jolla. That's where I got to know him. The Navy assigned me to the Eleventh Naval Headquarters for one month before I went overseas, so we lived in La Jolla for a month.

At approximately the same time, Margaret sold a book [*The Iron Gates*] to Warner Bros. and was hired by them to write a movie based on it. She wrote a pretty good script. So that was one reason why she stayed on here, I think, after the book. She wanted to. It made it possible for her.

In a couple of your books there are scenes in movie studios. Is that from the business when your wife worked there?

They probably draw on it. *The Ferguson Affair* has got a lot of movie stuff in it. That certainly draws on my experience being married to somebody who was working in the studios. I got to know the studio a little bit and some of the people who work there and so on. Enough to fake it, so to speak.

The story is pretty much true that Margaret picked out Santa Barbara as a place to live from a train window?

Yes, she was on her way north by train, on her way back to Canada. This was during the war. I had brought her and our daughter out here. The Navy had switched me from Boston out to San Diego, and from there I went overseas. Margaret, who had relatives in California, decided to go home to her father's in Canada. From Long Beach she got as far as Santa Barbara, and then she looked out the train window. That's how it really happened. She didn't have time to get off the train. It only stopped five minutes. So she got carried a hundred miles north, spent a night in a hotel, and went back.

Did you know what Santa Barbara was at all?

No, I'd never seen it. I'd seen references to it. It's mentioned in *The Great Gatsby*, for example. It's where, uh—Excuse me, sometimes I have a hard time remembering my name. It's where the girl had her honeymoon.

Daisy?

Yeah. That's where she had her honeymoon.

Margaret lived here from that point on and you joined her after the service?

Yes. You can tell a lot about a city by just looking at it.

And what did this one tell you when you first saw it?

I don't even remember. All I was seeing in the city was my wife and daughter. Margaret was seeing the city. I remember my first day or two here. It hasn't changed much. The population has greatly expanded. It hasn't really destroyed the city as a place to live.

How large was it then? In 1945.

Let's say that the difference would be between, say, 25,000 then and 70,000 now. That would be the city itself, but then the outlying areas, the municipal areas in

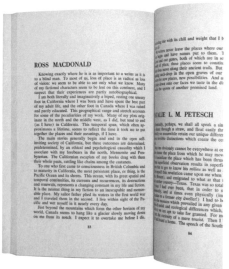

Left: Manuscript for Ken Millar's contribution to the Autumn 1975 issue of
South Dakota Review, *"The Writer's Sense of Place," a short essay that explores his roots in California and Canada.*

the county, would double that, I guess. Altogether I think there are about 200,000 people in this urban area.

Do you think it was cause and effect or fate that brought you to Santa Barbara?

It was sheer fate. Fate, of course, operates through all kinds of human instrumentalities. For example, the Navy brought me to California and the movie industry brought my wife to California, and what brought her to Santa Barbara was a train on which she was planning to go north back to Canada. The final cause was that she looked out the train window, as I told you, and saw Santa Barbara and got off at the next station. So there you have a wave of causality. Now we're making a plot out of this. The basic fact is that I was born in California and always wanted to come back. But, you see, my desire to come back didn't really affect any of these other causes that I mentioned to you. They were literally coincidental.

But you do have a case of cause and effect and fate coexisting in this case.

Yeah. But in a book you can't make things coincidental—or you shouldn't do it too much—so you have to relate all the causes to each other. Of course, while causality runs through my books, it really isn't what they are about. That merely is one aspect of the structure.

Did Margaret have any history of California?

No, she just plain liked it. *All* North American young people have a history of California. It's through the movies. It's very much a part of their donnée. It's the most powerful single source of images in our culture. Naturally, it's changed with California and California becomes changed with it. You don't think of the two separately. In fact, "Hollywood" is a way of seeing and it's a California way of seeing. It does have to do with the natural situation—the quality of the light is the reason why the movie industry is in California. It was here in Santa Barbara before it was in Hollywood, incidentally. It's an environmental reason. Environment really is a basic determinant in all human activities. That's one reason why we have to preserve it. It's part of our whole civilized heritage.

You said Hollywood "is a way of seeing." Could you elaborate at all on that?

Well, it's so obvious I don't know if I can find anything to say about it. Let's say in general it's an emphasis on the physical aspects of life by definition. It's a camera art, so naturally it's concentrated on the physical aspects: what can be photographed. *But* that doesn't mean there's any lack of symbolism. In fact, that's the source of major symbolism, not only in the movies but in all the plastic art that there is. You get what further meaning there is through a depiction of the physical. And that's symbolism. Movies are accidentally but profoundly symbolic, and they act in that way for everybody. And they haunt us.

Archer's first case on record, "Find the Woman," takes him to a beach house a few miles north of Santa Barbara. Is that a house you had at one point?

I lived on the beach here for just one year, but that was much later. I couldn't afford to live on the beach when I wrote that first story. Far from it.

In most of the books you don't usually call it Santa Barbara.

I probably called it Santa Teresa.

Pacific Point is another imaginary town, this one located south of LA.

Well, it's the same kind of city. Neither one of them represents Santa Barbara. I didn't want to be tied down to a specific group of people and buildings and so on. The only book I've written that comes fairly close to representing Santa Barbara physically is this last one. Even then I'm not writing about Santa Barbara.[1]

What is the equivalent city of Purissima?

I don't have any answer. Offhand I don't know anything about Purissima; it's just one of the names that I've put on cities. I just change the name because I don't want to give the impression that I'm just writing about the one city. I'm not. I change it around a bit, move it around a bit.

As a reader, I was unclear about the geography. When Archer said he would go to this town of Pacific Point, I figured it may have been closer.

That doesn't matter. Because, I mean, whether Pacific Point is seventy-five miles from Los Angeles or eighty miles away—Santa Barbara is—or whether it's immediately adjacent to Los Angeles, is not really terribly important. I'm not trying to write an exact portrait of a particular place, but I *am* trying to write about California as she is. That's one reason why my center *moves* a bit from one book to another. I get interested in one aspect or another of California and write about that. There's enough of all California in any California city to keep a California writer busy for the rest of his life. I'm a California writer, but most of my books are centered in the general area of Southern California.

Why are most of Archer's cases outside of LA?

You mean the idea of having him live in the city but move outside of it? I'm not a Los Angeles writer, and that's the basic reason why he moves outside of it. I couldn't make the sacrifice of living in Los Angeles [*laughs*], even in order to become a Los Angeles novelist.

Why did you condemn that fate to Archer? Why didn't you base him in Santa Barbara?

Well, that's his job. Lew Archer *is* a Los Angeles detective, but the cases of his that I write about are not Los Angeles cases. At least they're not primarily Los Angeles cases; they're all centered more or less in a smaller city. The reason is that I prefer to write in terms of a more understandable unit than Los Angeles. For one reason or another—primarily, the reason that I've been a small-city person most

of my life—I like to write about a small city rather than a large one. There are other reasons, too. If I were writing about Los Angeles, I would feel a necessity to present it in a realistic manner and to reflect its yearly changes and things like that. I don't want to be a tail tied to the enormous shaggy dog of Los Angeles. I'm not a historian of the development of Los Angeles. Those are all very interesting subjects, but they're not exactly mine. They're reserved for people who live or have lived for long periods of time in Los Angeles.

Have you spent much time in Los Angeles?

No, never for more than a few days at a time. I'm a Southern California writer but not a Los Angeles writer because I don't live in Los Angeles—and I don't go there either. I've only been there once or twice in the last few years. But you don't need Los Angeles because Los Angeles is just a vast area made up of many Santa Barbaras. I describe Santa Barbara or some other small city and people in Los Angeles say, "Gee, what a good portrait of Los Angeles." Well, it's just all the same.

I think it's sort of ironic that you're probably considered a big-city writer by most of your readers, but in fact the opposite is true.

Yeah, but the big city isn't in most of my books. I'm not a big-city writer, but the atmosphere of California and the peculiar civilization of California is so pervasive, it's the same really here as it is in Los Angeles. The feeling is the same and the people feel somewhat the same. There's this enormous openness and a sense of being on the moving rim of the present, and a sense of being on the edge of the vast unknown and misunderstood of the Pacific and so on.

I gather from your comments that you have mixed feelings about Los Angeles.

Well, I prefer to live in a smaller place myself. One thing about the technological developments … is that [they do] make it possible to avoid stifling concentrations of humanity and technology and so on. It's possible for a man to write a book in Santa Barbara and have it published in New York, but have the type set in Vail, Colorado. In fact that's what happened with the book we've been talking about, *The Blue Hammer*. The work that went into it was spread across the continent: here, Colorado, and New York. I don't have to live in New York or Colorado. Don't have to live here either. Now that business can be done by wire and all kinds of technical operations can be performed by wire, suddenly the city no longer has to exist in the old sense. There's no point in a lot of people jamming themselves together on one particular bit of land, because they don't have to be able to walk or take a taxi from their office to another guy's office. They just pick up the phone and plug in. They can talk just as easily or communicate just as easily to somebody in Denver or New York—*more* easily—as they can to somebody right in town. It's actually easier to communicate with New York than it is for one part of Los Angeles to communicate with another. I'm not wiping out the idea of Los Angeles as a gathering of people related to each other—I'm sure you understand that. But I'm just saying the definition of the city has been changed. It's no longer so terribly interdependent within itself.

We really are being *freed*, at least to some extent, by technology. God knows, like all other major scientific developments it has its threatening side, too. But that's true of all human things: they have their underside as well as their topside. Of course, our main technological problem is our capacity to wage war on us has become so terrible. But the only answer to it is that we have to stop waging war.

1 Nevertheless, when Millar worked with Burt Weissbourd on *The Instant Enemy* film project, he chose to base the story in Santa Barbara.

Even Los Angeles does not feel like a city to some of us who live in New York.

No, Los Angeles isn't a city, it's a *conjuriez* of many, many municipalities. But in effect, well, it's a new country. It isn't politically or legally a new country, but in its imaginative effect it's like going to another country, from the East, isn't it? In fact, it's as big as lots of countries historically have been.

It takes almost as long to cross Los Angeles as it does to fly from New York to Los Angeles. Really. It's enormous, you know. It's not really a city, it's practically a duchy or something. It's been put together by people who didn't care about how to build a city. It really isn't a city; it's, as I said, a collocation of neighborhoods, and it won't be a city until they have a decent means of getting from one part of it to another. You know, having to do it by car cuts you off from ever getting to know your own city.

This is a ridiculous, touristy question, but California seems to specialize—at least the East Coast feels that it does—in their own special breed of oddballs, particularly religious ones. This and that cult, this and that leader, and a lot of them that are crooks. You also have a lot of quack poets.

"Quack poets"?!

Well, I gather you don't like them very much.

On the contrary.

It doesn't come across that way sometimes. There are two or three Beat-type poet characters in your books that I don't find treated too sympathetically.

Well, anyway, that doesn't reflect my personal feeling about poets. I have a respect for poets beyond my respect for almost anyone else.

The way I read them, they're like half poet and half fakir. Like Chad Bolling in **The Galton Case,** *who seemed to have this quality of PR or fake about him, and he knew it.*

That's something else again. For every true poet there are ten semi-poets. It's quite true, I write about semi-people to a great extent, but this doesn't reflect my attitude towards people in general nor does it reflect my attitude towards poets. You see, the books, they're not just about my likes and dislikes, they're about certain stages in our *common* lives, and these people represent them.

Why do you think they lead semi-lives?

Because I do.

How would you define a "semi-life"?

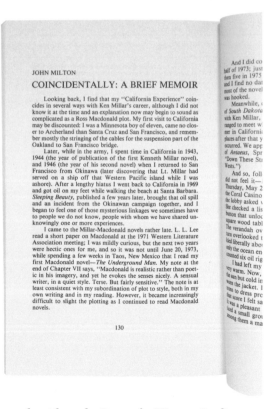

John R. Milton was the editor of the South Dakota Review. *Most of his typescripts and papers related to the journal reside at the Center for Western Studies at Augustana College. Generously, he made a rare exception with regard to his original typescript for his remembrance of Ken Millar, "Coincidentally: A Brief Memoir," which was published in the Spring 1986 Ross Macdonald tribute issue. In 1980, Milton met Millar for lunch at the Coral Casino Beach and Cabana Club (where many of the Paul Nelson interviews with Millar took place).*

By a semi-life I mean a semi-failed life. That's practically my subject matter. *But a semi-successful life, too. Semi-* works both ways. There are very few people, in my books or in life, that I can't find value in—and don't find value in. Very few people that I would consider worthless or beyond the pale.

I think most of us lead live semi-lives.

We do. Of course.

Maybe this is another touristy generalization, but California seems susceptible to religious fanaticism.

No, I think it's characteristic of California.

Is there a dark side to that?

Well, I don't know that it's a dark side exactly. This is a society in an economy which, in spite of its imperfections, does have the effect of liberating people to become whatever they want to become. I think people feel a lot freer. You know, the use of society is pretty definite and pretty formed historically. You have to have extraordinary strength or individuality or eccentricity in order to become different. I think it's more expected here that everybody should be different from everybody else. There are not the same economic pressures either which make people conform. I think it's easier for people to make a living. And they have more left over. However, traditionally, going far back behind the period that we're talking about, going back before the first World War, California has been a place where there's a lot of religious eccentricity. I use that word without attaching any value to it, pro or con. Religious differences have taken place to a great extent out here on the West Coast. I don't know why. Maybe it's easier on account of the nice weather and so on to become original. Or maybe religious people or people with new religious ideas sort of are the kind of people who go west. And everybody who goes west, if he keeps at it long enough, ends up in California. It's a tradition in California really.

A rootlessness. If indeed it is a rootlessness, you would say that it can represent the other side, which is freedom? Freedom of choice.

Well, of course, California hasn't been, you know, on the stage as long as New York state, obviously. There are great advantages in living in a society that has had a history and had time to build traditions. But, you see, we're not cut off from the traditions that New York represents. We're a nation as a whole and it's perfectly possible, though, to be highly civilized in California—more readily possible—than it is in New York, because you don't have the physical difficulties of actually getting to the places where civilization is taking place.

Do you think in a way California is like the new age as compared to the East Coast, which, specifically New York, is an old age or a dying age?

Not necessarily dying, because the possibility for renewal is there. But New York is stuck with the physical inheritance of the old age and it makes it difficult. And we're not. The sole advantage really that we have is that there's nothing here. I mean, that's the primary advantage: we don't *have to* vacate tenements. Of course, I'm using the physical, as always, as being symbolic of the human. New York is not just a physical object, it's also a place where people have been formed. The

people who have been formed by New York have often been crippled by it. I'm speaking historically about the effect of any urban colossus.

You think it doesn't hold true of California.

I didn't say that it didn't hold true, but it's just that California is still in the making and it's not terribly overgrown yet with unfortunate human creations.

I think parts of LA are.

I'm talking about the whole state being overgrown. I know that parts of LA are very unfortunate.

Is Santa Barbara an old California town?

Oh yes, it's just as old as Los Angeles. Within a few years. I think they were founded within the same decade, around about 1790.[2]

Would it be correct to say that Santa Barbara has always been planned with more foresight toward the future?

Milton saved this book of matches from the Coral Casino Beach and Cabana Club lunch as a keepsake.

Yes. There are reasons for that. One is that it is a nice place to be and has attracted the kind of people who are able to move. Santa Barbara, going back into the last decades of the nineteenth century—1860, 1870—attracted people literally from all over the civilized world. People who could live anywhere came here. People who could have homes in several places had one here. They brought in horticulturists and so on. The climate, which permits people to grow anything, attracted men who came here and planted trees, for example. Planted flowers. The rich people who moved here and set up their estates employed people of that sort to develop plantings. One result is that there's an enormous, rich variety of vegetation of all kinds here, much of it imported from other places. That's just a physical example of the reason why Santa Barbara is somewhat more civilized than some other parts of the West. Nearly 200 years since it was founded and the people who founded it were civilized. Throughout the latter half of the nineteenth century people came here because they were attracted by the salubrious climate and the beauty of the place. So there's a tradition of looking after what you have in Santa Barbara to a degree that you don't find in many other places. Although you go into a really good farming community in the Middle West and you'll find exactly the same *care* about the environment, although directed to slightly different ends. But an idea of permanence, an idea of putting down roots that will last not just for your lifetime but for your children's lifetime and for the next five centuries, is what we need. There's no reason why we should consider ourselves the final flower of civilization, after which everything goes bust. That's just foolish.

2 Los Angeles was settled in 1781, and Santa Barbara was settled the following year.

may 31, 1974   Jack Leonard

30. BEYOND ARCHER

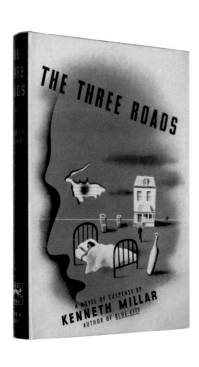

You said before that you don't know what you're going to write next. That must be a good feeling for a novelist in a way.

Yeah. It is for me.

Do you feel some of them may not be Archer books?

I would hope so. You can't predict what you're going to be seized by, you know. I think people as they get older tend to change more rapidly perhaps than they expect they will. It's like going into a reverse adolescence.

Do you feel yourself in a stage like this?

No, but I'm beginning to feel some of the freedoms of being over sixty.

Which are?

Well, it seems to me that you're not under such pressure in many ways, and I think, if the process continues, it would be possible for me perhaps to write something different, outside of my genre. I might even have the desire to do it.

Are you talking about the need to move the Archer novel in a direction toward, say, Gatsby, or to write a bigger book entirely within the detective tradition?

I don't know what I mean until I've tried it. The essential change that's required for me to write a different kind of book is to make my central character also my tragic figure. You see, as we've been discussing, the specific thing—differentia—of the Archer stories is that Archer is *not* the tragic center. He's at the center in a sense.

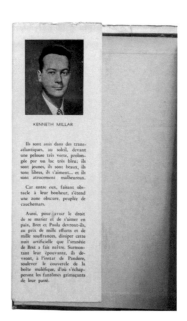

Left: US Knopf The Three Roads *(1948). Above: French* La boite de Pandore *(1948).*

This, of course, is typical of a whole series of novels going back for generations: the division between the hero as observer and recorder, and the hero as actor and tragic victim. The change, if there *is* any major change, it will be that. Both various aspects of the hero will come together in the central figure; whether in first person or third person doesn't really matter.

I did write a book of this sort a long time ago before I was equipped to do it terribly well. I mean *The Three Roads*. That doesn't have any intermediary between the reader and the tragic figure.

Do you feel a compelling need to do that?

Oh no, I just see it as a step that could be taken when and if I step away from what I've been doing. You see, I have managed to put enough of my own self—my own

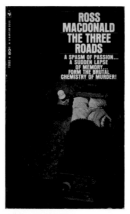

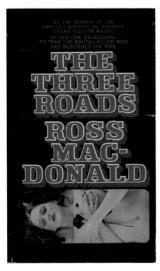
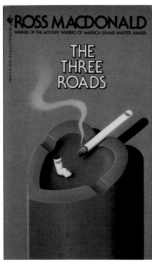
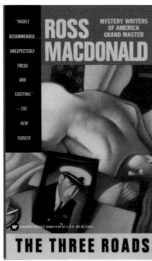
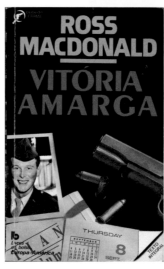
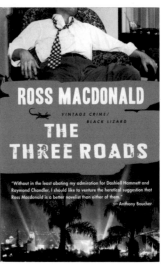

problems, my distresses and satisfactions, and all the things that go to make up life—into the various characters in my books. I don't mean Archer, I mean all the other people. Many of the people that Archer deals with are more important to *me* in a personal sense than Archer is in the Archer novels. I don't regard him as the one who represents *my* inner life. The other people—some of the other people—do.

Do you feel a need to take bigger risks, say, with the Archer novels as they are in concluding stages?

Yes, I would like to be able to do it. I don't know whether I will be able to. Because these things don't come from wanting; it actually has to reflect your needs and what you're prepared to do. I don't think any writer can sit down and write, more or less from the will, something that he wants to write. I'm really just playing one kind of wanting against another, but the kind of wanting that is valuable in writing is the kind that happens and continues to make things happen in oneself. In other words, you can't set up an ambition for yourself in relation to an unwritten book. At least I can't. The book has to gradually invent itself, in your mind, that you're writing. How it ends and so on. You have to give room for a book to develop. You can't tell it ahead of time what to be.

Do you think that would be the hardest book to do?

The danger is that it would be too easy and that it wouldn't incorporate the stresses that make the other books whatever they are.

Too easy in what sense?

In the sense that it wouldn't incorporate the emotional and experiential stresses that one writes from. I'm assuming that the strength in my books comes out of the handling of internal stresses which are in me and are reflected in the books. Basic internal stresses. They can be expressed in all kinds of ways. In the books they're expressed as conflict of character: with other character, with the situation, with his heredity, with his emotional needs, with his duty, and so on.

The danger is that one would simply pass over the deeply subjective in a willed book. It seems to me that if one were to aim at something larger it would have to be a development from what's already been done. Now, I'm perhaps alone or a small minority in thinking that Chandler's *The Long Goodbye* is not his best book.

I think it is.

From my standpoint it simply lacks the essential quality that makes his other books valuable. I'm not saying that it lacks it entirely, but there's a lack of dramatic and moral tension and stress in *The Long Goodbye* which makes it less interesting to me than the four other good novels.

THE THREE ROADS

by Kenneth Millar

I am afraid that the first part of this manuscript must be fairly severely cut. I sympathize with the author's effort to keep it out of the usual class of mysteries, but the second half is so much superior to the first from the point of view of technical execution generally and reader interest that it must be got to more quickly.

Furthermore the first half contains much repetition. This part, which would indicate a psychological story, is comparatively unconvincing and quite weak, especially since half way through the book the author tosses psychology out the window and has Taylor solve his problem by the usual strong-arm methods.

But the psychological undertone should be left and perhaps even heightened, for it helps to have the reader never quite sure of Taylor's sanity.

The opening scene is confusing. Too many emotions are conveyed to the reader and the result is blurred. It is several pages before the reader learns that Taylor was merely re-living the past. As for repetition Taylor tells the story of his childhood to Paula in the first flash-back; Paula repeats it all to a psycho-analyst; Taylor repeats the story to the analyst in his interview and the reader is present all three times.

The treatment of minor characters should be cut. Each new one is introduced with many pages of expository writing which holds up the narrative and it has very little relative material to the story, e.g., Clifter is introduced in six pages and then with his first scene with Paula is given 7 more pages before we get back to the main story. The same is true of Fahn. 6 pages are devoted solely to whim - 120-26. Is his presence necessary at all? There is little point in including the 9 page pulp-magazine piece about Taylor,

THE THREE ROADS

by Kenneth Millar

pages 128-35, since it simply hashes over details with which the reader is already acquainted. Page 164-65 - this obscene conversation has no bearing on the story and should be omitted.

Above: Two-page memorandum from 1947 from Knopf on Ken Millar's manuscript for The Three Roads *and how it needs to be cut.*
Right: Prompted by the memo, the first carbon typescript page of Millar's three-page response outlining his intended revisions to the manuscript.

That book seems to be very carefully structured.

It's not exactly hard-boiled mystery fiction structure, though. It's a dilution of it. I know it's structurally a good book, but that doesn't help it to be more interesting to me. Now, I'm speaking from a long-ago reading and I might have a different judgment if I reread it now. Anyway, I'm just using it as an example of what I would be afraid of. Because without tension, it seems to me, my books couldn't very well carry themselves. The material in them just simply wouldn't hold together.

***Well, I think there is tension in* The Long Goodbye.**

Again, I was now talking about what I might write. I'm not saying that there isn't tension in *The Long Goodbye.* Of course, there are other things in it, too, that are not as interesting to me as things in some of Chandler's other books. It seems to me that the introduction of friendship as an important element in the book is a poor substitute for the kind of real moral tension that there is in some of the earlier books. I'm just giving you a personal opinion. I'm not asking you to

2124 Bath Street,
Santa Barbara, California,
July 8, 1947

Alfred A. Knopf, Esq.,
501 Madison Avenue,
New York 22, New York.

Dear Mr. Knopf:

I have the memorandum about Three Roads which you gave Ivan, your kind letters of July 2, and a telegram from Ivan received this morning, stating that 'you want and expect to publish Roads but think contract discussion premature until you have my considered views about suggested revisions'. My views may best be illustrated by a brief outline of the revision which I began to plan on receiving your memorandum, and started to write this morning before the telegram came. No doubt my intentions will alter somewhat in detail, as they have a habit of doing, as I go along; but I intend to set up the first half of the book approximately as follows:

Section I: Saturday. Chapter 1. The book opens with Paula's first dialogue with Bret on the verandah of the Naval Hospital in San Diego, ending with his error about his marriage to Paula, and his retirement in confusion.

While she waits alone on the verandah for Dr. Wright to come and talk to her, she thinks back, motivated by doubt and fear about his present mental condition, to her first meeting with Bret: the La Jolla flashbacks, in shortened and sharpened form.

Then she talks to Dr. Wright about Bret's condition and its cause; and tells him about her single visit to Bret's wife Lorraine (using material from the later scene with Klifter). Another change: to speed up the sequence of events, Klifter's interview with Bret has already been half-arranged-for with Wright, and will occur on the following day, Sunday.

Chapter 2. Saturday evening. Opens with Paula telling Klifter about the murder of Lorraine, and their discovery of the body. The long passage about Klifter and his thoughts is removed entirely from the beginning of the chapter, cut perhaps 75%, and distributed within the chapter.

Section II. Sunday. Chapter 3. Bret's drowning dream, probably followed (though this is indefinite) by a brief reminiscence, as of something that happened a few days ago, of his delusion concerning Kerama Retto, using some of

Mr. Knopf
-2-

the material from the first chapter. Follows a somewhat
shortened version of his first meeting with Lorraine, which
leads up to his questioning of Dr. Wright, who won't tell
him what happened to Lorraine but does tell him that Klifter
is coming to see him this afternoon.

       Chapter 4. The interview with Klifter, in
the course of which Bret's confusion between mother and
wife, as in the original, is developed; and leads Klifter
to tell Bret about the murder of Lorraine. The passage about
Bret's projected book would be incongruous here, and is
dropped. Klifter's return train journey is dropped, not
without regrets, but dropped. (The obscene conversation on
pp. 164-5 will also be excised, without regrets.)

       Section III. Monday. Chapter 5. Paula comes
to take Bret to Los Angeles by car. Severely troubled by his
new knowledge of the murder, he questions her about it and
pries from her the reluctant details: the police facts of
the case which the pulp-story parody was devised to introduce
into the narrative. It will be noted that Fahn and his pulp-
magazine are dropped.

       Half-suspicious of Paula, Bret quarrels with her
and, when they get to Los Angeles, goes off by himself to look
up the old newspaper files on the case. Knowing that he's going
to do this, Paula anticipates his finding the name of the Golden
Sunset Cafe, and calls Larry to warn him to get out of town
and above all to stay away from the Golden Sunset Cafe.

       The above reorganization of the first half will
concentrate the whole story, except for the shortened flashbacks,
in four days, Saturday to Tuesday, of continuous action. I estimate
that it will reduce the first 150 pages by 25% or more; and I am
certain that it will take more effective hold of the reader's
interest. I have to admit that the first half of the book is
slow as it stands. I wrote it with the idea of "letting the
material secrete its own adrenalin," and evidently my experiment was not an unqualified success.

       If the revision I have outlined should turn
out to be too radical, and to lose more than it gains - which
I don't expect will be the case - I'll put it on the shelf
and apply the policy of straight cutting which you suggested
in your memorandum. But I'm inclined to think that actual
reorganization of the material will produce a better result.

book that I might not be able to do at all well. And by that I mean a longer book in which the basic tensions of the form are relaxed to some extent.

I was just wondering how much, if any, pull that type of book has for you. The longer, slower book, so to speak.

It's really difficult to answer that question. I really wouldn't know about any particular book or kind of book until I tried it. I could put it in a light way: I'm more interested in the length of sentences than I am in the length of books. To me that's the more essential thing. The book determines its own length in a way. You just go on until you've covered your subject or completed the family history or whatever.

Mr. Knopf
-3-

If you have any criticisms of my plan as outlined, I'll be
glad to have them. I expect that this work of revision will
take me at least six weeks.

       I understand your unwillingness to contract for
the book before having my definite reaction to your suggestions.
I need hardly add to the definite reaction given above that
I think, in spite of my earlier intentions for this book, that
you're right; that in a murder mystery of whatever kind,
readability comes first. (I intend, too, to do what I can to
underline the element of insanity.) Since I have your assur-
ance that you want to publish the book, I'm going right
ahead with the revision. I won't deny, however, that if you should
decide to go ahead pari passu with the preparation of the
contract, I'd feel happier about the whole thing.

       Thank you for noting the minor corrections on
the Blue City wrapper, which I thought I'd send in on the
chance of a reprinting. I liked the PW ad. It inflated
my ego.

       Yours sincerely,

Second and third pages (one penciled holograph addition to the second page) of Ken Millar's three page response to the Knopf memo.

If the time came when you decided that the book you're writing should be the last Archer novel, would that be synonymous with your stopping writing novels altogether?

No. And I wouldn't decide it until I finished the book. I think it would be extremely bad to sit down and say to oneself this is going to be the last of a certain series. I'd decide afterwards. No, I don't intend to give up writing as long as I'm alive.

share it. I'm using it not so much as an example of a book which I consider a failure; that's not my point. My point is that I myself would be fearful of moving in that more relaxed direction for reasons which are partly apparent in the structure of *The Long Goodbye*. I'm not saying that it isn't a good book, but it's the kind of

May 31, 1974   Jill Krementz

Ken and Maggie Millar at home. Photo by Rafael Maldonado Jr.

ACKNOWLEDGMENTS

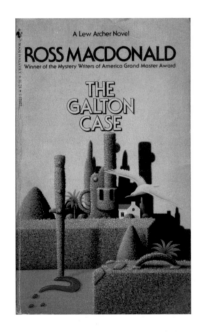

KEVIN AVERY

First of all, thank you to my publisher Gary Groth for proposing this project, to Paul Nelson's son Mark C. Nelson for giving it his blessing, and to Paul's old friend and confidant Jeff Wong for sharing the interview recordings with me in the first place and for opening his personal archive of Ross Macdonald collectibles—one of the world's largest—for everyone to see.

Special appreciation to Jill Krementz for her striking photographs and to Jerome Charyn for his wonderful foreword.

Thanks to Linwood Barclay, Norman J. Colavincenzo, Maureen Lamberti, Dave Marsh, Jim McBride, Tom Nolan, Kit Rachlis, Ralph Sipper, Craig Tenney, Burt Weissbourd, and Crystal Zevon. And, of course, Jann Wenner and *Rolling Stone*.

Most of all, I couldn't have done any of this without the support of my most beautiful and trusted editor, Deborah.

JEFF WONG

To the left is the copy of *The Galton Case* that started it all. Thank you to Martin Smith (aka Martin Martin), author of *Flora's Dream* and *Goodbye, Philip Roth*, whose 1983 detective fiction class at the School of Visual Arts introduced me to this book (the first Ross Macdonald novel I ever read); to Otto Penzler, who when asked, "Is there a book club edition or later printing hardcover of *The Galton Case*?" answered, "There might be, but collecting first editions is the only way to go"; to Rebecca D. Cyphert-Carlson, who bought me Otto's signed limited edition of *Lew Archer: Private Investigator* and really got the Ken Millar bug started; and to Glenn Horowitz, who gave me these sage words: "Collect what you enjoy." Thanks in advance to anyone who can locate a second printing of *The Name Is Archer* (Bantam 1295) from March 1955 for me. There's so much more I wish I could show from the collection, but there aren't enough pages.

My gratitude and love to Ralph and Carol Sipper, who opened up a world I never thought possible.

To Paul—I miss you and wish you could've seen this.

"A solution of writers is a pretty good liquid to swim in if you're another writer."
—*Ken Millar*

Ken Millar and Kurt Vonnegut in California. Photo by Jill Krementz.

SOURCES AND CITED WORKS

Avery, Kevin. Interviews with Dave Marsh, 2006 and 2014; Tom Nolan, 2007; Kit Rachlis, 2006 and 2013; Ralph Sipper, 2006; Burt Weissbourd, and Crystal Zevon, 2006 and 2007.

Bruccoli, Matthew J. *Kenneth Millar/Ross Macdonald: A Checklist*, 1971. Compiled by Matthew J. Bruccoli. Gale Research Company.

Bruccoli, Matthew J. *Ross Macdonald*, 1984. Harcourt Brace Jovanovich.

Bruccoli, Matthew J. *Ross Macdonald/Kenneth Millar: A Descriptive Bibliography*, 1983. University of Pittsburgh Press.

Cassuto, Leonard. 2003. "The Last Testament of Ross Macdonald." *The Boston Globe*. November 2.

Chandler, Raymond. *The Simple Art of Murder*, 1950. Houghton Mifflin.

Coulette, Henri. *The War of the Secret Agents and Other Poems*, 1966. Charles Scribner's Sons.

Davidson Films. *Ross Macdonald: In the First Person*, 1971.

Gale, Robert L. *A Ross Macdonald Companion*, 2002. Greenwood Press.

Goldman, William. 1969. "The Goodbye Look." *The New York Times Book Review.*" June 1.

Grogg, Sam, Jr. 1973. "Ross Macdonald: at the Edge." *Journal of Popular Culture*. Summer.

Hellman, Lillian. "Introduction." *The Big Knockover: Selected Stories and Short Novels by Dashiell Hammett*, 1966. Edited by Lillian Hellman. Random House.

Hoopes, Roy. *Cain*, 1982. Holt, Rinehart and Winston.

Kael, Pauline. 1975. "The Visceral Poetry of Pulp." *The New Yorker*. October 6.

Kitchener-Waterloo Collegiate and Vocational School (KCI), Ontario, Canada, *The Grumbler*, 1932.

Macdonald, Ross. "Foreword," *Archer at Large*, 1970, Alfred A. Knopf, Inc.; "Foreword," *Archer in Hollywood*, 1967, Alfred A. Knopf, Inc.; *The Blue Hammer*, 1976, Alfred A. Knopf, Inc.; *A Collection of Reviews*, 1979, Lord John Press; *The Doomsters*, 1958, Alfred A. Knopf, Inc.; *The Galton Case*, 1959, Alfred A. Knopf, Inc.; *The Instant Enemy*, 1968, Alfred A. Knopf, Inc.; *The Moving Target*, 1949, Alfred A. Knopf, Inc.; "The Writer as Detective Hero," *On Crime Writing*, 1973, Capra Press; and *The Zebra-Striped Hearse*, 1962, Alfred A. Knopf, Inc.

Millar, Kenneth. "Thought and English." *The School (Secondary Edition)*, 1941. Ontario College of Education.

Millar, Margaret and Kenneth. "Headnote to William Faulkner's 'The Hound.' *Murder by Experts*, 1947. Ziff-Davis Publishing Company.

McNary, Dave. 2011. "Studio Begins Exploring Lew Archer Franchise." *Variety.com*. October 31.

Nelson, Paul. "Book Proposal, Ross Macdonald: An Oral Biography," *Everything Is an Afterthought: The Life and Writings of Paul Nelson*, 2011, by Kevin Avery; "It's All One Case," *Inward Journey*, edited by Ralph Sipper, 1984; "Warren Zevon: How He Saved Himself from a Coward's Death," *Rolling Stone*, March 19, 1981.

Nelson, Paul. Interviews with Robert Easton, William Campbell Gault, Herbert Harker, Kenneth Millar, Margaret Millar, Larry Moskowitz, Carol Sipper, and Ralph Sipper. Used by permission. Courtesy of the Trustee of the Margaret Millar Charitable Trust and Special Collections and Archives, University of California, Irvine Libraries, Kenneth Millar Papers. 1976.

Nolan, Tom. *Ross Macdonald: A Biography*, 1999. Scribner.

Rachlis, Kit. 2006. "Essential." *Los Angeles Magazine*. October.

Ruoff, Jeffrey. *An American Family: A Televised Life*, 2001. University of Minnesota Press.

Sipper, Ralph. B. *Larry Moskowitz: Man of Esprit*, 1986, Cordelia Editions.

Smith, Cecil. 1974. "'Underground Man' to Surface on TV." *Los Angeles Times*. March 19.

Tuska, Jon. *The Detective in Hollywood*, 1978. Doubleday & Company, Inc.

Western Archives, Western University, London, Canada, *The Occidentalia 1935, 1936*, and *1938*.

Zevon, Warren. *Bad Luck Streak in Dancing School*, 1980. Elektra Records.

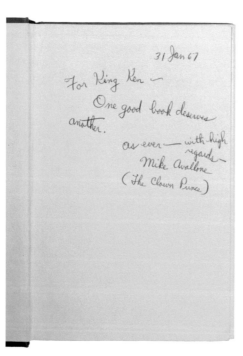

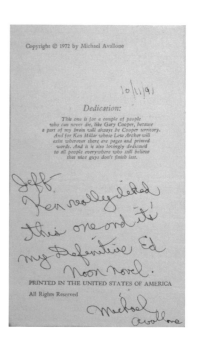

Prolific novelist Michael Avallone served as editor of The Third Degree, *the Mystery Writers of America newsletter, while Ken Millar was MWA president in 1965. In 1967, Avallone inscribed the UK edition of his novel* The Fat Death *to Millar, whom he felt was the superior writer: "For King Ken—One good book deserves another. As ever—with high regards—Mike Avallone (The Clown Prince)." The dedication in his definitive Ed Noon novel* Shoot It Again, Sam *(1972): "This one is for a couple of people who can never die, like Gary Cooper, because a part of my brain will always be Cooper territory. And for Ken Millar whose Lew Archer will exist wherever there are pages and printed words. And it is also lovingly dedicated to all people everywhere who still believe that nice guys don't finish last."*

INDEX

 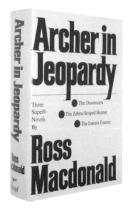 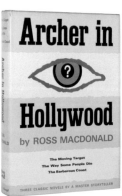 

Mark C. Nelson and his father Paul Nelson in Paul's apartment at Christmastime 1985.
The detail of the stack of books in the background shows Paul's copies of
Archer in Jeopardy, Archer in Hollywood, *and* Archer at Large *(Paul's books shown above).*

ABOUT THE AUTHORS

KEVIN AVERY is the author-editor of *Everything Is an Afterthought: The Life and Writings of Paul Nelson* and *Conversations with Clint: Paul Nelson's Lost Interviews with Clint Eastwood, 1979–1983*. Born and raised in Salt Lake City, Utah, he now lives in Brooklyn, New York, with his wife Deborah, stepdaughter Laura, and a four-legged muse named Mysti.

JEROME CHARYN is currently working on his twelfth crime novel about Isaac Sidel, who rises from police chief to President of the United States. His most recent book is *Bitter Bronx: Thirteen Stories*. The graphic novels he did with French artist François Boucq, *The Magician's Wife* and *Billy Budd, KGB*, are being reprinted.

ROSS MACDONALD, real name Kenneth Millar, was born in Los Gatos, California, in 1915 and raised in Ontario, Canada. Famous for his series of detective novels featuring private eye Lew Archer, he served as president of the Mystery Writers of America and was awarded their Grand Master Award. He died in 1983 with more than two dozen books to his name.

PAUL NELSON was, in the words of Bob Dylan, a "folk-music scholar." When Dylan went electric in 1965, so did he. A rock critic pioneer who became a legendary editor for *Rolling Stone* magazine, he also discovered the New York Dolls. He died in 2006 at the age of seventy. He never wrote the series of detective novels he dreamt of and never became, in his own words, "the next Ross Macdonald."

JEFF WONG is a graphic designer and award-winning illustrator who could be considered a "Kenneth Millar/Ross Macdonald scholar." He has proudly been affiliated with NoirCon, a biennial literary conference devoted to the dark, elusive, and seductive areas of art and life that we have come to call "noir," since 2010. He is currently working on *Collected Millar*, a publishing project by Syndicate Books to restore to availability the complete works of Margaret Millar.

ABOUT THE TYPE

Caledonia is a transitional serif typeface designed by William Addison Dwiggins in 1938 for the Mergenthaler Linotype Company. With the exception of the very first Lew Archer novel and two Archer omnibuses, all of Ross Macdonald's Knopf novels (including two under his given name, Kenneth Millar) were set in Caledonia. As a small tribute to Paul's love of Ken Millar's work, this book is set in a digital version called New Caledonia, introduced in 1982.